Diverse Voices in P

Through a variety of case studies by global scholars from diverse academic fields, this book explores photographic-album practices of historically marginalized figures from a range of time periods, geographic locations, and socio-cultural contexts. Their albums' stories span various racial, ethnic, gender and sexual identities; nationalities; religions; and dis/abilities.

The vernacular albums featured in this volume present narratives that move beyond those reflected in our existing histories. Essays examine the visual, material, and aural strategies that album-makers have used to assert control over the presentation of their histories and identities, and to direct what those narratives have to say, a point of special relevance as these albums move out of private domestic space and into public archives, institutions, and digital formats. This book does not consider photographic albums and scrapbooks as separate genres, but as a continuum of modern creative practices of photographic and mass-print collage aimed at self-expression and narrative-building that co-evolved and were readily accessible.

The book will be of interest to scholars working in art history, history of photography, visual culture, material culture, media studies, and cultural studies.

Mary Trent is an Assistant Professor of Art and Architectural History at College of Charleston, South Carolina, USA.

Kris Belden-Adams is an Associate Professor of Art History at the University of Mississippi, USA.

Routledge History of Photography

This series publishes research monographs and edited collections focusing on the history and theory of photography. These original, scholarly books may take an art historical, visual studies, or material studies approach.

The Materiality of Exhibition Photography in the Modernist Era
Form, Content, Consequence
Laurie Taylor

The Image of Environmental Harm in American Social Documentary Photography
Chris Balaschak

Hybrid Photography
Intermedial Practice in Science and Humanities
Edited by Sara Hillnhuetter, Stefanie Klamm and Friedrich Tietjen

The Selfie, Temporality, and Contemporary Photography
Claire Raymond

Photography in China
Science, Commerce and Communication
Oliver Moore

Visual Culture Approaches to the Selfie
Edited by Derek Conrad Murray

Italian Neorealist Photography
Its Legacy and Aftermath
Antonella Russo

Photography and Political Repressions in Stalin's Russia
Defacing the Enemy
Denis Skopin

Diverse Voices in Photographic Albums
"These Are Our Stories"
Edited by Mary Trent and Kris Belden-Adams

How Photography Changed Philosophy
Daniel Rubinstein

For more information about this series, please visit: https://www.routledge.com/Routledge-History-of-Photography/book-series/RHOP

Diverse Voices in Photographic Albums

"These Are Our Stories"

Edited by Mary Trent and Kris Belden-Adams

Routledge
Taylor & Francis Group
NEW YORK AND LONDON

Cover image: Frank Rinehart or Adolph Muhr, *Mother and Child, Wichita,* U.S. Indian Congress of the Trans-Mississippi and International Exposition in Omaha, 1898. Hand-tinted platinum print. Boston Public Library/Digital Commonwealth. Public Domain.

First published 2023
by Routledge
605 Third Avenue, New York, NY 10158

and by Routledge
4 Park Square, Milton Park, Abingdon, Oxon, OX14 4RN

Routledge is an imprint of the Taylor & Francis Group, an informa business

Library of Congress Cataloguing-in-Publication Data
Names: Trent, Mary, 1981- editor. | Belden-Adams, Kris, editor.
Title: Diverse voices in photographic albums : "these are our stories" / edited by Mary Trent and Kris Belden-Adams.
Description: First edition. | New York, NY : Routledge, 2022. | Series: Routledge history of photography | Includes bibliographical references and index.
Identifiers: LCCN 2022004348 (print) | LCCN 2022004349 (ebook) | ISBN 9780367743550 (hbk) | ISBN 9780367743574 (pbk) | ISBN 9781003157427 (ebk)
Subjects: LCSH: Photograph albums--History. | Vernacular photography--Case studies. | Storytelling--History.
Classification: LCC TR501 .D57 2022 (print) | LCC TR501 (ebook) | DDC 770--dc23/eng/20220414
LC record available at https://lccn.loc.gov/2022004348
LC ebook record available at https://lccn.loc.gov/2022004349

ISBN: 978-0-367-74355-0 (hbk)
ISBN: 978-0-367-74357-4 (pbk)
ISBN: 978-1-003-15742-7 (ebk)

DOI: 10.4324/9781003157427

Typeset in Sabon
by MPS Limited, Dehradun

Dedicated to James Wilson Trent, Jr. and Margaret Rose Vendryes

Contents

List of Figures ix
List of Contributors xiii
Acknowledgments xv

Introduction 1

1 The Album's Diverse Narratives 3
MARY TRENT

PART I
Complicating Family Narratives 25

2 Women on Holiday: Intergenerational Narratives in Photographic Albums from India 27
SURYANANDINI NARAIN

3 "Children of Shadowland": A Family's Scrapbook Story of Intellectual Disability 43
JAMES TRENT

4 Henry Darger's "Family" Album of American Orphans and Fugitives 56
MARY TRENT

PART II
Stepping Out of "the Closet," Privately 75

5 "Dropping Hairpins": Cisgender Performance and "Homosociality" in William Whitney's Fin-de-Siècle College Albums 77
KRIS BELDEN-ADAMS

6 A Scissored Gay Life of the 1930s and 1940s: The Scrapbooks of Ogden Salmon 97
JAMES A. KASER

7 In Plain Sight: Album-Making and Queer Identity in Mid-Twentieth-Century South Africa 115
DANIELLE KINSEY

PART III
Retelling National and International Histories 133

8 "We Carry the Weight of a 150-Year Legacy": Sharing the Memories of a Civil War Photograph Album 135
MICHÈLE GATES MORESI

9 The Politics of Floating: Space and Experience in G. Prat Photograph Album of China and Japan, 1874–1900 148
XINYUE YUAN

10 Collecting the Indian Congress: Reframing Indigenous Photography Albums from the Trans-Mississippi and International Exposition 164
KAREN BARBER

11 Secrets from the Family Album: Official and Silenced Knowledge on Migration 194
YA'ARA GIL-GLAZER

PART IV
Conclusions 209

12 Conclusions: Albums and Diverse Communities 211
KRIS BELDEN-ADAMS

13 Afterword 220
MARGARET ROSE VENDRYES

Index 227

Figures

2.1 Washington Monument, June ’93, 1993, color print, 4 in. × 6 in. © 2020 Mathur and Prashad Families 30

2.2 Mathur Home at Thoreau Drive, Bethesda, Maryland, 1993, color print, 4 in. × 6 in. © 2020 Mathur and Prashad Families 32

2.3 Monument, Washington D.C., April ’94, 1994, color print, 4 in. × 6 in. © 2020 Mathur and Prashad Families 34

2.4 Lilac Garden, Niagara, Canada, May ’94, 1994, color print. © 2020 Mathur and Prashad Families 35

2.5 Rekha, Asha, and Preeti on holiday in Kashmir, 1964, black-and-white print, 2.36 in. × 2.36 in. © 2020 Mathur and Prashad Families 37

3.1 Bernhard and Emily Kress, *New Lisbon Cottage*, *Kress Scrapbook* (1944–1966). James Trent Collection 44

3.2 National Association for Retarded Children, *Retarded Children Can Be Helped!*, Kress Scrapbook (1944–1966). James Trent Collection 48

3.3 Bernhard and Emily Kress, *Choo-Choo Train*, Kress Scrapbook (1944–1966). James Trent Collection 50

3.4 Bernhard and Emily Kress, *The “Jail,”* Kress Scrapbook (1944–1966). James Trent Collection 51

3.5 New Jersey Parents Group for Retarded Children, *Children of the Shadowland*, Kress Scrapbook (1944–1966). James Trent Collection 52

4.1 Henry Darger, *Album Cover*, left side, c. 1950s, collage, watercolor, pencil, carbon tracing, 31 ½ × 128 ¼ inches [whole cover]. Collection de l’Art Brut, Lausanne, Switzerland. © 2021 Kiyoko Lerner/Artists Rights Society (ARS), New York 57

4.2 Henry Darger, *Album Cover*, right side, c. 1950s, collage, watercolor, pencil, carbon tracing, 31 ½ × 128 ¼ inches [whole cover]. Collection de l’Art Brut, Lausanne, Switzerland. © 2021 Kiyoko Lerner/Artists Rights Society (ARS), New York 58

4.3 *Darger’s Table with Source Materials, Scrapbooks, and Art Supplies, Including a Stack of* Life Magazines. The Henry Darger Room Collection, Intuit: The Center for Intuitive and Outsider Art, gift of Kiyoko Lerner 61

4.4 Henry Darger, *Annabelle Aronburg Vivian*, c. 1940s, watercolor and pencil on paper, 35 ½ × 31 ½ inches. Collection of Robert A. Roth, Chicago, Illinois. Photographer, John Faier. © 2021 Kiyoko Lerner/Artists Rights Society (ARS), New York 64

4.5 Pan Am, *Find a New World*, 1958. Courtesy The Pan Am Historical Foundation/panam.org 67
5.1 William Belcher Whitney, *Class of 1887*, 1885–1887, hairpins, photographs, text, thread, ribbon, William Belcher Whitney Scrapbook. Amherst College Archives & Special Collections, Public Domain 78
5.2 *Class in Physics at So. Hadley and Amherst*, c. 1885, ink sketch on paper, William Belcher Whitney Scrapbook. Amherst College Archives & Special Collections, Public Domain 80
5.3 *William Belcher Whitney and Charles Amherst Chase*, May 25, 1887, William Belcher Whitney Scrapbook. Amherst College Archives & Special Collections, Public Domain 86
5.4 *Amherst College Baseball Team, Class of 1887*, William Belcher Whitney Scrapbook. Amherst College Archives & Special Collections, Public Domain 87
5.5 Henry N. Potter, *Three on Bed*, c. 1887, William Belcher Whitney Scrapbook. Amherst College Archives & Special Collections, Public Domain 88
6.1 Ogden Salmon, *Two Nightingales and a Swallow*, 1938, pencil and ink on paper, 12 × 8 3/4 in., Ogden Salmon Scrapbook. Collection of James Kaser, photograph © 2021 James Kaser 99
6.2 Ogden Salmon, *Before Tragedy Struck…*, 1938, pencil on paper, 8 ½ × 11 in., Ogden Salmon Scrapbook. Collection of James Kaser, Photograph © 2021 James Kaser 100
6.3 Ogden Salmon, *Scrapbook Page with Photograph*, 9 ½ × 6 in., Ogden Salmon Scrapbook. [Photograph is by Lee Weinstein, published in University of Chicago student publication, *Pulse*, April 1940]. Collection of James Kaser, photograph © 2021 James Kaser 103
6.4 Ogden Salmon, *Scrapbook Page with Two Photographs*, 9 ½ × 6 in., Ogden Salmon Scrapbook. [Top photograph is by Shapiro Studio, *Frank Overlees in Ponca Indian Dance*, 1936; Bottom photograph is by Shapiro Studio, *Ted Shawn and His Men Dancers in Ponca Indian Dance*, 1936]. Collection of James Kaser, photograph © 2021 James Kaser 106
6.5 Ogden Salmon, *Spring 1946*, 1946, photographic prints, 11 ¾ × 9 ¾ in., Ogden Salmon Scrapbook. Collection of James Kaser, photograph © 2021 James Kaser 110
7.1 *Self*, 1942, black-and-white photograph, 4 1/2 × 6 in. GALA Queer Archive, Johannesburg, South Africa, Renée Liddicoat Collection (AM2800). Photograph by Danielle Kinsey 119
7.2 *Last Lap*, 1945, black-and-white photograph, 3 × 5 in. GALA Queer Archive, Johannesburg, South Africa, Renée Liddicoat Collection (AM2800). Photograph by Danielle Kinsey 121
7.3 *Sex Mad!*, album page, 11 × 16 in. GALA Queer Archive, Johannesburg, South Africa, the personal photographic album of David, a Sailor (AM2823). Photograph by Danielle Kinsey 123

7.4 *Behave Yourself!*, n.d., black-and-white photograph, 2 × 3 in. GALA Queer Archive, Johannesburg, South Africa, the personal photographic album of David, a Sailor (AM2823). Photograph by Danielle Kinsey 124
7.5 *Bruno at a Party*, 1972, black-and-white photograph, 4 × 6 in. GALA Queer Archive, Johannesburg, South Africa, The Oral History Project Collection (AM2709), GALA Queer Archive, Johannesburg, South Africa. Photograph by Danielle Kinsey 128
8.1 *Album Cover*, 1864–1865, 2 × 1 13/16 × 7/8 in., photographic album of William A. Prickitt, 25th Regiment of the United States Colored Troops soldiers. Collection of the Smithsonian National Museum of African American History and Culture, Gift of Aneita Gates, on behalf of her son, Kameron Gates, and all the descendants of Captain William A. Prickitt 136
8.2 *George H. Mitchell*, 1864–1865, tintype, 1 3/16 × 7/8 in., photographic album of William A. Prickitt. Collection of the Smithsonian National Museum of African American History and Culture, Gift of Aneita Gates, on behalf of her son, Kameron Gates, and all the descendants of Captain William A. Prickitt 139
8.3 *John Walls*, 1864–1865, tintype, 1 3/16 × 7/8 in., photographic album of William A. Prickitt. Collection of the Smithsonian National Museum of African American History and Culture, Gift of Aneita Gates, on behalf of her son, Kameron Gates, and all the descendants of Captain William A. Prickitt 140
8.4 *William H. Morris*, 1864–1865, tintype, 1 3/16 × 7/8 in., photographic album of William A. Prickitt. Collection of the Smithsonian National Museum of African American History and Culture, Gift of Aneita Gates, on behalf of her son, Kameron Gates, and all the descendants of Captain William A. Prickitt 140
8.5 *Unidentified Union Soldier*, 1864–1865, tintype, 1 3/16 × 7/8 in., photographic album of William A. Prickitt. Collection of the Smithsonian National Museum of African American History and Culture, Gift of Aneita Gates, on behalf of her son, Kameron Gates, and all the descendants of Captain William A. Prickitt 144
9.1 G. Prat, *Canton: Vue de Shamien*, 1879, album page with albumen print and notes, 12.8 × 15.3 in., photographic album of China and Japan. Getty Research Institute, Los Angeles, CA 150
9.2 G. Prat, *Canton: Vue de Shamien*, 1879, album page with albumen print and notes, 12.8 × 15.3 in., photographic album of China and Japan. Getty Research Institute, Los Angeles, CA 151
9.3 G. Prat, *Canton: Vue de Shamien*, 1879, album page with albumen print and notes, 12.8 × 15.3 in., photographic album of China and Japan. Getty Research Institute, Los Angeles, CA 152
9.4 G. Prat, *Bal Masqué Chez Mr. & Mm. G. M. Smith (Jardine, Matheson & Co.)*, 1879, album page with albumen print and notes, 12.8 × 15.3 in., photographic album of China and Japan (Prat is seated on far left.) Getty Research Institute, Los Angeles, CA 157

9.5 G. Prat, *Canton: Messrs. Thomas, Row & Smith (Junior Men) Coté Nord, Pliée et Brûlée le 10 Septembre 1883*, 1883, album page with albumen print and notes, 12.8 × 15.3 in., photographic album of China and Japan. Getty Research Institute, Los Angeles, CA 159

10.1 Double-page album spread with handwritten "List of Tribes" and *Wichita Woman and Child in Cradle*, photograph by Frank A. Rinehart and Adolph Muhr, 1898, 22.8 × 8.26 in., American Indians Photographs album. Courtesy of Omaha Public Library. Public Domain 165

10.2 Double-page album spread with *Wichita Young Men, Fred Carruth and John Tatum* and *Group of Wichitas, Chief Tawaconi Jim and Wife in Center*, photographs by Frank A. Rinehart and Adolph Muhr, 1898, 22.8 × 8.26 in., American Indians Photographs album. Courtesy of Omaha Public Library. Public Domain 169

10.3 Cover, 1898, 11.4 × 8.26 × 1.96 in., American Indians Photographs album. Courtesy of Omaha Public Library. Public Domain 173

10.4 Frank A. Rinehart and Adolph Muhr, *Wichita Woman, Wife of Tawaconi Jim*, American Indians Photographs album, 1898, 4.3 × 6.29 in. Courtesy of Omaha Public Library. Public Domain 175

13.1 James Richmond Barthé, page from Barthé's Photograph Album (Paris, France), 1934, 12 × 14 inches. Richmond Barthé Papers, Amistad Research Center, New Orleans, Louisiana 221

13.2 Margaret Rose Vendryes, page from Lena Amabel Vendryes (1933–2012), 2012, digital memorial scrapbook. 223

13.3 Margaret Rose Vendryes, *New York City Pride*, page from author's photograph album, June 1995, 13 × 18 inches 225

Contributors

Karen Barber is a Visiting Assistant Professor of Art History at the University of Mississippi, and specializes in the history of photography, Modern art, and curatorial practice. Her research deals with interwar photography, camera-less processes, photography, and the medium's relationship to Native America.

Kris Belden-Adams is an Associate Professor of Art History at the University of Mississippi, and specializes in the history and theory of photography. She is the author of *Photography, Temporality, Modernity: Time Warped* (2019) and *Photography, Eugenics, 'Aristogenics': Picturing Privilege* (2020).

Ya'ara Gil-Glazer is the Head of the Education through Art Program, Department of Education, Tel-Hai Academic College, Israel. She researches and teaches courses in photography, visual culture, and critical art education. Gil-Glazer's research interests include Modern and contemporary art and visual culture and its educational integration into social contexts.

James A. Kaser is a Professor and Archivist at the College of Staten Island/City University of New York. He completed his doctorate in American Culture Studies at Bowling Green State University and is the author of four books: *At the Bivouac of Memory: History, Politics, and the Battle of Chickamauga*; *The Washington, D.C. of Fiction: A Research Guide*; *The Chicago of Fiction: A Resource Guide*; and *The New Orleans of Fiction: A Research Guide.*

Danielle Kinsey is an Assistant Professor in the Department of History, Carleton University, Ottawa, Canada. She is a co-collaborator for a Social Sciences and Humanities Research Council of Canada-funded project on "Photography and the Sexual Revolution," and is finishing a monograph on diamond consumption in Britain and its empire in the nineteenth century.

Michèle Gates Moresi holds a Ph.D. in American Civilization from the George Washington University. She is Supervisory Museum Curator of Collections at Smithsonian National Museum of African American History and Culture. She oversees collections acquisition and management activities, participates in exhibition development, and is co-editor of *Double Exposure,* a seven-book series about photographs from the NMAAHC collection.

Suryanandini Narain is an Assistant Professor of Visual Studies at the School of Arts and Aesthetics, Jawaharlal Nehru University, New Delhi. Her doctoral thesis addressed the feminine figure in family photographs from Delhi. She has written extensively on photography in India, especially around images of women, the family, and domestic and studio photography.

James Trent served as Visiting Scholar at Brandeis University's Heller School, and on the faculties of Gordon College and Southern Illinois University at Edwardsville. His writings include *The Manliest Man: Samuel G. Howe and the Contours of Nineteenth Century American Reform* (2012), *Inventing the Feeble Mind: A History of Intellectual Disability in the United States* (2016), and the co-edited *Phallacies: Historical Intersections of Masculinity and Disability* (2017).

Mary Trent is an Assistant Professor of Art and Architectural History at the College of Charleston who specializes in American and African American art and photography. She has published essays on the art of Henry Darger, and has forthcoming essays on the nineteenth-century photographic album of the formerly enslaved Ellen Craft and on the use of historical photographs in contemporary African American activism.

Margaret Rose Vendryes was an artist and art historian. Born in Jamaica, she held a doctorate in art history from Princeton University. She was the author of *Barthé, A Life in Sculpture*. Vendryes was a Professor of Art History, Performing, and Fine Arts, and was the Director of the Fine Arts Gallery at York College, City University of New York.

Xinyue Yuan is a Ph.D. candidate in Visual Studies at the University of California, Irvine. She works on Modern Chinese art and visual culture in a global context. Her dissertation project on transcultural histories of artists' books in Republican China is supported by the Metropolitan Center for Far Eastern Art Studies.

Acknowledgments

Academic research, especially in the humanities, is often not merely a professional endeavor, but one connected to personal experiences and histories. Research often originates with questions rooted in larger historical trajectories that nevertheless resonate with the circumstances of authors, who are, after all, historical subjects. This volume is a case in a point. Our study of albums documenting the complexities of everyday life was completed during the first two years of the coronavirus pandemic. It has not been an easy time and many of our contributors authored their studies from their homes during periods of lockdown, health precautions, and quarantine. Writing about domestic albums as sites that enable the recording of personal narratives about larger historical experiences became especially relevant.

We appreciate all of our contributors, whose voices we are glad are a part of this project. Our authors managed difficulties accessing research materials, and focused on writing and revising in the midst of pandemic shock, forced quarantines, and a variety of personal and professional losses. For many of us, our families (including children and others for whom we provide care) were home while we completed our scholarship, due to the closures or movement online of programs and schools. Over the course of the past two years, some of our authors became infected with coronavirus or had ill family members. Tragically, a couple even lost family members. One of the losses was James Trent, the author of Chapter 3 and father of co-editor Mary Trent. Our book includes his last academic publication, and we have dedicated the volume to him. Another loss was Margaret Rose Vendreys, who authored our book's Afterward. She passed away shortly before the book's publication, and we also dedicate the book to her.

We would like to thank Katie Armstrong and Isabella Vitti at Routledge for their belief in the project. We are also grateful for the insightful comments of our volume's anonymous peer reviewers, and we thank each other for taking this journey together. The book began with a November 2019 SECAC conference panel on "Photography and Album Making" organized by Mary Trent, with participation by Kris Belden-Adams, Michèle Gates Moresi, and Laura Coyle, whom we thank, along with SECAC, for its early support. Mary would also like to thank Marian Mazzone, Barry Stiefel, Jessica Streit, Tara Prakash, Brigit Ferguson, Mary Beth Heston, Patricia Dillon, and Jim Trent for reading early versions of the book proposal and her chapters. Mary also sends heartfelt appreciation to Drew for his unwavering support and to Julia and David for their regular distractions, which were a valued reminder to enjoy the everyday. Finally, Kris thanks John, Lily, and Avery for their love and support.

Mary Trent and Kris Belden-Adams

Introduction

1 The Album's Diverse Narratives

Mary Trent

Albums begin their lives as empty books that expect to be filled. A site of anticipation whether mass-manufactured or handmade, a freshly bound book of blank pages offers its owner a space for recording a personal history with photographs, mass-media print clippings, notations, and other added mementoes. Unlike a blank canvas, sketch pad, or unworked block of stone or clay, an unmarked album suggests the opportunity for documenting a life's narrative sequentially, over distinct moments of time. Albums created since the invention of photography and the expansion of mass print media also grant individuals a space for directing the visualization of their own identity in a manner that may depart from the stereotypes of dominant visual culture. Selecting and rearranging imagery and ephemera (ticket stubs, programs, flowers), photographic and scrapbook album-makers re-transcribe and reorient memories of daily life for themselves and their selected audiences.[1] These album-based archives are born in the gaps between dominant narratives. They introduce records that otherwise would fall through the cracks of recorded history in institutionalized acts of neglect, marginalization, misrepresentation, or erasure. Their pages voice needed additions to established historical narratives, including histories of photography.

As one of the most affordable and accessible media for recording, remembering, and memorializing daily life, bound albums of photographs and mass-media print ephemera sit in homes across the world as broad-reaching archives of social history. These creations became possible more than a century and a half ago, after the introduction of photography and subsequent nineteenth- and early-twentieth-century developments that enabled the mass distribution of printed photographic media in advertisements, newspapers, and magazines. Since then, people of diverse races and ethnicities, nationalities, gender and sexual identities, social classes, ages, and physical, mental, and intellectual abilities have been making photographic albums and scrapbooks to chronicle their lives in bound books of personalized visual and textual archives. Over the past two decades or so, developers and designers have also translated albums' analog language and traditions into formats for digital image storing and sharing across social media networks and clouds. Studying a diverse historical field of album-making practices offers an essential expansion of our existing histories of the global reception of photography and print media culture into a broadened understanding of the practices of daily life. These archives reach out from

DOI: 10.4324/9781003157427-2

the margins of established narratives to announce new terrains of what Sadiya Hartman might describe as wayward knowledge.

Like the history of art in general, histories of photography, visual culture, and mass media often privilege hegemonic and institutionalized voices from European and North American cultures. Our project's recovery of more diverse, localized, and everyday archives, however, explores new material representations of life stories that have otherwise been stereotyped, marginalized, or erased. Our definition of these personalized archives as "wayward" invokes Hartman's provocative use of the term to develop previously overlooked or maligned narratives of young Black women who managed to survive in spite of their absence or partial presence in historical archives.[2] Inspired by Hartman and other Black feminists who developed methodological and theoretical outlooks for working in the interstices of dominant archives, the chapters in this volume bring visibility to previously unrecognized or misinterpreted modes by which minor subjects have defined and recorded lives of survival and significance in everyday albums.[3]

Considered together, the albums discussed in this collection speak out and assert their makers' existences and experiences as vital to a full telling of history. These essays demonstrate the value of elucidating the history of photography and print media not simply from the echelons of the institutionalized, but also from a broadened field that includes acts of self-representation and self-memorialization in everyday life.

The Diversity of Domestic Albums

Domestic albums have historically been regarded as exhibiting conformity rather than diversity. This association relates to their production in the home, which has traditionally been gendered as feminine (and, hence, often viewed as sheltered and creatively derivative) in comparison to the public sphere's gendering as masculine (with its stereotyped qualities of active engagement and innovation). Laura Wexler, however, argues that, in contrast to these assumptions, photographic albums record the effects of state power as evocatively (if not more so) than official government documents.[4] It follows that, as the state exercises power in a range of means with distinct populations, albums illustrate how diverse individuals and their related communities absorb and respond to hegemony. Developing this perspective, this book explores ways domestic albums register a diversity of affective impacts of social, political, and economic restrictions on populations. If given due attention, these albums speak volumes about negotiations with public powers occurring in private formations of identity, status, belonging, and unbelonging.

Our interest in focusing on *diverse* albums and their stories includes a critical awareness of the range of historical meanings of the term. In many academic discussions today, the word may refer to the social and political ideals of including historically marginalized people from different social and ethnic, racial, gender, or sexual backgrounds in a society, community, or organization, an aim relevant to this book's reassessment of album history.[5] But, other, historical definitions are also important, including those which apply the term to singular beings or objects, rather than social groups. These definitions also vary, with one emphasizing difference between individual things that are "not of the same kind, not alike *in nature* [my emphasis]."[6] And, another focused on difference *within* one thing, "differing*from itself* [my emphasis] under different circumstances at different times, or in different parts."[7]

These definitions incorporate aspects of earlier, now obsolete uses of the word. One earlier use defines diverse as "different from, or opposed to what is right, good, or profitable: perverse, adverse."[8] Another frames diverse as "turning or impelling in different directions; diverting, distracting."[9] Thus, these two historically rooted definitions frame diversity as either marking 1) fundamental difference, rooted in *unalterable* nature *between separate things* or 2) situational, rooted in *changeable* experiences of time or space *within one thing* itself.

The first definition evaluates diversity as fundamentally in opposition to a (preferred) norm. It suggests that the word diverse holds within it the workings of hegemony. In this sense, a study of diversity in domestic photographic albums can follow Wexler's call to pursue ways albums reinforce on a personal, intimate level socialized ideals impressed upon their makers to which they cannot fully conform, a topic taken up in some of our chapters. Such studies indicate the power of structural forces on everyday experiences of self-alienation. The second definition poses diversity as a temporal and spatial shift in direction from an established path. It does not figure diversity as static but as a process of formation and allows for it within a single subject, whose self may perform different, seemingly conflicting, aspects of identity in different times and spaces. Taking this second definition into consideration adds to Wexler's call for an additional focus on albums as relevant for studying formations and presentations of self that incorporate movement, change, and fugitivity. In the realm of visual culture, there are few objects that can compete with a family album in terms of the temporal length of its durational creativity. Albums are additive, affective objects, and they often hold photographs, notes, and ephemera that were incorporated over spans of many years and even generations, and that may have originated in distinct locations many miles apart. As portable objects, albums may also have been uprooted and settled in new environments over time. For example, a photographic album made in London in the 1860s by the formerly enslaved woman Ellen Craft was still being preserved and annotated by her descendants in their home in Charleston, South Carolina, up until 2010, when it finally entered a public archive approximately 4,000 miles away from and 150 years after its original creation.[10] The presentation of self in an album is, thus, often the representation of diverse selves that formed and changed across time and space in reaction to different personal aspirations, social pressures, and historical conditions.

Our volume's emphasis on diversity in domestic albums thus engages a range of definitions, seeing in the diverse an ethic of inclusion and equity, the workings of hegemonic powers of normativity, and an acknowledgment of the forces of change in personalized experiences of history, which inherently challenge attempts at stasis and rigidity. Our volume aims to enliven and deepen these understandings of diversity in domestic albums by critically assessing the role of state power on the formation of album narratives while also acknowledging everyday modes of creative adaptation, refusal, and resistance in the formation of self. Thy Phu and Elspeth Brown refer to this as the "mixed feelings" of family photography, especially for marginalized subjects. They describe these objects as both aspiring to the conventions of normative family fictions, and as remaking the genre for those for whom it was never intended in "technologies of the otherwise."[11] This volume illuminates such technologies in the album's recordings of the self.

The Technologies of the Album

Like many album makers, our volume approaches the album as a medium with its own specific representational technologies and operations. An album is a tactile, multi-media production that includes not just photographic prints, but the pages upon which they are affixed, the covers and bindings, the additions of handwritten notes, scraps, clippings, drawings, and other ephemera, either affixed or loosely placed between pages. Wear and tear by fingerprints, smudges, etc., personally mark the pages, indicating years of hands thumbing through. Historians of photography have often sidelined the messiness and casualness of the domestic album to more directly focus on the visual operations within photographs. Yet, the very structure of an album, with its combination of a book format with photographs, tampers with intentions for considering and exhibiting the photographs in it as individual prints. Albums' existence as tactile material objects meant to be "read" by viewers like a book is also complicated by the art museum's conventions of placing such objects under vitrines to avoid degradation by touch.

Album makers regularly include other forms of media on their pages, as their documentary goals do not usually concern fine-art distinctions of medium specificity. The majority of our volume's album makers did not create their works to intervene in concerns and debates of fine-art photography, but to document personal experiences and respond to the broader visual culture. Rather than seeing this as a limitation, our volume regards such albums as opening up new possibilities for thinking through the reception of photographic and mass-media print media in a diversified field of everyday life beyond the traditions and constraints of fine art institutions. Thus, our volume embraces the messiness of our albums – approaching them not as vehicles for the delivery of photographs, but as examples of mixed media.

Albums often include diverse media across their pages. An album maker might incorporate photography, notations, ephemera, mass-media clippings, and handcrafted flourishes. This mixed-media approach reflects albums' origins in the domestic sphere, which foregrounded an album's narrative and memorial functions. Modern albums originated in nineteenth-century European and North American middle- and upper-class contexts, which were characterized by strictly reinforced gender roles aligning with divisions of public and private space. Albums primarily began as objects made and consumed in private or semi-private spaces that function adjacent to, but distinct from, the public sphere. They thus included media marketed for personal consumption and the recording of private history, more so than the media traditionally used to record the grand narratives in fine art.

Following the practices of many album-makers, this volume does not consider photographic albums and scrapbooks as separate genres, but as objects that occupy a continuum of everyday practices of photographic and collaged mass-print self-expression and narrative-building that co-evolved and were readily accessible. They each responded to the nineteenth-century's development of modern visual culture, via the growth in production of cheap, accessible photography and mass print visual media. With this expansion of visual culture, corresponding desires for visualizing, narrating, and memorializing one's identity and existence were met by the creation of archives of photographs and printed scraps in albums documenting personal life stories.

Personal albums had existed in Europe before photography's invention. Yet, these pre-photographic traditions of the Early Modern era were largely exclusive to an educated elite.[12] In the early nineteenth century, however, album making expanded into the middle-class format of the autograph and friendship books, corresponding with the first mass printing of blank books in the 1820s and growing in the 1840s alongside industrialization.[13] A new trend also developed in the 1820s for filling blank books not just with signatures and verses but with visual and textual scraps culled from the burgeoning popular mass print media, with this decade recording the first uses of the word "scrapbook."[14] The 1820s was also marked by proto-photographic explorations across different countries and continents that would lead to photography's public announcement at the end of the following decade in 1839.[15] Both mass-printed blank books and photography thus originated in tandem with industrialization, and both were marketed to an increasingly modernized population that sought to document themselves and their world, in detail, for their own domestic consumption.

The first blank books specifically made for photographs – with slots designed to hold standard size prints – would not be manufactured until the 1860s after the development of the carte-de-visite, the first highly detailed, inexpensive, easily reproduced photograph on a paper base.[16] The expansion of chromolithography in the late nineteenth century also brought cheap, colorful printed ephemera into homes in North America and Europe, where it was sometimes creatively combined with black-and-white photographs into photographic albums and scrapbooks.[17] The expanding popularity of scrapbooks and photographic albums in the 1860s resulted in their supplantation of the earlier friendship and autograph albums. Their rise in North America and Europe corresponded with these regions' shift from predominantly agrarian to increasingly industrial economies. As the middle class participated in a larger commercialized and mediated field, albums provided them with a personal space for asserting their position in the expanding and increasingly globalized world.

At the end of the nineteenth century, the Eastman Kodak Company began producing inexpensive, user-friendly cameras pre-filled with emulsion roll film. By the 1910s, the United States company's brilliant marketing campaigns persuaded consumers of the importance of keeping family photographic albums to document every milestone and preserve memories.[18] Twentieth-century printing and camera innovations subsequently resulted in what has been called "The Golden Age of Photojournalism," between the 1930s and 1960s, when press photographs became plentiful in cheap magazines and newspapers. This shift resulted in the incorporation of press photography into albums and scrapbooks.[19] Though the introduction of home video cameras in the 1950s and 1960s supplanted some of the memory-keeping functions of the photographic album, these books persisted. The subsequent development of digital cameras translated many of their functions into the digital field, where arranged collections of photographs and notations can now be shared instantaneously across globalized networks in social media "albums."

It is worth noting that the album and scrapbook share qualities with the archive. Each presents and preserves personal experience and identity using a collection of disparate objects for posterity. Yet, there are important distinctions. An archive's institutional roots are distinct from the album's. "Archive" derives from the Greek *arkheia* (public records) from *arkhē* (government). Its contents have been deemed of public importance by an authoritative body that grants it an institutional location, implicating it in large-scale systems of power delineated in critical theory scholarship. An archive's contents are indexed and inventoried according to a formal classification system that emphasizes institutionalized stasis In distinction, the photographic and scrapbook albums' roots in the Latin *album* (blank white writing tablet) from *albus* (white), foreground only the expectation of content being added by whomever takes over the blank book. What any individual places onto an album's white pages is not yet defined as either worthy or unworthy of institutional recognition. As Martha Langford suggests, albums' organization relates less to the modern taxonomies of the institutional archive, and more to an early Modern root in the cabinet of curiosities, with its less rigid organization and embracement of wonder.[20]

Though pre-printed albums sometimes point to a desire for organized taxonomy with the first page(s) holding pre-printed tables of contents and blank family trees for album makers to fill out, these lists (in practice) are most often never completed or only partially filled out. Instead, most everyday albums lack any standardized, professional system of organization or list of the book's contents. Unlike the finding aids that demonstrate a precise and legible overview of an archive, the technology of the album only ever offers a partial, fragmented view of the collection. An album can only open to two pages at a time. Viewing an album, like making one, is thus a series of connected (but also separated) moments in time and space. And, moving between these moments demands a physical act of turning pages. The technology of the album thus foregrounds movement and change, revelation and concealment in framings of identity in industrial and post-industrial societies.

Likewise, as objects often kept in the home and mended by generations of family or local record keepers, albums are not frozen in time, but built and rebuilt, with creators and their successors adding new content or even erasing, removing, or scratching out earlier media and notations. When albums switch hands, their meaning-making again takes a different path. Focusing on the work these albums performed for their creators and consumers over time, our volume approaches the album as a mixed medium with its own technologies for materializing the complexities of diverse experiences and identities in modern and contemporary life.

Albums of Everyday Life

Much of the scholarship on photography's history has ignored the album or marginalized it as a minor genre. Academic histories of photography, not to mention museum collecting and curating practices, traditionally highlight the canonical work of primarily professional photographers, both fine-art and commercial.[21] Though scholarship and collecting practices in the last several decades have turned more attention to the social functions of photography in place of their aesthetics, and to studies of image reception rather than their creation, albums' associations with women's history and the domestic realm have still often resulted in these objects' malignment as sentimentalized, hobbyist-made, aesthetically derivative objects unworthy of serious review.[22] Yet, groundbreaking work by a set of primarily female scholars over the last two decades has asserted the importance of albums for critical social histories. Following the general trends in material culture studies, feminist scholarship, and Black studies this work has considered how albums and their contents engage senses beyond the visual to also express layered narratives of sonic and tactile registers that together challenge views of the album's formulaic, straightforward evocations of sentimental memories and reveal albums and scrapbooks to be rhetorically and sensorially complex.

Langford's respected, foundational book, *Suspended Conversations: The Afterlife of Memory in Photographic Albums,* asserted that sharing albums is an act of oral tradition that privileges the spoken word over visual aesthetics. The original intention of most album-makers is not simply to create a visual experience, Langford asserts, but to repeatedly stage an "oral-photographic performance" in which one narrates a story around the imagery.[23] Also noting the role of senses beyond visuality in the creation, sharing, and reception of albums, Patrizia Di Bello explored the role of tactility in album-based memory-making and collage. The sense of touch, she argued, often has been gendered feminine and associated with the immediacy of domestic work with one's hands (washing, sewing, caring for children). She distinguished between the "femininized" sense of touch and the presumably male, distanced, privileged, analytical sense of vision. Di Bello foregrounded the interweaving of tactility and visuality in the album as reflecting aspects of women's embodied experiences. The cutting and gluing of photographs and other printed matter across albums, Di Bello argued, depicts women's pleasures of looking at and touching (photographs of) beloved family members, while also capturing more melancholic feelings of material and maternal "wounds" that are never fully "healed" or smoothed over into continuous surfaces.[24]

Stephanie Snyder also affirmed the connection between album-making and the traditional handiwork of women's domestic sphere, noting that albums participate in the cyclical rhythms of the home, including being updated or repaired as needed: "As with clothing, quilts, and other domestic artifacts, women regularly repaired albums against the damage inflicted by their use."[25] Considering the juxtaposition of photography's status as a medium of the industrial era and consumers' engagement with albums in the home, Elizabeth Siegel identified ways that album-makers interjected hand-crafted flourishes (added bits of lace, handwritten captions, etc.) into mass-produced blank albums, alongside mechanically produced photographs, to blend domestic/familial with commercialized/national identities and collective cultural memories.[26] These early examples foreground the generative uses of collage in albums as a creative representational strategy for individuals marginalized from professional networks of representational power. For women constrained by rigid nineteenth-century gender codes, the layering of imagery across an album's pages allowed for the expression of complex intertextual meanings not visualized in public forums.

These foundational texts primarily examined albums reflecting the viewpoints of white, middle-class, straight, and fully abled Canadian, British, and American women. Yet, album makers whose identities include another form of marginalization also used the strategies of orality, domestic tactility, and the integration of traditional handicrafts and mass-media artifacts (among others) to produce tangible expressions of their lived experiences. Our volume approaches a more diverse, global set of albums and scrapbooks to expand the analysis of layering and collage to albums and scrapbooks made by individuals experiencing a wider range of modes of difference. Tina Campt's foundational study of African diasporic photographs in Europe demonstrates how studies of such works can complicate established historical narratives, especially of diaspora and colonialism, by reviving previously silenced areas, including accounts beyond what is visible to the eye. By attending to other sensorial effects, including the sonic and haptic resonances of family photography, one can elucidate other disruptive and disorderly narratives.[27] A broader range of questions open up in this expanded field, such as: How do albums made by colonized, subaltern, and racially or ethnically minoritized subjects and their descendants absorb and adapt the medium of the album, which first developed under the technologies, conventions, and stereotypes of modern European and North American visual cultures? How have the oral histories of albums made by closeted members of LGBTQI+ communities communicated both publicly straight and privately queer narratives at the same time? How do the tactile qualities of an album reference the embodied experiences of differently abled persons?

Scholarship on global iterations of everyday photographic albums has historically focused on colonialist, missionary, and travel albums made by white Europeans and North Americans.[28] Working in the vein of critical Foucauldian studies, this scholarship illuminates how such albums typologize foreign "Others" and insert them into album-based Darwinian archives of racial hierarchies.[29] Additional studies have examined how travel albums assert class status via conspicuous consumption and affirm national identity in a global context.[30]

As Christopher Pinney argues in *Photography's Other Histories*, however, indigenous modes of photographic consumption have arisen in contrast to colonialist traditions. Pinney discusses how photography originally impacted global locations through a "disciplinary framework" that reflected an uneven distribution of power and that used the photographic archive as a system of oppression and control. Yet, he argues, local practices have not always simply reproduced pre-existent colonial structures. Rather, global photography has been "a *creator* of culture." Pinney calls this innovative work "a distinctive postcolonial popular aesthetic."[31] These smaller, local iterations of creativity are more easily overlooked than the larger systemic powers, but our volume aims to follow on the work of Pinney and others to address them. Essays in our volume pick up this thread. The albums and scrapbooks in our volume are informed by representational norms like those reproduced in colonialist archives, but they also creatively respond to such authoritative imagery in layered, everyday modes of survival in the interstices of dominant, institutionalized power.

Ignoring or excluding stories of minor subjects' survival, refusal, and resistance to the dominant powers of the archive and its historical narrative risks repeating its violence. For example, the focus shifts in significant ways in the 1850 daguerreotypes of the Black family members Renty and Delia Taylor who were enslaved in South Carolina are folded into the family narratives of Tamara Lanier, a great-great-great-granddaughter of Renty, rather than those of Louis Agassiz, a Harvard professor who commissioned the images to support his research into polygenism.[32] The oral histories of Lanier's family include proud memories of "Papa Renty" teaching himself and others to read even though literacy was illegal for the enslaved.[33] Yet, these narratives were not voiced in the recent, lengthy, edited scholarly volume on the photographs, which reproduced the forcibly taken images of the stripped subjects in full.[34] For more than a decade, however, Lanier has insisted on voicing the oral traditions preserved by five generations of her family. Her words evoke the traditions of the family photographic album to challenge photographic histories of subjugation and control in the afterlives of slavery. Her refusals pose important questions about who best speaks for images and how institutional powers attempt to silence the embodied knowledge of generations of minoritized families. As our volume's essays demonstrate, the family album work of wayward narratives provides ample content worthy of scholarly attention, theorization, and inclusion.

Our interest in albums as important sites for negotiating representational politics builds on Henri Lefebvre's groundbreaking *Critique of Everyday Life*. In it, Lefebvre argued that the habits of everyday life may seem, at first glance, trivial and unworthy of academic analysis. However, these practices are vital expressions of how individuals navigate the daily dialectics of "illusion and truth, power and helplessness, the intersection of the sector man controls and the sector he does not control."[35] Daily life is a site where one's local, or personal, actions and choices are woven into the larger socio-political structure. Thus, a study of the local reflects on the workings of the larger national and international power structures.

Following Lefebvre's study, Michel de Certeau examined how everyday actions include moments of resistance to bourgeois norms. These everyday actions are small enough to fly under the radar of dominant powers, and traditionally had not been recognized by academics as historically significant.[36] Others have expanded these arguments into specific studies of objects and practices within the fields of media studies and material culture studies. Daniel Miller and Henry Jenkins, among others, have explored the complex socio-political negotiations operating around so-called "low" objects, such as Coca-Cola's soft drinks or fan magazines.[37] These objects can both reassert limiting socio-political dynamics and provide opportunities for creative cultural resistance.

Building on this tradition, our study considers albums and scrapbooks as local recordings of the conscious and unconscious operations of power dynamics around identity. It asks several questions, including: To what degree does one control the representation of one's own identity in an album through conscious choices reflecting agency? To what degree does an album reinscribe and reinforce limiting ideals about identity from dominant media? Finally, how do albums balance a dialectics of creativity and conformity, agency and domination?

Important to our exploration of these questions is the expanding body of scholarship on photographs of everyday life. Pierre Bourdieu first explored in depth the underlying structural elements behind the practices of everyday photography, which he referred to in the title of his 1990 book as a "Middle-Brow Art." Bourdieu identified patterns of formal qualities and behaviors informing French citizens' uses of photographs to fortify family and community identities within the boundaries of what already was defined as socially acceptable. For Bourdieu, these photographs were much more focused on fulfilling a social function than an aesthetic one.[38] Those conventions, Richard Chalfen suggested in the 1987 book *Snapshot Version of Life,* were encouraged by Kodak's marketing and almost unconsciously adopted and assimilated on a widespread scale into homes worldwide.[39] These "rules" included documenting milestones of a child's life from babyhood to adulthood; celebrating upbeat rites of passage such as birthdays, weddings, and anniversaries; and sharing travel experiences. According to Chalfen, moments that might suggest negative counter-narratives and moments of family strife were deliberately and conspicuously *absent* from albums, such as mundane events like hair-washing and housecleaning, physical decline in old age, derailed marriages and the presence of former spouses, and other incidents that might contradict the "happy family" myth.

Drawing on Allan Sekula's essay "On the Invention of Photographic Meaning," Chalfen suggests that while credence frequently is given to the medium of photography's ability to document events with a degree of empiricism, images presented in albums are widely understood to create fictions, or "folk myths" that depart dramatically from the actual experience of family life.[40] Patricia Holland concurs in her essay "How Sweet it Is to Scan: Personal Photographs and Popular Photography," which further suggested that albums visualize tight-knit, happy families that affirm a fictional narrative of what the family *should* look like, rather than what it *does* look like.[41]

In their edited volume, *Family Snaps: The Meanings of Domestic Photography*, Jo Spence, Patricia Holland, and other feminists informed by psychoanalytic approaches looked beyond the seemingly innocent veneer of domestic photography to critique its role in naturalizing uneven power relations and psychological dynamics within the home.[42] Marianne Hirsch's studies of family photography and "the familial gaze" also expanded such studies to examine how these photographs transmute ideology not just in their own time but also across generations in ways that alter memory by asserting mythic visual narratives of the family as stable, happy, and uniform.[43] These studies largely approach the everyday album's form as reinforcing hegemony.[44] It is only from the perspective of looking back at the album with therapeutically informed memory, after time has passed and one's consciousness has been raised, that one can use a critical reinterpretation of the album's representation of family to liberate oneself from the book's original power.

Our volume recognizes albums' histories in reinforcing oppressive family norms, but is also interested in ways that albums creatively adapt, and sometimes even resist, these norms during the time of their creation and not just in hindsight. While the fictions of albums have been read for what they reinforce about state power, reception studies also have emphasized what these fictions may say about their audiences, including their evocations of aspiration and futurity. Building on Roland Barthes' discussion of snapshots in *Camera Lucida: Reflections on Photography*, Geoffrey Batchen has suggested that historians shift "the burden of imaginative thought from the artist and subject, where historians usually seek it, to the viewer, who is invited by such pictures to see much more than meets the eye."[45] Gil Pasternak has argued that the exaggerated display of happiness in family photographs, rather than simply conformist, may also be understood as enabling sitters to imagine a "utopian environment" outside of their "mundane realities" and that family photographs thus engage "political conflict and social destabilization."[46]

Like the foundational studies of photographic albums, the late-twentieth-century analyses of family photography by Chafen, Spence, and Holland, Hirsch primarily focused on examples depicting white, middle-upper class, able-bodied Europeans and North Americans. These studies emphasized the operations of dominant power over moments of local refusal.[47] Yet, notably, they sometimes made room for alternative potentials, especially when considering the perspectives on the family by individuals who sat on the margins of larger power structures. For example, Hirsch conceded that limited moments of resistance in family photography could be found with careful intertextual reading conducted by authors sensitive to their own subject positions. Her illustrative examples were not from actual photographs, but from literary accounts including Jamaica Kincaid's creation of "Lucy," a fictional character from her 1990 novel.[48] As Hirsch recounts, the Caribbean au pair works in an American household with family photographs whose visual myths do not match lived reality. Privately, Lucy is critically aware of this façade. She purchases a camera and begins photographing everyday life in order to privately document and acknowledge for herself ambiguities and contradictions not afforded recognition in her employers' mythologies.[49]

As approaches to everyday photography have expanded to include global examples and pieces made by people of color, studies have emphasized diverse approaches to the representation of family and identity. This work has broadened the understanding of everyday/domestic/family photography in distinct historical moments and locations. Pinney's scholarship, for example, raised awareness of global photographic "vernacular modernisms" not dominated by the Western emphasis on a Cartesian subject.[50] Pinney's study of everyday portraits from the central Indian town of Nagda argues that these examples frame identity not as stable and unchanging, but as multiple and contingent.[51] Deborah Poole has also explored how family portraits taken in studios in Cusco, Peru, demonstrate their subjects' negotiation of issues of race and class across European and indigenous formalist traditions to reveal race as a continuously contested and constructed category.[52] And, Deborah Willis, bell hooks, Tanya Sheehan, and others have demonstrated how African American everyday photography and albums can create a counter-archive to American visual culture's stereotypes about Black identity and its legacy of racist photography and visual mass print media to express pride and agency in the self-representation of personal and community identities.[53]

Recent Black and global feminist photographic scholarship has added innovative approaches to everyday and family photographs that are relevant to our volume's study of the album. Much of this work attends to the tensions in family photographs and albums, where seemingly inconsistent feelings of belonging and unbelonging, togetherness and distance, may be held in tension. Campt's expansive approach to Black photography evokes many ambiguities at play in photographic performances of Black "subjects in formation."[54] She discusses the importance of not only seeing, but of also listening to and feeling the haptics of family photographs to register their full meanings. This includes sitting with and paying attention to what the photograph does not show or narrate – what is hidden or quiet – including ways that marginalized and colonized subjects flee dominant narratives in moments of refusal.[55] As some of the archives she approaches are also absent or incomplete of full historical records, her scholarly attention to absence, stillness, and fugitivity is also an ethical practice that makes room for fragmentation and loss in her subjects' histories.

Deepali Dewan has argued that the very definition of family photography – which scholars have often approached as conformist and banal – becomes much less stable when the concept of family is viewed intersectionally with histories of race, colonialism, diaspora, and migration.[56] As she states, family photography then becomes a "category in flux, contingent on changing notions of photography and of family."[57] Phu, Brown, and Dewan together have explored these complicated, intersectional histories of family photography in their creation of "The Family Camera Network," a collaborative project and public archive that has documented the importance of oral history to photographs of families, especially those that have experienced dislocation due to state power. The scholars argue that this archive and its narratives have a performative function in "establishing, validating, and sustaining kinship relations that subvert or sidestep those authorized by state power."[58] These studies illuminate technologies of the album that enable marginalized individuals to enact personhood in spite of their exclusion from full socio-cultural participation in norms of family life.

Our study aims to build on the theoretical ground set by these accounts and bring to them additional, diverse, global, and historical case studies. The essays in this volume explore the ways specific albums reflect conformity to dominant norms, but also express identities and narratives that the norms do not adequately contain. While we recognize the importance of albums as sites for the re-inscription of dominant power, we also believe that scholarly accounts have overemphasized the dominance of European and North American, middle-class, white, heterosexual, feminized, ableist identity and visual power in the operations of photographic albums and scrapbooks. This book hopes to expand awareness of the value of wayward albums as interstitial records of historically diverse, global recordings of everyday life.

Chapter Sections and Summaries

Our volume's sections are structured around three modes by which our albums shift dominant narratives by telling new stories. The first section examines albums that both aspire to, and deviate from, normative ideals of the family. The chapters in *Complicating Family Stories* extend existing analyses of family photograph albums and their conventions beyond representations of united families, absent of ruptures or tensions. The essays consider mixed feelings in the telling of family history, including voices external to the family and those considered unfit for family life. These albums visualize framings of family that go beyond conventions to demonstrate survival, express ambiguities in the formation of self, and/or redefine familial community.

In Chapter 2, Suryanandini Narain focuses on family albums made by a grandmother, mother, and daughter based in Delhi. Narain considers the meanings of the family album across three generations of Indian women, the eldest of whom was born when the nation was still under British colonial rule. These women's albums blend Western and non-Western conventions across intergenerational narratives, Narain argues, to visualize themes around the women's relationships to their own bodies, their experience of time and aging, and the forces of patriarchy and modernity.

In Chapter 3, James Trent considers the scrapbook of a family whose son had an intellectual disability that led to his institutionalization. Emily and Bernhard Kress placed their oldest child, Bernhard Jr. in a state residential home in New Jersey when he was 11 years old during the post-WWII years. The Kresses produced a scrapbook of around 100 pages devoted to their son, but the majority of its objects are not personal family photographs, but clippings, correspondence, and newsletters related to the institution and parents' group. This scrapbook presents the Kresses' relationship with their son as channeled through the structures and policies of the authoritative institutions, not through the conventions of sentimentalized family photography. Trent provocatively argues that the scrapbook and its contents served as a material substitute for Bernard, whose presence was otherwise absent from the family home.

In Chapter 4, I consider the American artist Henry Darger's use of mass-media imagery including photographs of exotic landscapes, animals, and plants culled from popular magazines to make the cover of a monumental, handmade album that interrogates norms of the American family. The Chicago-based, self-taught artist, once an orphan, had been institutionalized as an adolescent in a home for the "feeble-minded" under Progressive-era, eugenics-informed policies meant to halt the breeding of supposed degenerates. After escaping from the institution, he spent the rest of his life privately reworking found photographic imagery and mass-media print clippings into large canvases that he bound together in oversized albums reaching ten feet in length. These works illustrate his epic fictional account of gender non-conforming child fugitives who flee from an evil society that oppresses them. This essay explores his reworking of found photography and clippings as a way of approximating family photography and travel albums for an individual with no family or economic ability to travel. It argues that Darger used the album format to absorb and adapt dominant mass-cultural imagery and its norms into albums that provided momentary flights from the daily realities of his extreme social marginalization.

Albums in the second section demonstrate the private, sometimes sub-coded presentations of queer intimacies and identities against the backdrop of heteronormative social spheres. The chapters in *Stepping Out of "the Closet," Privately* approach the album as a space for both hiding and revealing LGBTQI+ identity. The album makers in this section layer imagery, ephemera, and notations across blank pages in coded expressions of "closeted," societally oppressed LGBTQI+ identity. This section's essays consider albums and scrapbooks as candid forums for navigating cisgender and heterosexual norms and address the challenges of narrating the albums' hidden subcodes and of "outing" otherwise hidden identities. These essays illuminate how albums can represent self and community beyond biological kinship, as well as other forms of social affiliation, intimacy, and identity. These assertions of identity sometimes enact other forms of privilege, including those of race and social class, even as they navigate their makers' minoritized LGBTQI+ status. Prime examples of sites for "mixed feelings," these albums demonstrate the complex narratives and materiality of intersections between dominant and wayward aspects of identity.

In Chapter 5, Kris Belden-Adams argues that the album of Amherst College/Harvard law school student William Belcher Whitney both performs period expectations for elite hetero-masculine display while also communicating coded gay identity. Whitney's album collects and collages women's hairpin "trophies" from presumed romantic conquests, but these objects and others from his album also speak doubly, to in-group audiences, suggesting his engagement in "homosocial/sexual" relationships not only for subculture recognition, but also for posterity. This essay rebuilds his narrative, and it examines Whitney's struggle to conform to norms, while also addressing the methodological issues inherent in hindsight readings of queerness into the albums.

In Chapter 6, James Kaser analyzes aspects of several multi-media albums, scrapbooks, and journals dating from 1931 to 1949, created to affirm (in private) their maker's emerging identity as a man attracted to men by appropriating images from mainstream culture. Ogden Salmon remained closeted in public, but he recorded his sexual identity and private social life in his albums. In some of his books, the author created a fictional opera company, through which he projected his inner fantasies on romance-prone divas who engaged in socially inappropriate behavior (public nudity, stealing fiancés, and murder). Later albums use a more typical photographic format that depicts him and his friends as smiling, fashionable, and fit in the polished manner of mainstream media. Kaser explores how his albums were a space for visualizing an identity that he remained fearful of exposing in public.

Danielle Kinsey puts into conversation three personal photograph albums from the Gay and Lesbian Memory in Action archive in Johannesburg in Chapter 7. Her album-makers differ in how publicly open they were about their sexuality, and in their access to social power under apartheid. As such, the albums show both queer visibility and conformity. Kinsey's consideration of her album-makers' social positions highlights the intersectionality of their expressions of sexual and racial identity.

Her study emphasizes how South Africa's racial and class-based system of social stratification impact the navigation of queer sexuality.

The third section explores how albums can be activated in new tellings of traditional national and international histories by attuning to the everyday experiences of previously disregarded or misinterpreted populations. *Retelling National and International Histories* addresses albums that present fresh outlooks on prominent narratives from previously under-recognized perspectives. This section's essays are informed by recent scholarship like Pinney's, which consideres how colonialist and settler-era photographs and albums have not always simply asserted a dominant perspective on a passive landscape and its disempowered figures, but have absorbed the influence and pressures of local representational practices, politics, and traditions. Such studies consider how minority and indigenous peoples and traditions influence photographic albums produced by white Europeans and North Americans. These objects speak not just to the representational powers of their makers, but also to the influence of communities of color.[59] These examples demand reading against the grain of established histories that have privileged dominant powers, to instead regard ways that power can operate unexpectedly on the margins and below the radar. These chapters chart the historical value of sharing personal album memories that do not necessarily follow official histories. Additionoally, they demonstrate their relevance not only to academic scholarship, but also to public history and critical, activist pedagogy.

Chapter 8 is by Michèle Gates Moresi, the Supervisory Curator of Collections at the Smithsonian's National Museum of African American History and Culture. In it, Gates Moresi considers a rare microphotography album in NMAAHC's collection created by Captain William A. Prickitt, who oversaw Company G of the 25th Regiment of the United States Colored Troops during the U.S. Civil War. Measuring only about two inches by one inch, and less than one inch thick, this miniature album contains photographs of 17 soldiers who served under Prickitt, all but one of whom are identified by name. According to family lore, Prickitt collected the portraits to remember the men who saved his life during the war. Generations later, when Captain Prickitt's descendants donated their album to NMAAHC, they chose to share a family history and legacy not often evident in stories of the Civil War: that of interracial interdependence and respect. The album presents unique images of these soldiers and, along with the Prickitts' hand-me-down stories, helps us to witness their humanity. As such, this album assists NMAAHC in its endeavor to preserve African American experiences and to support projects that seek to recover memory.

Chapter 9 by Xinyue Yuan analyzes the "Chine-Japon" photographic album of G. Prat, a French silk inspector based on Shamian Island in Guangzhou (Canton). It considers how this late-nineteenth-century European traveler used his album to negotiate colonial anxieties around the political boundaries enclosing foreigners into separate geographic locations within semi-colonial cities. It argues that Prat assembled photographs into a floating tour on paper of East Asia that negotiated his own feelings of foreign precariousness. He did so, Yuan argues, by absorbing Asian representational traditions into the structure of his own European album in a manner that strove to exceed the embodied spatial limitations and vulnerability he felt as a foreigner. Yuan's essay thus charts how local visual cultures and indigenous pressures impacted Pratt's recordings of colonial experience in a photographic album.

In Chapter 10, Karen Barber addresses an album of photographs depicting

Indigenous delegates from the 1898 Indian Congress held at the Trans-Mississippi and International Exposition in Omaha, Nebraska, taken by Omaha studio photographer Frank A. Rinehart and his assistant Adolph Muhr in collaboration with Frank Mooney from the Bureau of American Ethnology. Barber argues that the album incorporated visual approaches to its subjects that presented Indigenous North Americans as racialized objects to be looked at and collected. However, more recent approaches to the album and its photographs by contemporary Indigenous communities and the artist Wendy Red Star have reclaimed the photographs in narratives of Indigenous ancestry and legacy. These contemporary projects vocalize the silences and refusals of the original archive to present a reframing of American Indigenous history and identity.

Ya'ara Gil-Glazer contributes the final piece in this section: Chapter 11. This essay recounts the author's use of critical educational theory in her practice of facilitating workshops between Arab and Jewish students in Israel that focused on family albums. These workshops employ concepts of *official* and *silenced* knowledge to elucidate shared themes of belonging and uprooting in stories of migration shared by both Jews and Arabs in ways insufficiently addressed in scholarly or daily discourse. Gil-Glazer's interactive work with album narratives gives collective voice to traumatic family histories and offers the potential of building trust and bringing students of diverse origins closer together. Based on insights from these discussions, her article proposes photo elicitation as a vehicle for broader critical educational discourse that merges the personal and the political, particularly in complex socio-political and war-torn contexts like Israel.

Publicizing Private Stories in a Digitized World

With the shift to digital photography at the end of the twentieth century, online platforms like Facebook and Google Photos have adopted the terminology of analog albums to describe their user-generated groupings of digital photographs into "albums," linking new technologies to traditions of the past. Yet, in spite of the digital shift, analog albums and scrapbook formats persist. Google Photos and other internet-based photographic companies offer opportunities to design and print paper albums from uploaded digital photographs. These formats increasingly include design options meant to mimic the handcrafted flourishes and notations of traditional scrapbooks, suggesting the continued desire even in the digital age for a relationship with the narratives and memories of material photographic albums.

With albums being a widespread, globalized form of increasing interest to scholars, formerly private albums are now reaching broader public audiences. More museums are recognizing their value to social history, and visual and material culture, and are collecting, displaying, and even digitizing examples. This shift offers the opportunity for bringing previously unheard stories to the public and for presenting a wider array of global photographic iterations of everyday culture. Our volume of essays, which is published in both print and digital volumes, is an example. Though all of the albums contributors discuss were originally crafted in private, most of them are now housed in public institutions and are readily available for access by researchers. With the current trends of digitization, it is also likely that some of these albums will eventually be scanned and uploaded to their institution's digital platforms where anyone online can open and virtually "flip" through their pages online.

Questions arise about what can be retained and what is lost when these objects leave their former, more intimate locations and are placed behind glass vitrines in formal, authoritative institutions or uploaded into open-access online content. Can the personal narratives and multi-sensorial, material qualities of an everyday album be experienced by a museum visitor seeing the object behind glass in a sterile, climate-controlled space or as pixelated images on a computer or smartphone screen? How is an album's presentation of identity and memory received differently when framed by the authority of an institutional context? Our volume's essays begin to address these questions by foregrounding ways that albums, from their very beginnings, balanced themes of public and private, formal and informal, and monumental and intimate, across their pages. The tensions around the dialectics of visibility and mixed feelings at the heart of albums' histories will likely continue as more of these formerly private albums become readily available in institutions and online.

New narratives, of course, inevitably develop as albums leave their original contexts and audiences to be viewed and discussed by a larger public. Our volume's objects of study have histories of reception past their original maker's lifetime that include important transfers of ownership between generations and private and public spaces, not the least of which is their inclusion in this very volume, where their stories are being retold by and for scholarly audiences. Cognizant of the challenges of this movement and of attempting to piece together the meanings of formerly private albums, our volume believes in the importance of these albums' inclusion in larger and more public narratives.

Our volume also recognizes that many albums were never made to be finished but, rather, grew with the passage of time and with the addition of new photos, notations, and other objects to be added over the years and often even by successive generations. In this vein, we consider our albums' histories as progressing and not as ending at the death of their original maker. We regard these continued narratives, and even the transformations of albums from analog to digital media, as acknowledging how retellings of history always shift to include concerns of the present. These albums' stories continue to grow, and by doing so, broaden our understandings of photography, media, diversity, and the navigation of identity.

Notes

1 Examples of photographs of everyday life have traditionally been referred to by professionals in the museum, gallery, and academy as "vernacular," to distinguish them from examples made to be "artistic." In this sense, the term "vernacular" has not worked so much to affirm qualities inherent to its subject, but to define it by what it lacks: fine-art status and intentionality. For this reason and others, Geoffrey Batchen proposed in 2020 putting the term "vernacular" to bed, and to speak only of "photography." This introduction is inspired by his call and thus largely refers to its objects, simply, as photographs. Or, when it is necessary to be more specific, it references them as photographs of everyday life made by everyday people. Geoffrey Batchen, "Vernacular Photographies: Responses to a Questionaire," and "Vernacular Photographies," *History of Photography*, Vol.24, No. 3 (Autumn 2000): 229–231, 266–275. Batchen, "Whither the Vernacular?" in *Imagining Everyday Life: Engagements with Vernacular Photography*, eds. Tina Campt, Marianne Hirsch, Gil Hochberg, and Brian Wallis (Göttingen, Germany: Steidl, 2020), 39.

2 Saidiya Hartman, *Wayward Lives, Beautiful Experiments: Intimate Histories of Social Upheaval* (New York, N.Y.: W.W. Norton & Company, 2019).

3 Christina Sharpe, *In the Wake: On Blackness and Being* (Durham: Duke University Press, 2016); Marisa Fuentes, *Dispossessed Lives: Enslaved Women, Violence and the Archive* (Philadelphia: University of Pennsylvania Press, 2016).

4 Laura Wexler, "The State of the Album," in "Seeing Family," eds. Jennifer Orpana and Sarah Parsons, special issue, *Photography & Culture*, Vol. 10.2 (July, 2017): 100.
5 "Diverse, adj." Oxford English Dictionary Online. December 2021. Oxford University Press. Accessed December 31, 2021: https://www-oed.com.nuncio.cofc.edu/view/Entry/56046?isAdvanced=false&result=1&rskey=dyORXZ&.
6 "Diverse, adj."
7 "Diverse, adj."
8 "Diverse, adj."
9 "Diverse, adj."
10 Mary Trent, "An Album is a Garden Spot:" Visualizing Freedom in the Family Photographs of the Formerly-Enslaved Ellen Craft, *American Art* (forthcoming).
11 Thy Phu and Elspeth Brown, "The Cultural Politics of Aspiration: Family Photography's Mixed Feelings," *Journal of Visual Culture*, Vol. 17.2 (2015): 155–156.
12 The earliest use of an album as a place for an individual to record detailed personal memories of one's life was the *album amicorum* in early modern German- and Dutch-speaking European countries. These pre-photographic albums made of handbound pages were filled with autographs and verses written in Latin by university students and nobles as a form of memento keeping and social networking. June Schlueter, "Michael van Meer's Album Amicorum, with Illustrations of London, 1614-15," *Huntington Library Quarterly*, Vol. 69, No. 2 (2006): 301–314.
13 Jennifer M. Black, "Autograph Albums and the Commercialization of Memory in the United States," in *Cultures of Memory in the Nineteenth Century: Consuming Commemoration*, eds. Katherine Grenier and Amanda Mushal (Cham, Switzerland: Palgrave Macmillan, 2020), 39–59.
14 Alexis Easley, "Scrapbooks and Women's Leisure Reading Practices, 1825-60," *Nineteenth Century Gender Studies* 15, no. 2 (Summer 2019), https://www.ncgsjournal.com/issue152/easley.html.
15 Geoffrey Batchen, *Burning with Desire: The Conception of Photography* (Cambridge, M.A.: The MIT Press, 1997).
16 Elizabeth Siegel, *Galleries of Friendship and Fame: A History of the Nineteenth-Century American Photograph Albums* (New Haven: Yale University Press, 2010), 69–111. Patrizia Di Bello, *Women's Albums and Photography in Victorian England* (Burlington, V.T.: Ashgate, 2007), 74–76.
17 Susan Tucker, Katherine Ott, and Patricia P. Buckler, eds, *The Scrapbook in American Life* (Philadelphia: Temple University Press, 2006) 8; Siegel, *Galleries of Friendship,* 141–143.
18 Nancy Martha West, *Kodak and the Lens of Nostalgia* (Charlottesville: The University Press of Virginia, 2000).
19 Liam Kennedy, "Securing Vision: Photography and US Foreign Policy," *Media, Culture & Society*, Vol. 30, No.3 (2008): 281.
20 Martha Langford, *Suspended Conversations: The Afterlife of Memory in Photographic Albums* (Montreal: McGill-Queen's University Press, 2001), 121.
21 Elizabeth Edwards and Janice Hart, "Introduction: Photographs as Objects," in *Photographs Objects Histories: On the Materiality of Images*, eds. Elizabeth Edwards, and Janice Hart (New York: Routledge, 2004), 79–80.
22 Di Bello, *Women's Albums*, 4, 13, 25-26. This has also resulted in the marginalization of scholarship by female scholars who write on women's albums and scrapbooks: Jennifer Black, "Gender in the Academy: Recovering the Hidden History of Women's Scholarship on Scrapbooks and Albums," *Material Culture*, Vol. 50, No. 2 (2018): 38–52.
23 Langford, *Suspended Conversations,* 122–157.
24 Di Bello, *Women's Albums*, 139–160. Sarah Parsons further elaborates on the role of feminine socialization, play with gender norms, and the activation of the sense of touch in Sarah Parsons, "Women in Fur: Empire, Power, and Play in a Victorian Photography Album", British Art Studies, Issue 18, https://doi.org/10.17658/issn.2058-5462/issue-18/aparsons
25 Stephanie Snyder, "The Vernacular Photo Album: Its Origins and Genius," in *Snapshot Chronicles: Inventing the American Photo Album*, eds. Barbara Levine and Stephanie Snyder (Princeton: Princeton Architectural Press, 2006), 33.

26 Siegel, *Galleries of Friendship*, 139–155.
27 Tina Campt, *Image Matters: Archive, Photography, and the African Diaspora in Europe* (Durham: Duke University Press, 2012).
28 Barbara Levine and Kirsten M. Jensen, *Around the World: The Grand Tour in Photo Albums* (New York: Princeton Architectural Press, 2007).
29 Langford, *Suspended Conversations,* 44–50.
30 Rachel Snow, "Tourism and American Identity: Kodak's Conspicuous Consumers Abroad," *American Culture*, Vol. 31, No. 1 (2008): 7–19.
31 Pinney, "Introduction: 'How the Other Half...'" in *Photography's Other Histories*, ed. Christopher Pinney and Nicolas Peterson (Durham, NC: Duke University Press, 2003), 11.
32 Agassiz, a professor of zoology and geology, commissioned the fifteen photographs by Joseph Zealy to illustrate his theories that races evolved separately and were distinct species. Maya McDougall and Garrett O'Brien, "Five Generations of Renty," *The Harvard Crimson* (March 18, 2021). Accessed March 30, 2022:, https://www.thecrimson.com/article/2021/3/18/lanier-v-harvard-scrut/.The enslaved subjects are Delia, Drana, Renty, Jack, Fassena, Alfed, Jem.
33 McDougall and O'Brien, "Five Generations of Renty."
34 Ilisa Barbash, Molly Rogers, and Deborah Willis, eds. *To Make their Own Way in the World: The Enduring Legacy of the Zealy Daguerreotypes* (Cambridge, Mass.: Peabody Museum Press; New York: Aperture, 2020).
35 Henri Lefebvre, *Critique of Everyday Life,* trans. John Moore (London, Verso: 1991), 21.
36 Michel de Certeau, *The Practice of Everyday Life*, trans. Steven F. Rendell (Berkeley, CA: The University of California Press, 2002),
37 Henry Jenkins, *Textual Poachers: Television Fans & Participatory Culture* (New York: Routledge, 1992); Daniel Miller, "Coca-Cola: A Black Sweet Drink from Trinidad," *Material Cultures: Why Some Things Matter* (Chicago: University of Chicago Press, 1997), 169–187.
38 Pierre Bourdieu, *Photography: A Middle-Brow Art*, trans. Shaun Whiteside (Cambridge, UK: Polity Press, 1990).
39 Richard Chalfen, *Snapshot Version of Life* (Bowling Green, Ohio: Bowling Green University Popular Press, 1987). For more about Kodak's female-focused marketing, please see: Dan Meinwald, "Picture Perfect: The Selling of the Kodak Image," *Frame/Work*, Vol. 1, No. 2 (1987): 15-25. As Jeremy Seabrook suggested, women were positioned as the dutiful custodians of family memory: Seabrook, "My Life is in That Box," in *Family Snaps: The Meanings of Domestic Photography,* eds. Jo Spence and Patricia Holland (London: Virago Press, 1991), 171–185.
40 Chalfen.; Allan Sekula, "On the Invention of Photographic Meaning," in Victor Burgin, ed. *Thinking Photography* (London: Palgrave, 1982), 84–109. The creation of fictional self-narratives is one of several continuities between analog (pre-digital) albums and their online counterparts, "shared album" digital social media practices: Kris Belden-Adams, "Everywhere and Nowhere, Simultaneously: Theorizing the Ubiquitous, Immaterial, Post-Digital Social Media Photograph," in *Mobile and Ubiquitous Media: Critical and International Perspectives*, Michael S. Daubs and Vince Manzerolle, eds. (New York and Bern: Peter Lang Inc./International Academic Publishers, 2017), 163–179.
41 Patricia Holland. "How Sweet it Is to Scan: Personal Photographs and Popular Photography," in *Photography: A Critical Introduction,* Liz Wells, ed. (New York and London: Routledge, 1995), 103–150.
42 Spence and Holland, eds. *Family Snaps.*
43 Marianne Hirsh, *Family Frames: Photography, Narrative, and Postmemory* (Cambridge, MA: Harvard University Press, 1997), 9–11.
44 A notable exception occurs in Motz's study of albums made by educated, unmarried, white women. Motz, "Visual Autobiography: Photograph Albums of Turn-of-the-Century Midwestern Women," *American Quarterly,* Vol. 41, no. 1 (1989): 63–92.
45 Geoffrey Batchen, "Snapshots: Art History and the Ethnographic Turn," *Photographies*, Vol. 1, No. 2 (2008): 121–142.
46 Gil Pasternak, "Intimate Conflicts: Foregrounding the Radical Politics of Family Photographs," *Photography, History, Difference*, ed. Tanya Sheehan (Hanover, N.H.: Dartmouth College Press, 2014), 218.

47 This dominant power was made visible in practices such as the baby book, which was influenced by eugenics and affirmed whiteness: Shawn Michelle Smith, "'Baby's Picture is Always Treasured': Eugenics and the Reproduction of Whiteness in the Family Photograph Album," in *The Nineteenth-Century Visual Culture Reader*. Vanessa Schwartz and Jeannene Przyblyski, eds. (London and New York: Routledge, 2004), 358–370.
48 Jamaica Kincaid, *Lucy* (New York, NY: Farrar, Straus Giroux Inc., 1990).
49 Hirsch, *Family Frames*, 72–76.
50 Pinney, "Introduction: 'How the Other Half…,'" 12.
51 Christopher Pinney, "Photographic Portraiture in Central India in the 1980s and 1990s," in *The Material Culture Reader*, ed. Victor Buchli (Oxford, U.K.: Berg, 2002), 87–103.
52 Deborah Poole, *Vision, Race, and Modernity* (Princeton, NJ: Princeton University Press,1997), 198–216.
53 Deborah Willis, ed., *Picturing Us: African American Identity in Photography* (New York: The New Press, 1994); Willis' volume includes bell hooks, "In Our Glory: Photography and Black Life," 43-53; Tanya Sheehan, "Revival and Subversion: Snapshot Performances from Kodak to Kara Walker," in *Study in Black and White: Photography, Race, Humor* (Philadelphia: The Pennsylvania State University Press, 2018), 132–162.
54 Campt, *Image Matters,* 8–9.
55 Campt, *Listening to Images* (Durham: Duke University Press, 2017), 9–10.
56 On family photography as banal see Geoffrey Batchen, "Snapshots: Art History and the Ethnographic Turn," *Photographies*, Vol. 1, No. 2 (2008): 121–142.
57 Deepali Dewan, "Introduction," in "Family Photographs," ed. Deepali Dewan, special issue, *Trans Asia Photography* 9, no. 1 (Fall 2018) http://hdl.handle.net/2027/spo.7977573.0009.101.
58 Phu, Brown, and Dewan, "'The Family Camera Network'" *Photography & Culture*, Vol. 10, No. 2 (July 2017), 153.
59 Nebahat Avcıoğlu, "Immigrant Narratives: The Ottoman Sultans' Portraits in Elisabeth Leitner's Family Photo Album, Circa 1862-72," *Muqarnas*, Vol. 35, No. 1 (2018): 193–228.

Bibliography

Avcıoğlu, Nebahat. "Immigrant Narratives: The Ottoman Sultans' Portraits in Elisabeth Leitner's Family Photo Album, Circa 1862-72." *Muqarnas*, Vol. 35, No. 1 (2018): 193–228.

Barbash, Ilisa, Molly Rogers, and Deborah Willis, eds. *To Make their Own Way in the World: The Enduring Legacy of the Zealy Daguerreotypes*. Cambridge, MA: Peabody Museum Press; New York, N.Y.: Aperture, 2020.

Batchen, Geoffrey. *Burning with Desire: The Conception of Photography*. Cambridge, MA: The MIT Press, 1997.

Batchen, Geoffrey. "Vernacular Photographies: Responses to a Questionnaire," and "Vernacular Photographies." *History of Photography*, Vol. 24, No. 3 (Autumn 2000): 229–231, 266–275.

Batchen, Geoffrey. "Snapshots: Art History and the Ethnographic Turn." *Photographies*, Vol. 1, No. 2 (2008): 121–142.

Belden-Adams, Kris. "Everywhere and Nowhere, Simultaneously: Theorizing the Ubiquitous, Immaterial, Post-Digital Social Media Photograph." In *Mobile and Ubiquitous Media: Critical and International Perspectives*, Michael S. Daubs and Vince Manzerolle, eds. (New York and Bern: Peter Lang Inc./International Academic Publishers, 2017), 163–179.

Black, Jennifer M. "Gender in the Academy: Recovering the Hidden History of Women's Scholarship on Scrapbooks and Albums." *Material Culture*, Vol. 50, No. 2 (2018): 38–52.

Black, Jennifer M. "Autograph Albums and the Commercialization of Memory in the United States." In *Cultures of Memory in the Nineteenth Century: Consuming Commemoration*, Katherine Grenier and Amanda Mushal, eds. (Cham, Switzerland: Palgrave Macmillan, 2020), 39–59.

Bourdieu, Pierre. *Photography: A Middle-Brow Art*. Shaun Whiteside, trans. Cambridge, U.K.: Polity Press, 1990.

Campt, Tina. *Image Matters: Archive, Photography, and the African Diaspora in Europe*. Durham: Duke University Press, 2012.

Campt, Tina. *Listening to Images*. Durham: Duke University Press, 2017.

Campt, Tina, Marianne Hirsch, Gil Hochberg, and Brian Wallis, eds. *Imagining Everyday Life: Engagements with Vernacular Photography*. Göttingen, Germany: Steidl, 2020.

Chalfen, Richard. *Snapshot Version of Life*. Bowling Green, Ohio: Bowling Green University Popular Press, 1987.

Certeau, Michel de. The Practice of Everyday Life, trans. Steven F. Rendell. Berkeley, CA: The University of California Press, 2002.

Dewan, Deepali. "Introduction." In "Family Photographs," edited by Deepali Dewan. Special issue. *Trans Asia Photography*, Vol. 9, No. 1 (Fall 2018).

Di Bello, Patrizia. *Women's Albums and Photography in Victorian England*. Burlington, V.T.: Ashgate, 2007.

Easley, Alexis. "Scrapbooks and Women's Leisure Reading Practices, 1825-60." *Nineteenth Century Gender Studies*, Vol. 15, No. 2 (Summer 2019). https://www.ncgsjournal.com/issue152/easley.html

Edwards, Elizabeth and Janice Hart, eds. *Photographs Objects Histories: On the Materiality of Images*. New York: Routledge, 2004.

Fuentes, Marisa. *Dispossessed Lives: Enslaved Women, Violence and the Archive*. Philadelphia: University of Pennsylvania Press, 2016.

Hartman, Saidiya. *Wayward Lives, Beautiful Experiments: Intimate Histories of Social Upheaval*. New York: W.W. Norton & Company, 2019.

Hirsh, Marianne. *Family Frames: Photography, Narrative, and Postmemory*. Cambridge, MA: Harvard University Press, 1997.

Holland, Patricia. "How Sweet it Is to Scan: Personal Photographs and Popular Photography." In *Photography: A Critical Introduction*, Liz Wells, ed. (New York and London: Routledge, 1995), 103–150.

Jenkins, Henry. *Textual Poachers: Television Fans & Participatory Culture*. New York: Routledge, 1992.

Kennedy, Liam. "Securing Vision: Photography and US Foreign Policy." *Media, Culture & Society*, Vol. 30, No. 3 (2008): 279–294.

Langford, Martha. *Suspended Conversations: The Afterlife of Memory in Photographic Albums*. Montreal: McGill-Queen's University Press, 2001.

Lefebvre, Henri. *Critique of Everyday Life*. John Moore, trans. London: Verso, 1991.

Levine, Barbara and Kirsten M. Jensen. *Around the World: The Grand Tour in Photo Albums*. New York: Princeton Architectural Press, 2007.

Levine, Barbara and Stephanie Snyder. *Snapshot Chronicles: Inventing the American Photo Album*. Princeton: Princeton Architectural Press, 2006.

McDougall, Maya and Garrett O'Brien. "Five Generations of Renty." *The Harvard Crimson* March 18, 2021. Accessed December 28, 2021: https://www.thecrimson.com/article/2021/3/18/lanier-v-harvard-scrut/

Meinwald, Dan. "Picture Perfect: The Selling of the Kodak Image." *Frame/Work*, Vol. 1, No. 2 (1987): 15–25.

Miller, Daniel. *Material Cultures: Why Some Things Matter*. Chicago: University of Chicago Press, 1997.

Motz, Marilyn. "Visual Autobiography: Photograph Albums of Turn-of-the-Century Midwestern Women." *American Quarterly*, Vol. 41, No. 1 (1989): 63–92.

Parsons, Sarah. "Women in Fur: Empire, Power, and Play in a Victorian Photography Album." *British Art Studies*, No. 18. https://doi.org/10.17658/issn.2058-5462/issue-18/aparsons

Pasternak, Gil. "Intimate Conflicts: Foregrounding the Radical Politics of Family Photographs." In *Photography, History, Difference*, Tanya Sheehan ed. (Hanover, N.H.: Dartmouth College Press, 2014), 217–240.

Phu, Thy and Elspeth Brown. "The Cultural Politics of Aspiration: Family Photography's Mixed Feelings." *Journal of Visual Culture*, Vol. 17, No. 2 (2015): 152–165.

Phu, Thy, Elspeth Brown, and Deepali Dewan. "'The Family Camera Network.'" *Photography & Culture*, Vol. 10, No. 2 (July 2017): 147–163.

Pinney, Christopher. "Photographic Portraiture in Central India in the 1980s and 1990s." In *The Material Culture Reader*, Victor Buchli, ed. (Oxford, U.K.: Berg, 2002), 87–103.

Pinney, Christopher and Nicolas Peterson, eds. *Photography's Other Histories*. Durham: Duke University Press, 2003.

Poole, Deborah. *Vision, Race, and Modernity*. Princeton, NJ: Princeton University Press, 1997.

Schlueter, June. "Michael van Meer's Album Amicorum, with Illustrations of London, 1614-15." *Huntington Library Quarterly*, Vol. 69, No. 2 (2006): 301–314.

Sekula, Allan "On the Invention of Photographic Meaning." In *Thinking Photography*, Victor Burgin, ed. London: Palgrave, 1982.

Sharpe, Christina. *In the Wake: On Blackness and Being*. Durham: Duke University Press, 2016.

Sheehan, Tanya. "Revival and Subversion: Snapshot Performances from Kodak to Kara Walker." In *Study in Black and White: Photography, Race, Humor*. (Philadelphia: The Pennsylvania State University Press, 2018), 132–162.

Siegel, Elizabeth. *Galleries of Friendship and Fame: A History of the Nineteenth-Century American Photograph Albums*. New Haven: Yale University Press, 2010.

Smith, Shawn Michelle. "'Baby's Picture is Always Treasured': Eugenics and the Reproduction of Whiteness in the Family Photograph Album." In *The Nineteenth-Century Visual Culture Reader*, Vanessa Schwartz and Jeannene Przyblyski, eds. (London and New York: Routledge, 2004), 358–370.

Snow, Rachel. "Tourism and American Identity: Kodak's Conspicuous Consumers Abroad." *American Culture*, Vol. 31, No. 1 (2008): 7–19.

Snow, Rachel. "Snapshots by the Way: Individuality and Convention in Tourists' Photographs from the United States, 1880-1940." *Annals of Tourism Research*, Vol. 39, No. 4 (2012): 2013–2050.

Spence, Jo and Patricia Holland, eds. *Family Snaps: The Meanings of Domestic Photography*. London: Virago Press, 1991.

Trent, Mary. "An Album is a Garden Spot:" Visualizing Freedom in the Family Photographs of the Formerly-Enslaved Ellen Craft. *American Art* (forthcoming).

Tucker, Susan, Katherine Ott, and Patricia P. Buckler, eds. *The Scrapbook in American Life*. Philadelphia: Temple University Press, 2006.

West, Nancy Martha. *Kodak and the Lens of Nostalgia*. Charlottesville: The University Press of Virginia, 2000.

Wexler, Laura. "The State of the Album." In "Seeing Family," edited by Jennifer Orpana and Sarah Parson. Special issue, *Photography & Culture* Vol. 10, No. 2 (July 2017): 99–103.

Willis, Deborah, ed. *Picturing Us: African American Identity in Photography*. New York: The New Press, 1994.

Part I

Complicating Family Narratives

2 Women on Holiday: Intergenerational Narratives in Photographic Albums from India

Suryanandini Narain

Author's Note: The names of the albums' makers and the subjects of the included photographs have been changed.

Preeti Prashad and her mother Rama Prashad documented their holiday travels from India to Washington, D.C., in two photographic albums in the summer months of 1993 and 1994. The women took the vacations to visit the U.S. home of Rama's elder daughter, Rekha Mathur, and her husband Ashok. Meera, Rekha's daughter, also recorded recollections about the trips in her diary. As members of my own extended family, they have shared these materials with me through conversations and interviews presented in this chapter. The Prashad women's documentation exemplifies single women of the Indian middle-class's motivations for vacationing in a foreign country: to visit family but also to gain exposure to a new culture in a globalized world. The subjectivity of these oral and photographic narratives aligns with geographer Gillian Rose's notion of a matrilineal and "traditional responsibility for domestic order," which places women in charge of domestic material objects and images.[1] Such a position enables them to steer the meanings that those artifacts inherit and create, and allows them to impart wisdom.

In addition to studying the two albums of U.S. trips, this chapter also looks at a 1964 album by the Prashads which they referred to as the "black album" due to the color of its cover. Additionally, it considers another of Preeti's personal albums, the "red album," which she made during her childhood and youth, and which includes photographs taken between 1957 and the 1970s. The four albums together cover the 1950s through the 1990s, encapsulating the touristic engagements of the album-makers/keepers over nearly four decades, from childhood to adult experiences. The albums belong to different time frames in the family's history, and also to alternative ideological phases in India's socio/political economies. As such, they generate alternative tourist visual narratives developed by Indian women. They provide photographic documentation of the women's shared family cohesion, which they played out in acts of mutual support and companionship in everyday life. This chapter explores the roles three generations of Indian women assumed in shaping and maintaining the "material and emotional economies" within their families, as keepers of the photographic archive of the Prashad family, and who also expressed resolved senses of place within that family narrative.[2]

Current scholarship on tourism and holiday photographs focuses on the white European/U.S. male tourist who bears his camera, pointed eastward toward "the Other." That touristic "gazer" seeks an experience that enables him to "get away" from everyday life.[3] Critiques of this literature have questioned the assumed binary

DOI: 10.4324/9781003157427-4

between "home" and "away," but do not necessarily account for differences in the identities and expectations of the traveler.[4] By exploring intergenerational narratives created and maintained by five women across three generations of a middle-class Indian family, this essay offers a new understanding of the tropes of tourist photography and its narration. Preeti and Rama present an alternative to predicted behaviors of the typical tourist featured in current scholarship. They are Westward-bound females who are not in possession of their own cameras. They also engage in domestic life even while on holiday, and thus experience "same-ness" with their lives back home while also encountering social and cultural differences. The women in this case study thus offer an antithesis to the Western male *flâneur* paradigm of the tourist photographer who freely negotiates his contemporary world.[5] Their documented travels redefine the boundaries of tourism, and their photographic albums bear equal instances of adventure and everyday-ness, of the seepage of the familiar into the unfamiliar, and of predictability amid novelty. As such, their narratives defy the binaries of the patriarchal symbolic order that seeks to separate home from abroad, domesticity from tourism, and leisure from work. Instead, they establish an alternative idea of space and temporal continuity.

The Washington, D.C., Family/Travel Albums

In the 1990s, the flow of Indians into America was noteworthy, as a large number made the move to garner jobs in the booming information technology and software sectors. The proliferation of the internet and global trade made the path to the U.S. a well-worn one for South Asians. The 1993 and 1994 Washington, D.C. vacations Rama and Preeti documented emulated this trend, even though Rama's son-in-law Ashok held a government office. These two single women of different generations used their photographic albums to negotiate their traditional family identities with the influences of American culture and materialism. Their oral accounts about the albums in interviews supplemented those that Rama's other two daughters and her granddaughter offered. The photographs in the 1993 and 1994 holiday albums are indicative of memory work, exemplifying the embellishment of facts in the recording of individual histories with a degree of presumed facticity. Un-self-conscious of the fictional additions to narratives, the images acquire uncontested meanings that fix "memories into the irreversibility of history" while they "immobilize the flow of family life into a fixed series of eternal snapshot identities," in the words of Jørgen Ole Baerenholdt and his co-editors.[6] This study exemplifies the central role oral narratives play in reinforcing familial identities, and in affirming familial cohesion and history. The preservation of visually guided oral narratives brings meaning to the lives of the women in question, while placing them in a broader historical continuum of class and gendered belonging.

The linked photographs of these albums make a personal claim to family integrity and narrative in a way that individual images cannot. The oral narration of memories that speak for and about family photographs, time and time again, remobilizes them, un-fixes them, and makes the albums into contingent entities with multiple possible meanings. These remobilizations take place when album narrators make changes to photography-prompted stories, and/or recontextualize them to suit different circumstances, especially across generations. This is not necessarily a "loss" of memory, where facts and faces are forgotten, but involves an expansion, embellishment, and enlivening of a "memory journey."[7]

"Mummy's" Trip

It was a matter of great pride for Rama to be invited to the U.S. in the summer of 1993 by her daughter Rekha and son-in-law Ashok Mathur. Ashok was then posted as Special Attaché (Personnel) at the Indian Embassy in Washington D.C. For four years between 1992 and 1996, they lived in a house on Thoreau Drive in Bethesda, Maryland. As it had been Rama's first (and final) international trip, later family conversations, including those with me, frequently referenced the treasured photographic album and its memories. Ashok took most of the photographs and developed them at the end of the trip while Rama was still in the U.S. He then gave them to her as a memento. Upon her return to Delhi, she later arranged the images in a paper-backed album from a local photography studio (Studio Parkash). Rama neatly inscribed the images with the names of the places and dates of her visits. She arranged the photographs chronologically, to allow every viewing of the album to be a sequential re-living of the trip.

Oral narrative is essential for telling the story behind and between the images. It references things that are not visible in the frame. The photographic album demonstrably functions as a mnemonic device for expanded narratives. With just 45 images standing in for a visit that lasted five months (from May to September of 1993), the oral storytelling is the dominant mode of remembrance. Typically, Rama, her daughters, and her granddaughters sit around the albums and discuss the images, recalling details about their travels.[8] They speak of their youths, their domestic preoccupations, growing up, raising children, the tourist spots they visited, and the extended family they met. They thus narrate their lived experiences beyond what is visible in the photographs – especially for the benefit of those who were not present on the trips, for those who were added to the family later, and for other extended family and visiting friends. Oral narratives are catalyzed by the photographs and go well beyond them.

Overall, the carefully composed photographs in the album are tableaus of seeing tourist spots and the family visiting friends and extended family, with Rama foregrounded as the chief occupant of every image. Conversations around the album often involve an older Rama narrating these images of herself and others made about three decades ago to make meaning through evoking memories in a visual and verbal exchange with other viewers of the album. Rama wields the privilege of imparting the fullest narrative, as she is both storyteller and protagonist.

For example, while sharing the album recently, she commented on moments extraneous to the photographs, such as the long flights. This trip had been the first time she had ever traveled by air. The Mathur family documented Rama's arrival on May 31, 1993 as a moment of great anticipation. Her 13-year-old granddaughter Meera mentioned it in the opening pages of her diary as a "countdown that was over" for "at last we would get to meet her."[9] The album did not include a photograph of her arrival or other moments of transit or departure between locations. The album bears consciously selected moments of active engagement with sites and sights, either domestic or touristic, that were deemed photography-worthy, rather than those that are in-between, transitory, or preparatory in nature. Of course, analog photography also produces fewer images than the compulsive image-making of digital photography today.

The first two images of the album show Rama, Rekha, Meera, and her sister Tara at the Washington Memorial on a June afternoon (Fig. 2.1). The memorial itself is not visible in the photographs, apart from the light-gray wall in the background. The focus instead is on the family group, which looks at the camera. A second photograph

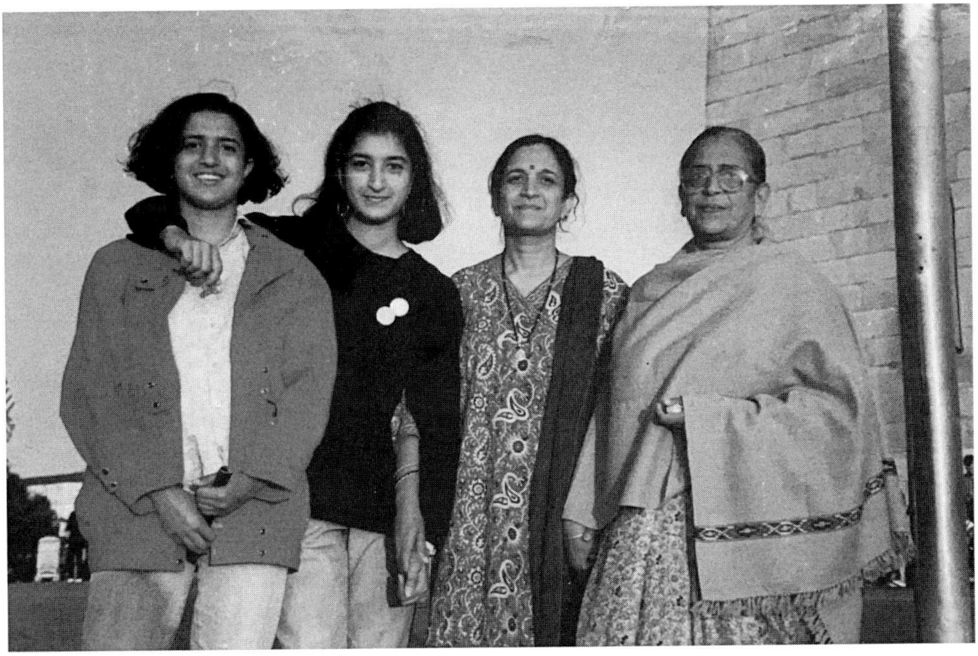

Figure 2.1 Washington Monument, June '93, 1993, color print, 4 in. × 6 in. © 2020 Mathur and Prashad Families.

shows them waiting in line to go into the memorial. But nowhere are they shown with the memorial in full view, even though its history and dimensions are vividly described in Meera's diary. Other photographs depict visits to the Air and Space Museum during the same month; the Statue of Liberty in July; Niagara Falls, Mount Vernon, Ocean City, and Great Falls in August; and Atlantic City in September. As photographer, Ashok builds a similarly tight frame around the family, usually the women. Even though Meera's diary mentions visiting sites such as the United Nations headquarters, the Twin Towers of the World Trade Center, the Empire State Building in New York, and the Luray Caverns in Virginia, the album includes no photographs of these sites. Every now and then, relatively nondescript fragments of these places appear in the background as the family's bodies are shown in full length and in close proximity to each other. The desired outcome of these images is the conscious and selective staging of the human subjects. As far as the sites are concerned, as geography scholars Michael Haldrup and Jonas Larsen have suggested:

> ... [T]ourism's attractions are transformed into theatres for staging a 'nice' family life. ... The family gaze revolves around the *production* of social relations rather than the consumption of places ... Places become scenes for acting out and framing active and tender family life for the camera. Family members and their performances make experiences and places extraordinary and full of enjoyable life ... When performing tourist photography, families are creating experiences and performing their "familyness" rather than an account of having been to destinations known for their historic or cultural significance.[10]

In accord with this performance of "familyness," Rama's relatives are photographed enjoying meals together in restaurants and picnic spots, resting on park benches, and boarding ferries. Emphasis is on time spent with each other rather than on laying a claim to having visited well-known American tourist spots. Without verso inscriptions and Meera's descriptive prose, it would be difficult to determine the locations of some of these images. As such, the photographs challenge an understanding of tourism that places the spectacular or the extraordinary in binary opposition to the ordinary and the everyday. These photographs seldom encapsulate the moment as one of having "arrived," or of being in the presence of the "wonderful" object or building. Instead, they favor the central subject as either Rama and/or her family.[11] The fragmentary nature of the tourist sites in these photographs bear repurposed meaning, as the focus is upon the human unit projecting itself and only tangentially referencing the monument, often in unrecognizable ways. The monuments and sites are fractured by the frame, appearing as abstract backgrounds or incidental occurrences to the family that is central. They strive "to stage the family within the attraction's socially constructed aura" rather than granting intrinsic value to the site itself.[12]

The notion of the everyday familial experience is embedded in these vacation photographs. Their purpose is the communication of familial unity and an absorption of Rama as a single mother into her daughter's nuclear family unit. This absorption occurs temporarily during the vacation but permanently in the photograph. The family is shown touching each other, standing in "corporeal proximity" to each other, and collectively holding the direct gaze of the photographer and viewer.[13] These poses articulate an expression of togetherness, of "bonding family members as *one* social body."[14] Photography historian Elizabeth Edwards explains the deliberate comportment of bodies:

> Staged pictures ... disclose specific intentions, as opposed to promising to reveal a priori meanings lodged in configurations of the world. There is also a theatricality ... that the subjects project themselves or the drama forward to something external - the camera and the viewer. Hence we can attribute some significance to the self-conscious, intentional content of the photograph.[15]

Rose corroborates this proposition by regarding "family photographs as a technology for performing familiality."[16] Indeed, the photographs in Rama's albums are a collation of performed familial relations, set against the backdrop of well-known American landmarks, and appropriated for their function as backdrops and little else. The photographic moments that make the album's narratives are a conjunction of the performance of familial belonging and of the triumph of one's arrival at a tourist destination. The result is a hybrid photographic album that is part-family focused, part-tourism-focused.

In contrast to photographing sites that are public, spectacular, and touristic, the album also visualizes the domestic space of the Mathur home on Thoreau Drive.[17] Some photographs mark the travelers' wonderment at tourist sites – such as an image of Rama on her first escalator ride in Atlantic City, or of her sitting in front of a floral clock at Niagara on the Canadian side. This parallels representations of the Mathur home. The album marvels at the home's technological, atmospheric, and architectural novelties, such as its basement, attic, fireplace, and even the snow that its owners shoveled from the driveway. The album allows for a reconstruction of the extraordinary within the ordinary precincts of the home by narrativizing these novel elements. For example, a photograph of the house covered in snow is the only image in the album that is devoid of people. It stands as a highlight for the family as they recall their pleasure and excitement of the experiences within the home. Photographs of Rama sitting on the steps of the house, or seated beside a large fireplace, or on her granddaughter's bed, are composed to include the domestic setting more fully than the spatial contextualization used at tourist spots, so the bed or the fireplace appear unfragmented in the frame (Fig. 2.2).

These photographs deliberately focus on the house as a site for the family holiday experience, locating the family and Rama within it, and putting it on par with the tourist sites they visited – if not more of a focus. It is important to note that the images of the family in the home deviate from the normative tourist practice of being photographed at "viewpoints," or in the company of historic monuments. The domestic setting is instead celebrated as an important site for image-making in what is still seen as a holiday experience by the visitor and her family. The home also conveys generational accomplishment in a new country, and its presence suggests family pride in that achievement.

Scholars of tourism studies have argued that vacations are intended as an escape from the "paramount reality" of everyday living.[18] Yet they have also asserted that "ultimately, lasting escape is not possible, as individuals must inevitably reassume their place in the everyday social structure."[19] The photographs in this album suggest instead that vacation time also offers a continuum of their identities, by virtue of their gender, familial positions, and social class. While on vacation, Rama and Preeti occupy a liminal

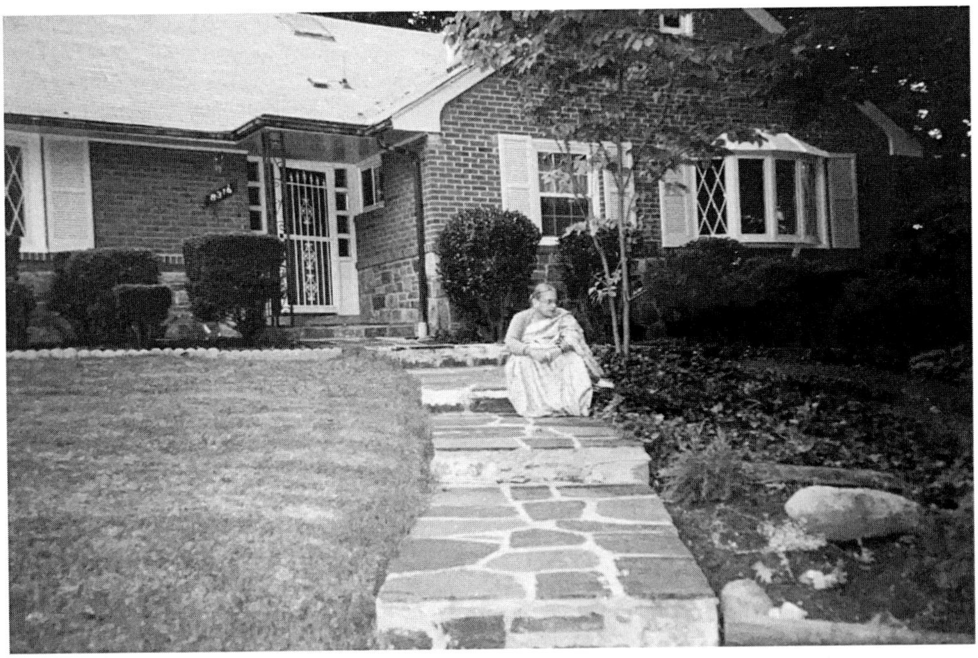

Figure 2.2 Mathur Home at Thoreau Drive, Bethesda, Maryland, 1993, color print, 4 in. × 6 in. © 2020 Mathur and Prashad Families.

zone between reality and a break in the routine. They carry over their home identities to the house on Thoreau Drive, while also occupying identities as tourists when visiting landmark monuments and natural sites on the American East Coast. "Residences," or second homes where tourists picture themselves during holidays, provide a "stage" for familial bodies, and enable "familyness" to be enacted, often in greater measure.[20] The vacation album is as much a testament of the familiarity essential to the familial, and the self, relocated within the domestic, as it is about the family unit's encounter with "the Other," the spectacular, and the unfamiliar.

Periods of time not visualized by the album also inform my reading of Rama's D.C. vacation. The album's 45 photographs only highlight key moments from Rama's five-month-long trip. Meera's diary fills in these gaps with a substantial narrative account. Its meticulous details combine a tourist guide's factual narrative about monuments and sights with a personal outpouring of emotional tidings toward her grandmother.

Conversations with trip participants indicate that the photographs do not always picture the times that were most memorable.[21] Often, memorable parts of the vacation included the domestic engagements of housekeeping and personal conversations shared by mother, daughter, and granddaughters. These domains also are gendered, and not photographed because they were not deemed unusual, and/or because they transpired in the absence of Ashok, the man wielding the camera. Although fondly remembered during my discussions with them, these moments are not photographed as exceptional experiences, but they stay embedded within the everyday-ness of memories of domestic life in India. The family was the subject of photographs in the album, mostly when it was outside of the home, engaged in travel and tourism. Domesticity occurred as a timeless continuum during Rama's trip, which did not generate any spectacular moments worthy of taking photographs unless it offered a reflection of the differences in lifestyle in America, or the backdrop for special occasions such as parties.

While viewing the albums together, Rama and her daughters would orally recollect the many house parties hosted by the Mathurs for professional acquaintances in the local Indians community, along with friends and family. Photos in the album depict Rama at parties in the drawing rooms of other homes that she visited during her stay in New York City and Baltimore. Rekha mentions the food she cooked in vast quantities for parties, and the house that she kept with pride for her family and visitors alike. Meera's diary names people who hosted Rama, and she details what was eaten, which films were watched, and what jokes were cracked.[22] A few photographs portray family seated around dining tables with an Indian food spread. Such images reinforce a liminal zone for Rama between cultural familiarity and the novelty of being abroad. As such, the definition of a "vacation" as "time away" from domesticity and its routines does not apply to Rama's album, which detailed the routines of her daughter's household on special occasions.

Preeti's Trip

There are several similarities, overlaps as well as significant differences between Rama's and Preeti's albums, both covering trips to the United States. Preeti traced her mother's footsteps and visited her sister the following year in 1994, staying nearly four months between March 27 and July 11. As a 36-year-old woman, she, like her mother, was a single traveler on this vacation, and she was ensconced in her sister's family for the length of her stay. As such, her identity was co-opted as "sister," "aunt," and "sister-in-law," and her single marital status was allayed for these months. The concept of "familyness," albeit temporarily enacted for the vacation period, became permanently memorialized in the album. Viewing the album reactivates memories of the album's events through conversations that enable Preeti and the other women in the family to relive familial identity.

Preeti's album includes exactly twice the number of photographs taken during her mother's visit or 90 images. She printed and archived the images in a brown, leather-bound album she purchased in the U.S. The additional photographs depict new destinations she visited during her vacation, and a larger number of solitary portraits. Preeti's album also bears multiple photographs of every destination; whereas Rama's only includes single photos of visits to the same sites. The Statue of Liberty appears by herself in an image in Preeti's album, while it is entirely absent from Rama's. Additionally, Preeti is foregrounded in photographs of the ferry ride and at the Statue itself. Similarly, the Washington Monument is uncropped and in full visual glory as Rekha and Preeti pose before it (Fig. 2.3).

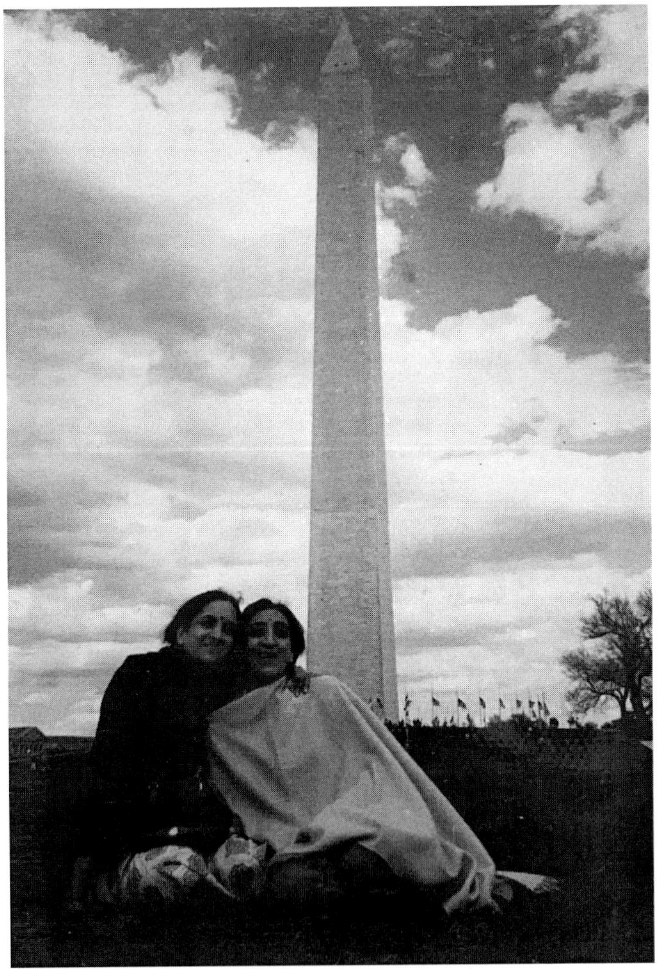

Figure 2.3 Monument, Washington D.C., April '94, 1994, color print, 4 in. × 6 in. © 2020 Mathur and Prashad Families.

Preeti's album features the new spectacle of the shopping mall more prominently. Although Rama visited up to six malls, they do not appear in any of her album's photographs. Meera reiterates an ambivalence about them by writing in her diary the names of these malls followed by the line: "you can write what you thought about the malls yourself."[23] While Preeti appears on the same golden escalator in Atlantic City that Rama visited the previous year, she also stands in front of the slot machines with a box of popcorn. Photographic documentation of the family at meals during their drives to Canada or New York replicate the ones taken with Rama but are far more numerous. Unlike on Rama's trip, Preeti does not visit extended family, which suggests an affinity between sightseeing and spending time with her sister's family over engagement with extended family and D.C.'s Indian community.

Another point of departure in Preeti's album is the presence of many solo portraits of Preeti, with cherry blossoms and tulips at Kenwood, at the bottom of a flight of steps at Niagara, and against the stalactites of Luray Caverns. These photographs set her apart from the family and give her the space for self-expression and independence (Fig. 2.4). Hence, within the seemingly familiar framework of repetitive traveling and familial bonding, Preeti's persona emerges as one that is different from her mother's.

In one self-portrait, Preeti appears, seated on the windowsill of the Mathur household. She is dressed like her nieces, Meera and Tara, in jeans and a white t-shirt that she bought during the trip. Her makeup was done by Meera, and she smiles confidently at the camera. As such, her place is a fluid one, perched between an older and a younger generation. As a single woman, her status aligns with that of her

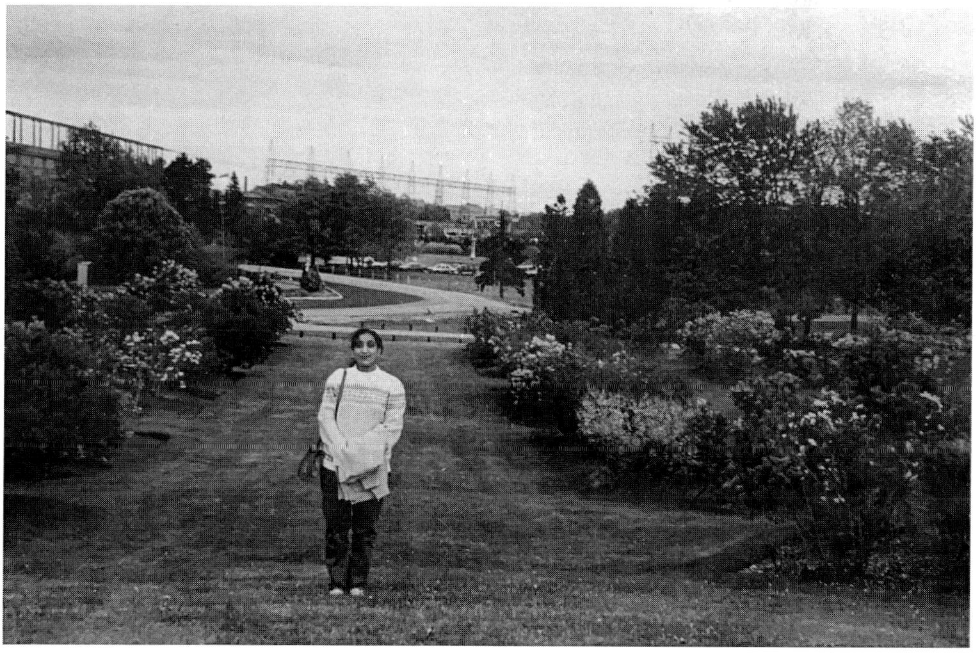

Figure 2.4 Lilac Garden, Niagara, Canada, May '94, 1994, color print. © 2020 Mathur and Prashad Families.

nieces, while her sister and mother take on maternal roles. Preeti's album is as much about her individuality as it is her familial membership. It also addresses the single woman's ambivalent status in family social situations including holidays.[24] Indeed, from within the frame, Rekha's family absorbs the precariousness of both Rama's and Preeti's single statuses in different ways, re-establishing maternal relations for the former, and aligning the latter's identity either with the single status of her two young nieces, or with her own sister in appearance, gestures, and postures, re-enacting their relationship before her sister's marriage.

Scholars have not explored the family vacation album as a testament to the single individual's kinship relations as a method of social assimilation. But this idea is worth closer study. U.S. vacation albums by both Rama and Preeti reveal the integration of single women into the familial fold, while allowing room for negotiating individual identities. Photographic albums like theirs allow a family to display itself to itself, as well as to others. As such, through the act of archiving family photographs in the album, the process of "using – producing, selecting, ordering, displaying – photographs, the family is actually in the process of making itself."[25] The albums are testaments to how Rekha's family identity influences the fundamental nature of Rama's and Preeti's representations of their vacations. Familial relationships over the holidays absorb the two single women and remain part of the albums' re-narration after the trips as the family folklore narratives globally scatter.[26]

The "Red" and "Black" Albums

In the 1960s, summer vacations for middle-class Indian families included going to hill stations (popular tourist destinations in elevated vistas), located in the northern states of Himachal Pradesh, Kashmir, and Uttarakhand. International travel was usually reserved for professionals such as diplomats, academics, and businesspeople, and recreational family travel was restricted to the very elite.[27] The Prashads' Kashmir trip photographs are loose, unbound images showing Rama's family on vacation in 1963. The family was then comprised of Rama, her daughters (Preeti, Rekha, and Asha), Rama's widowed sister-in-law, and Rama's husband Anil Prashad. Anil took ten photographs with a Rolleiflex camera, and occasionally unidentified guides/locals/fellow tourists photographed the family with it too. He was likely the photographer of images of the family frolicking by the river, sitting on the snow on a mountainside, and riding a *shikara*.[28] A local studio photographer also captured the girls dressed in local Kashmiri costumes (Fig. 2.5).[29]

Rama organized her photographs of early married life as well copies of the Kashmir photos into her "black album." Several images from the Kashmir trip are copies that were shared by family members. The poignancy of the photographs and the unmade album lies in the fate that would strike the family later that year. Anil Prashad would die suddenly from heart failure while down in a mine at the Asansol coal fields, where he worked as General Manager.

The ten Kashmir photographs were assimilated into the overall narratives of other albums, instead of enjoying a separate status and relating to other later vacation photographs and narratives. This confirms the notion of vacation time as existing in narrative continuum, rather than as a break from a paramount reality. For example, in Rama's "black album," rites of passage that define the family – such as the marriage of Rama and Anil Prashad, and the latter's death – are punctuated by the

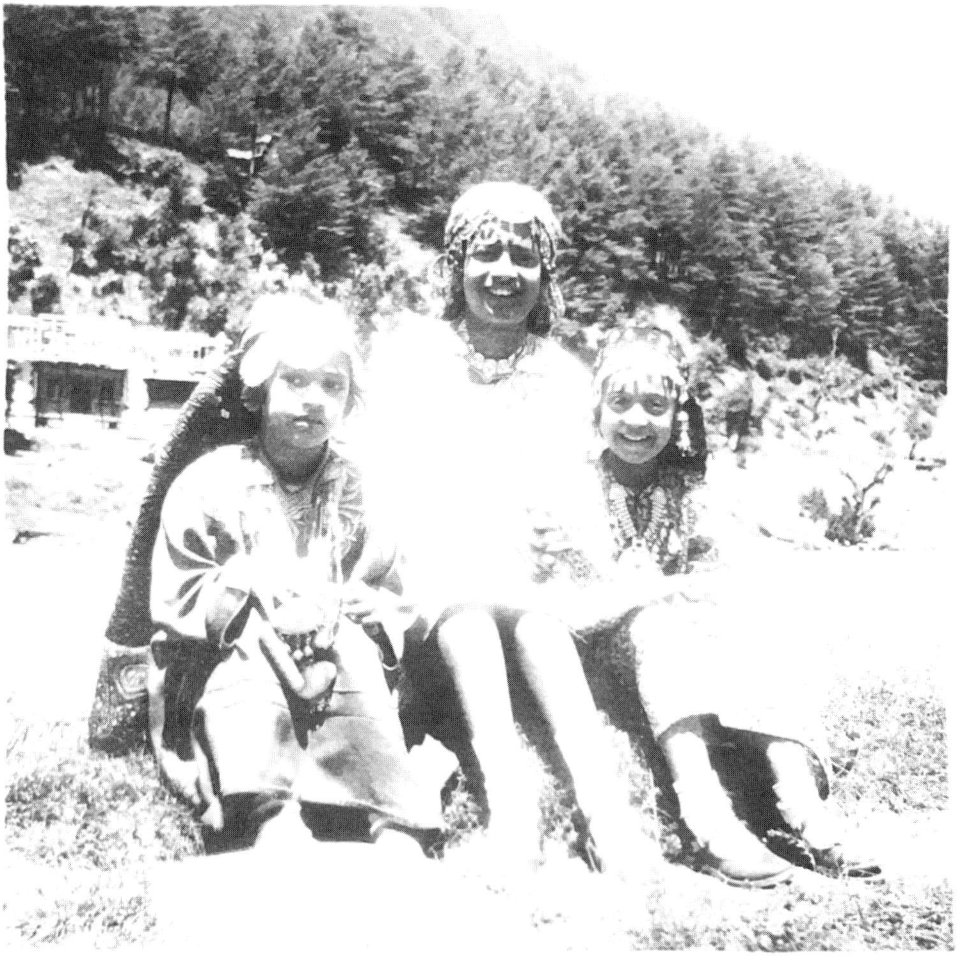

Figure 2.5 Rekha, Asha, and Preeti on holiday in Kashmir, 1964, black-and-white print, 2.36 in. × 2.36 in. © 2020 Mathur and Prashad Families.

photographs of everyday life from this 13-year period in a horizontal format, leather-bound album. The Kashmir images are distributed across the pages of this album and are interspersed with other holidays, festivals, and everyday images of the family. The album includes 83 photographs portraying Rama as a housewife and a mother of three daughters. Among those are photographs from her wedding to Anil, of their two homes in Asansol, of daily routines on a sunny verandah and in a spacious drawing room, and of visiting guests photographed on the large front lawn. There are photographs of the family at festivals such as Holi, and of Anil with his office seniors and colleagues at the mines. The trip to Kashmir, the first and last holiday that they took together as a family, joins the scenes of everyday life in Rama's albums, forming part of an integrated time of happiness. After Anil's death in 1964, life for the family was mired with struggle and transformation as they moved to Delhi. They recall that they did not take many photographs until at least 20 years later.

Preeti's "red album," is a Rexine-covered album containing mostly black-and-white images and a spattering of full-color photographs from later years, all chronologically arranged and neatly labeled. The first few pages start with Preeti's photographs as a baby. The album then presents images of her childhood with her sisters and parents in Asansol, followed by the post-1964 years in Delhi. Single photographs reference the vacation to Kashmir, another trip to Mussoorie with extended family, and college trips she took to Dhanbad and Mumbai. Preeti clarifies that relatives and friends with cameras sent them photographs up until the 1970s, when the family purchased an automatically focusing "point-and-shoot" camera.[30] Professional photographers took school and college functions where Preeti performed on stage or wore a graduation gown.

In the "red" album, Preeti makes the effort to create her own narrative as an individual from the larger familial context by painstakingly putting together her own timeline, a subset of the larger familial chronology. Preeti would compile more albums with her as the central character. These albums contained family photos with those of professional engagements such as office functions and award ceremonies. As such, Preeti's albums were decade-long temporal encapsulations, rather than organized by themes based on specific vacations or other events. Her selection and arrangement of images is autobiographical.

The two women's assimilation of the Kashmir photographs into the "black" and "red" albums allows them to remain a part of the family narrative and a coherent past. Even though the photographs of the Kashmir trip remind them of Anil's death and the family's relocation in about a year, they choose to evoke photography's "complex and even contradictory relationship to memory," and to enjoy the "crevices between myth and reality … [where] happy photographs have the power to evoke contradictory memories."[31] As such, the "black" and "red" albums evoke and transcend the contiguity between photography and death. The envisioned future of a happy family in the photographs of the Kashmir trip are upbeat moments made bittersweet by the un-photographed fact of Anil's death that both women know will occur when they narrate the album in hindsight.

Conclusions

Unlike other kinds of souvenirs, the vacation photo albums are a miniaturized presentation of the self for the self.[32] Ironically, they are a means of identity construction that partly relies on the veracity of facts held up by the image, and partly on subjective retellings of stories that are not necessarily bound by these facts. During a re-narration of the vacation through a sharing of the album, these images can acquire additional narratives, or suffer a loss of meaning, depending on the circumstances and authorship of the re-narration. What may have once induced a sense of pleasure may be tinged with embarrassment, ambivalence, or nostalgia. For example, Preeti's photographic portrait taken by Meera shows Preeti wearing a new pair of jeans and makeup. It reflects a changing body. This is especially relevant in the case of photographic subjects who may have gained or lost weight, aged noticeably, or in objects that have been discarded or continue to be used – such as Meera's white bedroom furniture set that still is kept by Rekha in her flat in Delhi. Every re-visitation of the album's pictures may introduce embellishments or erosions of narrative, contingent upon who views and who narrates the album, and under what circumstances.

Often, an identifiable tension emerges between the photographs' functions to fix or trigger memory and the narratives' innate malleabilities.[33] In the examples cited here, meanings embedded in albums about vacations are more flexible, and their afterlives continually evolve in time and in changing contexts.[34] This flexibility is granted by the differential inclusion or exclusion of images from albums that bear loose images. Oral narrativization may differ according to the audience involved. In the case of the four albums belonging to the Prashad family, narratives are layered in complementary ways, building a palimpsest in an "active process of creation of meanings" as the memories of one woman compensate for the loss or absence of another woman's recollections.[35] Rama's memories of Asansol speak of a time that her daughters were too young to remember, while Preeti's numerically larger number of photographs from her U.S. trip create a more detailed remembrance of the vacation than that commemorated by her mother a year earlier. As Preeti recounts retracing her mother's steps to several tourist sites, their responses concur and overlap. They recall the same things about Rekha's home, as if both were there together and not visiting a year apart. The "red" and "black" albums, on the other hand, bear childhood photographs that optimistically anticipated the future, even if their activation in a context beyond the photographic frame sometimes simultaneously foretold and recalled the loss of their father/husband.

These four family albums engage the intersections of the "family gaze" and the "tourist gaze."[36] The albums demonstrate how the context of tourism allows the family to produce itself as a social unit, and to become visually enshrined as such in the form of a photograph. The vacation albums of these middle-class Indian women reveal generational differences and continuities in their production of "*desired* togetherness, wholeness and intimacy."[37]

The album, as a document, exceeds the individual photographs between its leaves. It grants viewers space for narrativization, and gives its subjects meaning in surprisingly flexible ways. Gender and relational specificities in Rama's and Preeti's albums enable them to offer accounts that go against the conventions of tourist and familial views. In the hands of these generations of women, the album is part of a larger restorative historical practice, in which family members, vacations in idyllic spaces, and the comforts of domesticity absorb the single subject in the embrace of belonging and a story much larger than just one person's.

Notes

1 Gillian Rose, *Doing Family Photography: The Domestic, The Public and The Politics of Sentiment* (New York: Routledge, 2016), 58. Some of the reasons outlined by Rose, in her bid to understand why the maintenance of family photographs is stereotyped as "women's work," include the feminized responsibility of the "maintenance and display of family togetherness, which is part of what Munro and Madigan call 'women's traditional responsibility for domestic order' (Jamieson 1998)." Rose cites: Moria Munro and Ruth Madigan, "Negotiating Space in the Family Home," in *At Home: An Anthology of Domestic Space.* Irene Cieraad, ed. (Syracuse: Syracuse University Press, 1999), 114.; Lynn Jamieson, *Intimacy: Personal Relationships in Modern Societies* (Cambridge: Polity Press, 1998).

2 Tanya Evans, "The Use of Memory and Material Culture in the History of the Family in Colonial Australia," *Journal of Australian Studies*, Vol. 36, No. 2 (2012): 212. A rich

history of the role of Kodak in making women the custodians of family memory can be seen in its advertisements in the U.S., but the Indian case is still under exploration.

3 Jørgen Ole Baerenholdt, Michael Haldrup, Jonas Larsen, and John Urry, *Performing Tourist Places* (New York: Routledge, 2004), 115–116.

4 Karen Stein, "Getting Away from It All: The Construction and Management of Temporary Identities on Vacation," *Symbolic Interaction*, Vol. 34, No. 2 (Spring 2011): 290–308.

5 John Urry is credited for drawing attention to "the activity now emblematic of the tourist: the democratised taking of photographs — of being seen and recorded and seeing others and recording them. The role of the gaze connects flâneurs and tourists ... Moreover, the figure of the flâneur seems to resist feminine aspects." Chris Rojek and John Urry, *Touring Cultures: Transformations of Travel and Theory* (New York: Routledge, 1997), 25.

6 Baerenholdt, et al., *Performing Tourist Places,* 111.

7 Baerenholdt, et al., *Performing Tourist Places,* 119.

8 This information was gleaned over several conversations in the decade that I have known the family, and in more focused interviews in 2020.

9 Meera Mathur, *Unpublished Diary Entry* (1993), pp. 2.

10 Michael Haldrup and Jonas Larsen argue that the key role of tourist photography is to construct a sense of family: "Tourist photography is one of the uniquely modern ways through which families produce life narratives that are constructing them as families in a mobile world. Tourist photography is part of that theatre, producing personal narratives and memories. Rather than being an alienating add-on, photographing is an integral component in producing identity, social relations and 'familyness.'" Michael Haldrup and Jonas Larsen, "The Family Gaze," *Tourist Studies* (London: Sage Publications, 2003), 25–26.

11 Haldrup and Larsen, "The Family Gaze," 52.

12 Rojek and Urry, *Touring Cultures*, 91.

13 Rojek and Urry, *Touring Cultures*, 112.

14 Rojek and Urry, *Touring Cultures*, 96.

15 Elizabeth Edwards, "Photography and the Performance of History," *Kronos*, No. 27, Visual History (November 2001), 20.

16 Gillian Rose, "Family Photographs and Domestic Spacings: A Case Study," *Transactions of the Institute of British Geographers* Vol. 28, No. 1 (March 2003): 126.

17 Rose's concept of "feminist geographies" is worth evoking while examining the domestic space within which Rama, Rekha, Meera, and Tara spend vacation time. Rose writes of the domestic spaces where women live and work as mapping a distinctly feminist geography, where image making, archiving, and display also takes place. Rose, "Family Photographs and Domestic Spacings," 5.

18 Stanley Cohen and Lauri Taylor, *Escape Attempts: The Theory and Practice of Resistance to Everyday Life* (New York: Routledge, 1992), 136.

19 Karen Stein: *Symbolic Interaction*, Vol. 34, No. 2 (2011): 292.

20 Haldrup and Larsen, "The Family Gaze," 29.

21 Suryanandini Narain, *Interview with Album Participants* (September 2020).

22 Meera Mathur, *Unpublished Diary Entry* (1993), 10, 13, 15, 18, 19, 23, 29.

23 Meera Mathur, *Unpublished Diary Entry* (1993), 8.

24 Kinnaret Lahard, "Time Work: Keeping Up Appearances" *A Table for One*: *A Critical Reading of Singlehood, Gender and Time* (Manchester: Manchester University Press, 2017), 90.

25 Annette Kuhn, *Family Secrets: Acts of Memory and* Imagination (Ann Arbor: University of Michigan Press, 1995), 19.

26 Daina Harvey and Janet Lorenzen, "Signifying Practices and the Co-Tourist." *Tourismos: An International Multidisciplinary Journal of Tourism* Vol. 1, No. 1 (2006): 9–26.; Marianne Hirsch, *Family Frames: Photography, Narrative, and Postmemory* (Cambridge: Harvard University Press, 1997), 8.

27 Families and individual women, such as Rama and Preeti, also traveled abroad to visit extended family. This is mainly because in the pre-digital age, before tour companies offered pre-planned vacation packages, planning travel itineraries abroad took an incredible amount of expense, research, and effort.

28 A *shikara* is a wooden boat or houseboat found in Kashmir's Dal Lake.

29 David MacDougall, "Photo Hierarchicus: Signs and Mirrors in Indian Photography," *Visual Anthropology*, Vol. 5, No. 2 (1992): 103–129.
30 Suryanandini Narain, *Interview with Preeti Prashad* (September 2020).
31 Alexander Freund and Alistair Thomson (eds.), *Oral History and Photography (London and New York:* Palgrave Macmillan, 2011), 169.
32 Karen Stein, *Getting Away from It All: Vacations and Identity* (Philadelphia: Temple University, 2019) 302, 304.; Susan, Stewart, *On Longing: Narratives of the Miniature, the Gigantic, the Souvenir, the Collection* (Baltimore: Johns Hopkins University Press, 1985).
33 Harald Welzer, "Re-Narrations: How Pasts Change in Conversational Remembering," *Memory Studies*, Vol. 3, No. 1 (2010): 5–17.
34 This understanding of variable narratives from family photographs and albums concurs with Welzer's position: "Acquisitions and applications of pasts always follow the needs and demands of the present, and in this way individuals as well as memory communities always choose those aspects from the endless inventory of existing historical narratives and images that make the most sense for them in the real time of narrating and listening. Research on re-narrations and research on the transmission of historical consciousness in intergenerational communications both deal with the question how human beings interpret and narrate biographical events." Welzer, "Re-Narrations," 6.
35 Julia Hirsch, *Family Photographs: Content, Meaning and Effects* (New York: Oxford University Press, 1981), 5.
36 Haldrup and Larsen, "The Family Gaze," 39.
37 Baerenholdt, et al., *Performing Tourist Places*, 71.

Bibliography

Baerenholdt, Jørgen Ole, Haldrup, Michael, Larsen, Jonas, and Urry, John, eds. *Performing Tourist Places*. New York: Routledge, 2004.

Cohen, Stanley and Taylor, Lauri. *Escape Attempts: The Theory and Practice of Resistance to Everyday Life*. New York: Routledge, 1992.

Edwards, Elizabeth. "Photography and the Performance of History." *Kronos*, Vol. 27 (November 2001): 20.

Evans, Tanya. "The Use of Memory and Material Culture in the History of the Family in Colonial Australia." *Journal of Australian Studies*, Vol. 36, No. 2 (2012): 207–208.

Freund, Alexander and Thomson, Alistair, eds. *Oral History and Photography*. London and New York: Palgrave Macmillan, 2011.

Gibson, James J. *The Senses Considered as Perceptual Systems*. Ithaca: Cornell University Press, 1996.

Haldrup, Michael and Larsen, Jonas. "The Family Gaze," *Tourist Studies*. London: Sage Publications, 2003.

Harvey, Diana and Lorenzen, Janet. "Signifying Practices and the Co-Tourist." *Tourismos: An International Multidisciplinary Journal of Tourism*, Vol. 1, No. 1 (2006): 9–26.

Hirsch, Julia. *Family Photographs: Content, Meaning and Effects*. New York: Oxford University Press, 1981.

Hirsch, Marianne. *Family Frames: Photography, Narrative, and Postmemory*. Cambridge: Harvard University Press, 1997.

Kuhn, Annette. *Family Secrets: Acts of Memory and Imagination*. Ann Arbor: University of Michigan Press, 1995.

Lahard, Kinnaret. "Time Work: Keeping Up Appearances." *A Table for One: A Critical Reading of Singlehood, Gender and Time*. Manchester: Manchester University Press, 2017.

MacDougall, David. "Photo Hierarchicus: Signs and Mirrors in Indian Photography." *Visual Anthropology*, Vol. 5, No. 2 (1992): 103–129.

Rojek, Chris and Urry, John. *Touring Cultures: Transformations of Travel and Theory*. New York: Routledge, 1997.

Rose, Gillian. *Doing Family Photography: The Domestic, The Public and The Politics of Sentiment*. New York: Routledge, 2016.
Stein, Karen. "Getting Away from It All: The Construction and Management of Temporary Identities on Vacation." *Symbolic Interaction*, Vol. 34, No. 2 (Spring 2011): 290–308.
Welzer, Harald. "Re-Narrations: How Pasts Change in Conversational Remembering." *Memory Studies*, Vol. 3, No. 1 (2010): 5–17.

3 "Children of Shadowland": A Family's Scrapbook Story of Intellectual Disability

James Trent

On Friday, July 16, 1948, the parents of Bernhard Kress, Jr. placed him in the State Colony for Boys at New Lisbon, New Jersey. He was 11 years old. The state residential facility housed males who were identified as either "mentally deficient" or "mentally retarded." At the time, Americans regarded these labels as less offensive than previously used terms – "feebleminded," "idiot," "imbecile," and "moron." Today, of course, all these labels are regarded as inappropriate. Bernhard Jr., or "Bernie," as he was called, had one type of "mental deficiency:" Down syndrome. At Bernie's birth, physicians labeled the condition "Mongolian Idiocy" or "Mongolism," and they referred to people with the condition as "Mongoloids." Although obsolete in the twenty-first century, the labels used in much of the twentieth century represented the racist claim that people with Down syndrome resembled so-called "inferior" people of northeast Asian descent.

Bernie's parents, Emily and Bernhard Sr., kept a photographic scrapbook. Although each parent contributed to the contents of the scrapbook, it was Emily who likely maintained the selection and placement of items into the album.[1] The scrapbook's exterior is made of hard, thick brown cardboard. Its exterior dimensions are 15 inches long, 11.5 inches wide, and 2.5 inches deep. The interior contains 108 pages of heavy, brown paper. There are also several loose pages with additional items – clippings, photographs, letters, brochures, and papers written by institutional authorities. As a result, more than 400 objects fill the Kresses' scrapbook. Each affixed item was placed with congruent spacing between the other items and was carefully glued to the page. The scrapbook dates from 1944 to 1966. Its contents are, without exception, about living with intellectual disability in a residential institution, and the Kresses' engagement with their son's disability. As such, the items in the scrapbook tell a family's story of having a child with intellectual disability, with its contradictory images, institutional control, conflicting labels, mixed meanings, and ambiguous hope.

Emily and Bernhard Sr. were both 33 years old at the time of the placement of their son at the State Colony for Boys. The elder Bernhard was a typographer, and Emily was a stay-at-home mother. The Kresses had a second child, Ann, who was younger than her brother. They were a typical post-war middle-class family. Prior to his admission to the state institution, Bernie lived with his parents in Cliffside Park, New Jersey, just west from Manhattan across the Hudson River. New Lisbon was in the sparsely populated South Jersey pinelands, about one-hundred miles south of Cliffside Park. Given the absence of interstate highways at the time, it took nearly four hours to drive between the two New Jersey communities, thus making it difficult for the Kresses to visit Bernie and for Bernie to visit his family.[2]

DOI: 10.4324/9781003157427-5

At the time, the state of New Jersey had four public institutions like the one at New Lisbon. Two facilities housed males and two contained females. On January 1, 1951, two and one-half years after Bernie's placement, the census of the four institutions was 4,750 inmates, with 675 "retarded children" on a waiting list for admission.[3] The institutional population and long waiting list left no doubt that the facilities were overcrowded. Although the ages of the inmates varied from young children to senior adults, they were all referred to as "boys," "girls," and "children." This assumption was most clearly apparent during the Christmas season. As shown in the Kresses' scrapbook, staff members wrote letters to Santa Claus for each of the institution's inmates. The letters asked for "candy and a toy," and were sent to each inmate's parents or nearest family member. The prevailing perspective was that inmates of any age were still children and, as such, wanted Santa Claus to bring them candy and toys. Thus, the institutional staff viewed the inmates as perpetual children. The Kresses and most of the public had little reason to doubt the institutional staff's perspective.[4]

On the grounds of the State Colony for Boys at New Lisbon were so-called "cottages" that housed the inmates (Fig. 3.1). At New Lisbon, and in many similar facilities throughout the nation, the cottage usually contained a day room, a congregate sleeping room, a bathroom with several toilets and showers, a small kitchen,

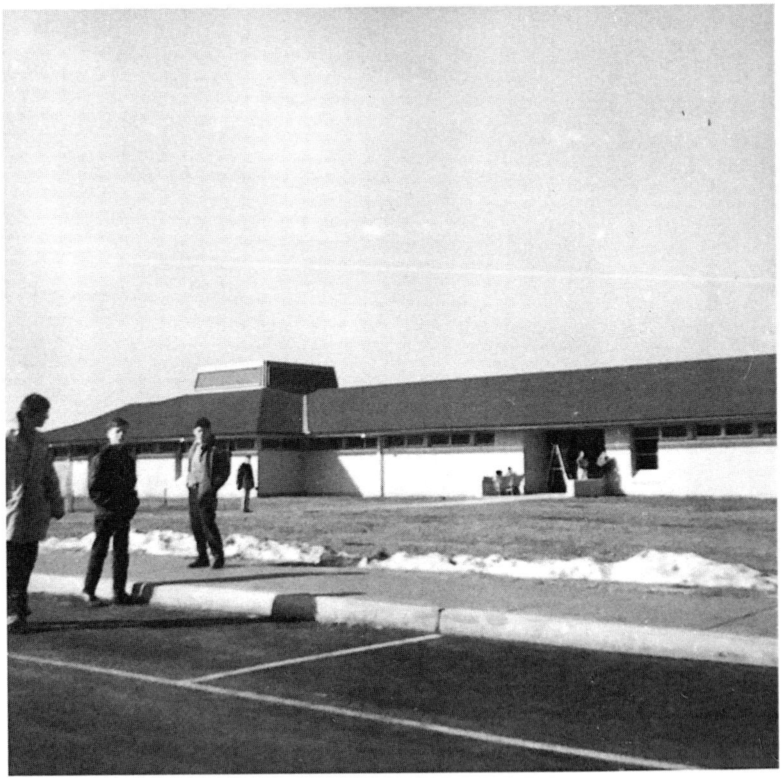

Figure 3.1 Bernhard and Emily Kress, *New Lisbon Cottage*, Kress Scrapbook (1944–1966). James Trent Collection.

and an office for the staff. The cottage staff were usually called "cottage parents" or "house parents." Because New Lisbon was in an isolated location in southern New Jersey, the institution's cottage staff consisted primarily of residents of surrounding small-town, rural communities. They worked in three shifts of eight hours each. Besides the cottages, the institution had two operations that allowed it to approximate self-sufficiency – a hatchery to supply eggs and a 400-acre farm where crops were grown and cattle for milk and meat were raised. Consuming the bounty were the institution's inmates, and working the hatchery and the farm were many of its "high functioning boys." In addition to the cottages, and the hatchery and farm, the institution had a hospital with 30 beds and a dental clinic, a chapel for religious services, a building that served as living quarters for some of the staff, a school where the institution provided basic academic and vocational education to its inmates, a building that housed the offices of the institution's superintendent and his professional staff, and another serving as the staff dining hall and inmates' barbershop. In 1965, with a gift from an architect and a construction company, the institution added a swimming pool with an adjoining bathhouse to its structures. In short, the New Lisbon institution was nearly a self-contained village.[5]

The population of the State Colony for Boys was exceptional in two ways. Some of its inmates were boys and men with intellectual disability who were also labeled "emotionally deficient." Others were inmates with intellectual disability who had committed petty crimes in their home community and had been sent to New Lisbon by court order. Often these inmates were "high functioning," that is, they could work on the institution's farm or have day work on the "outside." Supervising the inmates, who were on what the institution called "extended vacations" or day jobs in the nearby communities, were social workers and psychologists, who were members of the institution's professional staff.

A few letters in the Kresses' scrapbook date to before Bernie's 1948 institutionalization. In one, a friend wrote to Bernhard and Emily shortly before Bernie's New Lisbon placement. The friend noted that he was "thinking of you in these hours of mental and spiritual anguish." He implied that Bernhard and Emily's marriage had been strained by the care needed for Bernie. Yet, he acknowledged that the Kresses felt guilt about Bernie's forthcoming institutionalization, and that they would likely be criticized by their parents for not keeping Bernie at home. Nevertheless, the friend wrote, "I am still of the opinion … that for Bernie to go to an institution is wisest and best for each of the four individuals in your immediate family."[6] Thus, from the friend's perspective, Bernie's placement at the State Colony for Boys was necessary for the Kresses' family stability and preservation. This perspective was the prevailing one held by professionals and much of the general public in the post-war era. Before World War II, residential institutions had existed primarily for members of the underclass. For many social scientists who championed eugenic sterilization and institutional segregation, these "feebleminded" people were considered a menace to society. According to this outlook, such people required institutional segregation because in the community they would be reproducing more of their own degenerate kind. During and after the war, however, disabled family members of the middle class joined the institutional population to "save the family" from perceived disorder and disruption. Supported by friends, professionals, and most of the public, institutional segregation for intellectually disabled members of middle-class families seemed to be the only reasonable choice for the family's well-being. By the end of the 1950s, it had become the norm.[7]

Another letter in the scrapbook was addressed to Bernhard. Dated April 1, 1944, the letter was from A. H. Meese, the Superintendent of the New Jersey Training School at Totowa, one of the two facilities for females. Bernie's parents had taken him to Superintendent Meese for an evaluation because, at the time, Totowa was the closest institution to Cliffside Park. They reported that Bernie "is exerting a great mental and physical strain" on the family.[8] In his letter, the superintendent confirmed what the Kresses already knew but also feared, "Bernhard Junior is what is called a Mongolian and he is of a low-grade type so far as mentality is concerned. There is no hope of any appreciable improvement mentally." The Kresses would have "to struggle along and do the very best you can for him," because at the time the crowded institutions had no room for Bernie.[9] That Meese wrote such an uncompromising evaluation reflected a policy that was firmly in place by the World War II years. Especially for educated middle-class families like the Kresses, authorities believed that they should not withhold an assessment no matter how disconcerting the evaluation might be. By adopting such a policy, authorities like Meese controlled labels and hope.

Authorities also controlled treatment. Since experts in the mid-1940s believed that they could do nothing to cure or alleviate "mental deficiency," the best recourse, the only good recourse, was the placement of people with intellectual disability in a residential facility "with their own kind."[10] In his letter, Meese articulated a common reason for institutionalization. Mothers who care for their "mentally retarded child" will succumb to insanity. Meese wrote Bernhard:

> It is quite apparent that you and Mrs. Kress have given little Bernhard loving and devoted care and I know you will continue to do so. However, it seems evident that the boy is already proving to be quite a strain on your wife. Always in these case [sic] I am more concerned with the mother than I am about the child, as mothers are with their children morning, noon, and night, whereas the father does get away from it during the workday. I am going to offer the suggestion that you do all in your power to take the load off of Mrs. Kress whenever you are home, and you should watch carefully to see that she does not break under the strain. That sort of thing happens over and over again. It has happened that many times mothers in this position finally break and have to be taken to a private or State hospital. I don't want to frighten you unduly, but it is better to be forewarned about such things and then do all in your power to prevent the break.[11]

Under the threat of the mother's descent into insanity, authorities like Meese provided treatment not so much to the disabled family member, but, as they reasoned, for the sake of family preservation and stability. From their perspective, residential institutionalization for the "retarded" member became the only reasonable treatment to save the family. It had nothing to do with the treatment of people with a disability. Instead, their supposed treatment became life-long institutional incarceration, segregated from family and ordinary community life.

New Jersey's institutional superintendents were exceptional in one respect. In most states these authorities were physicians, but in New Jersey most of the superintendents were psychologists. Prior to Bernie's institutionalization, institutional authorities, whether physicians or psychologists, were the only recognized experts on "mental retardation." They had their own professional association – the American Association on Mental Deficiency.[12] Through that association, they championed segregation, eugenic sterilization and, of course, institutionalization. Their diagnoses and their opinions were taken as unquestionable. For this reason, physicians and psychologists identified, determined, and labeled those people who were intellectually "normal," and those people who were intellectually inferior. In short, they were the arbiters of the ordinary and the "abnormal." It is not surprising, then, that the Kresses included several articles by institutional authorities in their scrapbook.

From Bernie's eleventh year until his thirty-first, the Kresses kept their scrapbook to remove any doubts they may have had about his placement and to remind themselves that what they had done to their son was the right thing to do. In the process, their scrapbook revealed the contradictions of residential institutionalization. When one looks through the entire scrapbook, one notices the absence of images of Bernie. Bernie is pictured in only one clipping (probably from an institutional newsletter), dated 1951. He is with a group of eleven New Lisbon inmates who made up a rhythm band of percussion instruments.[13] His mother drew an arrow to his image and wrote his name. His portrait does not appear again among the more than 400 items in the scrapbook. Even the photographs taken by the Kresses for the album are consistently of buildings and objects at the Colony for Boys, and not of Bernie. Bernie's absence indicates that the Kresses' scrapbook was not intended to represent their son. Instead, its purpose was to assuage their misgivings about their son's institutionalization by filling the album with items about the institution and their involvement in emerging parent groups that were developing in the late 1940s and early 1950s. The best known of these groups was the National Association for Retarded Children (NARC), an organization of parents and other family members that emerged in the early 1950s.[14] The scrapbook, then, provided a way of substituting their son for a compilation of material that responded to his institutionalization. Now, with Bernie segregated in a residential institution, his mother and father could reassure themselves that what they had given their son was the best option. As such, the scrapbook became their virtual son. In the process of this reassurance, the scrapbook also revealed mixed messages given to intellectual disability.

Much of the scrapbook is filled with clippings, all carefully cut and delicately placed on the pages. Besides articles from newspapers, 4 sources provide most of the clippings. They are the newsletters from the NARC, the New Jersey Parents Group for Retarded Children (later known as the New Jersey ARC), the Bergen-Passaic Unit of the New Jersey ARC, and the State Colony Association for New Lisbon Boys. The organizations' newsletters, and the articles in them, had titles that reflect the Manichean claims that parents like the Kresses experienced. "Children Limited," "Living Dead," "Progress for Retarded Children," "Parents' Voice," "Secret Children," "Retarded Children Can Be Helped," "Forgotten Children," "Ill-Finished Children," and "Children of Shadowland" – the names claim both despair and hope. For despair, the "children" are referred to as the "living dead," and they are "ill-finished children," existing in a "shadowland." For hope, there is the label, "progress for retarded children" and the claim, "retarded children can be helped."

This dualistic phrasing is well illustrated by an image of the head and shoulders of a young boy who appears in both dark and light (Fig. 3.2).[15] The left side of the boy's face and neck is in shadow, while the other side is in the light. He fits in with period standards for the appearance of proper American children, appearing white and able-bodied with nicely parted hair and a handsome face. But his expression looks sad as if someone told him he was not normal. The Janus-like image, used by the NARC in

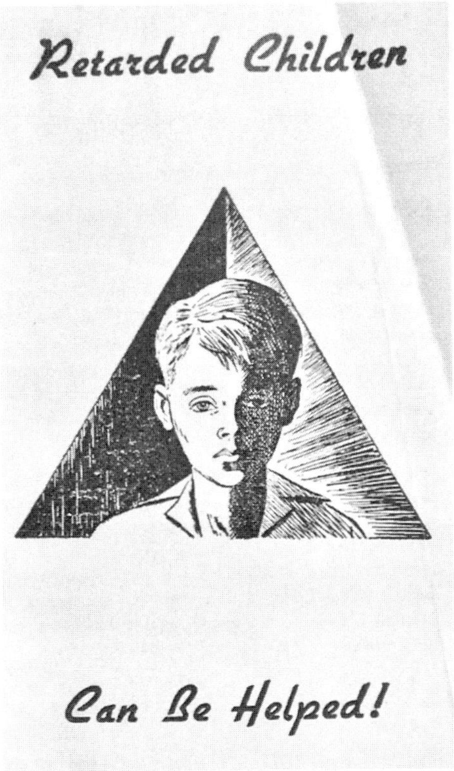

Figure 3.2 National Association for Retarded Children, *Retarded Children Can Be Helped!*, Kress Scrapbook (1944–1966). James Trent Collection.

some of its literature and advertisement in the 1950s and early 1960s, and carefully placed in the Kresses' scrapbook, suggests both hope and despair. It reflected the mixed conception of intellectual disability that pervades the scrapbook. "Retarded children," it seems, could be helped, but there were always the questions, why do they need help and to what end are they helped?

The Kresses involved themselves in two organizations related to Bernie's institutionalization: The Bergen-Passaic Unit of the New Jersey ARC and the State Colony Association for New Lisbon Boys. Bernhard was president of the State Colony Association in 1954 and 1955. Also, Emily became the chair of the Bergen-Passaic Unit's institutional relations committee, and she spoke frequently to women's clubs and at Parent-Teacher Association meetings about "mental deficiency."[16]

In 1948, the year they placed Bernie in the New Lisbon facility, the Kresses noted in their scrapbook one of the institution's most egregious scandals. The newspaper headline was "Feebleminded Bury Young Inmate Alive." The piece reported that a group of inmates at the New Lisbon facility was playing together in a mound of sand. They would place one "boy" at a time in a ditch, and then cover him in the sand. He would then escape from the mound of sand. This game of sand covering and escape continued for several "boys." At some point, however, the inmates were called to come back to their cottage, whereupon they left one of their mates buried in the sand. When institutional authorities found him, the 27-year-old inmate was dead. At the time the scandal occurred, the Kresses had only recently placed Bernie in the New Lisbon residential facility. They recorded the event by clipping the newspaper account and placing it in their scrapbook.[17] But they were hardly aware at the time of the full dynamics and dangers of the institution. In any case, they kept Bernie at the facility; for the sake of the family's stability, they were content to have him remain "with his own kind."

In 1961, when another scandal occurred, the Kresses were fully aware of the comings-and-goings of the New Lisbon facility. On this occasion, there were three different complaints in newspaper clippings that Emily added to the family's scrapbook. The first had to do with "boys" being tied to their beds to control them from misbehavior and noncompliance. Staff members with the approval of the institution's superintendent were doing the restraining. Some recalcitrant inmates were tied to their beds for days, only being allowed to visit the toilet. The second complaint was identified as homosexuality. Visitors to the institution, including New Jersey lawmakers and members of their staff, had witnessed sexual behavior among the "boys." The sensationalized newspaper headline called the institution a "New Sodom and Gomorrah." Of the finding, New Jersey State Senator Anthony J. Grossi claimed, "If it weren't for the lives of innocent people there, it [the institution] long ago would have been visited with fire and brimstone." The third and most damning criticism involved the institution's superintendent himself. According to the complaint, he had beaten three inmates who had escaped and then been returned to the institution. Emily dutifully glued the newspaper clippings to the pages of the scrapbook.[18]

As a result of the 1961 scandals, the New Jersey governor appointed a committee to investigate the facility. Shortly before Christmas of that year, the committee released its report. The report put the blame for the wrongdoings in the hands of the institution's superintendent. The headline of a newspaper clipping read, "Retarded Children's Home Head Chided." Interestingly, the members of the State Colony Association for New Lisbon Boys, including the Kresses, supported the superintendent against the charges of abuse and neglect. So, even though long-term restraint, beatings, and in 1961 homosexuality were considered illegal and shameful, the Association defended the superintendent because they did not want to disrupt the status quo.[19] Their disabled family member was at the New Lisbon facility, away from them, and they wanted it to stay that way. In 1948, the year of Bernie's placement, a group of parents found that across the state's four institutions "900 children were forgotten and unvisited." There is little reason to suppose that matters had changed by 1961.[20] Although the Kresses defended the superintendent, the publicity about the scandals meant that they could not avoid seeing the dangers of the institution.

As members of the State Colony Association for New Lisbon Boys, the Kresses supported a 1961 state bond issue that resulted from the investigation, and they placed fliers about the bond issue in their scrapbook. The bond referendum provided funds for the improvement of New Jersey's residential institutions. The passage of the bond issue had special significance for the New Lisbon colony because it allowed state authorities to build additional cottages that were newer, more comfortable, and less crowded. For families like the Kresses, the improvements also reassured them that the segregated institution, even with scandals, remained a good placement for their son.

Of course, in a short time, the new cottages would themselves become crowded with boys and men from the institution's ever-burgeoning waiting list.

In the early 1960s, the facility experienced a major expansion. Then-President John F. Kennedy's principal charitable backing was "mental retardation." Indeed, Emily added to the Kresses' scrapbook Eunice Kennedy Shriver's much-read article "Hope for Retarded Children," that appeared in the September 22, 1962, edition of the *Saturday Evening Post*. The Kennedys ensured that "mental retardation" had never had more public and legislative attention. Yet, the attention presupposed that "hope for retarded children" depended on residential institutionalization. In the early 1960s, Emily placed several photographs of the old and new buildings in a group of four pages of snapshots.

This group of photographs had two curious items. Emily entitled one photograph, "choo-choo train," and the other she identified as "the jail" (Figs. 3.3 and 3.4). The first was an image of a train on wheels that could seat about two dozen "boys." Occasionally the institutional cottage staff filled the train with inmates and drove them over the roads and sidewalks of the facility. Emily wrote "choo-choo train" under the photograph in the scrapbook. The train resembled a ride found at a county fair or at an amusement park. It was an object designed for children, even "retarded children," many of whom were adults. The second image was of a building. Emily wrote "the jail" under this photograph. A building with this name was odd for an

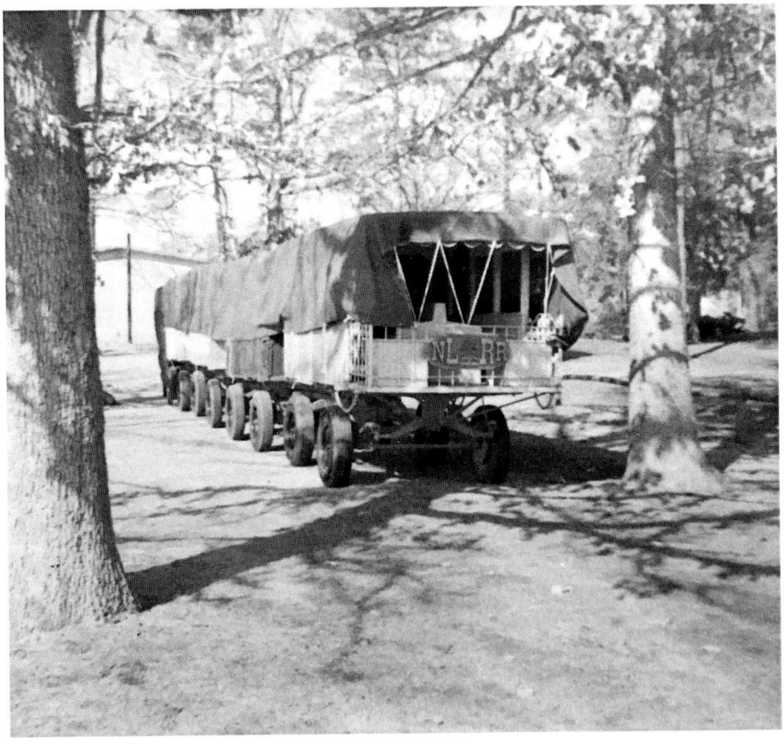

Figure 3.3 Bernhard and Emily Kress, *Choo-Choo Train,* Kress Scrapbook (1944–1966). James Trent Collection.

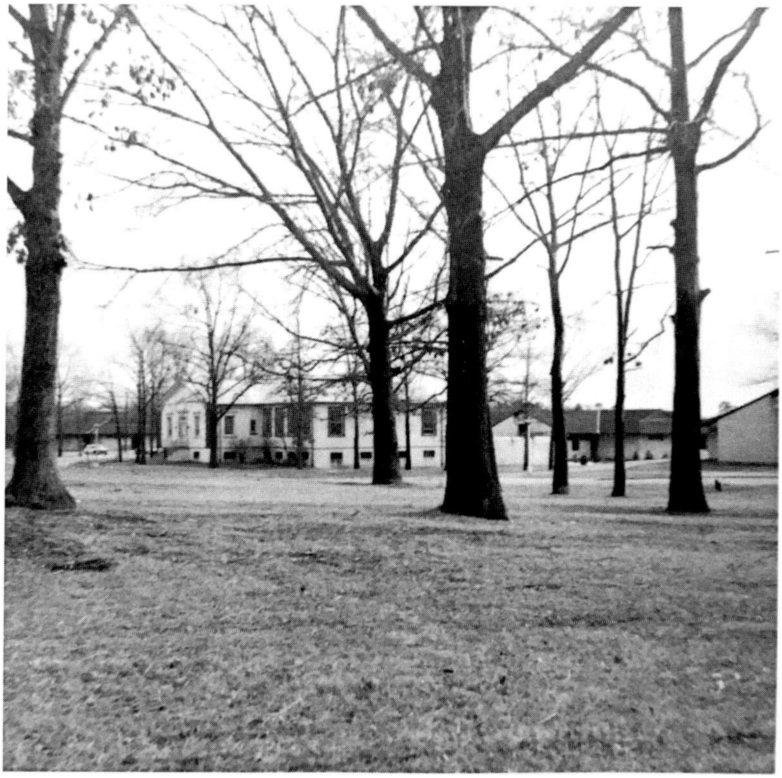

Figure 3.4 Bernhard and Emily Kress, *The "Jail,"* Kress Scrapbook (1944–1966). James Trent Collection.

institution for "the retarded." Why did such an institution include a jail on its grounds? Parents with boys and men at New Lisbon knew that the jail housed misbehaving "mentally deficient" petty-crime offenders, whom New Jersey courts had sent to the facility, as well as for other residents of the institution whose behavior had become problematic. Usually, authorities said the latter residents were "out of control." Once again, the two photographs portrayed mixed meanings.

Indeed, the images of the choo-choo train and the jail were filled with paradox. In one, the object represented fun and good times for children, but at the institution, also for adults. As we have seen, however, fun and good times were for "retarded children." Such "children" were "eternal children." Their bodies grew, and their ages increased, but they were still treated like children. In the other photograph, we find an image of a facility that is usually associated with criminal adults. In the jail, then, were the deviant of deviants. In it were disabled boys and men who were doubly institutionalized. They were in a jail for wrongdoers in an institution for "the retarded." At the same time, the images of the train and of the jail revealed the contradictory nature of the New Lisbon facility. It was a place both for adult children, and for children adults – in both cases the conflicting images spoke to the irony of help for people with intellectual disability.

Several years before this time, in the late 1950s, a parent association began to use another image in their promotional pamphlet and brochure. Emily placed the item in the Kresses' scrapbook. The image is of a young girl holding a white rabbit (Fig. 3.5). We are to assume that the rabbit is her pet. She is dressed for winter and wears a coat with a toboggan hat on her head. She looks up to the viewer's left with a smile on her face. The girl fulfills post-war middle-class expectations for white, able-bodied children; there is no visual suggestion that she is living with a disability. However, in bold print on both the pamphlet and the brochure, we find the title, "Children of Shadowland." Once again, there is a conflicting message of hope and of hopelessness. Inside, the pamphlet promotes the "Retarded Children's Fund," sponsored by the New Jersey Parents Group for Retarded Children, the original name for the New Jersey ARC. The organization distributed the pamphlet and brochure in order to raise $100,000 for community-based programs for "retarded children."[21]

In the mid-1950s, some parents of children and adults with intellectual disability began to call for programs and activities based in communities. Some parents wanted to keep their child in the community; other parents had become discouraged with the long waiting lists for admission to New Jersey's residential institutions. For them , it seemed impossible that their child would ever be admitted to an already crowded

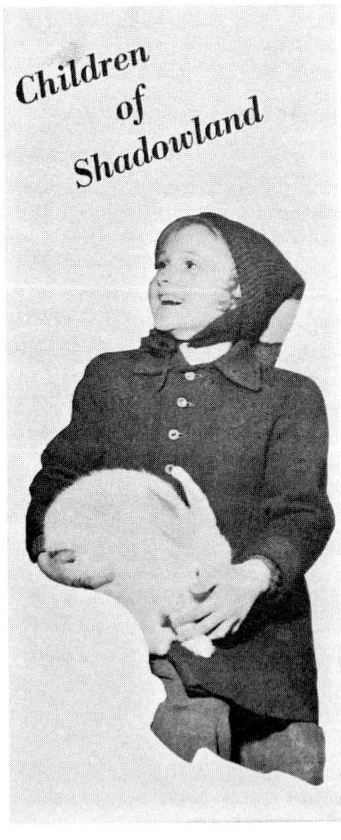

Figure 3.5 New Jersey Parents Group for Retarded Children, *Children of the Shadowland*, Kress Scrapbook (1944–1966). James Trent Collection.

facility. In like manner, an early 1960s pamphlet and brochure reminded the reader that there were 38,000 "retarded" people remaining in New Jersey homes, who without services "advanced only in years."[22] Although Bernie was at the Boys Colony at New Lisbon, the Kresses added the pamphlet and brochure to their scrapbook. As members of the Parents Group for Retarded Children, they included these items because, like other parents and professionals at the time, they began to see that residential institutions could not house all people with intellectual disability. This was especially the case given the growth in the general population as a result of the post-war "baby boomers," some of whom would soon be having their own babies.[23]

What would the $100,000 "Retarded Children's Fund" provide? The literature from the Parents Group in the Kresses' scrapbook indicates four services for "trainable retardates" who remained in the community. They noted that trainable identified about one-fourth of the state's "children" with intellectual disability. The remaining "children" were not trainable and were destined for institutional care. For some of the "trainable retardates," then, the four community services were diagnostic clinics, preschool-age day nursery programs, vocational training in sheltered workshops, and summer camps.

The obvious purpose of diagnostic clinics was testing to confirm the suspected disability. The brochure noted that such clinics could also provide data for research, which we know today would include anything from IQ-testing data to the use of people with intellectual disability as subjects for experimenting with polio vaccines.[24] The nursery programs were intended for parents who could not afford existing private daycare centers. They were assumed to be only for children with intellectual disability, thus ensuring segregation from "normal" preschoolers. The third service provided by the fund was vocational training primarily in community-based sheltered workshops. Parents and professionals believed that high functioning "mentally retarded" teenagers could begin learning a manual trade if vocational training meant especially for them was provided. For "boys," this training usually meant farm work or shop work; for "girls," it usually meant so-called domestic science. The assumption was that such special training would be segregated from vocational training for non-disabled students. Although many parents hoped that their child would one day find gainful, independent employment while living in the community, most teenagers and adults continued over the years to work at the sheltered workshop, turning the training facility into a community-based, long-term care institution. Almost always the sheltered workshop provided below-minimum wage and routinized work for its long-term disabled trainees, who now functioned as employees. Teenagers with intellectual disability became adults while working at the sheltered workshop, thus never experiencing independent employment.[25] The final service was summer day camps. Even though New Jersey institutions had occasionally provided summer camping experiences for their inmates, summer camping programs did not exist for "retarded children" living in the community. There was no question that people with intellectual disability would benefit from a camping experience, but like other services, the summer campers had to be segregated from other "normal" children and adults.

The services anticipated by the New Jersey Parents Group for Retarded Children had mixed meanings. Like the boy with the Janus-like face and the girl with the white rabbit, the services for which the parents' group were asking private funding suggested a conflicting split between hope and hopelessness. The services, like the boy and the girl, were gentle and non-threatening. But they were also a "shadowland."

For every activity funded by the campaign, people with intellectual disability were segregated from nondisabled people. Activity was certainly better than inactivity, but keeping "retarded people with their own kind" held them in the specter of "the abnormal." They would have no encounters with the wider world, and the wider world would continue to avoid and fear them. In short, the so-called community services soon became institutions.

Although the Kress family visited Bernie (as indicated by the photographs they took of the choo-choo train and the buildings of the State Colony for Boys), it is likely that their contact with their son was infrequent. They lived in northern New Jersey and Bernie lived one-hundred miles south in remote, rural New Lisbon. Likewise, as noted earlier, they included in their scrapbook a newsletter clipping of only one image of Bernie with several other inmates. There is no indication that the family felt ashamed for having a son with Down syndrome. But they were content to have Bernie live with "others of his own kind," because they could then be an ordinary post-war, middle-class family. Their scrapbook, then, became a way for the Kresses to chronicle numerous aspects of Bernie's institutionalization, without having Bernie as a cohabitating member of the family.

As we have seen, having an institutionalized family member with intellectual disability in the 1950s and 1960s was an ongoing contradictory experience. Adults, as well as children, could have intellectual disability, yet intellectually disabled adults were consistently labeled as children. It was assumed that mothers would go insane if they had to care for a "mentally deficient child," yet "retarded children can be helped." Some teenagers and adults could learn farm work or a manual trade, yet these teenagers and adults were "eternal children," not destined for gainful community employment. Some "retarded children" could live in communities, yet segregated community special education classes and sheltered workshops ensured that their community presence would always be marginalized. The Kresses' scrapbook told a story that continued for more than 20 years. It was a story about a post-war middle-class family's engagement with intellectual disability and institutionalization, with its conflicting images, institutional control, contradictory labels, mixed meanings, and ambiguous hope.

Notes

1 I have credited Emily Kress with the maintenance of the scrapbook because women were most often maintainers of family albums and scrapbooks. In her book, Jessica Helfand examines several scrapbooks, and she notes that men like Mark Twain kept scrapbooks. However, nearly all of the scrapbooks that she studied were kept by women. See: Jessica Helfand, *Scrapbooks: An American History* (New Haven: Yale University Press, 2008), 3.
2 Bernhard Kress and Emily Kress, *Kress Scrapbook* [In the Possession of the Author] (1944–1966), 56.
3 Kress and Kress, *Kress Scrapbook*, 21.
4 Kress and Kress, *Kress Scrapbook*, 10.
5 Kress and Kress, *Kress Scrapbook*, 1.
6 Kress and Kress, *Kress Scrapbook*, Letter from First Name? Rowland to Bernie and Emily, July 12, 1948, 56.
7 James W. Trent Jr., *Inventing the Feeble Mind: A History of Intellectual Disability in the United States* (New York: Oxford University Press, 2016), 229.
8 Kress and Kress, *Kress Scrapbook*, Letter from A.H. Meese to Bernhard J. Kress, April 1, 1944, 55.
9 Kress and Kress, *Kress Scrapbook*, 55.

10 C. Mackenzie, "Families Advised on Retarded Child," *New York Times* (May 26, 1947): 26. During World War II, the American Psychiatric Association recommended that people with intellectual disability be euthanized, and their parents be given psychotherapy to deal with their guilt. See: Wolf Wolfensberger, "The Extermination of Handicapped People in World War II Germany." *Mental Retardation*, Vol. 19, No. 1 (1981): 1–7.
11 Kress and Kress, *Kress Scrapbook*, 55.
12 The American Association on Mental Deficiency has had several names over its 144-year history. They include the Association of Medical Officers of American Institutions for Idiotic and Feeble-Minded Persons, and the American Association for the Study of the Feeble-Minded. Its current title is the American Association on Intellectual and Developmental Disabilities.
13 Kress and Kress, *Kress Scrapbook*, 33.
14 The National Association for Retarded Children has had three names over its nearly seventy-year history. The second name was the National Association for Retarded Citizens. Today it is known as "The Arc."
15 Kress and Kress, *Kress Scrapbook*, 75.
16 Kress and Kress, *Kress Scrapbook*, 16, 18, 31, and 53.
17 Kress and Kress, *Kress Scrapbook*, 47
18 Kress and Kress, *Kress Scrapbook*, 47, 82, 89–90.
19 Kress and Kress, *Kress Scrapbook*, 90.
20 Kress and Kress, *Kress Scrapbook*, 7.
21 Kress and Kress, *Kress Scrapbook*, 29.
22 Kress and Kress, *Kress Scrapbook*, 29.
23 James W. Trent Jr., "Historical Foundations of the Field of Intellectual and Developmental Disabilities," in *APA Handbook of Intellectual and Developmental Disabilities*, Vol. 1, ed. Laraine Glidden (Washington, D.C.: APA Books, 2020), 19–1.
24 Trent, *Inventing the Feeble Mind*, 257.
25 Even today, many sheltered workshops are operated by local ARCs, which pay their workers subminimum wages and, thus, find little reason to train their workers for community-based, independent employment.

Bibliography

Helfand, Jessica. *Scrapbooks: An American History*. New Haven: Yale University Press, 2008.

Kress, Bernhard and Kress, Emily. *Kress Scrapbook*. 1944-1966. James Trent Collection.

Mackenzie, C. "Families Advised on Retarded Child," *New York Times*, (May 26, 1947): 26.

Trent, James W. Jr. "Historical Foundations of the Field of Intellectual and Developmental Disabilities," in *APA Handbook of Intellectual and Developmental Disabilities*, Vol. 1, Laraine Glidden, ed. (Washington, D.C.: APA Books, 2020), 19–21.

Trent, James W. Jr. *Inventing the Feeble Mind: A History of Intellectual Disability in the United States*. New York: Oxford University Press, 2016.

Wolfensberger, Wolf. "The Extermination of Handicapped People in World War II Germany." *Mental Retardation*, Vol. 19, No. 1 (1981): 1–7.

4 Henry Darger's "Family" Album of American Orphans and Fugitives

Mary Trent

Self-taught Chicago artist Henry Darger (1892–1973) is well known for creating a large body of visual and written work alone in his small apartment over many decades. His landlord, photographer Nathan Lerner, accidentally discovered his art just before the artist's death, and was responsible for bringing it to public attention. Otherwise, it likely would have been lost. Darger wrote what has been claimed to be the longest fictional work in the English language: a more-than-15,000-page novel titled *The Story of the Vivian Girls, in What Is Known as the Realms of the Unreal, of the Glandeco-Angelinnian War Storm, Caused by the Child Slave Rebellion*, or *In the Realms of the Unreal*.[1] And, he created hundreds of mixed-media depictions of scenes and characters related to his tale of an epic war between nations who enslaved and oppressed children and an army of child rebels fighting for freedom. Many of these artworks are monumentally large in scale, stretching beyond ten feet in length. Though they now hang in galleries around the world as individual, framed pieces of fine art, the works were created as pages in domestic albums that Darger hand-constructed in his apartment.

This essay restores the original interpretive significance of Darger's art as pages in albums. To do so, it foregrounds the importance of an understudied piece in his oeuvre: the mixed-media, collaged cover he made for the largest of his hand-bound albums, a work which one would have originally viewed before seeing any of the interior pieces (Figs. 4.1 and 4.2). By identifying and analyzing the appropriated source imagery of this album cover, this chapter argues that Darger constructed a monumental spin-off of the traditional American family album that expressed mixed feelings of both longing for and disavowal of the nation's twentieth-century familial norms.

An orphan and lifelong bachelor who lived alone, Darger demonstrated in his art the persistent influence (even on the socially marginalized) of twentieth-century visual culture's idyllic presentation of the American dream of middle-class family bliss. Yet, his art also includes a stark critique of those ideals' hypocracies in light of oppressive American social polices against those who could not conform. Darger's art is a powerful example of how domestic albums can both rhetorically reinforce the notion of the primacy of family, while also adapting crerative modes of self-expression and survival beyond a family unit's supportive and nurturing norms. As such, Darger creates a new kind of non-bloodline-based "family" in his album, one of the unwanted and the outcast.

Orphans and Fugitives

Darger's more than ten-feet-long cover originally bridged a threshold between the outside of the album and the paintings inside. At first glance, the cover might appear

DOI: 10.4324/9781003157427-6

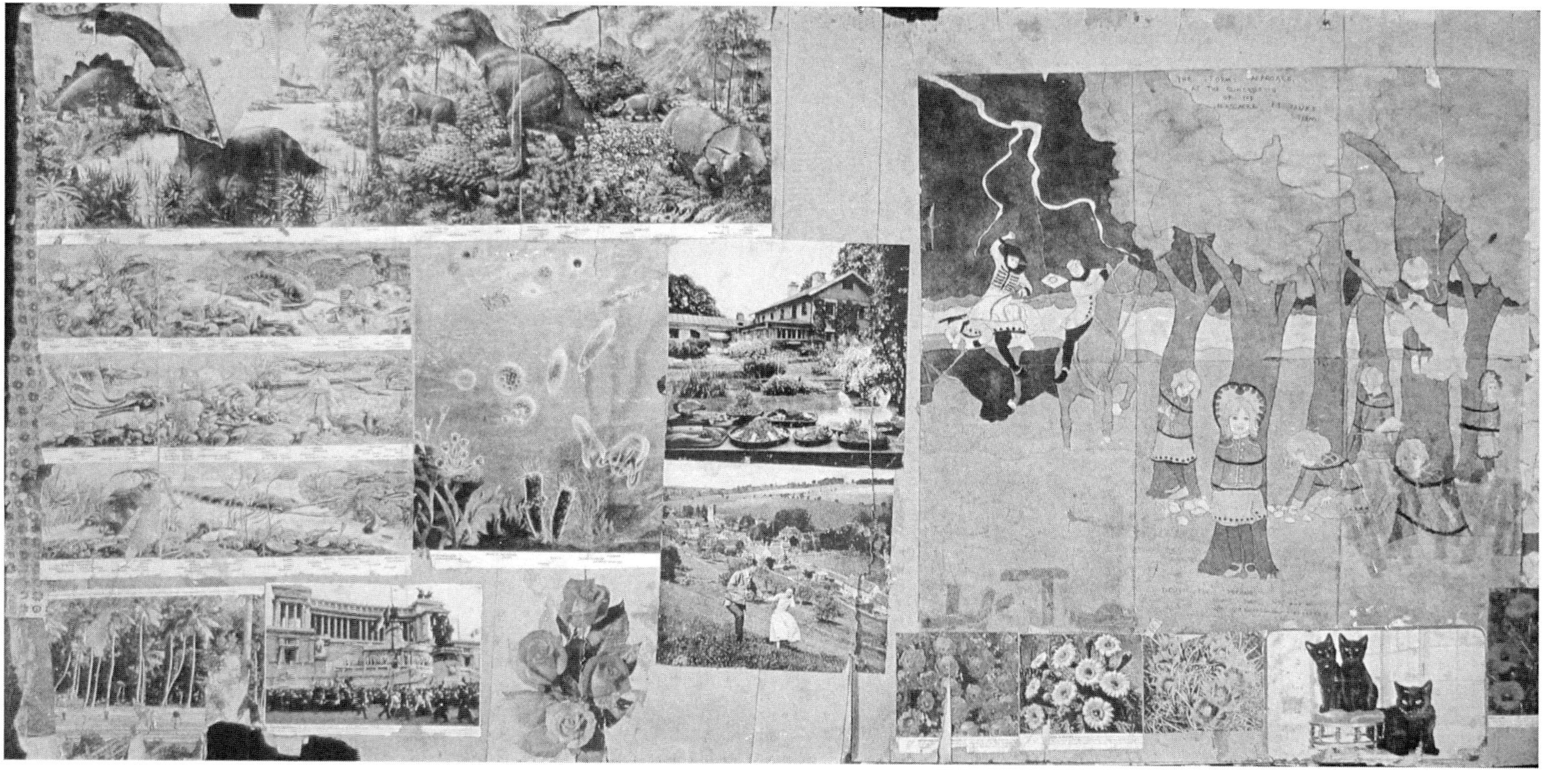

Figure 4.1 Henry Darger, *Album Cover*, left side, c. 1950s, collage, watercolor, pencil, carbon tracing, 31 ½ × 128 ¼ inches [whole cover]. Collection de l'Art Brut, Lausanne, Switzerland. © 2021 Kiyoko Lerner/Artists Rights Society (ARS), New York.

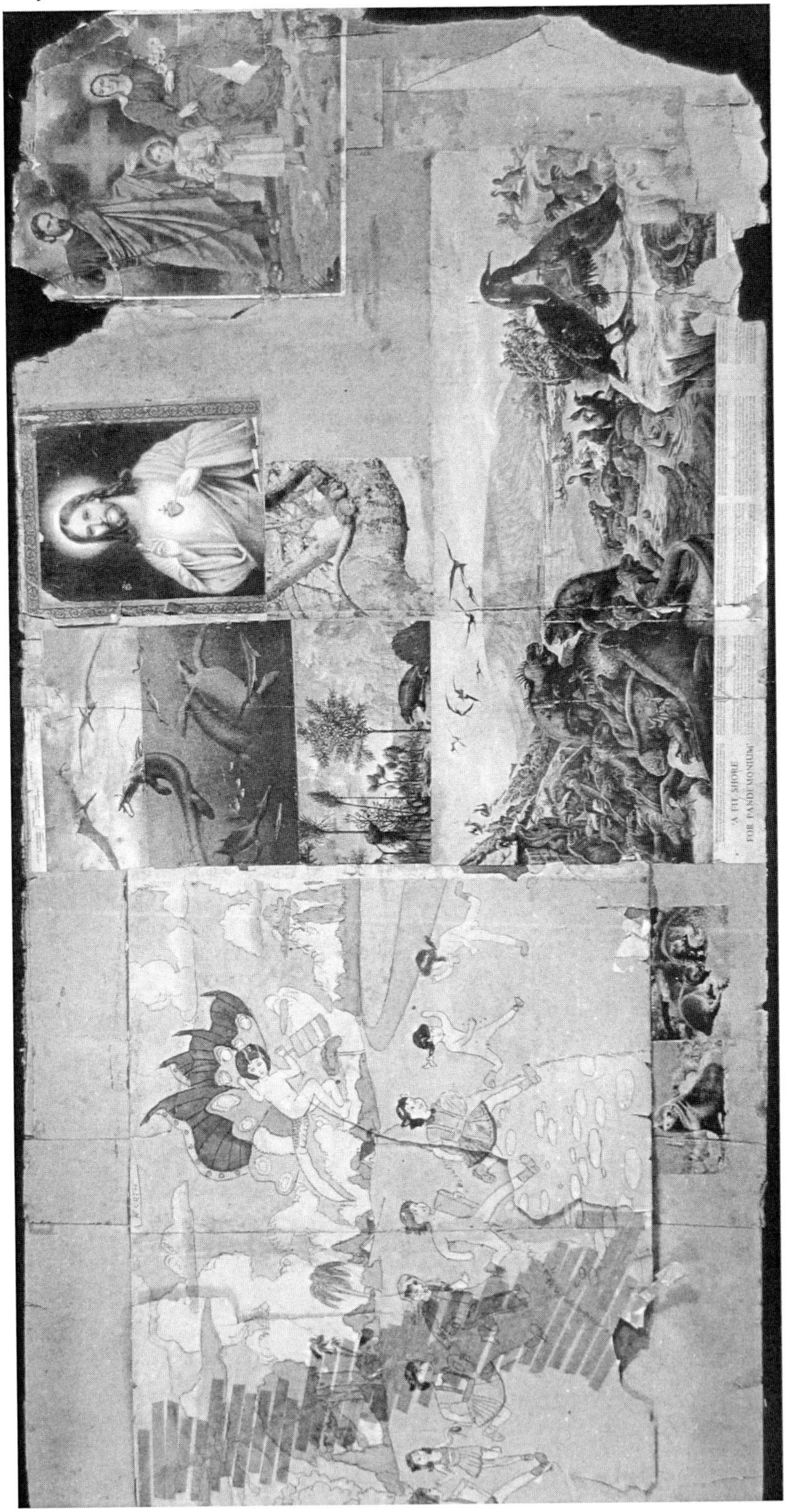

Figure 4.2 Henry Darger, *Album Cover*, right side, c. 1950s, collage, watercolor, pencil, carbon tracing, 31 ½ × 128 ¼ inches [whole cover]. Collection de l'Art Brut, Lausanne, Switzerland. © 2021 Kiyoko Lerner/Artists Rights Society (ARS), New York.

as a messy, hodgepodge of unrelated material not recognizably significant to the artworks inside. It includes two of Darger's own smaller watercolor and graphite paintings. Alongside them, he collaged twenty clippings of mid-century American popular visual culture depicting dinosaurs, a happy couple in the countryside, cute cats, Christ and the Holy Family, cactus flowers, lizards, and other seemingly random items. The nearly two dozen scraps around the paintings primarily derive from articles or advertisements published in *Life* magazine from September 1953 to October 1958. By considering the original sources of these materials and how they resonate with themes from Darger's larger body of work, this essay will show that the selections of items on the cover was not random, but introduced the overall concerns of the album, including the artist's response to twentieth-century American visual culture's representational ideals of the family.

To begin, Darger included two of his smaller paintings on the cover that address themes common in many of the paintings held within the album: they depict children on their own, fleeing violent and oppressive adults (Figs. 4.1–4.2). The image on the left (Fig. 4.1) includes three soldiers on horseback who wear grey uniforms modeled on Confederate soldiers from the United States Civil War. These characters are citizens of Darger's fictional nation of Glandelinia, which seceded from the fictional Abbiennia in order to continue its practice of child slavery. The men approach the seven young Vivian Sisters, Abbiennian princesses who wear their hallmark scouting outfits of purple, yellow, and red. Each of the girls has been tied to a tree by two thick bands of black rope. The men advance vigorously, and Darger's work invites the viewer to indulge in the thrill of an almost cinematic scene. Yet, the captions at the top and bottom reassure the viewer that the intervention of the thin streaks of lightening crackling against the black sky will save the girls: "The storms approach ... it saves them ... not one of the Glandelinians escapes alive." Through the welcome intervention of nature – not any adult saviors – the girls are free.

The second painting has no caption, but Darger's familiar iconography identifies it as another scene of flight (Fig. 4.2). As in the work on the left, the painting alludes to struggles faced by girls at the hands of adults, while also reassuring the viewer of their escape with the aid of forces from the natural world via the help of a human/dragon hybrid that Darger called a Blengin. These child-protecting creatures live on the imaginary planet in which he works take place and show up regularly in his writing and art to aid child fugitives. The eight children have recently escaped from a Glandelinian camp and they run across a rural landscape of billowing clouds and grassy fields, with a few homes peeking up from the horizon. They seek the safety of invading Abbieannian troop encampments where they will officially be granted their freedom. One of the ways the Glandelinians punish children is by stripping them of their clothing, and three of the fugitive children are still naked. Their nakedness reveals their gender non-conformity: though they wear girlish bows and braids in their hair, they have male genitalia. Darger crafts his children's hair and faces in line with standard styles of midcentury children's advertisements and illustrations (like Dick and Jane readers) that communicate clear male and female roles, yet he subversively shifts society's gender norms by giving his girl children penises. These transgressive youths are punished and shamed by the Glandelinians. But, the children in Darger's novels and texts refuse to submit to oppression and flee their captors.

Like these two paintings, the majority of Darger's visual works focus on children absent from parents – orphans and fugitives who refuse to submit to governing norms. Many of these he developed from pre-existent orphan characters from American popular culture like *Little Annie Rooney*, a plucky comic strip character who remains ever optimistic that she will one day get a family, in spite of her many undeserved hardships across her long run in comic strips from 1927 to 1966. Darger transforms these idealistically cute, but ever-orphaned and never-homed, characters of popular culture into more radical figures whose bodies cannot and will not conform or submit to the laws of the state. Darger repositions Annie and other orphans who had previously remained wistful for ideals of family enfoldment, even as they have been repeatedly denied such promises, into dozens of children in the act of collective flight from structural forces of oppression.

Darger's method of transforming these images was complex. To transfer a mass-print clipping or enlargement into his compositions, he often first used tracing paper to copy it. Then, he would make alterations to the tracing-paper drawing, such as changing or removing clothing, adding props or accessories, or changing the original figure's facial expression. After making these manipulations on the tracing paper, he would employ carbon paper to transfer the manipulated image from the tracing paper onto the paper of his final work. He then would paint his traced forms in with watercolors.[2]

Because Darger kept his source materials, one can find the original clippings for much of his imagery. In fact, he did not just trace the children in his works from mass print clippings, but the majority of his imagery across his compositions. In any one of his canvases, roughly 80–90% of the imagery has likely been traced from pre-existent mass print sources. For example, in the image of the eight children fleeing on the right side of the cover, the girls' heads would have been traced from Little Annie Rooney orphan characters and possible one or two characters from a coloring book (Fig. 4.2). Their outfits and bodies likely derived from sewing pattern illustrations or photographic clothing advertisements, which were frequent sources for Darger. Six of the girls' sets of running legs are from the same template, which Darger flipped for the right-most figure. The Blengin was likely made from a Little Annie Rooney clipping for the head, a clipping of butterfly wings possibly from a coloring book, and a lizard or dinosaur tail scrap. Darger would have traced the clouds, trees, shrubs, and homes from other clippings from mass print photographs, comics, or coloring book imagery.[3]

To get his (often small) appropriated clippings to be the right size for his large works, Darger had photo-enlargements made. Starting in the 1940s, he began taking his mass-print scraps to his local drugstore to have them sent off to a professional photography studio. He would give the drugstore specific instructions for how he wanted the studio to crop the image before enlarging it into a negative and new print. Though this process was costly, it allowed him to amplify small clippings to 11-by-14-inch reproductions that he could then trace into his increasingly monumental album pages. He kept his valuable sources well-organized, filing his negatives neatly in a wooden box and storing the enlargements in manila envelopes. On the envelope's exteriors he wrote brief notes indicating their contents and how they were to be repurposed in his paintings: "Girl on bike, drawn twice," "Male Blengin, drawn always," or "Special picture girl bending w/ stick & another jumping away in terror."[4] He also kept dozens of scrapbooks with carefully pasted mass-print sources filling the pages, which no doubt provided visual inspiration for his art. A planning journal includes lists of all the paintings he wanted to make and whether or not he had yet "pictured" them. His recorded notes indicate that (for at least part of his career) he spent about a month on each painting, drawing the composition first, then painting it.[5]

Thus, though his finished pieces are colored in with paint, their forms were created via the use of photographic enlargement technologies and the reproduction and recombination of imagery appropriated from print media. His finished pieces are palimpsests that carry traces of manipulated photographic media underneath a multicolored sheen of paint. And, the sources Darger consulted over his many decades of active production suggest that works were intended to intervene in histories of photographic reproduction and mass print imagery, more so than histories of painting. His home was not filled with sources addressing fine art traditions of painting, but with stacks upon stacks of popular print imagery (Fig. 4.3). Additionally, his materials and writing leave no indication that he was invested in the discourses, debates, or traditions of fine art painting, or that he even attended the expansize collections of histocially-significant paintings nearby, such as at institutions like The Art Institute of Chicago. Rather, his archive of print sources focus on the dominant and widely accessible imagery of American mass media, especially its traditions of representing American children, the family, and the home.

wDarger also extensively appropriated from the words of published texts, often copying passages of several pages into his fictional writings.[6] The Glandelinian war with Abbiennia, for example, was based on elements and sources covering the history of enslavement in the United States and the Civil War, including *Uncle Tom's Cabin*by

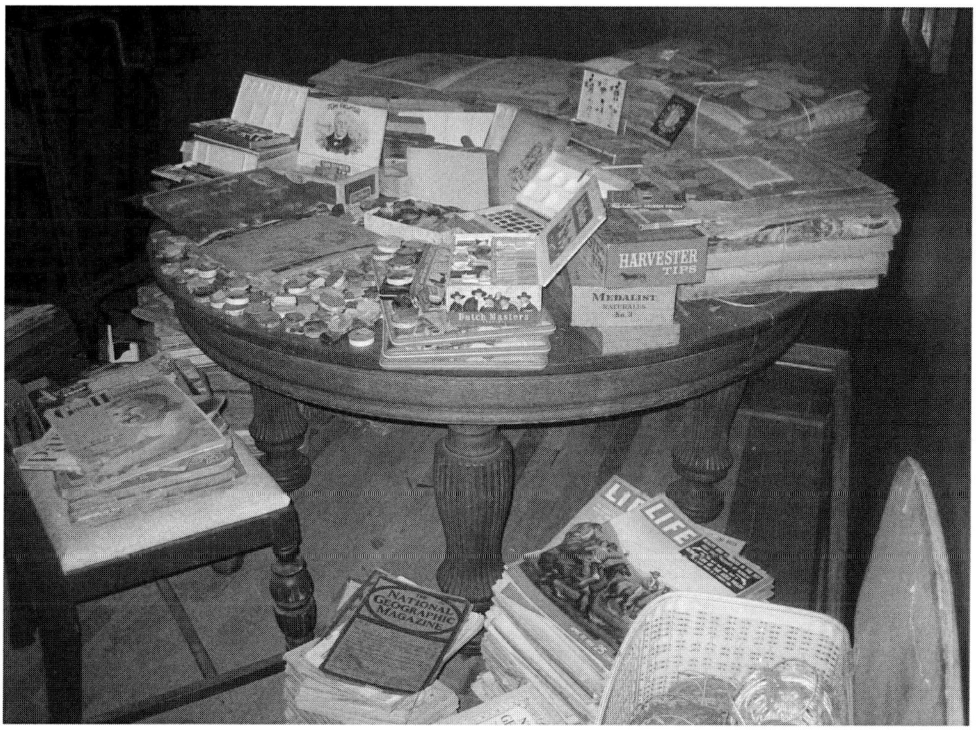

Figure 4.3 Darger's Table with Source Materials, Scrapbooks, and Art Supplies, Including a Stack of Life Magazines. The Henry Darger Room Collection, Intuit: The Center for Intuitive and Outsider Art, gift of Kiyoko Lerner.

Harriet Beecher Stowe, from which he liberally appropriated text.[7] Yet, Darger's characters – like his source materials – were almost exclusively white. The artist shifted the history and historical fiction of his sources to make it not his characters' race that led to their oppression and enslavement, but another marginalizing factor: their inability to conform to norms of gender. The artist borrowed from the historical precedent of the Civil War with its roots in the racially based system of enslavement in American to create his own fictional account of the forced institutionalization and oppression of gender aberrant children. His many illustrations of children fleeing enslavement on foot across vast panoramic landscapes also resonate with the visuals produced by narratives like Stowe's, which she wrote just after the 1850 passage of federal legislation supporting the return of formerly enslaved individuals to enslavement in the South after they had successfully escaped to freedom in the North.[8]

Darger's stories of child enslavement also find a historical resonance in Progressive Era eugenicist policies that attempted to control the behavior and sexual reproduction of delinquent and/or developmentally disabled children, who were often lower-class and immigrant. During his childhood, state institutions confined persons with intellectual and developmental disabilities in single-sex quarters during their reproductive years to enact the recommendations of eugenicists that such persons should not be allowed to reproduce.[9] In some states, forced sterilization was also performed, though not in Illinois. It was not uncommon for immigrant adolescents to be swept off American city streets and sent to the country out of fear of their weak genes spreading uncontrollably through the American population.[10] Darger himself had been incarcerated to one such institution in 1904: the Illinois Asylum for Feeble-Minded Children. This large state-run facility in Lincoln, Illinois, housed 1,200 youths and adults with developmental or intellectual disabilities. Cases of neglect and abuse were documented during the years of Darger's stay.[11] The Asylum also operated a farm, which higher functioning inmates were required to work during the agricultural season. It was during one of these seasons of forced labor that Darger managed to escape, which likely deepened the connection he later felt between his own experience of the state-sanctioned incarceration and forced labor of those deemed "feeble-minded" and the nation's longer history of race-based enslavement.[12]

Darger himself was born of a working-class German immigrant father and an American-born mother in Chicago in 1892.[13] His mother died when he was four while giving birth to a younger sister who was put up for adoption. In 1900, his father entered Chicago's St. Augustine Poor House. Then effectively orphaned, Darger was first taken in by a Catholic charitable home for boys. Darger was quite intelligent and excelled at his studies, but he had disciplinary problems.[14] Four years after entering the home, his caretakers hired a doctor to examine him, likely because of his poor behavior. The doctor arranged for the boy's confinement in the Asylum, listing only "self-abuse" on the intake form.[15] "Self-abuse," a euphemism for masturbation, was a common fear among eugenics-influenced doctors. They believed that the supposedly excessive, unrestrained sexuality of "feeble-minded" and differently abled individuals and immigrants threatened to overpower the hearty genetic stock of American Anglo-Saxons Darger was imprisoned to control his seemingly out-of-control sperm. Yet, in 1909 he fled the institution, successfully escaping from it and walking more than 150 miles back to Chicago. Reading *Uncle Tom's Cabin* later, Darger felt a resonance between his travails and the character Eliza who fled enslavement in Kentucky with the hopes of reaching Canada. Upon arriving back in the city, Darger would live the rest of his life without a family, working as a menial laborer, predominantly as a janitor in local hospitals. In his free time, he began writing and making art about orphaned, gender-non-conforming children whom the Glandelinian state had held in captivity, but who then took their lives into their own hands and fled.

Eugenicist's fears about Darger reproducing did not come to pass. He fathered no children and, in fact, lived in extreme social isolation. Though he was free from the institution, his life was characterized by economic hardship and marginalization. For 54 years, he worked as a janitor, dishwasher, and bandage roller in three Chicago Catholic hospitals, never rising to higher positions, before surviving on meager Social Security checks in his final years. Darger had little disposable income and, as far as we know, he did not own a camera. He never cohabited with a lover or married, and no photographs of blood relatives were found in his apartment at his death. In fact, he only owned three photographs of himself. Two of these were studio portraits taken at the same location with the one person with whom Darger seemed to have formed a loving relationship in adulthood: his "pal" William Schloeder. Darger historian Jim Elledge has speculated that Schloeder and Darger were lovers.[16]

Michael Moon offers another interesting possibility by considering Darger's assertion in his writing that he had wanted to adopt a child. In text from the nineteen-teens and twenties, when Darger would have been in his mid-twenties through late-thirties (prime childrearing years), Darger writes that he petitioned God to help him adopt children.[17] This would have also been during the time that Schloeder lived in Chicago, and when he and Darger were close. Moon speculates that if Darger had attempted to adopt a child, he may have wanted to do so with Schloeder, who presumably would have also served as a father. Their hopes for creating this unusual family structure of two male parents, Moon asserts, may have been boosted by mass-press fictional accounts of cobbled-together families that exceed the normative male-female model, like Dick Tracey's adoption of a boy street urchin "The Kid" as his sidekick detective. As Moon recounts, however, homophobia would have made it difficult for this atypical couple to adopt.[18] Thus, though Darger may have wished to integrate into a non-biologically reproductive family unit with Schloeder and a child, this did not come to pass. Schloeder moved with his sister to Texas in the 1930s and died there in 1959.

Documentary pictures of Darger's apartment after his death reveal that, rather than photographs of friends or family members, his walls and mantle were filled with portraits he had made of his fictional characters.[19] One framed example is a drawing of Annabelle Aronburg Vivian, a heroine from his novel (Fig. 4.4). In it, the young girl poses in a manner familiar from photographic portraiture. She is finely dressed with neatly coiffed hair that is decorated with a large bow, rendering her a cute picture of girlishness fitting for the era of Shirley Temple. She sits in a plush chair, her body at a slight angle, with her head and gaze turned toward the viewer. Her mouth is closed, unsmiling, and at rest. She is aware that she is being looked at and she presents herself to the viewer with poise and confidence. Darger likely traced this image from a photograph (possibly of Temple) originally printed in the mass press.[20] Temple had famously played orphans in Hollywood films [Curly Top (1935), The Little Princess (1939), Miss Annie Rooney (1942)]. Traced and painted over, Darger adopted this orphaned image as a surrogate member of his imagined family.

In her exploration of vernacular photographs of the African diaspora in Europe, Tina Campt explores the invocations of orphaned photographs, largely anonymously made works that have been mostly dislodged from recorded histories, including those

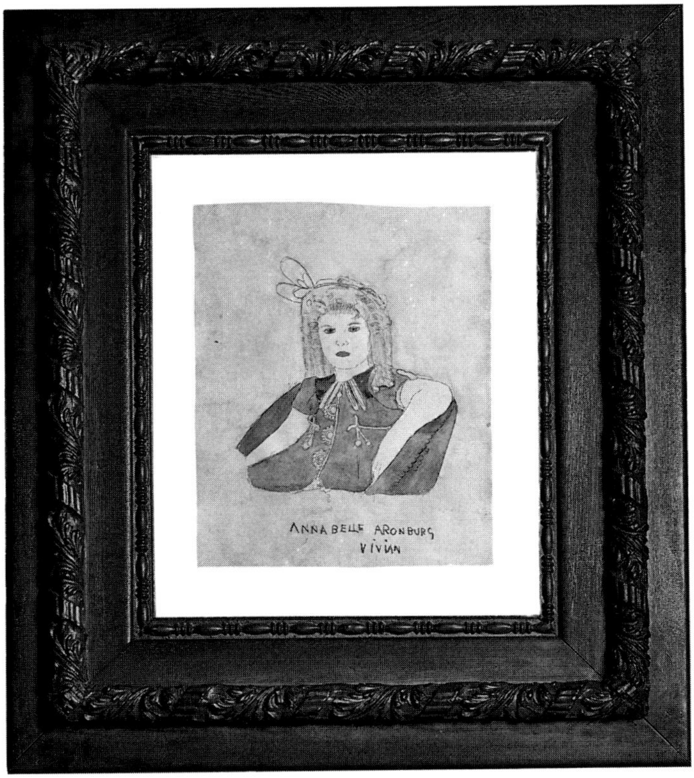

Figure 4.4 Henry Darger, *Annabelle Aronburg Vivian*, c. 1940s, watercolor and pencil on paper, 35 ½ × 31 ½ inches. Collection of Robert A. Roth, Chicago, Illinois. Photographer, John Faier. © 2021 Kiyoko Lerner/Artists Rights Society (ARS), New York.

of their creator and subjects.[21] Building on the metaphor, she notes the "potentially disruptive capacities of the unruly, orphaned child," who both longs for family inclusion, while also being rebelliously disengaged.[22] Campt considers how such unattached family photographs of the Afro-Europeans "simultaneously claim a place of both of belonging and unbelonging."[23] Campt also develops the idea of Black fugitivity in relation to the performativity of Black family photographs in the afterlives of enslavement. By evoking both norms and alterity, these everyday family photographs can undermine the seeming "clarity and legitimacy" of hegemonic social expectations: Often an elusive presence, the fugitive has an ability to pass that camouflages difference while highlighting the very distinctions on which identity and community are based.[24] Though developed in response to family photographs made by Afro-Europeans who held a distinct racial and diasporic history and identity that Darger did not share, Campt's terminology of orphans and fugitives is helpful for thinking through Darger's approach to the appropriated and recontextualized images in his "family" album. Darger's history was different, but his domestic albums offer a related outlook on photography's performative uses around navigating positions of belonging and unbelonging.

Many of the sources Darger used for his art are clippings from mass-media print sources that he would have likely picked up from the hospital trash and brought to his home after others had discarded them. These images had been abandoned by their original owners, and would have ended up buried in a landfill if the artist had not "adopted" them. Darger lived on a paltry budget and had no fine-art training. But, working as a janitor, he had access to countless newspapers and magazines discarded in hospital waiting rooms. He carefully saved and reused these cast-away materials, and his apartment was filled with stacks and stacks of periodicals he salvaged from the trash (Fig. 4.3). Rehoming these orphaned images first to his apartment and then into his art, Darger both stabilized and destabilized this mainstream American material. He grounded these images in a new narrative and a visual world of his creation, one that radically defied dominant American notions of the family and its photographs.

Michel de Certeau has described how marginal members of society like Darger, whose lives are seemingly absent of political power, nevertheless find minoritarian means of assertion. Such figures do not hold access to spaces in which they can publicly project authority and influence (like in an exhibition at an art gallery or museum), but they nevertheless find ways to frequently *poach* from the property of dominant media producers, much as peasants in feudal systems would covertly hunt on the lands of nobles.[25] Marginal figures can thus shift the cultural economy to their own interests in little day-to-day ways that go unstopped because they are never visible enough to directly challenge dominant powers.[26] In the field of media studies, de Certeau's theory has been employed as an alternative to the idea that audiences only passively consume the messages of hegemonic media, to instead explore ways that the audience "talks back."[27]

Considering de Certeau's theories about media alongside Campt's writing about orphans and fugitives in the afterlives of enslavement suggests how Darger's art resonates as an example of fugitivity in the practice of everyday life. According to de Certeau, the socially marginalized perform small acts of refusal that are not noticed by authorities but build up over time.[28] Over six decades, Darger's creations performed daily fugitivity to normative ideals of the American family and its visual documentation. For one who had lost the freedom of his youth due to the state deeming his procreative abilities threatening, he sustained a practice of imaginative alternative family creation that flew under the radar, evading detection, until a new media landscape was more ready to receive his visual commentaries about reimagined family norms.

A Cut-Up and Cut-Out Album

A Neo-Bauhaus photographer and member of the faculty at the Illinois Institute of Technology, Lerner recognized the importance of Darger's art when he stumbled upon it in 1973. He gradually embarked on a decades-long mission to care for and bring it to the public. By the time the work was first exhibited at the Hyde Park Art Center near the University of Chicago campus on the city's south side in 1977, it had been altered to align with audience expectations for showing and selling two-dimensional fine art. The albums' pages were cut out of their bindings so that each could be framed, enabling it to be exhibited to large audiences and, ultimately, sold as individual pieces to collectors and institutions. Because most of Darger's pieces are illustrated on both sides (as they were originally pages in a book), his art is usually framed in double-sided glass and hung from the ceiling.

The removal of Darger's art from its original home in his domestic albums enabled its exhibition in fine art institutions. What was lost in the process, however, was the work's important engagement with the conventions of family album-making, which have been documented in social theory and histories of photographjy. Pierre Bourdieu's foundational analysis foregrounds the ritual role of photography in supporting the social integration of groups, most importantly the middle-class family unit.[29] Following Bourdieu's lead in analyzing this "middlebrow art," additional sociologically inflected studies have presented family photograph albums as instruments of socialization that assert one's successful participation in the norms of middle-class family life.[30] Buttressing these arguments is a century of advertising from Kodak encouraging consumers to preserve "picture perfect" moments in family albums.[31]

Darger's album cover includes some clippings that are akin to the types of photographs that typically show up in family albums, as charted by such studies. Darger pasted a photograph on his cover of three cats posed like family pets, though the artist had no pets (Fig. 4.1). The image came from a Puss n' Boots cat food advertisement published on page 108 of a November 19, 1956, *Life* issue. The ad depicted an idealized picture of perfectly clean, calm, well-behaved cats with a caption indicating pet-owners' tendency to anthropomorphize pets: "Don't be alarmed children. It's only a camera!" Further text proclaims the nutritional superiority of Puss n' Boots, with its ability to turn a "half-starved orphan" stray cat into a "beautiful, healthy, and loveable" family member. The ad was originally meant to sell cat food, but Darger "adopted" this stray as one more "orphan" image in his own imagined family album.

In addition to photos of beloved pets, the "middlebrow" art of family photograph albums also frequently include pictures of family vacations. Darger's album cover includes two photographs related to family vacations taken in Europe, even though Darger himself did not have the finances to take trips, especially abroad, nor a family with which to travel. Just to the left of Darger's paintings are two clippings that suggest an imaginative form of family travel. One shows a couple frolicking in the British countryside, which Darger clipped from a Pan-Am advertisement printed on page 108 of a June 16, 1958, issue of *Life* magazine (Fig. 4.5). The photo's caption reassures readers that such a trip is worth the cost, "The other 50 weeks are richer for the two you spend abroad." Though Darger could never afford such a trip, he used the ad's photograph imaginatively. Above it, Darger pasted a scrap from an article in the same issue documenting top restaurants in Europe.[32] The clipping shows a "superb smorgasbord" from the oldest restaurant in Stockholm meant to delight American travelers abroad. This ephemera introduces elements of Darger's practice as in line with Bourdieu's discussion of using popular photography to assert one's fulfillment of social norms, here the expectation of albums as a reel of family highlights, including happy memories on vacations. Yet, Darger's album documented other sorts of flight as well, not the consumption-filled travel splurges encouraged by advertisements, but moments of fugitivity from the demands of a heteronormative, ableist, capitalist, white-supremacist, American system in which his life was always already marginalized.

Within the album, Darger's art transformed images of Temple, Little Annie Rooney, the Dionne Quintuplets, and other sources of orphan images and/or pictures of parentless children into fugitive characters of his fictional world. At least at the end of his life, Darger was also known to search the trash cans and dumpsters of his populous Chicago neighborhood for material. Darger was not one to throw anything

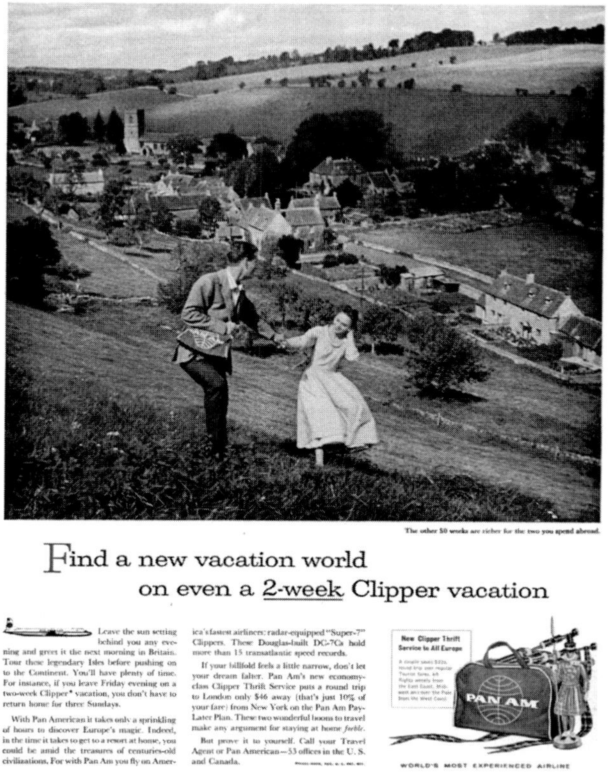

Figure 4.5 Pan Am, *Find a New World,* 1958. Courtesy The Pan Am Historical Foundation/ panam.org.

away, even damaged art, and he gladly worked with and found value in that which others had thrown out and deemed no longer of value. Note the long diagonal rip that stretches across the left half of the right-most watercolor painting collaged on his album cover (Fig. 4.2). Visible marks show where the artist taped the page to save it, rather than discard it. Darger created his imagined family album as a collage of cast-off detritus from America's visualization of its family ideals.

"A Living Laboratory of [Media] Evolution"

Flowers are also a historical album convention. Actual dried flowers may be pasted in as mementos of important days, and album photographs sometimes include flowers as props in the rituals of weddings, graduations, births, and even funerals. Darger's album cover has several photographs of flowers, including a sentimental bouquet of red roses recalling the types of flowers given on Valentine's Day or pasted into Victorian scrapbooks. Yet, the artist also included four other photographs of flowers that come from a less expected source. These images derive from a *Life* magazine article titled "The Land of the Sun," from its April 5, 1954, issue. The article is the ninth installment of a 13-chapter series about the natural history of the Earth called

"The World We Live In." It focused on the environmental conditions of deserts and how species have adapted remarkable abilities to survive, and even thrive, in these climates. It argued that people are mistaken to believe that deserts are "remote and uncharted terrain must either be too perilous or too worthless to know."[33] To illustrate its claims that deserts are in fact filled with life, it presents photographs of flowering cacti that "burst into bloom" after surviving "the breaking of a bitter drought."[34] The article acknowledges that life is hard in the desert, but that cacti and other species triumph against the odds: "The desert's stark domain supports creatures bred to its harsh demands."[35]

Darger's inclusion of *Life*'s photographs of hardy, little flowers on his cover indicates that he saw a connection between these tough plants and his work's heroines. Art historian Leisa Rundquist has charted correspondences between Darger's conception of girlhood and flowers, particularly as represented by the Vivian Sisters, several of whom are named after flowers, and who he depicted on the canvas on the left of his album cover, just above the collaged cacti.[36] Yet, his selection of these desert flowers, specifically, is significant as they are not hothouse blossoms, but emblems of survival despite the odds, much like Darger's orphaned, fugitive children.

Darger also may have felt an alliance with these flowering cacti himself. After escaping the Asylum, he faced extreme limitations – both financial and social – for the rest of his life. Yet, in spite of his "drought" of flowers related to family weddings, births, graduations, or other milestones, Darger saved orphaned images of hearty cacti as flowers that better reflected the circumstances of his own life. *Life*'s description of the surprising success of desert species could also be extended as a metaphor for the creative practices of anonymous, untrained artists like Darger. Like *Life*'s flowers, Darger's art breaks down assumptions of barren cultural "deserts." The uneducated, marginalized artist's apartment may have been a "stark domain," barren of traditional fine art or elite culture, yet it evolved "creatures bred to its harsh demands."[37]

Darger also included on his cover clippings from the fifth installment of "The World We Live In" series, which was published in *Life*'s September 7, 1953, magazine. Titled "The Pageant of Life," this edition discussed the origins of life on Earth and the long history of evolution. It addressed the existential question "What is life?"[38] Darger's selected illustrations of dinosaurs from the Jurassic and Cretaceous periods, sea reptiles from the Mesozoic era, a three-tiered image of sea creatures from the Cambrian, Ordovician, and Silurian periods, in addition to a menagerie of soft-bodied, simple sea creatures from the Pre-Cambrian era. By including such clippings on his cover, he suggests that his massive album takes an exceptionally long historical view when considering the notion of "family." The scraps also indicate that Darger's interest in creation goes beyond a human-centric viewpoint to consider the ways diverse species have developed on Earth.

Life described the dinosaurs as a great success of evolution that, though extinct today, survived for millions of years by adapting to the particular demands of their prehistoric world. Darger may have felt a resonance between the development of these powerful monsters and his own "wondrous workings of evolution" in his album, in which he merged mass-media clippings of everyday American girls with the tails of dinosaurs to create the Blengins.[39] Unlike Darger's depictions of fugitive children, who often only have the strength to assert agency by fleeing, the Blengins' adaptations give them superhuman skills and strengths, enabling them to more aggressively fight back. Though he did not produce biological offspring, Darger's album enabled imaginative generation.

Riffing on the powers of evolution, he manipulated media to produce not just individuals but new species like the Blengins and whole new worlds.

Other clippings on Darger's cover explore examples of the impact of isolation on evolutionary adaptation. An illustration of iguanas and cormorants resting on a volcanic isle has the heading "A Fit Shore for Pandemonium," which indicates the clippings' origins in a September 8, 1958, *Life* magazine article called "The Enchanted Isles." The essay was the second in a *Life* series on "Darwin's World of Nature." It addressed the "untouched sanctuary" of the Galapagos Islands, a prime case study of natural selection made famous by Charles Darwin.[40] Darger also included on his cover three additional photographic clippings from the article depicting baby penguins, a small seal, and an iguana lounging in a tree. The article called the islands of black rock located far off the western coast of Ecuador "a living laboratory of evolution."[41] It describes how remarkable mutations in species' genes granted them selective advantage over time, helping them master the particular challenges of their locales. It names the land "The Realm of the Rocks," which no doubt would have delighted Darger in its proximity to his own name for the fantastic world of his characters introduced in the subtitle of his novel: *The Realms of the Unreal*.[42]

The article identified the Galapagos as a fascinating case study of evolution because it remained sequestered as "a little world within itself."[43] The species on the Galapagos evolved into unique, one-of-a-kind creatures over centuries without any intervention. Upon their discovery by Darwin and others, the Galapagos expanded human understandings of biodiversity and evolution. Precisely because of their isolation, these animals producing something unusual, different, and unexpected that taught Darwin fundamental truths about existence.

Darger may have understood himself as like the creatures on the Galapagos, whose development was influenced by their isolation. He kept his small apartment private, completing his work there, then binding it in an album that he closed and (as far as we know) opened only for himself. Darger received no known critical feedback from audiences during his six decades of artistic creation. His art originated in content first made for mass-mediated audiences, but then it evolved in isolation in his apartment, absent from external feedback.

Interestingly, De Certeau references biological metaphors in his explanation of the practice of everyday life. In some wonderfully creative flights of metaphor, he compares poaching to the evolutionary developments of camouflage and other tricks by which smaller, less powerful plants and animals survive over time either as parasites or in mutually beneficial symbiotic relationships by taking resources from larger animals who do not detect them or see them as posing a threat. De Certeau suggests that this "ageless art … goes back much farther than our histories and forms strange alliances preceding the frontiers of humanity."[44] The actions of these creatures, in other words, offer an ancient evolutionary strategy of survival analogous to the poaching practices de Certeau saw practiced in modern daily life by marginalized individuals.

Campt, as quoted at the end of the proceeding section, also asserts fugitivity as invoking camouflage in its most powerful moments, when a fugitive is able to pass for the norm while simultaneously challenging and expanding its boundaries. Without being noticed, Darger collected stacks and stacks of orphaned images that had originally repeated myths of the American nuclear family. Over 60 years, he created a massive, monumental body of work that recast those idealized characters as heroic fugitives from oppressive norms. To others, Darger camouflaged as just one more member of the urban marginalized and dispossessed population rummaging through the trash. All the while, his living laboratory of media evolution grew.

Darger's Spiritual Family

Darger was a lifelong Catholic and his photographic album cover incorporates Catholic imagery alongside its other media. Darger kept many devotional images in his apartment that sat alongside his framed portraits of his fictional characters. Like him, his fictional child characters were also faithful Catholics. He even collaged Catholic prayer cards into a few of his canvases.

In absence of a biological family, Darger found an important model of a spiritual family in visions of Christ and his Earthly family with Mary and his adoptive father Joseph. His cover includes an illustration of the boy Jesus holding a sacrificial lamb with white doves at his feet, and with Mary and Joseph standing behind them. A clipping next to it features Jesus pointing to his Sacred Heart. Darger's convergence of these images aside clippings from articles about the evolutionary wonders of the prehistoric era and the Galapagos islands indicate that the artist likely associated the Catholic miracles of immaculate conception, visionary experience, and the Holy Family with the extraordinary natural wonders and abundant creations of life on Earth.

Another clipping references the funeral procession of Pope Pius XII. Albums sometimes will include memories of end-of-life moments, funerals, and wakes for beloved family members. The orphaned, socially isolated Darger did not have photographs of any of his family members' funerals to include in his album. His father had died in the Poor House while Darger was at the Asylum, so he had no photograph with which to remember him or his passing. But, he pasted on his cover a photograph of the funeral procession of another "father," the Holy Father, Pope Pius XII, passing by the Il Vittoriano monument in Rome, which is also called the "Altar of the Fatherland.[45]

Life's articles about evolution presented science as compatible with Christian beliefs. With its mission of bringing pictures and stories into every home in America, *Life* approached the subject of evolution sensitively. It framed a clear presentation of well-researched scientific information with respectful references to the Bible, including quoted passages meant to appear compatible with the scientific arguments. In this way, the magazine educated Americans about the most up-to-date science of natural history in the comfort of their own living rooms without threatening their religious beliefs. "The Pageant of Life" from which Darger clipped his dinosaur imagery, for example, opens with a quote from Genesis.[46] Its summary of the controversial historical reception of Darwin's theory of Evolution asserts that humans have always questioned where they came from and that Darwin was a spiritual man whose statements on religion suggested that he believed that the process of evolution followed an original divine creation.[47] As it did for many American readers, *Life*'s arguments fit comfortably alongside Darger's spiritual beliefs.

Life's articles emphasize nature's incredible power to adapt, even in the harshest conditions, and to produce miraculous solutions to environmental difficulties beyond any powers of human control. Human intervention had no hand in the creation of the dinosaurs or the animals of the Galapagos – these creatures survived on their own and adapted via the powers of random genetic mutations. Human powers of reproduction are also absent from the Christian story of Christ's immaculate conception and miraculous resurrection. The Catholic church has traditionally resisted human attempts to control reproduction or life via birth control, abortion, the death penalty, or through the artificial selection of eugenics.[48] The discourses of Christ and of natural selection thus come together on Darger's cover and offer counter-narratives to the eugenicist emphasis on selective breeding and reproductive control that had so negatively impacted Darger in his youth. In his fugitivity from norms of the American family and its ideals of reproductive fitness, Darger found support both in stories of evolutionary wonders and of Christ's miraculous conception. His album folds these discourses into his adapted version of a family album.

Conclusion

The album-based roots of Darger's art offer an opportunity to not only better understand his work but also to expand the scholarly awareness of examples of the performative workings of the family album and its photographic and non-photographic media. Having been orphaned and institutionalized in a eugenicist asylum in his youth, Darger was aware of the oppressive potentials of ideals of "picture perfect" American families. In adulthood, he found ways to "make do" through practices of everyday life in which he rescued orphaned images from mainstream culture, while keeping his activities camouflaged from the notice of others. His adopted and adapted images became characters in his imaginative family albums, which substituted for the documentation of a family he never had. These creations provide a powerful example of how albums can both express deep desires for family belonging and acceptance while also performing fugitivity from those ideals.

Notes

1 A good introduction to Darger's productions is: Michael Bonesteel, *Henry Darger: Art and Selected Writings* (New York: Rizzoli, 2000).
2 Brook Davis Anderson and Michel Thevoz, *Darger: The Henry Darger Collection at the American Folk Art Museum* (New York: Harry N. Abrams, 2001).
3 Examples of these clipped sources are housed in the archives at the Henry Darger Study Center.
4 Henry Darger Study Center, Box 72.
5 Henry Darger Study Center, Box 18 and Box 50, folder 2.
6 Moon, Michael. *Darger's Resources*, (Durham, N.C.: Duke University Press, 2012).
7 Leisa Rundquist, "Little Ways: Girlhood According to Henry Darger," *Southeastern College Art Conference Review*, Vol. 15, No. 4 (2009): 443.
8 Joan Hedrick, "Stowe's Life and *Uncle Tom's Cabin,*" *Uncle Tom's Cabin & American Culture*. Stephen Railton and the University of Virginia, 2007, http://utc.iath.virginia.edu/interpret/exhibits/hedrick/hedrick.html.
9 Patrick A. Curtis, "Eugenic Reformers, Cultural Perceptions of Dependent Populations, and the Care of the Feebleminded in Illinois, 1909-1920," (Ph.D. diss., University of Illinois at Chicago, 1983), 68.
10 On the practice of exporting urban "children at risk" to rural homes see: Paula Fass, *Kidnapped: Child Abduction in America* (New York: Oxford University Press, 1997), 42–45. On the institutionalization of feeble-minded children see: James Trent, *Inventing the Feeble-Mind: A History of Intellectual Disability in the United States (*Cambridge, UK: Oxford University Press, 2017), 67–88, 98, 131–183.
11 Trent, *Inventing the Feeble-Mind*, 119–123.
12 Darger, *The History of My Life*, undated and unpaginated. A copy of this autobiography can be found in: Klaus Biesenbach, ed. *Henry Darger* (New York, NY: Prestel, 2009), 281–313.

13 The basic outlines of biography come from Darger, *The History of My Life*, unpaginated. Additional biographical information is established in: John MacGregor, *Henry Darger: In the Realms of the Unreal* (New York: Delano Greenidge Editions, 2002), 30–84.
14 Darger, *The History of My Life*, undated and unpaginated.
15 MacGregor, *Henry Darger*, 45.
16 Jim Elledge, *Henry Darger, Throwaway Boy: The Tragic Life of An Outsider Artist* (New York: Harry N. Abrams, 2013).
17 The three instances of Darger's writings that mention a desire to adopt occur in Volume 1 of *The Story of the Vivian Girls*, 285-303, a journal dated to 1916 kept in the Henry Darger Study Center Box 46, Folder 1, and a loose sheet of typed paper dated to 1929 kept in HDSC, Box 49, Folder 29. MacGregor also quotes from these sources in: *Henry Darger*, 641–643. He identifies another instance of the petitions in: *The Story of the Vivian Girls,* 3487–3497.
18 Michael Moon, *Darger's Resources* (Durham, N.C.: Duke University Press, 2012), 7.
19 Kyoichi Tsuzuki, *Henry Darger's Room: 851 Webster* (Tokyo: Imperial Press, 2007). These photographs assisted with the recreation of Darger's apartment, which is on permanent display (in slightly smaller scale) at the Intuit Center for Intuitive and Outsider Art in Chicago.
20 Michael Bonesteel, "Henry Darger and the Aronburg Mystery" *Epidemiology and Psychiatric Sciences*, Vol. 27, No. 3 (June 2018): 226.
21 Tina Campt, *Image Matters: Archive, Photography, and the African Diaspora in Europe* (Durham, N.C.: Duke University Press, 2012), 83–114.
22 Campt, *Image Matters,* 90.
23 Campt, *Image Matters,* 112.
24 Campt, *Image Matters,* 87.
25 Michel de Certeau, *The Practice of Everyday Life*, trans. Steven F. Rendell (Berkeley, CA: The University of California Press, 2002), 174.
26 Michel de Certeau, *The Practice of Everyday Life*, 18.
27 Henry Jenkins, *Textual Poachers: Television Fans & Participatory Culture* (New York: Routledge, 1992).
28 De Certeau, *The Practice of Everyday Life*, xiii-xv, 18, 25.
29 Pierre Bourdieu, *Photography: A Middle-Brow Art,* trans. Shaun Whiteside (Stanford University Press: Stanford, CA, 1990), 30.
30 Susan Sontag, *On Photography* (New York, NY: Picador, 2001).; Richard Chalfen, *Snapshot Versions of Life* (Bowling Green, OH: Popular Press, 1987).; Marianne Hirsch, *Family Frames: Photography, Narrative, and Memory* (Cambridge, MA: Harvard University Press, 1997).; Jo Spence and Patricia Holland, eds. *Family Snaps: The Meanings of Domestic Photography* (London, UK: Virago Press, 1999).; Marianne Hirsch, ed. *The Familial Gaze* (Hannover, N.H.: Dartmouth College Press, 1999).
31 Nancy Martha West, *Kodak and the Lens of Nostalgia* (Charlottesville: University of Virginia Press, 2000).
32 "The Fabulous Food of Fabeled Restaurants," *Life Magazine* June 16, 1958: 59.
33 Lincoln Barnett, "The Land of the Sun," *Life Magazine* (April 5, 1954): 72.
34 Barnett, "The Land of the Sun," 90.
35 Barnett, "The Land of the Sun," 72.
36 Rundquist, "Little Ways:" 437, 435.
37 Barnett, "The Land of the Sun," 90.
38 Barnett, "The Pageant of Life," *Life Magazine* (September 7, 1953): 54.
39 Barnett, "The Pageant of Life," 54. Examples of paintings where you can see dinosaurs or Blengins made from dinosaur sources are reproduced in: Klaus Biesenbach, *Henry Darger* (New York: Prestel, 2014), 218, 216, 108, 216. Intuit: The Center for Intuitive and Outsider Art in Chicago also has in its archives tracing paper showing Darger's use of dinosaur parts in his creation of Blengins.
40 Barnett, "The Enchanted Isles," *Life Magazine* (September 8, 1958): 62.
41 Barnett, "The Enchanted Isles," 57 and 76.
42 Barnett, "The Enchanted Isles," 58–59.
43 Barnett, "The Enchanted Isles," 57.

44 De Certeau, *The Practice of Everyday Life,* 40.
45 The clipping is from "Village and World Pray for Pope Pius XII: A Simple End to a Pope's Splendid Life" *Life Magazine* (October 20, 1958): 28. (21–29 total pages)
46 "Let the waters bring forth the creeping creature having life … " Genesis 1:20, in Barnett, "The Pageant of Life," 54.
47 Barnett, "The Pageant of Life," 54.
48 Sharon M. Leon, *An Image of God: The Catholic Struggle with Eugenics* (Chicago: University of Chicago Press, 2013).

Bibliography

The Henry Darger Study Center Collection. The American Folk Art Museum, New York.

Anderson, Brook Davis and Michel Thevoz. *Darger: The Henry Darger Collection at the American Folk Art Museum*. New York: Harry N. Abrams, 2001.

Barnett, Lincoln. "The Land of the Sun," *Life Magazine* (April 5, 1954): 72–93.

Barnett, Lincoln. "The Pageant of Life," *Life* (September 7, 1953): 54–73.

Barnett, Lincoln. "The Enchanted Isles," *Life Magazine* (September 8, 1958): 56–75.

Bonesteel, Michael. *Henry Darger: Art and Selected Writings*. New York: Rizzoli, 2000.

Bonesteel, Michael. "Henry Darger and the Aronburg Mystery." *Epidemiology and Psychiatric Sciences*, Vol. 27, No. 3 (June 2018): 225–226.

Bourdieu, Pierre. *Photography: A Middle-Brow Art*, trans. Shaun Whiteside. Stanford, CA: Stanford University Press, 1990.

Campt, Tina. *Image Matters: Archive, Photography, and the African Diaspora in Europe*. Durham, N.C.: Duke University Press, 2012.

Chalfen, Richard. *Snapshot Versions of Life*. Bowling Green, OH: Popular Press, 1987.

Curtis, Patrick A. "Eugenic Reformers, Cultural Perceptions of Dependent Populations, and the Care of the Feebleminded in Illinois, 1909-1920." Ph.D. diss., University of Illinois at Chicago, 1983.

De Certeau, Michel. *The Practice of Everyday Life*, trans. Steven F. Rendell. Berkeley, CA: The University of California Press, 2002.

Elledge, Jim. *Henry Darger, Throwaway Boy: The Tragic Life of An Outsider Artist*. New York: Harry N. Abrams, 2013.

Fass, Paula. *Kidnapped: Child Abduction in America*. New York: Oxford University Press, 1997.

Hedrick, Joan. "Stowe's Life and *Uncle Tom's Cabin*." *Uncle Tom's Cabin & American Culture*. Stephen Railton and the University of Virginia, 2007. http://utc.iath.virginia.edu/interpret/exhibits/hedrick/hedrick.html

Hirsch, Marianne. *Family Frames: Photography, Narrative, and Memory*. Cambridge, MA: Harvard University Press, 1997.

Hirsch, Marianne. ed. *The Familial Gaze*. Hannover, N.H.: Dartmouth College Press, 1999.

Jenkins, Henry. *Textual Poachers: Television Fans & Participatory Culture*. New York: Routledge, 1992.

Leon, Sharon M. *An Image of God: The Catholic Struggle with Eugenics*. Chicago: University of Chicago Press, 2013.

Life Magazine. "The Fabulous Food of Fabled Restaurants" (June 16, 1958): 50–62.

Life Magazine. "Village and World Pray for Pope Pius XII: A Simple End to a Pope's Splendid Life" (October 20, 1958): 21–29.

MacGregor, John. *Henry Darger: In the Realms of the Unreal*. New York: Delano Greenidge Editions, 2002.

Moon, Michael. *Darger's Resources*. Durham, N.C.: Duke University Press, 2012.

Rundquist, Leisa. "Little Ways: Girlhood According to Henry Darger." *Southeastern College Art Conference Review*, Vol. 15, No. 4 (2009): 434–447.

Sontag, Susan. *On Photography*. New York: Picador, 2001.

Spence, Jo and Patricia Holland, eds. *Family Snaps: The Meanings of Domestic Photography*. London, U.K.: Virago Press, 1999.
Trent, James. *Inventing the Feeble-Mind: A History of Intellectual Disability in the United States*. Cambridge, U.K.: Oxford University Press, 2017.
Tsuzuki, Kyoichi. *Henry Darger's Room: 851 Webster*. Tokyo: Imperial Press, 2007.
West, Nancy Martha. *Kodak and the Lens of Nostalgia*. Charlottesville: University of Virginia Press, 2000.

Part II

Stepping Out of "the Closet," Privately

5 "Dropping Hairpins": Cisgender Performance and "Homosociality" in William Whitney's Fin-de-Siècle College Albums

Kris Belden-Adams

Dozens of long, V-shaped metal women's hairpins from the late-nineteenth-century radiate from a heart-shaped blank space in the center of an album page to which they have been stitched, leaving larger tortoise-shell-patterned pins, and a pin decorated with a red bow, resting near the page's margins (Fig. 5.1). Almost all of the twenty-two pins are labeled with handwritten initials or names – presumably of the women who formerly owned them – and the dates when they came into the possession of owner William Belcher Whitney (b. 1866, d. 1936). One initialed spot houses a pin that fell out of the book, or perhaps was returned to "M.O.," its former owner. Whitney collected these pins, according to this layout, from December of 1885 until he graduated from Amherst College in 1887. Variations in the designs of the pins underscore their variegated nature as a collection, and index the multitude of women whom young, single Whitney met and courted during his Amherst years. Two small mugshots of well-coiffed, hat-wearing women are tucked behind three metal pins that were stitched by Whitney with white thread onto the album page.

The hairpins rest like cisgender courting trophies acquired from the many Massachusetts college women whom Whitney persuaded to literally, and perhaps figuratively, let down their long locks from the confines of their proper "up-dos." Many of the pins are associated with specific social events that are mentioned in programs and other souvenirs on other pages of Whitney's four albums, including receptions, dances, orchestra concerts, plays at various nearby colleges or venues, and special events – such as Wellesley College's "Tree Day" and Smith College's "Mountain Day." A few are accompanied by sketches and references to inside jokes Whitney shared with several of the women.

Whitney represents himself for posterity in his albums as a girl-chasing, cisgender male, in accord with class expectations. But the presence of gay-subculture-encoded objects ("dropped hairpins"), as well as several snapshots and portraits suggesting same-gender attraction, present a counter-narrative for Whitney, who engages in casual, familiar poses with male classmates – some of whom are photographed in bed together. Photographs reveal that a homosocial relationship existed between Whitney and classmate and renowned baseball/tennis player, Charles Amherst Chase. They also suggest that Whitney – who never married or had children – did not conform to the heteronormative masculinity expected of men of his social class. For Whitney, album-based photo collage was a medium for absorbing and parroting cisgender gender norms that pervaded his social class, while expressing a quiet, closeted homosocial rebellion in these private albums that were laden with LGBTQI+

DOI: 10.4324/9781003157427-8

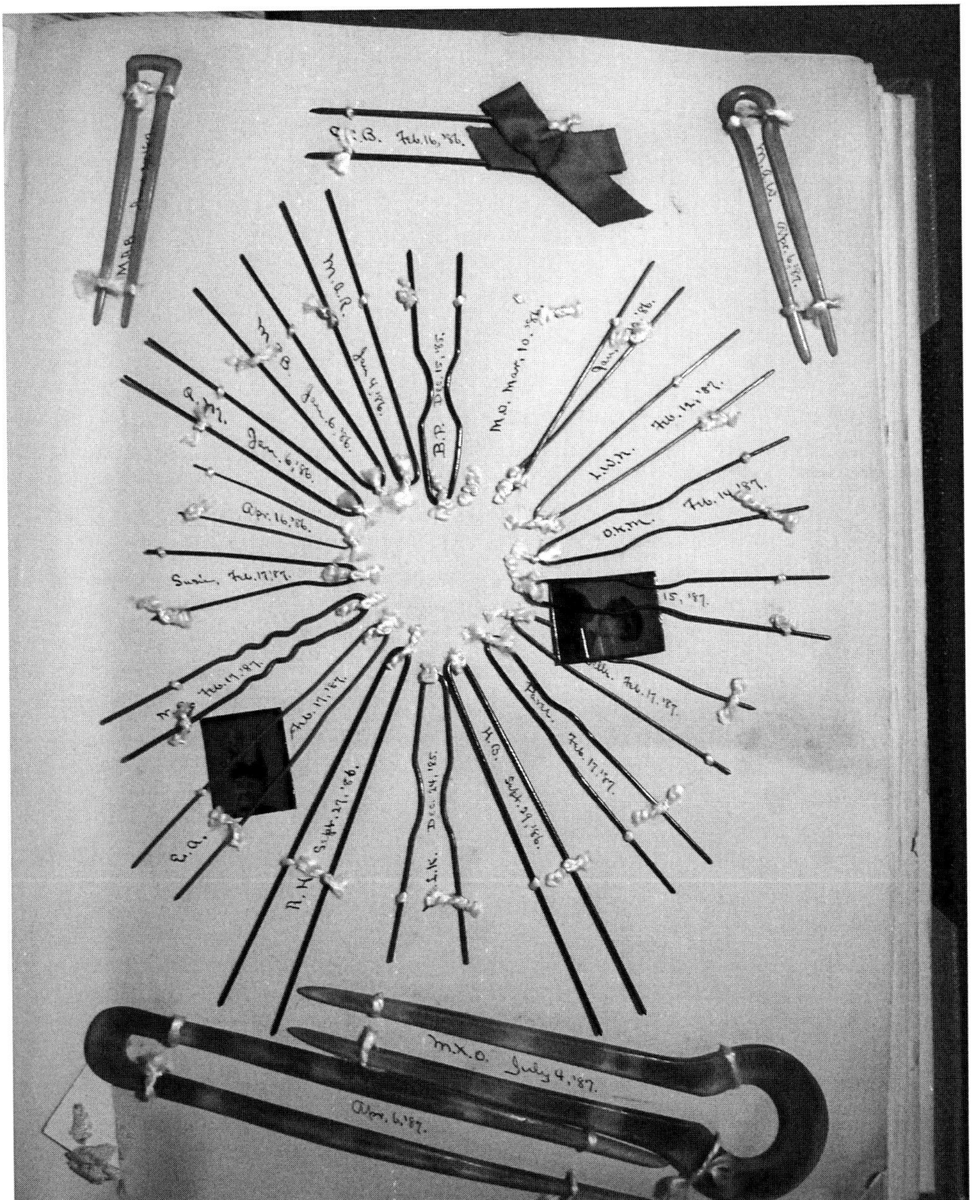

Figure 5.1 William Belcher Whitney, *Class of 1887*, 1885–1887, hairpins, photographs, text, thread, ribbon, William Belcher Whitney Scrapbook. Amherst College Archives & Special Collections, Public Domain.

subcultural codes. The narratives implied by the photographs, sketches, memorabilia, and letters in several pages of Whitney's albums are examined here through the lens of the pressures that upper-class men were under to conform to class expectations while struggling to fulfill and conform to cisgender "norms."[1]

Introducing the Whitney Albums

Whitney's four richly adorned, sculptural, multimedia albums – detailing his life and active social engagements while studying as an undergraduate at Amherst College (BA, 1887) and as a graduate student at Harvard Law School (degree, 1890) – provide an account of a bustling social life that involved chasing and courting many women at once, bonding with classmates, indulging in the decidedly "masculine" activities of baseball, football, and crew, and upholding his family's social-caste expectations as a marriage-worthy and social "Whitney."[2]

Whitney's impressive hairpin collection, for example, speaks to his plight as a *very* socially active young man who was popular with young women at colleges (and at least one high school) throughout the northeastern U.S. as a prospective suitor. A comparison of the hairpins, their dates, and the initials added by Whitney to the memorabilia and personal letters he pasted into the four volumes of his photographic scrapbooks reveals more context to his bustling social life. Whitney began his hairpin collection over winter break of 1885, and added two pins from women with the initials "B. P." (dated – chronologically and romantically – December 15, 1885) and "M. S. K." (Mabel Kidder, dated December 24, 1885). A comparison of the pins with memorabilia from Whitney's various albums suggests that "B. P." was a woman whom Whitney fondly called "Becky," who misidentifies Whitney as "Ted" in an apparent and ongoing inside joke. Her name, memorabilia, and photographs of her reappear in other albums throughout his time at Amherst College.

Next to one small note bearing the words "Ted from Becky," a small piece of paper bears the lighthearted ink-on-paper sketch. Drawings such as *Class in Physics at So. [South] Hadley [home to Mount Holyoke] and Amherst*, dated Christmas Day of 1885 (Fig. 5.2), appear periodically in the 1885–1886 album. In it, a crowd of young women and men sit, segregated by genders, in an auditorium. The South Hadley women, presumably Mount Holyoke students, sit reservedly with their arms folded. Amherst men, on the other hand, make themselves comfortable, and "manspread" their legs to consume as much space as possible. They smile, and several men speak casually with each other. Men and women do not interact. Clearly, the college classroom is a space where men are at natural ease, and women sit tentatively and uneasily.

This quick sketch, and others with its line quality and detail, make lighthearted fun of the behavior of Amherst men, who are shown as comfortable, self-assured, and well-dressed in full suits. The Mount Holyoke women appear socially awkward, properly dressed, quiet, and uptight. Whitney was not an artist and took no coursework in the visual arts at Amherst. It is possible that "Becky" of Mount Holyoke, whose notes appear near the sketches, or another classmate was their creator. The content of this drawing further suggests that "Becky" may have met Whitney during a shared-instruction physics course taken by students at both colleges. If this commentary about the lack of interactivity between the young men and women was more than just satire, then the meeting and friendship of "Becky" and "Ted"/William was even more unusual – not to mention, subversive – of the normative, expected, gender-conforming behaviors.

As Carroll Smith-Rosenberg points out, gender-segregated colleges were the norm, because they preserved the "protective rituals that surrounded 'visiting' between young women and men within the traditional Victorian home."[3] For schools such as Amherst and Mount Holyoke to combine instruction "threatened the very principle of gender polarity," and "[p]arents, administrators, and faculty observed the experiment with

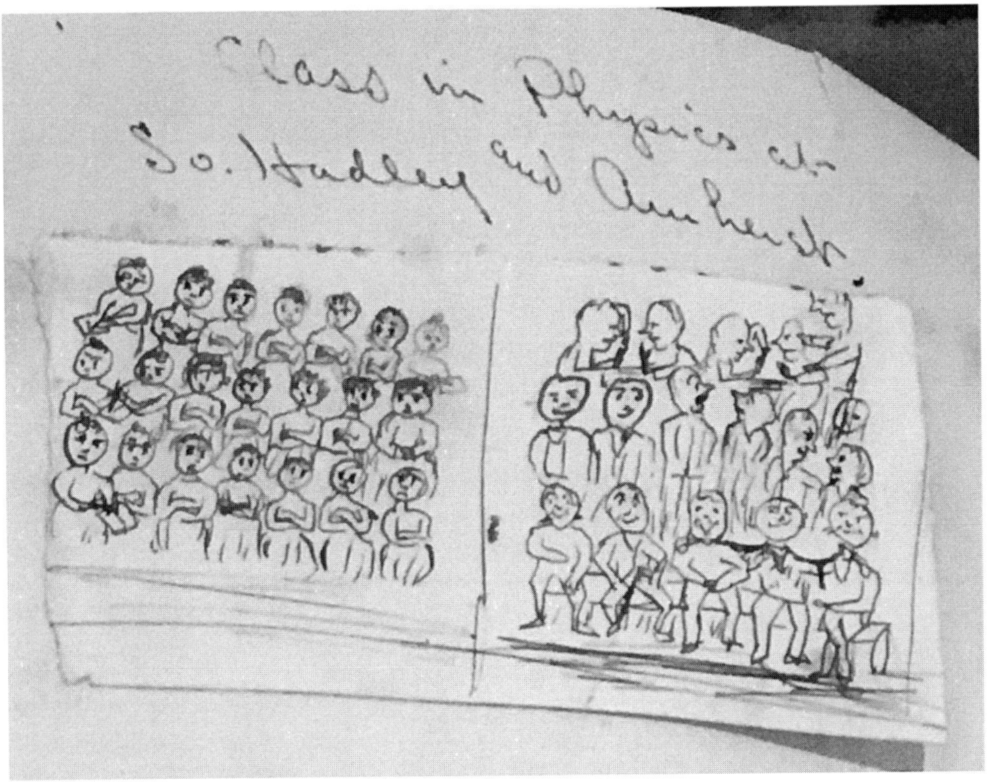

Figure 5.2 Class in Physics at So. Hadley and Amherst, c. 1885, ink sketch on paper, William Belcher Whitney Scrapbook. Amherst College Archives & Special Collections, Public Domain.

concern."[4] For young women, the experience of joining the co-ed classroom was sometimes embarrassing, as student M. Carey Thomas vividly described in a letter to her parents:

> There are three hundred boys in the present Freshman class. … There is nothing disagreeable here about the men except that they collect by fifty's [sic] on the steps of different buildings and to pass between them into the lecture rooms is quite an ordeal. The stare so – usually I find myself perfectly crimson by the time I am past them.[5]

Women were discouraged from interacting with the young men in their classes, as student Ellen Cort Brown noted:[6]

> We never talked to the men in the halls or the classrooms when coming or going, nor walked anywhere with them – on the campus. In the large lecture halls and the small class rooms [sic], filled mostly with our brothers and cousins and future

> husbands, we walked demurely as inconspicuously as we could manage, and took seats, always at the front. ... We were not insulted – only tolerated and ignored.[7]

Katherine Hulburt, one of several women of the Smith College Class of 1886 who continued her education in graduate school at Yale University, described what was like to be one of the very few females pursuing advanced degrees: "Here ... Kant lives, and groans, I fancy, in the undisturbed soil of some twenty graduate minds, while the feminine portion of the class challenges in silence and discreetly holds its peace."[8] Her Smith and Yale classmate Leona Peirce noted that female graduate students were addressed as "gentlemen" in co-ed classrooms at Yale and Cambridge University (U.K.), or they were ignored.[9] Historian Allen Johnson points out that for women college students, "the better she did [at] it, the worse for her reputation."[10] Upper-caste society feared that educated women would make the vision of women as boring, overeducated, over-masculinized, uncharming, disengaged domestic managers supervising the cooking of bland, tasteless meals a reality:

> No longer are the theatre and the ball-room terrestrial heaven. The woman *de nos jours* [of our day] gives her time to serious matters. She goes in her hundreds and thousands (so they say) to lectures – not pretty little lectures with magic-lantern slides, but lectures that provide intellectual oatmeal porridge. Lectures which are, speaking metaphorically, bone-making food, lectures on the Economic System of the Middle Ages and the Metaphysic[s] of the Will, and fine, large things of that kind. So say the scaremongers. And thereafter enthusiastically inquire "If all this does not make women into men, what does it do?"[11]

The fear of an educated, "masculinized" female population reached a fever pitch in 1890 as the first "bold New Women" began appearing "unescorted on Boston streets, using big vocabularies to defend themselves from forward strangers."[12] The New Woman was demonized by the mass press as a threat to the very existence of proper femininity, let alone a woman's willing acceptance of her child-bearing destiny: "The proper thing to give to a girl of today, we are told, is a walking-stick or a cigarette case or a matchbox. Something business-like and masculine is her only joy."[13] To discourage such behavior, wholesale scorn for the New Woman was encouraged among the upper class, which characterized feminists as prostitutes, as historian Jane H. Hunter points out: "Girls who appeared in public and walked the streets were historically 'public women,' prostitutes."[14] And dignified upper-class women did not want to mistakenly be identified as one of *those*.

Therefore, for "Becky" and Whitney to strike up a friendship in a co-educational physics class was quite remarkable, considering the norms of gender dictated decorum that their interactions (beyond demure courtship) violated. "Becky" later boldly sends Whitney an invitation to an unspecified social event at Mount Holyoke, and calls him "Ted." This invitation overlaps and is overlapped by two additional sketches that are affixed to the page near a train ticket to Amherst from Mount Holyoke. In one sketch, two young, precocious boys draw pictures of people on a wall of a *School for Girls* as a schoolmarm with a switch sneaks around the corner and catches them. Perhaps Whitney was the naughty schoolboy infiltrating Mount Holyoke, much to the chagrin of the dormitory matrons? Amherst was a short train ride away from two schools that only enrolled women – Mount Holyoke and Smith

College. Trains to Northampton, Mass. (home of Smith) and Hadley, Mass. (home to Mount Holyoke) would have provided the men of Amherst with an opportunity to meet intellectually challenging, yet non-threatening women of a similar social station.

In another second cartoon sketch, a corsage-wearing, well-coiffed woman with pointy, frog-like, outstretched fingers reaches her hands toward an unfinished sketch of a lightly drawn, suited, dandy of a man – perhaps an effigy of Whitney, who always appears meticulously dressed and well-coiffed in class and alumni pictures. Such sketches do not reappear regularly in Whitney's albums, and they usually refer to Mount Holyoke. Therefore, it is possible that they belonged to one of the women of that college who are mentioned in Whitney's four albums: "Becky" or Mary A. Rogers, the presumed former owner of hairpins marked "M. A. R.," who would invite Whitney to her Mount Holyoke graduation in June of 1890. It is also possible that "Becky" and Rogers could be the same person, although "Becky's" later appearance with five other women in photographs taken while out with Whitney to visit the New England Conservatory of Music suggests that she also could have been a woman who contributed the hairpin and photograph by the label "A.P.F." Incidentally, in those later photographs of "Becky" and her Conservatory cohort from the Whitney album show the women dressed in drag in men's suits and wearing fake mustaches. Whitney's playful friendship with "Becky" proved subversive of gender norms in more ways than just one: it defied decorum for male-female social contact, and it offered a place where gender non-conformity was welcome.

By February of 1886, Whitney already was exchanging letters with other female acquaintances, in addition to the recurrent appearances of "Becky," and of Rogers – who only appears a couple of times in his albums. Whitney reminisced in letters with Grace C. Blake (whose red-bowed hairpin appears at the top of the layout, accompanied by the initials "G. C. B.") from Providence, R. I., about moonlit sailing during the summer of 1885, and he takes her to a piano/vocal concert by Henry G. Tucker on February 19, 1886. Whitney's second album contains a brochure from Hotel Neptune on Block Island, along with a tourism brochure featuring views of sailing. According to the hand-written dates added to tourist literature in the albums, Whitney spent many of his summers at Block Island, a sandy-beached destination off the coast of Rhode Island, throughout college and law school. As a filled dance card from the Hygeia Hotel in Block Island dated August 8, 1888, attests, Whitney socialized often with many young women during these summers. But three days after Whitney took Blake (with whom he shared memories of moonlight sailing on Block Island) to a concert, he accompanied Mary A. Carter of Smith College to a social event on her campus, although he did not collect a hairpin from her.

A few weeks later, in March of 1886, Whitney attended an event called "Paper Festival" at Village Church with Maddie Orr ("M. O."), an event from which he brought home not only a hairpin, but souvenir women's paper gloves and a paper red rose. Orr also gave Whitney a notice of an unpaid bill levied against her by "Mrs. Flannagan" for an unnamed expense accrued the night before their date. Whitney also took Orr to a musical performance again that month in Boston. Orr does not appear again in the hairpin lineup until April and July of 1887.

Whitney's hairpin-collecting slowed from April until December of 1886, when he accrued just two pins from two women "A. K." and "H. B." (although he kept no other memorabilia or correspondence from them) in September. Whitney took Hannah Noble to a fraternity reception in October (although he missed the opportunity to snag a pin), and he accompanied Smith College student "Miss A. W." (Alice Walton) to a play in December. Next to a note about that play, Whitney pasted a pressed flower, stitched-in a penny, and affixed an "Old Maid" playing card that had been ripped in half – perhaps by "ladies' man" Whitney, or by "Old Maid"-stereotype-resisting Walton, whom he initially met while returning a lost book – and who would become a Classical archeologist and pursue a Ph.D. and a career in academia, rather than marriage.[15] Incidentally, starting in the fall of 1886, Whitney started to live in his fraternity house, and he attended several initiation events that typically were not co-educational or date-friendly.[16] Memorabilia saved in those albums suggest that other male students accompanied him to fraternity events, which consumed a lot of his time in late 1886.

On February 12, 1887, Whitney collected a pin from Lura W. Nelson ("L. W. N."). Two days later, on Valentine's Day, he snagged another one from "O. K. M.," whose full name and context could not be determined by consulting the memorabilia in his albums. But February 17, 1887, was a banner hairpin-collecting day for Whitney: He archived five pins and two tintype photographs for that date from "Little Belle," "Paree," "Estelle" (noted as "E. A.," and accompanied by a tintype mugshot), "Nell" ("N. C."), and "Susie" at the New England Conservatory of Music in Boston. But he then took a break from building his pin collection until April of 1887, when he added one from "M. A. W." (April 6), and another from "A. P. F." (April 15, accompanied by a small tintype portrait), followed by "M. A. B." in June. Orr reappears for a date with Whitney and contributes two more large pins to the layout on July 4 and April 6 of 1887.

On May 26, 1887, "Becky" reappears and gives "Ted" several tintype photographs of women – including one with two women (one was "Becky" herself), dressed in drag in men's suits, and wearing oversized fake mustaches.[17] In the other two photos, "Becky" and four other women play tennis rackets like musical instruments in an indoor room for the photographer, allowing their bloomers underneath their formal dresses to rise to view. The same young woman pretends to sing as six other young, formally dressed women play music with violins and a tambourine as if they are entertaining guests in a "music room." The photographs collectively reinforce the narrative of "Becky's" playful relationship with Whitney. But the integration of women in drag and mustaches, along with the visible bloomers, Whitney expresses a willing subversion of not only the demure, passive sophistication expected of women from his social caste, but of the prevailing, normative, binary conceptions of gender.

By the summer of 1887, Whitney's hairpin collection page was full. Rather than start a new page, he stops documenting the women in his life by archiving and displaying their hairpins, but he still keeps date-related memorabilia (such as gloves, sunglasses, and scarves), and women's letters. He also makes notes regarding his copious social engagements with a long list of young women. Although obviously, Whitney fairly could be described as a man who dated frequently, he also includes rejections to attend events from women and their parents in his scrapbook. For example, Wellesley College student Jeanette C. Welch turns Whitney down to go to a fraternity party.[18] Orr politely declines an invitation on two occasions when she has "other plans." "G. Leonard" politely rejects the opportunity to attend an event with Whitney. And Emily ("Emy") Hills – whose rejection note was mailed to Whitney in the same envelope as the one from Leonard – turns down an invitation from him because "mamma does not think it would be prudent for me to accept your kind invitation." (Hills was still in high school at New Salem Academy when Whitney began asking her out on dates.) That both Leonard's and Hills's letters arrived in the same envelope suggests that Whitney was extending his social invitations to many women simultaneously, to increase his odds of finding dates. "Miss Cook" also declines an invitation to an event on June 27, 1887, and the very terse rejection note was written on her behalf by an irate parent.

Such dramatic turns in his romantic life occurred fairly regularly for Whitney, whose relationship with Orr was tumultuous by late-nineteenth-century standards and involved an unpaid bill issued by "Miss Flannagan." Nevertheless, Orr accepted his invitation to a reception in June of 1887, and invited Whitney to call on her and meet her new friend, "Miss Ridley." Something awkward occurred during that visit, because she sent a letter of apology to Whitney to let him know that she was not angry with him that night, but with someone else. Orr's apparent attempt to match Whitney with one of her friends suggests that her relationship with Whitney was platonic.

Jeanette Welch of Wellesley College (Class of 1889) does not have a hairpin in Whitney's collection because she entered his life after his hairpin collage was complete. But she becomes a recurring character in Whitney's social life starting just months before his Amherst graduation in 1887, as he was about to relocate to Boston to attend Harvard Law School. The two had known of each other previously, though – as Welch sent Whitney a note in December of 1886, to thank him for dropping by to visit her in her hometown of Boston. After Whitney's move to Boston, he and Welch attended many social events together, including baseball games, classical music concerts, and "Tree Day" at Wellesley. In a scrapbook kept by Katherine Lane of the Wellesley Class of 1990, who assigned unique nicknames to many of her classmates, the physically diminutive Welch was assigned the moniker "Welsh rabbit."[19]

Welch's letters to Whitney are consistently polite and proper, and always signed with first and last name to denote a formality or propriety that stood in contrast to "Becky's" use of her nickname only, and of the familiar nickname "Ted" to address Whitney. This suggests that perhaps Welch may have considered her social engagements with Whitney as professionally(?) formal events, and not necessarily relationship- or intimacy-building personal ones. Perhaps this was because Welch had plans for her future after graduation that did not involve fulfilling the expectations of women of her social class: marrying, supporting her husband's career, tending the family's social profile within the community, and having children. Following her graduation from Wellesley College, Welch got a Ph.D. in physiology at the University of Chicago, became a medical doctor at a time when very few women did, and set up a medical practice in Grand Rapids, Michigan.[20] She never married or had children. Such achievement was entirely fitting for a person of her social caste – albeit not of her gender.

Collectively, the many hairpins, letters, photographs, and memorabilia in Whitney's albums suggest a narrative of a young, hyper-social, marriage-seeking college man who enjoyed girl-chasing, in adherence to heteronormative expectations of masculinity in the late-nineteenth-century, New England upper class. Whitney – then an aspiring lawyer – would have been a fine prospect for marriage for women at nearby all-female colleges. In his scrapbooks, Whitney conjures and supports a persona of the hairpin-trophy-collecting "ladies' man." Like Victorian-era women's albums, Whitney's scrapbooks also attest to the lengths a Brahmin man went to in the 1880s to find a wife – only to end up an eternal bachelor.

"Dropped Hairpins" and Other "Homosocial" Tendencies in Whitney's Cisgender Album Performance

In several places in his four scrapbooks, hints of counter-narratives to the pervasive Brahmin masculine cisgender normativity appear. These call into question the degree to which Whitney merely may have been *performing* as a cisgender "ladies' man" to appear to adhere to pervasive upper-social-caste expectations.[21] The phrase "dropped hairpins" commonly was used among gay men in the late nineteenth and early twentieth centuries as a means of communicating a socially encoded message to other gay men, according to historian George Chauncey:

> Many men kept their gay lives hidden from potentially hostile straight observers (by "putting their hair up") ... but that did not mean they were hidden or isolated from each other — they often, as they said, "dropped hairpins" that only other gay men would notice. Leading a double life in which they often passed as straight (and sometimes married) allowed them to have jobs and status a queer would have been denied while still participating in what they called "homosexual society" or "the life."[22]

Chauncey argues that "[f]or some, the personal cost of 'passing' was great. But ... many men positively enjoyed having a 'secret life' more complex and extensive than outsiders could imagine."[23] For Whitney, who mingled in prestigious circles while in New York, such as the University Club and Harvard Club, "passing" was an absolute must for maintaining his/ his family's social positions and status, and keeping up appearances with his patent-law clients and colleagues.[24] Perhaps it was entirely coincidental that the items Whitney collected from various women to display his voracious courting efforts were hairpins. But if considered as *intentional* objects, ones that were encoded with a message that was legible only within gay subculture, Whitney's hairpin collage is means of reflecting both the reality of being gay, and of the reality of being obligated to pretend to live a Brahmin/Puritan-caste "straight" life, which required "putting one's hair up" and participating in the cisgender courting pageant.

In addition to the *actual* "dropped hairpins," other metaphorical "dropped hairpins" appear in Whitney's scrapbooks. Whitney was such an avid baseball and tennis fan that he owned season tickets to all of Amherst's games and followed the teams when they played locally and on the road. He consistently includes baseball-game programs, to which he added detailed notations about the performance of each athlete. Specifically, Whitney also was a keen follower of the athletic pursuits of baseball- and tennis-playing classmate Charles Amherst Chase (1864–1937), a Chicago native and descendant of both Aquila Chase, who settled in Newbury, Mass., and James Thompson, the settler of the towns of Charleston, Mass. (now part of north-central Boston) and Woburn, Mass. (a northern Boston suburb).[25] Newspaper clippings including images of a lanky, mustachioed young Chase appear in several areas of Whitney's scrapbooks. Articles recounting Chase's athletic accomplishments and his obituaries often comment on his demeanor: "He was a man of attractive personality, energetic, just, straightforward, generous, public-spirited and fond of fun."[26]

By the time Chase started at Amherst, he already was known nationwide as a top-notch, competitive athlete. Chase was nationally recognized on collegiate and professional tennis circuits, despite having his small stature, which was noted as a presumed disadvantage by sports commentators.[27] However, Chase's slight build made him an exemplar of the traditional Brahmin ideal, who also happened to possess athleticism. (Incidentally, like Chase, Whitney also had a relatively compact physical build. According to Whitney's biometric card, he went from being a diminutive 99.4-lb crew-team coxswain to a 156.5-pound athlete in the course of just one semester in 1888, after his time on the Harvard crew team ended.[28]) As a tennis player, Chase won five Western Championship titles, the Wright & Ditson Tournament, finished second in the Intercollegiate National Championships, and reached the semi-finals and quarterfinals of the United States National Championships consistently from 1886 until 1890. Whitney affixed a cardboard-framed tintype mounted to the album, in which a clean-shaven Whitney clad in athletic wear poses with Chase. Whitney's hand rests familiarly on the shoulder of a mustachioed, baseball-cap-wearing Chase. Both hold tennis rackets, shift their weight to one side, and stand before an indoor photography studio backdrop representing foliage (Fig. 5.3). Their feet touch, revealing a hint of intimacy.

Amherst alumni files claim that Chase's baseball abilities were "way more phenomenal than at tennis."[29] Chase played second base while at Amherst, and his undergraduate years marked the peak of his athletic career, lending Chase a semi-

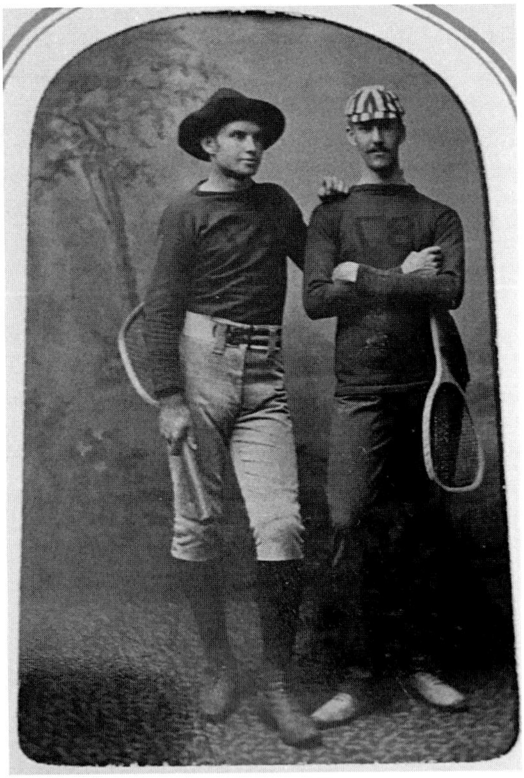

Figure 5.3 William Belcher Whitney and Charles Amherst Chase, May 25, 1887, William Belcher Whitney Scrapbook. Amherst College Archives & Special Collections, Public Domain.

celebrity status on campus. Whitney's album includes not only newspaper clippings covering Chase's numerous tennis victories, but a group portrait of the Amherst College baseball team – a group to which Whitney did not belong, personally. In this group portrait, Chase lounges in the front row, second from left, with his striped uniform open to reveal his Amherst team t-shirt below it (Fig. 5.4). Chase looks toward the camera with downcast, sultry eyes, with legs spread, and a bat descending suggestively from his crotch and out of the picture plane. Chase leans back on the legs of his teammate in the back row. The team's catcher, seated just to Chase's left, rests a leg and arm with great familiarity on Chase's right open leg. Another teammate on the other side of Chase holds himself up by hooking his left arm around the knee of another member of the group, while also pressing his buttocks right up against Chase's. Other men make bodily contact with each other and overtly express their affection by placing a hand on another young man's shoulders, or leaning on each other (back row, the second, third, and fourth players from the left). But the ease and familiarity shared by the men in the front row are decidedly more suggestive of intimacy than that of the men in the back row. Arms hook around the insides of legs, derrieres touch, and the men rest their bodies and limbs into and onto each other with a casual closeness that suggests more than just affection defined by friendship. Had these gestures and gazes been shared by subjects of opposite genders, we would not hesitate to read them as expressions of sexual desire, if not sexual relations.[30]

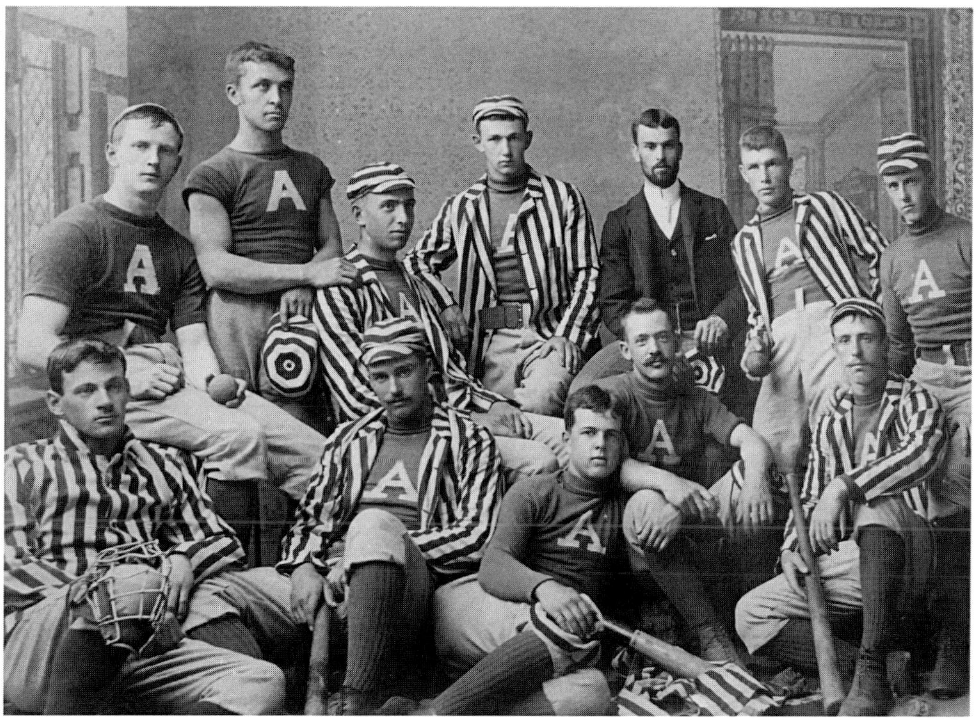

Figure 5.4 Amherst College Baseball Team, Class of 1887, William Belcher Whitney Scrapbook. Amherst College Archives & Special Collections, Public Domain.

The Amherst baseball team frequently traveled together to play games against other colleges nationwide and had ample opportunity to develop tight-knit relationships. Also, while upper-class men and women were encouraged to go on dates, spending an extended amount of time along with a member of an opposite gender generally was restricted until marriage. As Carroll Smith-Rosenberg points out, the rigid sequestering of the college-age upper classes by gender enabled men and women to separately develop "homosocial" worlds of intimacy with their gender, while enjoying their independence from their immediate family and sometimes – erotic passion, love, and intimacy.[31] Whether the nature of their same-gender relationships was sexual, Susan Martha Vicinus argues, many were indeed intimate and based on meaningful, life-long bonds – not unlike the romantic conception of marriage.[32] Photographs of the baseball team suggest not only camaraderie and joy of male brotherhood, but physical ease in each other's company.

In another photograph from the Whitney scrapbook taken by Henry N. Potter studio in Rochester, N.Y., Chase lies with two other men (presumably also baseball players) in a bed, with their striped baseball jerseys slung over the chair nearby (Fig. 5.5). The same trio of men also is photographed playing cards at a table while wearing their sleepwear in another photograph kept by Whitney. On the back of the photograph of the men playing cards, one of the young men is identified as Andrew P. "Pete" Alvord, who also never married or had children, lived in New York City, and was a member of the University Club (with Whitney), according to genealogy and Amherst alumni records.[33] Whitney's involvement in the making of this photograph is unclear. But Whitney's albums include baseball-ticket stubs and programs containing detailed scoring notations added in his handwriting, suggesting that he traveled to some out-of-town games with the team. That Whitney owned and kept these

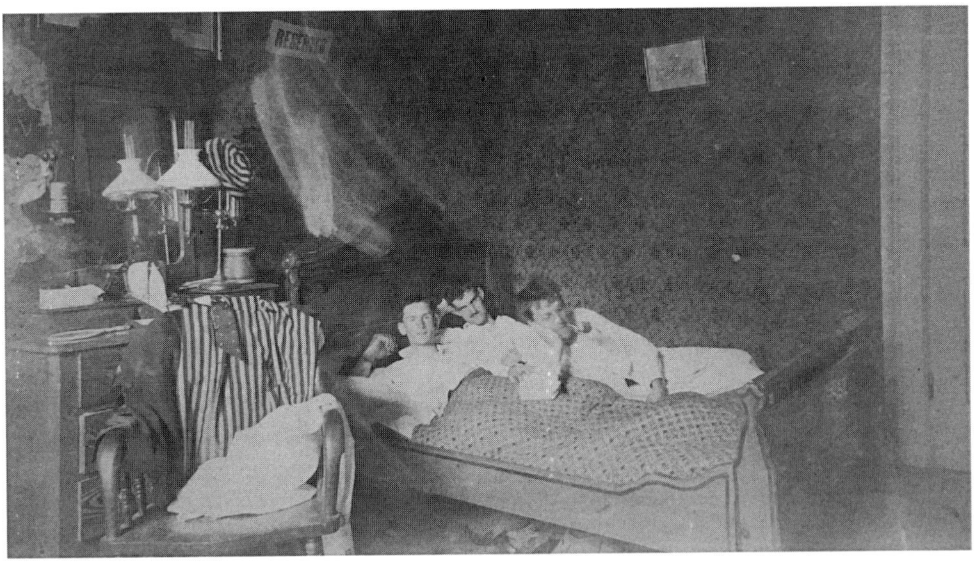

Figure 5.5 Henry N. Potter, *Three on Bed*, c. 1887, William Belcher Whitney Scrapbook. Amherst College Archives & Special Collections, Public Domain.

photographs for his scrapbook can be interpreted as a desire to commemorate his relationships and time spent with these men, as well as a sense of belonging with, and among, several members of the baseball team, including Chase. And finally, in an undated alumni reunion photograph showing both men around age 40, Whitney sits next to Chase, who rests an arm and leg on Whitney's inner thigh.[34]

Archiving "Queer"-ness or "Queer"-ing the Archive?: Methodological Reflections

Many literary scholars have suggested that it is risky to over-read homoerotic desire with hindsight into artifacts such as journals, and they instead have advocated for the use of the label "homosocial," which acknowledges same-gender relationships, yet maintains an ambiguous position toward subjects' sexual orientations.[35] Such an approach reinforces cisgender normativity. David Deitcher, author of the book *Dear Friends: American Photographs of Men Together, 1840-1918*, has pointed out that this is not always the best strategy: "[H]omophobic self-censorship, masked as strategic discretion" is often extended to the subjects of photographs, for fear of "outing" (read: "shaming") them in the eyes of surviving relatives.[36] Deitcher discusses his initial approach to discussing photographs of men expressing mutual affection: "Rather than admit to their emotional and erotic resonance as historic representations of same-sex love, I maintained an academic attitude, preferring to dwell instead on the 'historic mutability' of friendship and masculinity."[37] Such an approach is applicable for interpreting Whitney's albums.

As Deitcher points out, our histories focus by reflexive default and habit on reading images of same-gender affection as "non-romantic," and he proposes that we not be afraid to acknowledge and historicize artifacts as expressions of LGBTQI+ desire. To reinforce a pervasive and persistent cisgender normativity by automatically assuming the subjects of photographs are "straight" by default obligates them to conform to abide by cisgender norms in historical perpetuity. As such, it denies the possibility of unveiling and working to dismantle the oppression of LGBTQI+ self-expression. Deitcher argues that a queer history for photographs not only helps to reveal suppression, but it also acknowledges, validates, and humanizes LGBTQI+ relationships, as they have been commemorated in historic artifacts.[38]

Nevertheless, Whitney's photographs of the baseball team and his tintype made with Chase testify to the importance of his relationships with other men (especially Chase). Whitney never married or had children, despite the tremendous amount of energy he dedicated during his college years to courting young women, collecting their hairpins as trophies (or, as a nod to the cisgender courting pageant in which gay men of his caste were obligated to participate), and displaying them in his album. Whitney became a patent lawyer and lived in New York City, and kept in touch with Alvord. Chase graduated from Amherst and got a law degree from Northwestern University. Then Chase married Nellie Green, the daughter of a prominent industrial leader and owner of the Superior Stove Works company, and settled into a profession as a banker in Superior, Wisconsin. Neither Whitney nor Chase had any children. Whitney died first, on December 8, 1936, and Chase died a few weeks later.[39] Unfortunately, no correspondence survives to attest to the nature of their relationship beyond their time at Amherst. Only the alumni photograph of them in their forties remains, and in it, Chase places an arm and leg on Whitney's thigh.

Being members of prominent, successful, U. S.-founding families, both Whitney and Chase would have been under substantial pressure to marry a woman of similar elevated social standing, to have children, and to further their respective family's bloodline as a dutiful student of a late-nineteenth-century college curriculum that integrated eugenics ideas as scientific fact – especially within Brahmin/Puritan-descendant social circles. Bearing children was directly connected to the religion, ideals, and principles on which these men's Puritan forefathers founded New England. Historian Elaine Tyler May notes that "[f]or the Puritans, 'be fruitful and multiply' was a biblical dictum, and fruitfulness itself conferred status. Pregnancies were viewed as 'a contribution … to the common task.'"[40]

Patriarchs of the late-nineteenth-century New England upper classes viewed LGBTQI+ desire as an active threat to the bloodline. In Oliver Wendell Holmes Sr.'s short story "A Moral Antipathy" (1885), same-gender relationships are conveyed to readers as "pathological conditions" that actively block heterosexual marriage. In her analysis of Holmes's story, Marylynne Diggs further states that "these [same-gender] relationships form the conflict which must be overcome in order for the narrative obligations of the marriage plot to be fulfilled."[41]

Similarly, when same-gender desire did exist in the Victorian age, Martha Vicinus notes, "[e]rotic attraction to one's own sex was often defined as a 'passing phase,' common to adolescence."[42] This is to say, young men and women sometimes dabbled in same-gender relationships while in college, but tradition and social pressure mandated that they settle into their "proper," gender-dictated, roles in heterosexual marriages upon graduating. "Deviant" masculinities, Kaja Silverman suggests, were defined as "perverse" because they threatened a "dominant fiction" in late-nineteenth-century culture: that we have absolute "faith above all else in the unity of the family, and the adequacy of the male subject."[43] That "male subject" was the hub of society, comprised and ran its economy, formed its power structures, and made its decisions. In order to maintain that status quo, however, the important white cisgender "male subject" also must reproduce.

However, David Getsy has suggested that the word "queer" – and its embodiment (by individuals including Whitney) – are synonymous with the frequently quiet "attitude of defiance" against the presumed stability and hegemony of identity.[44] But it also is a source of empowerment, in Getsy's words: "a recognition that the fear of the un-normal is also a source of power."[45] Whitney thus enjoyed the innate privilege of a white, cisgender-"passing" man of the upper-class, while also subtly signaling his "apart-ness," layered identity, and resistance, in the form of the feminized, disjointed, sometimes chaotic, assemblage of photomontage. Whitney's hairpin-trophy collecting, copiously documented dating life involving a revolving door of female companions provided an ideal performance of Brahmin cisgender masculinity expected of a man of his social caste. To spite this, Whitney's collage of women's hairpins also operates as an enormous, subcultural-encoded "dropped hairpin" that sends a message for posterity about the plight of gay men "passing" within the Brahmin/Puritan upper class at a time when eugenics ideals were pervasive. He also shows photographs of gender-expectation-deviant, mustachioed women who resisted cisgender class norms and expectations. His album thus reveals a narrative of a young man's (and some women's) conflicted navigation(/s) of a social and cultural world that demanded that he (/they) stay in the "closet" and embrace cisgender normativity, as he was (/they were) taught that anything other than heteroerotic behavior was "deviant." Yet Whitney's private scrapbooks describe the great lengths to which a man will go to appear to conform to society's expectations while also celebrating, and perhaps boldly declaring (to an initiated audience) his innate desires.

Notes

A version of this essay first appeared in: Kris Belden-Adams, *Eugenics, "Aristogenics," Photography: Picturing Privilege* (New York: Routledge, 2020). Reproduced with permission of Taylor and Francis Group, LLC, a division of Informa plc.

1 Whitney was from one of the highest social classes in the northeastern U.S. in the late–nineteenth century. Oliver Wendell Holmes Sr. described this social caste of wealthy "New England aristocrats" who were "robust," "well-bred," came from well-known families who were descended from the original Puritan American settlers. Holmes suggests that this group possessed a sense of "inherited moral responsibility," which – combined with their Protestant beliefs, staunch Puritanical work ethic, and mental acumen – positioned them (or, the *male* versions of them) to be genetically predisposed to be "honorable" scholars and captains of industry. Oliver Wendell Holmes, Sr., "The Professor's Story," *Atlantic Monthly*, Vols. 5–7 (1860–1861): 1–4.; For more, please see: Frederic Cople Jaher, "The Politics of the Boston Brahmins: 1800–1860" in Ronald P. Formisano and Constance K. Burns, eds. *Boston, 1700-1980: The Evolution of Urban Politics* (London: Greenwood Press, 1984), 59–86. As Karla F. C. Holloway points out, white-male privilege is central to U.S. society throughout the country's history: "His gender and his race (he is a white male) placed him among society's most privileged and outside of the coded social identities that have an embedded vulnerability." Karla F. C. Holloway, *Private Bodies, Public Texts: Race, Gender, and a Cultural Bioethics* (Durham and London: Duke University Press, 2011), 8.

2 Whitney was a descendant of John Whitney, who settled in Watertown, Mass., in 1635. Whitney also was distantly related to Gertrude Vanderbilt Whitney, founder of the Whitney Museum of American Art in New York City. Incidentally, William Belcher Whitney would amass an impressive Tibetan Buddhist art collection after becoming a New York City patent lawyer. After his death, the artwork was donated to the American Museum of Natural History. According to Amherst College alumni records, Whitney's law degree was a three-year Master's level credential that allowed him to pass the bar exam in 1892. He would receive a Juris Doctorate from New York University in 1905. That degree allowed him to teach patent law classes at NYU from 1902–1915. Alumni Biographical Files, Class of 1887 – William Belcher Whitney. Entry 379. Amherst College Archives.

3 Carroll Smith-Rosenberg, *Disorderly Conduct: Visions of Gender in Victorian America* (New York and Oxford: Oxford University Press, 1985), 250.

4 Smith-Rosenberg, *Disorderly Conduct,* 250.

5 M. Carey Thomas is quoted in: Marjorie Houseian Dobkin, *Making of a Feminist: Early Journals and Letters of M. Carey Thomas* (Kent, Ohio: Kent State University Press, 1979), 103.

6 Upon having her social "coming out" party, or "debutante ball," upper class women were told that even if they were to attend college, it was *not* for eventually working outside of the home (which would interfere with childbearing, supporting one's husband, and would take a job away from a more-deserving man or lower-class woman), but to become more interesting companions and socialites. William Hill-Climo, "Race Betterment: The Nation's Duty," *Eugenics Review* (No. 3, Oct. 1, 1909): 194–202.

7 Charlotte Williams Conable, *Women at Cornell: The Myth of Equal Education* (Ithaca: Cornell University Press, 1977), 117. Conable continues to describe how the women of co-ed Cornell were insulted by their male colleagues, who sang this song about them: "The coed leads a wretched life / She eats potatoes with a knife." Conable, *Women at Cornell,* 116.

8 Katherine Hurlburt, Various Authors, "Letters of the Class of 1886," Unpublished. Smith College Archives, Class Records, Box 80.CLA.1426. 1888.

9 Leona Peirce, "Letters of the Class of 1886," Unpublished. Smith College Archives, Class Records, Box 80.CLA.1426. Feb. 1892.

10 Peirce, "Letters of the Class of 1886," n. p.

11 Womanly Mannishness," *Democrat and Chronicle* (Rochester, N.Y.), (April 7, 1906): 13. This article is affixed in the following student scrapbook: Scrapbook of Newspaper Clippings 1886–1898, Lucia R. Briggs Scrapbook. Schlesinger Library, Radcliffe Institute, Harvard University, Cambridge, Mass. Page (seq. 47). Repository Schlesinger Library on the History of Women in America. 2012–M149.

12 Jane H. Hunter, *How Young Ladies Became Girls: The Victorian Origins of American Girlhood* (New Haven: Yale University Press, 2002), 273.; Allen Johnson, ed., *The Chronicles of America*, Vol. 33 (New Haven: Yale University Press, 1921), 233.

13 "Womanly Mannishness," 13.

14 Hunter, *How Young Ladies Became Girls*, 291.

15 Katherine A. Geffcken, "Walton, Mary Alice," *Database of Classical Scholars, Rutgers School of Arts and Sciences*. Accessed Jan. 4, 2019: https://dbcs.rutgers.edu/all-scholars/9200-walton-mary-alice.

16 Charlotte Williams Conable explains that fraternity rules forbade members to invite female students to their parties, and they actively encouraged the young men to shun them as worthy for marriage and/or introduction to "fashionable society." Conable, *Women at Cornell*, 116–126.

17 It is possible that "Becky" is also the woman whom Whitney calls "A.P.F." in the hairpin collage. A thumbnail portrait of "A.P.F." appears in the collage, and another photograph of the same woman, wearing the same clothing and hat, taken on the same day, is captioned by Whitney as "New England Conservatory," and is pasted into the album by a note from "Becky." The same woman also appears in photographs of a group of five women who are pretending to play musical instruments with tennis rackets, seven women who are pretending to be playing parlor music and singing together, and a group of two women who are dressed like men and wearing fake mustaches. As it soon will be argued, women who were too focused on their college educations faced the allegation of becoming too "excessively masculinized." Allen Johnson, ed., *The Chronicles of America*, Vol. 33 (New Haven: Yale University Press, 1921), 233.

18 Whitney's 1887 rejection letters are preserved in: William Belcher Whitney, Class of 1887, Scrapbook. Vol. 3 – 1886–1887. Amherst College Archives. MA.00099.

19 Katherine Lane, *Class of 1890: Scrapbook*, Wellesley College, Wellesley College Archives. n. p. Oliver Weendell Holmes, Sr., argued that typical upper-class university students were quietly athletic but not over-muscular, possessed tempored vigor, and had "a handsome face – a little too pale, perhaps," a narrowed jaw, light or non-existent facial hair, and a calm expression. The mental image of this gentry is synonymous with the calm, focus and dignity expected of leaders in education, culture, business, and social life, he suggested: Holmes, "The Professor's Story," 1-4. Both Welch and Whitney personified the slight physical type conjured by Holmes as the ideal for their social class. Whitney's anthropometric card – which he affixes to his albums – reveals that he was five-foot-two-inches tall. Kris Belden-Adams, *Eugenics, Aristogenics, Photography: Picturing Privilege* (New York: Routledge, 2020), Chapter 3. Upper-class women were expected to be cultured, educated, interesting, pleasant in appearance, well-mannered, graceful, demure, modest, make supportive wives and dutiful future mothers, in accord not only with the expectations of her gender and class, and with the goals of positive eugenics. In essence, they were sent to college only to become more interesting conversationalists and socialites, rather than to find and have careers. In this sense, Jeanette Welch's life path – like Whitney's – departed from its gender and class expectations, too. Belden-Adams, *Eugenics, Aristogenics, Photography*, Chapter 4. In effect, upper-class women's ability to replicate themselves and their bloodline could help stave off the decline of moral society that many feared was an inevitable result of waves of late-nineteenth-century immigration's dilution of the W.A.S.P./Puritan-descendant bloodline. Women like Welch were told that their capacity to reproduce was seen as the social caste's last line of self-defense. Dudley Allen Sargent, who

ran Harvard's physical education program starting in 1879, even encouraged women to build "a large well-developed pelvis with plenty of muscular and organic power behind it," which would naturally help her produce more "large brainy children." Adam S. Cohen, "Harvard's Eugenics Era," *Harvard Magazine* (March-April 2016), n. p. Accessed April 17, 2017. Available at: http://harvardmagazine.com/print/52049?page=all.

20 Wellesley College, "Alumnae Notes," *The Wellesley Magazine,* Book 40 (April 13, 1897): 409.; University of Chicago, "College of Medicine Alumni," *The Alumni Record of the University of Illinois Chicago Departments of Medicine and Dentistry* (Chicago: Rogers Printing Co., 1921): 93.

21 Judith Butler, "Performative Acts and Gender Constitution: An Essay in Phenomenology and Feminist Theory," *Theatre Journal*, Vol. 40, No. 4 (Dec. 1988): 519–531. Although decades separated Whitney from Butler's ideas on gender performativity, her work informs this chapter's view of his performance of masculinity.

22 George Chauncey, *Gay New York: Gender, Urban Culture, and the Making of the Gay Male World, 1890–1940* (New York: Basic Books, 1995), Kindle Locations 329-331. "Hairpins" were "dropped" in visual art of this period, as well. For example, Patricia McDonnell has suggested that Marsden Hartley's paintings were rife with "dropped hairpins": Patricia McDonnell, "'Essentially Masculine': Marsden Hartley, Gay Identity, and the Wilhelmine German Military," *Art Journal*, Vol. 56, No. 1 (Summer 1997): 62–68.

23 Chauncey, *Gay New York*, 332–333.

24 "William Belcher Whitney," Alumni Biography Files, Amherst College, Class of 1887.

25 Leander Thompson, *Memorial of James Thompson of Charleston, Mass.,1630–1642, and of Eight Generations of His Descendants* (Boston: L. Barta & Co., 1887), 204. Specifically, Charles Amherst Chase's lineage in the U.S. can be traced back to Aquila Chase, who received the first land grant at Hampton, N.H., in 1640, and later settled in Newbury, Mass. Chase's ancestors also fought in the Revolutionary War. "Charles Amherst Chase (1864-1937)," *The National Encyclopedia of American Biography,* Vol. 28 (1940): 229.

26 "Charles Amherst Chase (1864–1937)," 229.

27 "Charles Amherst Chase," Alumni Biography Files, Amherst College, Class of 1887. n. p.; "Illness Fatal to Bank Head at Age of 73," *The Evening Telegram*, Superior, Wisconsin (Jan. 27, 1937), "Charles Amherst Chase," Alumni Biography Files, Amherst College, Class of 1887. Record 953. n. p.

28 William Belcher Whitney Scrapbooks. Class of 1887. Amherst College Archives, Series 1 (Personal Scrapbooks). Vol. 4 (1887–1890).

29 "Charles Amherst Chase," Alumni Biography Files, Amherst College, Class of 1887. n. p.; "Charles Amherst Chase," *Amherst Graduates' Quarterly,* Vol. 26–27 (1937): 245.

30 While many late-nineteenth-century baseball team photographs show teammates with arms around each other, the physical familiarity shared by this Amherst Baseball Team group portrait exceeds the usual amount. For example, the scooting of derrieres into other teammates, and the hooking of arms around other men's limbs does not usually appear.

31 Carroll Smith-Rosenberg, *Disorderly Conduct: Visions of Gender in Victorian America* (New York and Oxford: Oxford University Press, 1985), 28.

32 Martha Vicinus, "Distance and Desire: English Boarding School Friendships, 1870-1920," in Martin Duberman, Martha Vicinus, and George Chauncey, Jr., eds. *Hidden from History: Reclaiming the Gay and Lesbian Past* (New York: Penguin Books/Meridian, 1989), 283.

33 "Andrew Porter Alvord, 1864–1947," Ancestry.com, Accessed Nov. 1, 2018: https://www.ancestry.com/family-tree/person/tree/18025647/person/130127036380/story?_phsrc=HVb1162&_phstart=successSource-
; "Andrew Peter Alvord," Alumni Biography Files, Amherst College, Class of 1887. "Pete" Alvord was a member of the social fraternity/literary society Alpha Delta Phi, as well as Theta Nu Epsilon ("Skull and Bones" secret "class society"). Charles Chase was a member of the social fraternity Chi Psi, and lived in the fraternity lodge as he neared graduation. William Whitney also lived in his fraternity house as an upper-classman. Whitney was a member of Delta Kappa Epsilon, a social brotherhood of substantial pedigree that has included six U.S. presidents: Rutherford B. Hayes, Theodore Roosevelt, Franklin D. Roosevelt, Gerald Ford, George H. W. Bush, and George W. Bush. Whitney posed for the

tintype photograph with Chase on Wednesday, May 25, 1887, the same day as his Delta Kappa Epsilon initiation. It would not have been unusual for a photographer to be present at the event, and for Whitney to bring a male companion with him. "Class of 1887," *Amherst College Olio*, Amherst, Mass., 1888. Amherst College Archives. xLH1.A43 O44. Accessed Dec. 17, 2018: https://acdc.amherst.edu/view/asc:321764. An entry in the College Olio also suggests that Whitney was a member of "Skull and Bones" in 1886: Amherst College Memorabilia/Olio, 1888, for the Senior Class of 1887. No. 77839. Amherst College Archives.

34 "William Belcher Whitney," Alumni Biography Files, Amherst College, Class of 1887.

35 Susan Van Dyne, "'Abracadabra': Intimate Inventions by Early College Women in the United States," *Feminist Studies*, Vol. 42, No. 2 (2016): 280.

36 David Deitcher, *Dear Friends: American Photographs of Men Together, 1840-1918* (New York: Harry N. Abrams, Inc., 2001), 36.

37 Deitcher, *Dear Friends*, 36. According to Susan Van Dyne, it was not unusual in the 1880s for Massachusetts college students to engage relationships with people of the same gender that defied definition by today's standards, because the modern concepts of "lesbian" or "gay" desire did not yet exist: "Not fully articulated, but passionately felt, same-sex desires emerged from widely shared rituals and intimacies that constitute residential college life. In the early 1880s, these desires were not yet consolidated into a separate matrix that intermittently both sustained and constrained desire." Van Dyne, "'Abracadabra,'" 280–281.

38 Deitcher, *Dear Friends*, 150.

39 Charles Amherst Chase died on Jan. 27, 1937.

40 Elaine Tyler May, *Barren in the Promised Land* (Cambridge: Harvard University Press, 2007), 24–25.

41 Marylynne Diggs, "Romantic Friends Or A 'Different Race of Creatures'? The Representation of Lesbian Pathology in Nineteenth-Century America," *Feminist Studies*, Vol. 21, No. 2 (Summer 1995): 317.; Oliver Wendell Holmes, Sr., *A Mortal Antipathy* (1885), Reprint. (Boston: Houghton Mifflin, 1892), 294.

42 Martha Vicinus, "The History of Lesbian History," *Feminist Studies*, Vol. 38, No. 3 (Fall 2012): 575.

43 Kaja Silverman, *Male Subjectivity at the Margins* (New York and London: Routledge, 1992), 2, 15–16.

44 David J. Getsy, "Introduction: Queer Intolerability and Its Attachments," in *Queer* (Cambridge, MA: The MIT Press, 2016), 12.

45 Getsy, "Introduction," 15.

Bibliography

Adams, Bluford. *Old and New New Englanders: Immigration and Regional Identity in the Gilded Age*. Ann Arbor: University of Michigan Press, 2014.

Alcott, William A. *The Young Wife: Or Duties of Woman in the Marriage Relation*. Boston: George W. Light, 1837.

Alumni Biographical Files. Class of 1887 – William Belcher Whitney. Entry 379. Amherst College Archives.

"Andrew Peter Alvord," Alumni Biography Files, Amherst College, Class of 1887.

Amherst College – Memorabilia/Olio, 1888, for the Senior Class of 1887. No. 77839. Amherst College Archives.

Anonymous. "Woman and Home: The Management of Husbands – To Succeeding in Dressing Well, Kiss the Children Good," *Plain Dealer*. Cleveland, Ohio (Dec. 27, 1883): 3.

Bederman, Gail. *Manliness and Civilization: A Cultural History of Gender and Race in the United States, 1880–1917*. Chicago: University of Chicago Press, 1995.

Belden-Adams, Kris. *Eugenics, Aristogenics, Photography: Picturing Privilege*. New York: Routledge, 2020.

Burke, Chloe S. and Castaneda, Christopher J. "The Public and Private History of Eugenics: An Introduction." *The Public Historian*, Vol. 29, No. 3 (Summer 2007): 5–17.

"Charles Amherst Chase," Alumni Biography Files, Amherst College, Class of 1887.

"Charles Amherst Chase (1864–1937)," *The National Encyclopedia of American Biography*, Vol. 28 (1940): 229.

Chauncey, George. *Gay New York: Gender, Urban Culture, and the Making of the Gay Male World, 1890–1940*. New York: Basic Books, 1995.

"Class of 1887," *Amherst College Olio*, Amherst, Mass., 1888. Amherst College Archives. xLH1.A43 O44. Accessed December 17, 2018: https://acdc.amherst.edu/view/asc:321764

Cohen, Adam S. "Harvard's Eugenics Era." *Harvard Magazine*, (March-April 2016), n. p. Accessed April 17, 2017. Available at: http://harvardmagazine.com/print/52049?page=all

Conable, Charlotte Williams. *Women at Cornell: The Myth of Equal Education*. Ithaca: Cornell University Press, 1977.

Deitcher, David. *Dear Friends: American Photographs of Men Together, 1840-1918*. New York: Harry N. Abrams, Inc., 2001.

Di Bello, Patrizia. *Women's Albums and Photography in Victorian England*. London: Routledge, 2017.

Diggs, Marylynne. "Romantic Friends Or A 'Different Race of Creatures'? The Representation of Lesbian Pathology in Nineteenth-Century America." *Feminist Studies*, Vol. 21, No. 2 (Summer 1995): 317–340.

Dobkin, Marjorie Houseian. *Making of a Feminist: Early Journals and Letters of M. Carey Thomas*. Kent, Ohio: Kent State University Press, 1979.

Edwards, Elizabeth. "Homoerotic Friendship and College Principals, 1880-1960." *Women's History Review*, Vol. 4, No. 2 (1995): 149–163.

Geffcken, Katherine A. "Walton, Mary Alice," *Database of Classical Scholars, Rutgers School of Arts and Sciences*. Accessed January 4, 2019: https://dbcs.rutgers.edu/all-scholars/9200-walton-mary-alice

Getsy, David J. *Queer*. Cambridge, MA: The MIT Press, 2016.

Hasian, Marouf Arif, Jr. *The Rhetoric of Eugenics in Anglo-American Thought*. Athens: University of Georgia Press, 1996.

Hill-Climo, William. "Race Betterment: The Nation's Duty." *Eugenics Review*, Vol. 1, No. 3 (Oct. 1, 1909): 194–202.

Holloway, Karla F. C. *Private Bodies, Public Texts: Race, Gender, and a Cultural Bioethics*. Durham and London: Duke University Press, 2011.

Holmes, Oliver Wendell, Sr. *A Mortal Antipathy* (1885). Reprint. Boston: Houghton Mifflin, 1892.

Holmes, Oliver Wendell, Sr. "The Professor's Story." *Atlantic Monthly*, Vols. 5–7 (1860-1861): 1–4.

Hurlburt, Katherine. Various Authors, "Letters of the Class of 1886," Unpublished. Smith College Archives, Class Records, Box 80.CLA.1426. 1888.

Hunter, Jane H. *How Young Ladies Became Girls: The Victorian Origins of American Girlhood*. New Haven: Yale University Press, 2002.

Huntington, Ellsworth and Whitney, Leon F. *The Builders of America*. New York City: William Morrow & Co., 1927.

Jaher, Frederic Cople. "The Politics of the Boston Brahmins: 1800-1860," in *Boston, 1700-1980: The Evolution of Urban Politics*, Ronald P. Formisano and Constance K. Burns, eds. (London: Greenwood Press, 1984), 59–86.

Johnson, Allen, ed., *The Chronicles of America*, Vol. 33. New Haven: Yale University Press, 1921.

Kraut, Alan M. *Silent Travelers: Germs, Genes, and the 'Immigrant Menace'*. New York: Basic Books/HarperCollins Publishers, Inc., 1994.

Lane, Katherine. *Class of 1890: Scrapbook*. Wellesley College: Wellesley College Archives.

Maxwell, Anne. *Picture Imperfect: Photography and Eugenics, 1879-1940*. East Sussex, U.K.: Sussex Academic Press, 2008.

May, Elaine Tyler. *Barren in the Promised Land*. Cambridge: Harvard University Press, 2007.

McDonnell, Patricia. "'Essentially Masculine': Marsden Hartley, Gay Identity, and the Wilhelmine German Military," *Art Journal*, Vol. 56, No. 1 (Summer 1997): 62–68.

Our Famous Women: Comprising the Lives and Deeds of American Women. Hartford, Conn.: A.D. Worthington and Co., 1883.

Peirce, Leona. "Letters of the Class of 1886," Unpublished. Smith College Archives, Class Records, Box 80.CLA.1426. Feb. 1892.

Roosevelt, Theodore. *The Strenuous Life: Essays and Addresses*. New York: Century Company, 1901.

Sekula, Allan. "The Body and the Archive." *October*, Vol. 39 (Winter 1986): 3–64.

Sheldon, William Herbert. *Atlas of Men: A Guide for Somatotyping the Adult Male At All Ages*. New York: Harper and Brothers, 1954.

Siegel, Elizabeth, ed., *Playing with Pictures: The Art of Victorian Photocollage*. Chicago: The Art Institute of Chicago, 2009.

Silverman, Kaja. *Male Subjectivity at the Margins*. New York and London: Routledge, 1992.

Smith-Rosenberg, Carroll. *Disorderly Conduct: Visions of Gender in Victorian America*. New York and Oxford: Oxford University Press, 1985.

Thompson, Leander. *Memorial of James Thompson of Charleston, Mass.,1630–1642, and of Eight Generations of His Descendants*. Boston: L. Barta & Co., 1887.

University of Chicago, "College of Medicine Alumni," *The Alumni Record of the University of Illinois Chicago Departments of Medicine and Dentistry*. Chicago: Rogers Printing Co., 1921.

Van Dyne, Susan. "'Abacadabra': Intimate Inventions by Early College Women in the United States." *Feminist Studies*, Vol. 42, No. 2 (2016): 280–310.

Vertinsky, Patricia. "Physique as Destiny: William H. Sheldon, Barbara Honeyman Heath and the Struggle for Hegemony in the Science of Somatotyping." *Canadian Bulletin of Medical History*, Vol. 24, No. 2 (Feb. 2007): 291–316.

Vicinus, Martha. "Distance and Desire: English Boarding School Friendships, 1870-1920," in *Hidden from History: Reclaiming the Gay and Lesbian Past*, Martin Duberman, Martha Vicinus, and George Chauncey, Jr., eds. (New York: Penguin Books/Meridian, 1989), 212–232.

Vicinus, Martha. "The History of Lesbian History." *Feminist Studies*, Vol. 38, No. 3 (Fall 2012): 566–596.

Wellesley College, "Alumnae Notes." *The Wellesley Magazine, Book*, Vol. 40 (April 13, 1897): 409.

Whitney, William Belcher. Class of 1887, Scrapbook. Vol. 3 – 1886–1887. Amherst College Archives. MA.00099.

"Womanly Mannishness," *Democrat and Chronicle* (Rochester, N.Y.) (April 7, 1906): 13.

6 A Scissored Gay Life of the 1930s and 1940s: The Scrapbooks of Ogden Salmon

James A. Kaser

Ogden Salmon (1915–1990) constructed a remarkable series of scrapbooks from 1931 to 1949. During this time, he negotiated his gay identity in the homophobic culture of the early-twentieth-century United States.[1] These artifacts of his identity formation utilized four different formats to provide a dynamic response to his changing circumstances between the ages of 16 and 34. They include clippings of "high" and "low" cultural artifacts that reflect on his marginalized status.[2]

The earliest scrapbooks, dating from 1931 to 1939, were made while Salmon lived with his parents in suburban Chicago as an only child. His effeminacy prompted his father to enroll him at Morgan Park Academy, an all-male military academy.[3] Begun as a school-boy pastime, he continued to make opera-diva scrapbooks in this format through his early twenties. He comprised these scrapbooks of hand-drawn materials accompanied by made-up stories about romance-prone divas engaging in socially inappropriate or scandalous behaviors (such as public nudity, stealing fiancés, and murder). Rather than clipping printed content in these early albums, Salmon drew his own images based on cultural stereotypes and themes. He also wrote stories for imaginary opera newspapers, which he then assembled into "back files."

His next phase of scrapbooking dates from 1938 to 1940. In this period, he created "journal-scrapbooks" in which he "queered" mass-cultural content by arranging clipped ephemera interspersed with sanitized, coded, third-person, magazine-style accounts of his personal experiences and thoughts as a young man whose social life centered on Chicago's "Fairytown." While he was creating these journal-scrapbooks, Salmon was still financially dependent on his father, who had arranged employment in the family's real-estate business.[4] The books focus particular interest on news stories that recognize homosexuality (e.g., the coverage of Leopold and Loeb), cultural productions that indulged (and, perhaps, validated) a gay male gaze (e.g., photographs of shirtless male actors), and instances of gender non-conformity (like cross-dressing). He included no images of friends and curiously remains invisible himself. His impersonal tone effectively "normalizes" his attraction to men and his homosocial activities: attending public events, eating restaurant meals, socializing in private, participating in nude life-drawing sessions, and visiting public cruising areas. Salmon stops using the journal-scrapbook format after relocating to New York City.

The format of Salmon's next scrapbook, made around 1942, consists solely of clipped images of nearly-naked men. It was entirely different from his earlier productions and is the least personalized of them all. Perhaps this is appropriate, since Salmon then was living as an enlisted man and was under the control and surveillance of superior officers and fellow soldiers. Kept in a Manhattan Beach Coast Guard

DOI: 10.4324/9781003157427-9

Training Station binder, Salmon's scrapbook included clipped images of athletic men exercising or striking bodybuilder poses to show off their physiques. From the cisgender perspective of the mainstream publications from which such images were clipped, the depictions were aspirational celebrations of male athleticism. Only through knowledge of his sexual orientation of Salmon do we read the images as objects of his desire. Unlike earlier scrapbooks in which Salmon foregrounded actors and dancers and relished instances of gender non-conformity, here Salmon embraced homoerotic attraction to athletic male bodies that characterized a culturally emergent homosexual masculinism that dominated gay culture after World War II.[5]

Salmon's final surviving scrapbooks, made from 1944 to 1949, include vernacular snapshots and photographic portraits of himself and his friends in the polished manner of mainstream (cisgender) visual culture. While the images are personal, Salmon still treats his subjects distantly, providing full name annotations – even for himself. The men wear uniforms or business suits, except when they sunbathe in swimsuits or wear nothing at all. Even when nude, they exude an air of a sexual, playful camaraderie, typical of "physique magazines" like *Grecian Guild Pictorial* that popularized homosexual masculinism in the post-war era. The effeminate boy who expressed himself in the 1930s through the guise of fictional opera divas and re-appropriated images of actors, celebrities, and people in the news found in 1940s homosexual masculinism an identity he could willingly present to others, despite the self-oppression of outwardly identifying with the heteropatriarchy.

Salmon's scrapbooks and photographic albums express a journey of self-discovery. Although Salmon escaped his restrictive family by moving to New York City (where he had a career as a visual merchandiser, male lovers, and a circle of gay friends), he always led a cautious and closeted life.[6] His scrapbooks do not tell a simple story of liberation and gay pride. They do, however, document evolving strategies for navigating his way through a world hostile to his effeminacy and sexual orientation and show how his intentions, source materials, narratives, and formats changed over time.

The Diva Scrapbooks

Salmon's two earliest scrapbooks, dating from 1931 to 1939, primarily consisted of hand-written and hand-drawn newspapers with various titles. Like actual newspapers, Salmon gives his "newspapers" mastheads, subscription forms, advertisements, signed articles, column illustrations, and a "Picture Section." While he mentions actual opera companies, he most often writes of the fictional, Chicago-based, La Paz Opera. His early content was clearly inspired by the opening of the Chicago Civic Opera House in 1929. Although he mentions a few actual opera singers, most of Salmon's story deals with fictional opera stars' performances, stage costumes, and offstage wardrobes and lives (Fig. 6.1).

In writing on opera's appeal for gay men, Wayne Koestenbaum points to its aesthetic as an "art of excess and display, of exteriority...[that] became an art of introspection and interiors" with the advent of radio and recordings.[7] In the symbolic prison of Salmon's home, where his emotional expression was constrained by his father and oppressive expectations of cisgender normativity, Salmon could listen to opera recordings and broadcasts and experience passionate emotions, excess, and a form of escapism. By creating his fictional opera company on paper, Salmon could perform "an oblique variety of drag," as Koestenbaum describes the behavior of

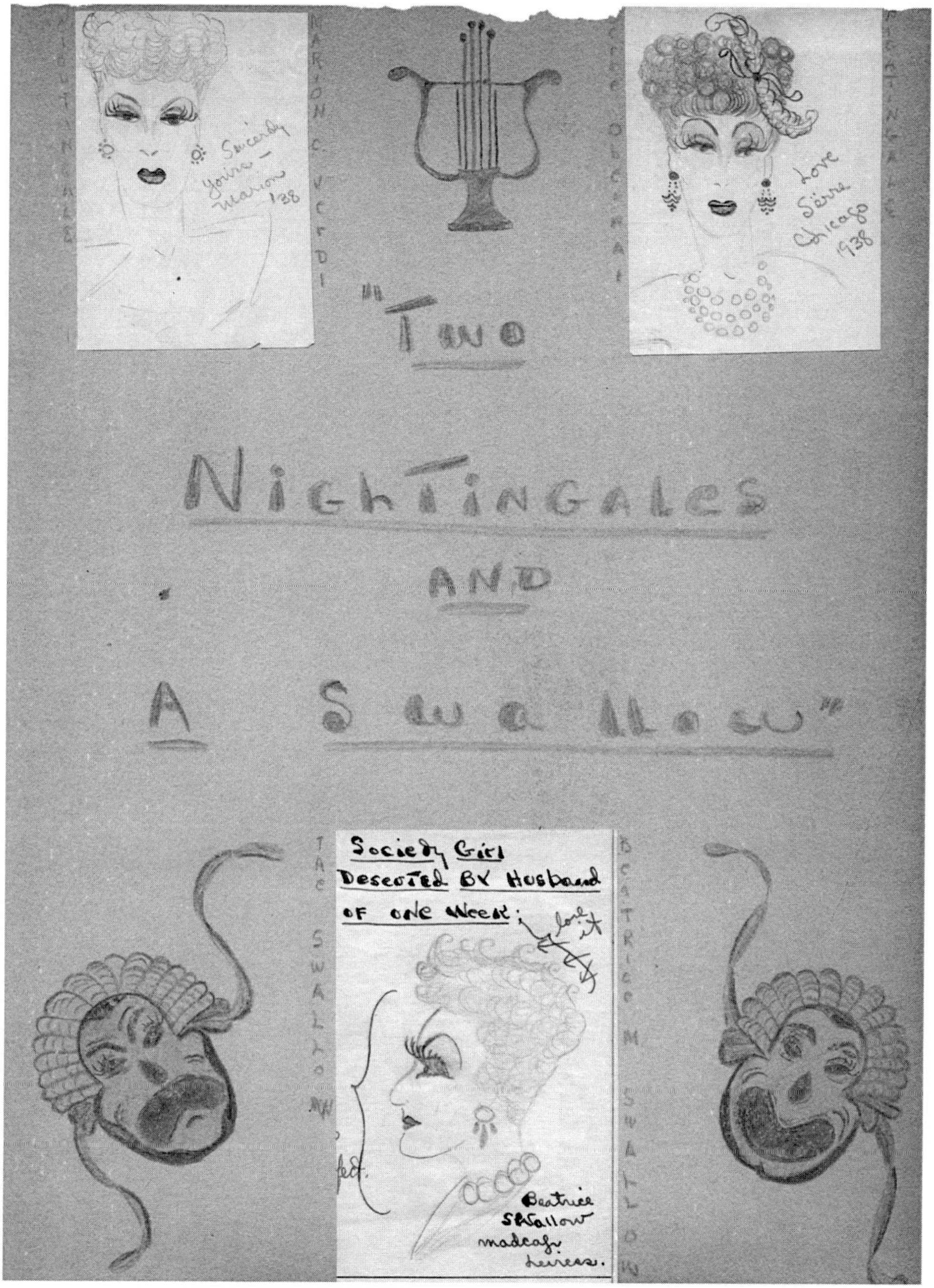

Figure 6.1 Ogden Salmon, *Two Nightingales and a Swallow*, 1938, pencil and ink on paper, 12 × 8 3/4 in., Ogden Salmon Scrapbook. Collection of James Kaser, photograph © 2021 James Kaser.

1940s fans who staged operas, complete with costumed figures, on miniature stages.[8] Like them, Salmon "cuts and restitches gender to suit his fancy."[9]

Salmon's fictional divas – accomplished, famous, and wealthy females – live as independently as men. Historian Paul Robinson calls such divas "gender bending," since they present an exaggerated female gender expression, while their powerful voices put them on an equal footing with men.[10] In his albums, Salmon creates three fictional divas. The oldest, Amelia Samper, a native Chicagoan, marries at a young age to an elderly French nobleman. Samper, with a face taut from repeated lifts, divorces in 1938, and plans to wed 24-year-old danseur Charles Danielli. A second diva, Serre Obernai, is 16 years younger than Samper, yet Salmon creates an extensive biography for her that includes a British aristocrat/diplomat father and Italo-Russian mother, marriage at fifteen to an elderly Italian count, volunteer nursing in World War I Paris, and a stage career, before employment as a high-paid diva with the Chicago Civic Opera (Fig. 6.2). Salmon's account falls off after Obernai debuts at the Civic Opera. However, he included many hand-rendered illustrations of her with elaborate coiffures, diamonds, orchids, and Pekinese dogs. Salmon takes the least interest in his third diva, American Marion Verdi, but gives her an exotic ancestry,

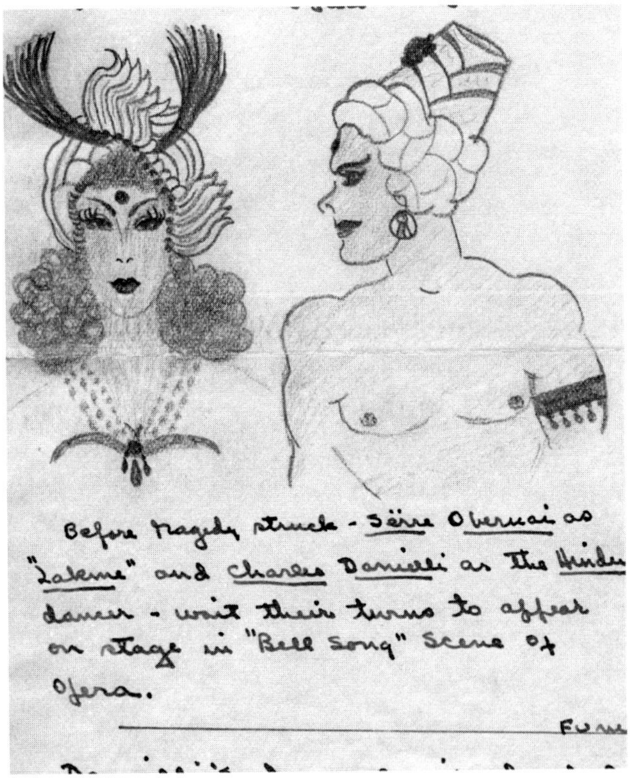

Figure 6.2 Ogden Salmon, *Before Tragedy Struck…*, 1938, pencil on paper, 8½ × 11 in., Ogden Salmon Scrapbook. Collection of James Kaser, Photograph © 2021 James Kaser.

which Verdi herself learns about only after inheriting a fortune from a distant Egyptian relative.

If Samper's and Obernai's narratives are interpreted as projections of Salmon's concerns, they show his desire for independence, creative achievement, and a striking personal appearance. As we learn from later scrapbooks, Salmon enjoyed dressing in an attention-getting fashion by violating sartorial boundaries, although there is no surviving documentation of his cross-dressing. While Salmon created distinctive appearances for his divas through fashion, he also gave them ethnicities he considered "exotic" (German, Italian, Russian, and Egyptian) to add to their glamour. In conversations with friends, Salmon claimed an "exotic" Native-American ancestry for himself. The veracity of this claim is unclear – his father's family took pride in their descent from a Plymouth Colony ancestor.[11]

As a man expected to repress his own emotions, the histrionic divas of his opera scrapbooks provided Salmon with an expressive and oblique means of "drag." Paul Robinson suggests that closeted men (such as Salmon) might experience liberation in the "lyrical shouting" by opera singers. However, Salmon problematizes his divas' emotional expressions by imagining their life stories beyond the boundaries of the stage. For instance, after Verdi lost most of her inherited wealth, she destroyed her dressing room in a "demented" rage.[12] His other divas also go mad while expressing emotions off stage, hinting that Salmon himself may have feared losing emotional control, perhaps because homosexual attraction was considered in the 1930s in the U.S. to be a mental illness.[13]

Salmon created the opera scrapbooks from age 15 to 24. Thus, the books might be expected to chronicle adolescent and early-adult sexual longings. Yet, they contain surprisingly little sexualized content until Salmon is 23 and introduces a new character, Beatrice Swallow. The earlier opera scrapbooks present an opera company newspaper with appreciative articles about divas. With Swallow's introduction, Salmon's news takes on a tabloid quality. His articles focus on Swallow's scandalous behavior and include sexualized illustrations of Swallow and her intended lover. The surname "Swallow" also has sexual connotations. While the surname is a witty reference to Swallow's cough syrup industry fortune, the surname also refers to a bodily function with both operatic and erotic intentions. *In Opera, Sex, and Other Vital Matters*, Robinson parallels operatic vocalization to sexual expression, pointing to the athletic employment of the mouth and throat, body parts second only to the genitals as erogenous zones.[14] Beyond the opera world, swallowing is an oral sexual act selectively undertaken by those performing fellatio, combining all the erogenous zones, Robinson mentions.[15]

In an early scrapbook appearance, Swallow becomes enamored with Danielli, Samper's corps de ballet fiancé. Previously an opera fan and supporter, she becomes determined to outshine Samper as an opera diva and win Danielli. She attends the opera wearing a dress without undergarments that is so revealing that the top does not hold shut. Her torso is revealed and it is as though her aroused emotions have escaped as well as her breasts. Curiously, Salmon illustrates this spectacle without creating a titillating image of Swallow. However, his illustration of the male Danielli is highly masculinized. Danielli's figure is cartoonishly accentuated with broad shoulders, a deep chest, and muscular legs. Salmon's proclivity to eroticize only the male figures also is evident in his representation of the divas, whose bodies are obscured under elaborate costumes. Additionally, their faces are distorted by sneering hauteur and/or overshadowed by elaborate hairstyles and millinery.

Soon after the dress incident, Swallow debuts as Flora in *Tosca*. The performance, meant to win Danielli, merely outrages the audience with inferior singing and overacting. Abandoning her plan, she instead conquers Danielli with promises of wealth, and they elope. However, their marriage is unconsummated and quickly ends, since the fastidious Danielli cannot stomach Swallow's rose-tinted peignoirs and beauty regimen. Danielli returns to the corps de ballet until an enraged Swallow shoots him dead from on stage. Judged criminally insane, Swallow is remanded to the Asylum for Insane Criminals at the Illinois State Penitentiary at Menard. When her sanity returns, she is released from prison and reappears in the final newspaper issues pledging to give up the "gay life" and become a schoolteacher. Koestenbaum argues that "diva conduct" is a culturally available means "to dramatize the problematics of self-expression."[16] That is, by creating a fictional, larger-than-life identity – even satirically – one advances one's own identity formation. Through this elaborate and dramatic Swallow plot, might Salmon have been expressing his resolve to resist either homoerotic desires, or an infatuation with a heterosexual male?

Parallels between "diva behavior" and Salmon's own life are difficult to ignore, especially given the storyline he created for Marion Verdi that references the experience of one of his closest friends. In his account of Verdi, she earned acclaim as Lady Godiva in the imaginary opera *Hellzadamarung* until her revealing costume drew censorious attacks and arrest. Salmon's coverage of Verdi is in the 1939 "World's Fair" edition of his mock newspaper. Like his divas, Salmon visited New York World's Fair in 1939, prompted by his friend John Callaghan's appearances in the Broadway revue *Hellzapoppin*. Callaghan acted in the role of Lady Godiva and was costumed to appear nude. Although he was not arrested, his performance must have seemed a daring act of gender-bending. We do not know enough about Salmon's friends and family to know if there are other personal details incorporated into his diva characters. However, it seems clear that Koestenbaum's concept of "oblique drag" illuminates the ways Salmon employed his diva scrapbooks to work through issues of his own personal gender and sexual expression as a school boy, adolescent, and young man living with his censorious family in Chicago from 1931 to 1939.[17]

The Journal-Scrapbooks

In 1938, while still creating fictional opera narratives, Salmon began making scrapbooks that incorporated dated journal accounts of his own activities. He wrote these entries like magazine reports on the activities of public figures. These journal-scrapbooks are housed in loose-leaf notebooks with monthly tab divisions, and cover 1938, 1939, and 1940. At the end of each year, Salmon lists the books he read, movies he viewed, and plays he attended. In his journal entries, he includes the full names of personal friends, as though writing for readers, but he includes no images of them. Salmon also intersperses personal content with editorial observations about celebrities, fashion, news events, and live performances, movies, and plays he attended. He illustrated much of this content with clippings from programs, newspapers, and photographic magazines (such as *Life*). Salmon uses the journal-scrapbooks to document his activities and to clarify his thoughts about cultural productions and current events. The resulting artifact also manifests Salmon's emerging identity as a gay man (Fig. 6.3).

Motion-picture content predominates the album and includes reactions to films, clippings of actors' photographs, and comments on actors' personal lives. Salmon

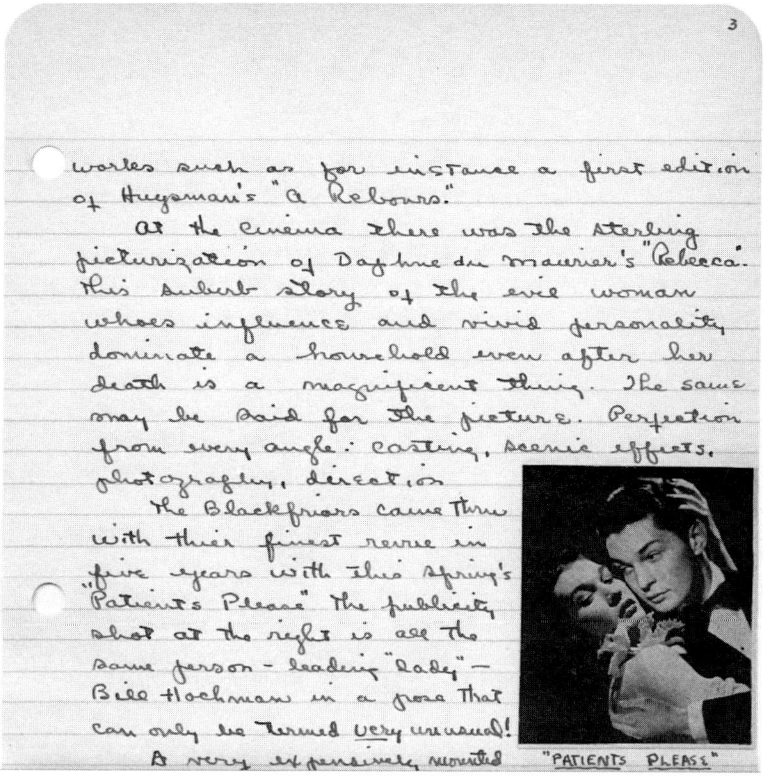
3

works such as for instance a first edition
of Huysman's "A Rebours."
At the cinema there was the sterling
picturization of Daphne du Maurier's "Rebecca."
This superb story of the evil woman
whoes influence and vivid personality
dominate a household even after her
death is a magnificent thing. The same
may be said for the picture. Perfection
from every angle: casting, scenic effects,
photography, direction.
The Blackfriars came thru
with their finest revue in
five years with this spring's
"Patients Please." The publicity
shot at the right is all the
same person – leading "lady" –
Bill Hochman in a pose that
can only be termed very unusual!
A very expensively mounted

Figure 6.3 Ogden Salmon, *Scrapbook Page with Photograph*, 9½ × 6 in., Ogden Salmon Scrapbook. [Photograph is by Lee Weinstein, published in University of Chicago student publication, *Pulse*, April 1940]. Collection of James Kaser, photograph © 2021 James Kaser.

sometimes viewed four movies in a single day. He was a fan of a few female stars but paid most attention to male actors, commenting on their relative attractiveness and noting revealing scenes (often accompanied by clipped illustrations). For example, he recalls actor George Raft bathing in the 1932 Mae West movie *Night After Night*. In April of 1939, Salmon includes a press clipping of actor Tyrone Power emerging from a shower. Discussing the 1939 film *Lucky Night*, he observes that Robert Taylor looks attractive throughout, particularly when wearing pajamas. Salmon also adds shirtless images to the album of the Dead End Kids and Sabu, whom he describes as "luscious."[18]

Koestenbaum claims gay men assemble collages of clipped images as a means of addressing their "policed, curtailed sexual condition."[19] By pasting images into an album, the gay man creates an object that gives voice to his secrets, references past experiences, and makes desire tangible, tactile, and realized – even if only to a small degree. In her recent work on celebrity culture, Sharon Marcus uses fan scrapbooks to study the complex relationships among celebrities, publics, and media, and she shows how fans use scrapbooks to "pursue, intimacy, connection, and proximity, not with real people," but with the ephemera generated by celebrity culture.[20]

While Salmon's desires are made tangible by these private scrapbooks – not surprisingly, given the stigmatization and criminalization of homosexuality – he leaves no explicit record of his sexual activities. However, in journal-scrapbook entries during the first months of 1938, Salmon notes overnight stays with other young men, and four entries are set off with inked stars.[21] Although he gives the full names of his male hosts, he provides no description of their activities. Perhaps, these were sexual encounters.

The only other entries that might be construed as documentation of sexual activities are visits to locker rooms and "cruising" areas – both popular places for gay men to have sexual encounters with other gay men. The locker rooms he mentions are at the Lake Shore Athletic Club and the Chicago Civic Opera, where he was a supernumerary.[22] Cruising at the Indiana Dunes is evidenced by references to outdoor voyeurism: watching men in towels, sunbathing, and swimming nude.

Salmon also mentions figure-drawing classes as opportunities for voyeurism. One of his friends taught Works Progress Administration (W.P.A.) art classes in Evanston, Ill., and Salmon indulged the thrill of seeing attractive nude men under the guise of art-making. Although the environment was not homosocial or private, it offered safe and prolonged visual stimulation. The classes also included a more private corollary. Salmon and the instructor socialized with the male models after class, taking them for a meal and/or providing them with transportation.

The main content of Salmon's social record is concerned with homosocial activities in public and private spaces. Unlike later generations of gay men, Salmon and his friends only occasionally went to bars and nightclubs. When they went, it was usually to attend a performance, like those by popular New York nightclub singer/pianist Dwight Fiske.[23] Much more frequently than going to bars, they socialized over dinner, usually selecting restaurants with "exotic" décor and food, such as Japanese or Russian. However, their favorite Chicago eatery was The Men's Grille, operated by Carson Pirie Scott & Co. A group of Salmon's friends met there regularly, calling themselves "the lunch club." Since many of them worked as window dressers at area department stores, the location was convenient. However, the men-only establishment also made a homosocial gathering unremarkable.[24] Of course, the easiest homosocial gathering to orchestrate was in a private dwelling. Perhaps because so many of Salmon's friends were designers or artists, their events in apartments and houses were often elaborate, and featured themed dinners, costume parties, and listening to new recordings or radio broadcasts of opera or symphonic music.

Chicago, like New York, went through a "pansy craze" in the 1920s and 1930s, when "effeminate" men became visible.[25] The Near North neighborhood Salmon frequents and refers to with popular slang as the "Boul Mich" (for "Michigan Boulevard") and "Towertown" (after the Chicago Water Tower neighborhood) was popularly dubbed "Fairytown." Here young men lived in rooming houses or shared apartments, dressed in eye-catching fashions, and worked in area department stores in such large numbers that by the late 1930s, gay male store clerks had become a stereotype. Although it was possible for gays to go to a public venue and see "pansy" performances, audiences were often cisgender and middle- or upper-class people "slumming," as they also did at venues showcasing people of color. So private gatherings were still the safest venues for gay men. This was particularly true after Illinois passed a "sexual psychopath law" in 1938 that meant that anyone even suspected of deviance could be incarcerated in the psychiatric division at Menard (like Salmon's fictional character Swallow).

However, Salmon's journal-scrapbook shows how public performances could take on a homosocial and identity-affirming dimension similar to what George Chauncey describes in New York City in a later time period.[26] Salmon notes his pleasure in unexpectedly seeing friends at events, and lists them by name. Salmon also delightedly notes anonymous males wearing attention-getting clothing. For instance, at a Sonja Heine show, he espies a "young-man" wearing a camel's hair coat with an oversized orchid corsage. At a Harald Kreutzberg dance recital, there was "near riot in the balcony" when a man appeared in a white fur vest.[27] Clearly, unusual sartorial choices could signal to other knowing men. Furthermore, by observing reactions, one could discover other gay men among prosaically dressed cisgender men. Of course, such signaling could be read by unsympathetic people, and so was mostly engaged by men who had little social status at risk. Salmon took great care in constructing his own appearance and signaled his gay identity subtly by wearing rings he commissioned. He describes his rings and the pleasure he took in wearing an "immense topaz" to the opening night of the 1939 Civic Opera season.[28]

Salmon's ring-wearing was not peculiar to him. Samuel M. Steward (1909–1993), living in Chicago at the same time as Salmon, categorized men who wore well-tailored suits and distinctive rings, as "elegants."[29] Although Steward was educated, he had working-class origins and sneered at the "elegants" ("my God, the rings!"), even while, like them, he used the lobby of the Civic Opera House to pick up men.[30] It is obvious from Steward's comments that Salmon's appearance was calculated to make himself identifiable to fellow gay men who understood these subtle subculture-identifying codes.

While sartorial choices might transform Salmon's audience experience, comments by fellow attendees might also "queer" an otherwise straight performance for an inner circle. Salmon would have been familiar with opera-performance claques (professional applauders) who signaled their displeasure or enthusiasm in a sycophantic manner. In the midst of a claque comprised instead of "elegants," a man could comment audibly to those around him without disrupting the performance. For instance, Salmon sought out dance performances featuring male soloists. Based on the evidence in his journals and scrapbooks, other "elegants" coveted such performances as well. At a Ballet Russes recital, a danseur appeared in an "amazingly brief" costume. He prompted whispered comments among the block of men seated around Salmon and "all went for a gayer afternoon."[31]

Clipped illustrations of two companies that featured male ballet dancers – and even danseurs partnering each other – appear repeatedly in Salmon's journal-scrapbooks (Fig. 6.4). However, his enjoyment was problematized by company avowals of the danseurs' masculinities. For instance, The Philadelphia Ballet (founded by Catherine Littlefield in 1935) was a mixed-gender group but featured danseurs as farmhands, cowboys, and Native Americans. Salmon was rapturous over the latter performers, who wore nothing except body paint and loincloths. However, Littlefield's comment that "the men in her troupe are all of the masculine type" outraged him.[32] When Salmon saw men dancing with other men, he interpreted the performance as a confirmation of the men's gayness. Salmon dismissed Littlefield by claiming that: "a ballet boy is a ballet boy, all clever publicity to the contrary."[33] Salmon was even more enthusiastic about Ted Shawn and His Men Dancers, an all-male company that celebrated male athleticism with choreography in which men partnered each other.

Salmon also recorded several different instances of men performing in women's

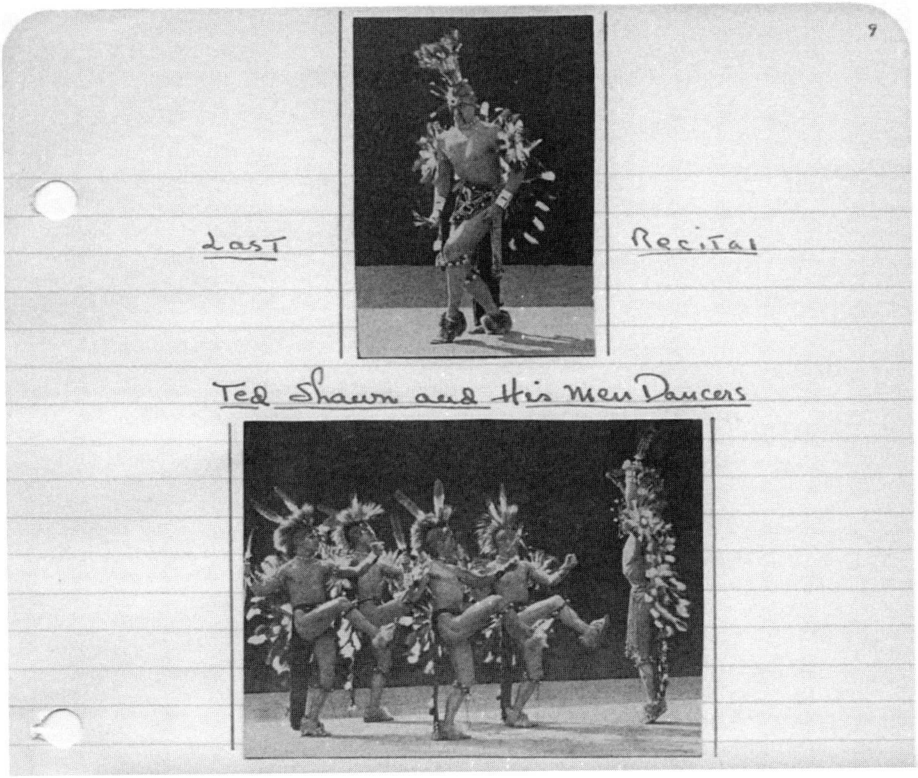

Figure 6.4 Ogden Salmon, *Scrapbook Page with Two Photographs,* 9½ × 6 in., Ogden Salmon Scrapbook. [Top photograph is by Shapiro Studio, *Frank Overlees in Ponca Indian Dance*, 1936; Bottom photograph is by Shapiro Studio, *Ted Shawn and His Men Dancers in Ponca Indian Dance*, 1936]. Collection of James Kaser, photograph © 2021 James Kaser.

clothing, taking most interest in "naturals," who seem to be letting an inner femininity emerge. For the combined hilarity and titillation, Salmon went to every Blackfriars performance to see beefy football players clomp about in female or revealing clothing.[34] His appreciation of a 1939 Blackfriars production is different because a male actor convincingly plays both the female and male starring roles. In addition to writing a rave review, Salmon clips a manipulated image showing the actor in both roles simultaneously.

Salmon takes the greatest interest in a fictional male, Ferdinand the Bull (from Munro Leaf's book) who rejects aggressive masculinity in preference of feminine-identified behaviors, like smelling flowers. The enthusiastic Salmon notes hearing two book readings, seeing the 1938 Disney film short, and lists products with Ferdinand images on them, including clothing, fabric, and cereal packages. After describing the Chicago store window displaying Ferdinand "look[ing] coyly at the crowds from under 6-inch eyelashes and lavender eyelids, all the while sniffing an enormous flower," Salmon writes: "The strangest part of the whole thing is how a nation which prides itself so strongly on being masculine has taken the gentle, pansy, bull to its hearts."[35]

While Salmon notes examples of "pansies" receiving positive receptions, he also records negative receptions, from the mild to the murderous. When Leslie and Sewall Stokes's *Oscar Wilde* opened in New York in 1938, starring Robert Morley, Salmon includes a full-page clipping of the star. However, he also adds a quote from Walter Winchell's syndicated column referring to "whoops-my-dearies leaving the *Oscar Wilde* show."[36] When *Esquire* prints an article claiming that "pansy" male designers schemed to "make women unattractive to men," Salmon comments at outraged length.[37] Likewise, when news stories raised questions about actor Robert Taylor's virility, Salmon disgustedly notes that Taylor is given fight scenes so that he can get disheveled and bloody and appear shirtless with artificially enhanced chest hair.

Salmon reacts at most length to news stories that he felt referenced homosexual deviants. In November 1938, Salmon clipped newspaper stories about then-jailed murderer Nathan Leopold. In his commentary on Leopold, Salmon declares that all school children should be given physical and mental examinations to prevent them from eventually becoming criminals. Leopold was convicted as a 20-year-old along with his accomplice Richard Loeb for kidnapping and murdering 14-year-old Robert "Bobby" Franks in Chicago in 1924.[38] Leopold had claimed he was driven to kill Franks and to commit earlier adolescent thefts and arson to prove his intellectual superiority. He was in the news in 1938 for passing his 34th birthday in jail. The Leopold and Loeb case would have loomed over Salmon's childhood and adolescence. David S. Churchill has analyzed the changing public discourse regarding the case as a reflection of the increasing stigmatization of homosexuality between the murder trial during Chicago's 1920s "pansy craze," when Leopold and Loeb's relationship, deemed evidence of mental illness, was used to argue against the death penalty. In the trial of Loeb's murderer in 1936 – by which time homosexuality was censored and policed – a jury, influenced by the "deviance" of Loeb's homosexuality, found his murderer, James Day (who had slashed Loeb's throat and then stabbed him more than 55 times) not guilty.[39]

Although Salmon expressed his dismay over news articles in which homosexuals were associated with mental illness, sexually transmitted diseases, and violent crimes, the coverage that was most upsetting to him involved the exposure and censoring of private behavior. Newspapers including the *Chicago Daily Tribune* reported that Gale Franklin Davison, a Galesburg, Ill., resident, was found dressed in women's clothing and hanging dead from a tree.[40] Salmon incorporated a clipped photograph of the handsome Davison, providing his gloss to the story.[41] In Salmon's version, Davison's mother said he frequently attended "masquerades," and police found a much-used cosmetics case in Davison's locked car. Salmon concluded:

> this poor young man would have been highly distressed had he lived on and found that the lovely creation he had worked on and fussed over was referred to, as it was in one news hash, as, "a hideous masquerade."[42]

Salmon's focus on the ideas of exposure and censorious commentary in the case of Davison probably reveals his fear that his activities at the Indiana Dunes, or even just his homosocial outings with other effeminate young men could make him the focus of mental health interventions, police harassment, or random physical attacks.

Even though Salmon's journal-scrapbooks cover his social life, reading habits, and his attendance at public events, he provides only general references to any personal life events. He mentions his first day working for his father, March 17, 1938. However, he records little about the job. By contrast, Salmon devotes extensive coverage to his week-long trip to New York City in August of 1939, as well as his year-long preparations. Salmon's trip to Manhattan from August 18 to September 1, 1939, to visit John Callaghan and see the World's Fair is clearly transformative. His New York City account is embellished with clippings of the Fair, stage productions he attended, and city sights. He also includes clippings of stage and screen stars he sees in public or actually meets, including Rosalind Russell and John Garfield. He also lists designers and stage personalities he meets through Callaghan, like fashion designers Adrian (Adolph Greenburg, 1903–1959) and Raoul Pene du Bois (1914–1985), as well as actors Sydney Chatton (1918–1966) and Michael O'Shea (1906–1973), whose physical attractiveness makes a big impression on Salmon.[43] Despite his focus on his touristic experience of New York City, unlike other travel-focused albums, Salmon includes no photographs of his own.

The most personal aspect of the trip is the time Salmon spends with a new acquaintance, Manhattanite Ludlow White, whom he addresses with a series of nicknames.[44] Although circumspect, he references White enough to make it clear that their time together is special. Once "La Blanc," (i.e. White) arrives in Chicago from New York in July of 1940, Salmon writes that he "began living instead of just existing, knowing instead of hoping."[45] The two spent a week at South Haven, Michigan. Then, in August of 1940, Salmon notes: "I'm going to New York to try to find myself...I can't help feeling just a bit uncertain one minute and joyous the next."[46] He uses a plural pronoun when describing the trip to New York City and mentions a shared apartment in the city.[47] After summing up the rest of the year in one extended entry, the journal-scrapbook culminates in the inclusion of a program for a Christmas Eve concert in which White's name appears as a soloist. Salmon concludes: "New York has proved a decidedly happy experience, and ahead lies even better things...Next year is vacation year for this journal."[48]

The War Years and Beyond

In his year-end summary for 1940, Salmon included images of boxer-clad, barechested military inductees that may reflect an intensification of his earlier anxieties over the private becoming public. On September 16, 1940, draft registration began. John D'Emilio has written about the impact of the draft on gay men.[49] Since a history of homosexual behavior was grounds for exclusion, induction interviews began to include questions about sexual practices. According to D'Emilio, the anticipation of the physical and verbal examination induced intense anxiety in many men. Induction began in October of 1940, but Salmon was not called. He worked as a retail display manager for almost two years before enlisting on August 8, 1942, at Fort Jay, New York, as a private in the Warrant Officer Corps. We cannot know his motivations, but Salmon may well have been encouraged by the experiences of his friends. Alan Bérubé's research has shown that many gay men thrived during military service in World War II, and Salmon, a military-school graduate, may have anticipated serving in the context of a social network.[50] In fact, within the first week of basic training, he made a life-long friend who would become a post-war lover.[51]

His scrapbook from around 1942 consists entirely of clipped images of men, but not casually shirtless actors and celebrities. These men wear the abbreviated garments of bodybuilders and display their physiques for admiration. The departure of this scrapbook from Salmon's earlier collage activities lies in both the lack of aestheticization and commentary. Salmon collected and pasted images of nearly naked men posing for admiration onto his scrapbook pages with no captions or intentional arrangement, other than to cover the pages without overlapping the images. For Salmon, the images would have been exciting novelties. The comments of author Paul Monette help us understand this perspective. When Monette encountered such photographs as a 15-year-old in the 1950s, he found them self-affirming evidence of other gay men, and used them as masturbation aids.[52] The images are also early examples of the sort of photographs David K. Johnson presents as manifestations of homosexual masculinism.[53] Although clipped from military publications and weightlifting magazines, such images would later be created for sale to gay men. Such depictions – photographs of bodybuilders (judged on appearance), rather than weightlifters (judged on strength) – became associated with an iteration of gayness that connected gyms and bodybuilding with ancient Greece where male beauty was admired and homosexuality was openly expressed by athletes and soldiers. Craig Loftin shows how this manly version of same-sex attraction appealed to middle-class and white-collar men in the post-War years who disdained the effeminate behavior associated with "pansies."[54] The appeal homosexual masculinism would hold for Salmon – scorned from childhood for his effeminacy – is probably evidenced in this clipped physique photography.

Salmon's military service ended in January 1944 after he spent time in a military hospital with a disease that predated his enlistment.[55] He returned to New York City and resumed working in visual merchandising for department stores. The scrapbooks he created after the war are the only others known to survive (Fig. 6.5). Dating from 1944 to 1949, they are entirely different from the "oblique drag" of the diva scrapbooks and the journal-scrapbooks with a movie magazine format. These post-war scrapbooks are personal photograph albums that consist mostly of snapshots, a few studio photographs, a handful of event programs, and a scattering of clipped items. Although carefully arranged chronologically, they do not evoke the aesthetic of a mock publication. The clippings and programs document the activities of Salmon and his friends, some of whom were actors, dancers, designers, and vocalists. When the images are not simply portraits, they depict men in public New York City venues, day trips to the country or the beach, and vacationing at Fire Island and Provincetown. While he noted similar homosocial activities in his 1938 through 1940 journal-scrapbooks, previously there had been no photographic documentation of these trips. Yet, these albums, with no fantasized divas or journal-scrapbook-style commentary, seem the least personal of Salmon's creations. Salmon's full-name captions and inking of his own first name under photographs of himself lend the album a distant, third-person quality. Furthermore, even when the images are snapshots, the men in them pose. They look directly into the camera and smile, even in the few images in which they are sunbathing nude on the beach. The beach photographs, taken in segregated and isolated homosocial environments, have the same playful innocence that made possible the sale of bodybuilding magazines on newsstands at this time. Finally, even though Salmon may

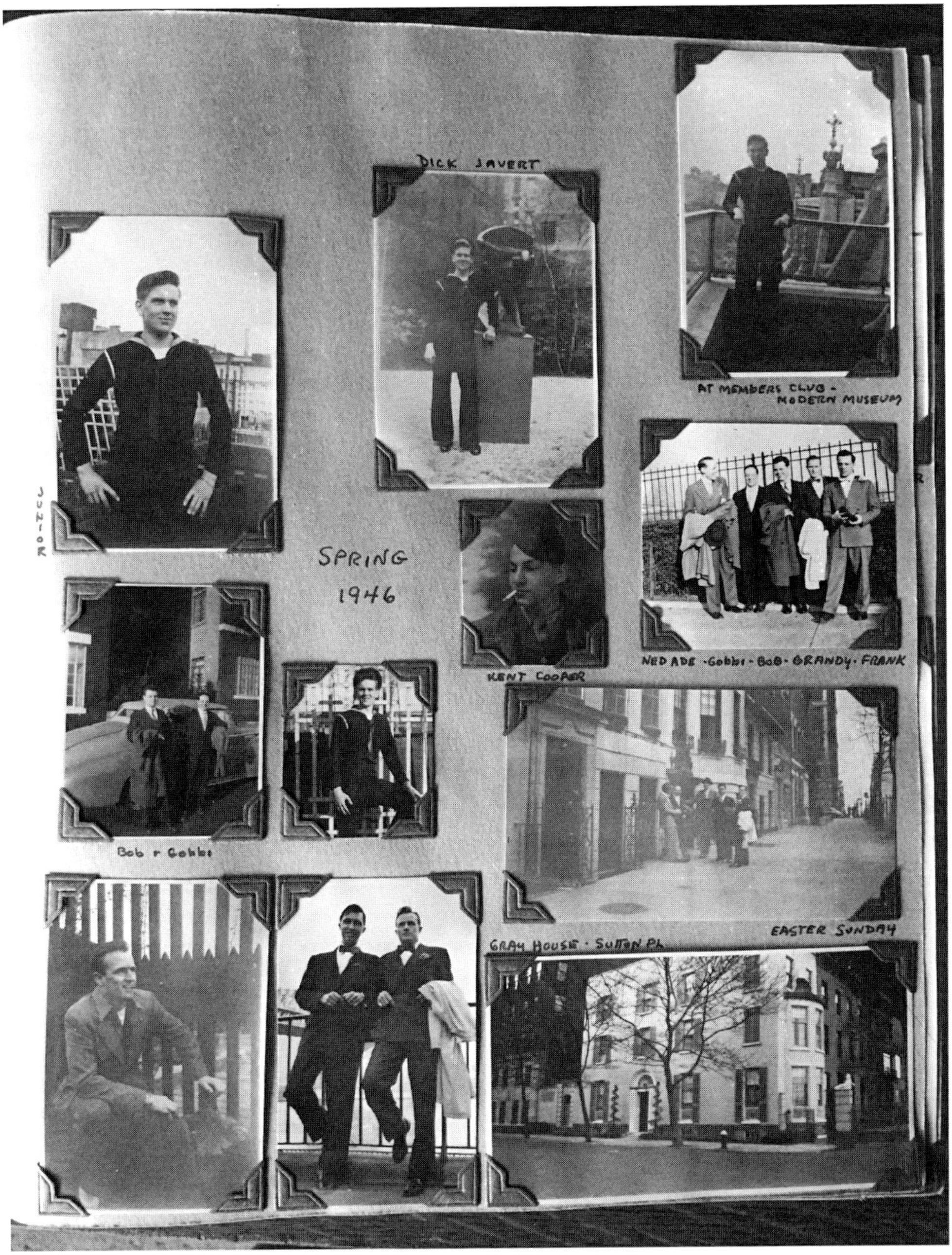

Figure 6.5 Ogden Salmon, *Spring 1946*, 1946, photographic prints, 11¾ × 9¾ in., Ogden Salmon Scrapbook. Collection of James Kaser, photograph © 2021 James Kaser.

appear in a photograph with his current domestic partner, the men pose far apart from each other and look directly at the photographer, rather than each other. Presumably, the in-house photography studios at Salmon's workplace and his friendship with other gay men in the images made him comfortable with taking and printing the photographs. In combination with his earlier bodybuilder scrapbook, these last scrapbooks, evidence his final stage of negotiating gayness. He embraced homosexual masculinism, admiring straight-acting bodybuilders, and concealing any indication of his effeminacy. Clad in respectable suits and ties, appearing at highbrow cultural events, working hard at a career in a corporate business environment, he remained deeply closeted and fearful of being outed until the end of his life. His gayness was confined to a segregated world of gay friendships, experienced secretively in private and physically isolated settings.

Conclusion

As a group, Salmon's scrapbooks document the ways he came to terms with his gayness in a homophobic culture. In the absence of positive images of openly gay men, he queered mainstream cultural productions, selectively focusing on aspects of books, current events, films, and stage performances that resonated with him, literally clipping them for his scrapbooks and then providing his own interpretive frameworks. In the early scrapbooks, he found an outlet for his emotional life through fantasized accounts of fictional opera divas. When he began establishing a social life, he sought out images that validated a gay male gaze – shirtless actors and male ballet dancers partnering each other. As an enlisted man, confronted with the homoeroticism of military life, Salmon collected images of men posed to invite admiration of their bodies. By the period documented in the materials from 1944 to 1949, Salmon no longer validated his emotions by queering contemporary cultural productions. He instead embraced an image of same-sex desire made respectable by association with Classical Greek culture. His friends do not appear in drag, but in their military uniforms or suits and ties. He depicts them in work and cultural settings and hardly ever at bars. When they appear nude, the images are not salacious but associated with fitness and health.

An analysis of the Salmon scrapbooks as tangible artifacts of identity formation is useful in understanding the motives for scrapbook creation by gay men. Other examples of such materials may survive but are rare. Some men who kept them likely feared they would fall into the wrong hands, and destroyed them. Surviving relatives regarded such materials as deviant and worthy of destruction. Even gay friends destroyed such scrapbooks if they were depicted in them, or if they felt the creator's reputation needed protecting. When such materials do survive, they are often taken apart, and the images sold separately (the treatment to which the Salmon scrapbooks were being subjected by a photograph dealer before I bought them). While scholars have discovered some aspects of gay culture that Salmon's scrapbooks document, the scrapbooks have the dynamism of a first-hand account that demonstrates the creative effort and self-oppression required to adopt an image acceptable to the dominant homophobic culture.

Notes

1 Salmon was born in Chicago and lived there until 1940. He was the son of Walter Ogden Salmon (1877–1969) and Gertrude (Ogden) Salmon (1880–1968), who married in Cook County, Illinois, in 1903. He relocated to Pound Ridge, N.Y., in the early 1970s. He was a visual merchandiser employed by Lord & Taylor for most of his career. In addition to information from genealogical databases, his scrapbooks are my main information source. I also interviewed a man who knew Salmon through his life partner, who was a man from Salmon's generation. Anonymous. Interview by James Kaser, August 29, 2019.
2 This paper draws upon a growing body of scrapbook scholarship. Books by Ellen Gruber Garvey and Georgeanne Scheiner were particularly relevant. In *Writing with Scissors*, Garvey shows how a scrapbook can be read as its maker's attempt to - at least, visually - make a place for themselves in a world in which they may feel disenfranchised. This often features an assemblage of reaffirming clippings from a wide range of diverse sources, and the exclusion of most of the vast sea of marginalizing content to which they were exposed. Ellen Gruber Garvey, *Writing with Scissors* (Oxford University Press, 2013). Georgeanne Scheiner's reading of the movie-fan scrapbooks of girls as "tangible artifact[s] of identify formation" appears in: Georgeanne Scheiner, *Signifying Female Adolescence: Film Representations and Fans, 1920–1950* (New York City: Praeger, 2000), 130.
3 Anonymous. Interview by James Kaser, August 29, 2019.
4 The family real-estate company was W. O. Salmon and Co., of 30 N. LaSalle Street, Chicago, Illinois.
5 For an overview of the emergence and prevalence of homosexual masculinism, please see: David K. Johnson, *Buying Gay* (New York: Columbia University Press, 2019).
6 Anonymous. Interview by James Kaser, August 29, 2019.
7 Wayne Koestenbaum, *The Queen's Throat* (New York: Poseidon, 1993), 47.
8 Koestenbaum, 82.
9 Koestenbaum, 82.
10 Paul Robinson, *Opera, Sex, and Other Vital Matters* (Chicago: University of Chicago Press, 1992), 167.
11 Salmon's paternal grandmother, Blanche Ogden Salmon (1853–1936), descended from Pilgrim John Ogden and held office in ancestry organizations like Daughters of Founders and Patriots. "Blanche Ogden Salmon," *Chicago Daily Tribune* (Nov. 3, 1936): 18.
12 Salmon, Diva Scrapbook, *Universal Opera News*, November 18, 1931.
13 According to John D'Emilio, the rise of psychoanalysis after World War I. added mental illness to the stigmatization of homosexual behavior, which already had been regarded as a sin, a criminal act, and a disease: John D'Emilio, *Sexual Politics, Sexual Communities: The Making of a Homosexual Minority in the United States, 1940–1970* (Chicago: University of Chicago Press, 1983), 16–18.
14 Paul Robinson, *Opera, Sex, and Other Vital Matters* (Chicago: University of Chicago Press, 2002), 164.
15 Robinson, *Opera, Sex, and Other Vital Matters,* Chs. 9, 10.
16 Koestenbaum, 133.
17 Koestenbaum, 82.
18 Salmon includes a clipping of the shirtless actors appearing in *The Dead End Kids in Crime School* (Warner Brothers, 1938), who were nicknamed the "Dead End Kids." Born Selar Sabu, the actor was commonly known as Sabu Dastagir (1924–1963). Salmon commented on Sabu's appearance in *The Thief of Baghdad* (United Artists, 1940).
19 Koestenbaum, 64.
20 Sharon Marcus, *The Drama of Celebrity* (Princeton: Princeton University Press, 2019), 96.
21 Salmon, Journal-Scrapbook, January–February 1938.
22 "Super," abbreviates "supernumerary," the term for a non-singer who helps fill an opera stage. Koestenbaum writes: "the super is like the fan: a backstage spy, an onlooker, not a participant." Koestenbaum, 71.
23 Dwight Fiske (1892-1959) presented story songs that seemed nonsensical, but included references meaningful to an "in-group," often, of gay men.

24 The Men's Grille opened in 1931. Meant to attract shoppers, the menu included a daily .75-cent special and a $1.00 *table d'hote* luncheon. John Drury, *Dining in Chicago* (New York: John Day, 1931), 232.
25 David K. Johnson, "The Kids of Fairytown," in *Creating a Place for Ourselves*, ed. Brett Beemyn (New York: Routledge, 1997), 97–118.
26 George Chauncey describes gay men's covert appropriation of public spaces in several works. For his account of appropriation of theater performances, see: George Chauncey, *Gay New York* (New York: Basic Books, 1994), 351.
27 Harald Kreutzberg (1902–1968) was one of the first ballet dancers in the United States to develop an audience attracted by male solo performances.
28 Perhaps due to limited commercial styles of men's rings, Salmon purchased stones or antique coins and commissioned rings to be made by a friend.
29 Justin Spring, *Secret Historian* (New York: Farrar, Straus and Giroux, 2010), 207.
30 Spring, 207.
31 Ogden Salmon, Journal-Scrapbook, 1938–1939, April 2, 1938.
32 Salmon, Journal-Scrapbook, November 1938.
33 Salmon, Journal-Scrapbook, November 1938.
34 Formed in 1903, the University of Chicago Blackfriars Club was an all-male club. During the 1920s and 1930s, professional designers and directors helped with club productions.
35 Salmon, Journal-Scrapbook, November and December 1938.
36 Salmon, Journal-Scrapbook, November 1938.
37 Anonymous, "Fashion Is a Fairy, *Esquire* (April 1938), 35ff.
38 Salmon, Journal-Scrapbook, November 1938.
39 David S. Churchill. "The Queer Histories of a Crime: Representations and Narratives of Leopold and Loeb." *Journal of the History of Sexuality*, Vol. 18, No. 2: 287–324. doi:10.1353/sex.0.0046.
40 "Find Man Dead Chained to Tree in Woman's Garb: Face Rouged, Hands Tied Behind Back," *Chicago Daily Tribune* (Dec 11, 1938): 15.
41 Salmon quotes: "Press Inquiry in Death of Man Clad as Woman," *Chicago Daily Tribune* (Dec 12, 1938): 16.
42 Salmon, Journal-Scrapbook, December 1938.
43 Sydney Chatton made short films with The Three Radio Rogues. Michael O'Shea became known as a character actor in film and television after 1943.
44 Born William Ludlow White (b. 1908), White grew up in Evanston, Ill. He appeared in 1940s New York City directories at 155 E 33rd Street.
45 Salmon, Journal-Scrapbook, July 1940.
46 Salmon, Journal-Scrapbook, August 1940.
47 Later city directory entries list Salmon with the same address as White.
48 Salmon, Journal-Scrapbook, December 1940.
49 John D'Emilio, *Sexual Politics, Sexual Communities* (Chicago: University of Chicago Press, 1983), 25.
50 Alan Bérubé, *Coming Out Under Fire* (New York: Free Press), 1990. In particular, see the chapter, "Fitting In," 34–66.
51 Anonymous, Interview with Author, August 29, 2019.
52 Paul Monette, *Becoming a Man: Half a Life Story* (New York: Harcourt, Brace, Jovanovich, 1992), 82–83.
53 David K. Johnson, *Buying Gay* (New York: Columbia University Press, 2019).
54 See: Craig Loftin, "Unacceptable Mannerisms: Gender Anxieties, Homosexual Activism, and Swish in the United States, 1945–1965," *Journal of Social History*, Vol. 40 (2007): 557–596.
55 Due to Health Insurance Portability and Accountability Act laws, details are withheld from the archival record. See, National Archives and Records Administration, *Hospital Admission Card Files, ca. 1970 – ca. 1970*, NAI: *570973*; Record Group Number: *Records of the Office of the Surgeon General (Army), 1775–1994*; Record Group Title: *112*.

Bibliography

Anonymous. Interview with James Kaser, August 29, 2019.
Bérubé, Alan. *Coming Out Under Fire*. New York: Free Press, 1990.
Chauncey, George. *Gay New York*. New York: Basic Books, 1994.
Churchill, David S. "The Queer Histories of a Crime: Representations and Narratives of Leopold and Loeb." *Journal of the History of Sexuality*, Vol. 18, No. 2: 287–324. doi: 10.1353/sex.0.0046.
D'Emilio, John. *Sexual Politics, Sexual Communities*. Chicago: University of Chicago Press, 1983.
Garvey, Ellen Gruber. *Writing with Scissors*. New York: Oxford University Press, 2013.
Johnson, David K. *Buying Gay*. New York: Columbia University Press, 2019.
Johnson, David K. "The Kids of Fairytown," in *Creating a Place for Ourselves*, Brett Beemyn, ed. (New York: Routledge, 1997), 97–118.
Koestenbaum, Wayne. *The Queen's Throat*. New York: Poseidon, 1993.
Loftin, Craig. "Unacceptable mannerisms: Gender Anxieties, Homosexual Activism, and Swish in the United States, 1945–1965." *Journal of Social History*, Vol. 40 (2007): 557–596.
Marcus, Sharon. *The Drama of Celebrity*. Princeton: Princeton University Press, 2019.
Monette, Paul. *Becoming a Man: Half a Life Story*. New York: Harcourt, Brace, Jovanovich, 1992.
Ogden Salmon Journals, 1931–1949. Collection of the Author.
Robinson, Paul. *Opera, Sex, and Other Vital Matters*. Chicago: University of Chicago Press, 1992.
Scheiner, Georgeanne. *Signifying Adolescence*. New York: Praeger, 2000.
Spring, Justin. *Secret Historian*. New York: Farrar, Straus and Giroux, 2010.

7 In Plain Sight: Album-Making and Queer Identity in Mid-Twentieth-Century South Africa

Danielle Kinsey

Vernacular photographic albums are valuable sources for understanding public presentation and private identity for white LGBTIQ persons in apartheid South Africa. When these albums are housed in a public archive dedicated to queer histories, such as the Gay and Lesbian Memory in Action (GALA) LGBTIQ Archive in Johannesburg, their public/private or frontstage/backstage dynamics take on greater historical significance.[1] This chapter investigates three albums in the GALA collection to show how each differently represented the hiding and revealing of LGBTIQ identity in mid-to-late twentieth-century South Africa. Each foregrounds its maker's control over their own narrative but also reveals how album-makers were forced to work within dominant paradigms that could be empowering at times and "closeting" at others. Each presents the quotidian naturalness of queerness as empirical fact – a queerness lived "in plain sight." Though each album functioned as a personal archive, they had (and continue to have) public functions as shared objects between friends and family members. As art historian Patrizia di Bello has argued, albums have a community-building dimension when other people are invited to view them. As a tool of policing queerness, however, they can also be used as evidence of a certain way of life in the event of an official inquiry.[2] In the space of GALA, the albums' public functions are amplified and queer histories can take form.

Renée Liddicoat created her album during World War II and details her experience in the South African Women's Auxiliary Army Services. It presents a coming-of-age narrative that anticipates her career in psychology and her openly lesbian life in the apartheid era. The album *David, A Sailor, 1950s* documents military life in the mid-twentieth century, but almost nothing is known about its maker – compelling us to imagine "David's" queer life and community in ways he might not have intended. Michel/le Bruno, a well-known queer Johannesburg hairdresser and gay-rights pioneer, also created an album now housed at GALA that had both public and political functions.[3] Many of Bruno's personal photos are in the archive's collection along with the album. The album depicts parties he attended in 1972 and, within the context of GALA, it also becomes evidence of queer liberation.

Liddicoat's and "David's" albums operate on two levels: as a (mostly) straight-appearing frontstage available to the casual viewer, and as a more ambiguous, queer-er backstage for hands-on users who turn over the photos and read the captions on the other side. Liddicoat's verso captions discuss a life entwined with another woman's. "David's" verso captions evidence a world of explicit gay sex and community. In contrast to these two, Bruno's album appears to only have a frontstage, as it celebrates his easy queerness at public parties. Yet homophobic legal and policing systems and state

DOI: 10.4324/9781003157427-10

oppression in the 1960s and 1970s form the album's backstage. By making the album, Bruno took what had been used against him by the legal system – pictures taken at parties – to not only create a touchstone of personal pride but as a way of ensuring his own safety by documenting his extensive ties within Johannesburg (Joburg) society.

Much as photographic albums are invaluable repositories of queer history, there are limits to what they can tell us about the past. As with other minority and persecuted figures, the lack of primary-source material for writing queer histories is not just frustrating but integral to the story. Queer people in the twentieth century were less likely to have children to whom to pass memorabilia. Inheritance laws did not recognize same-sex partnerships and would award estates to blood- or marriage-related family members, despite family estrangements. In contexts where queerness is considered shameful, families share artifacts suggesting straightness with local archives but withhold queer references. This was the context GALA was fighting against from its inception in 1997. The project to create an archive for LGBTIQ experiences is synonymous with movements to write that history and to advocate for LGBTIQ rights. How each album entered the archive (preserved in collection notes) reflects the contingent ways Liddicoat, "David," and Bruno lived their queer lives in plain sight between the 1940s and 1970s, as well as the contingencies alive in the political project of writing histories of queer life in South Africa in today's context. This chapter discusses how questions around Bruno's security, Liddicoat's psychological career, and everything having to do with "David" belie complicated histories.

The Renée Liddicoat Photograph Album[4]

We do not know what the Liddicoat album meant to its maker (presumably Liddicoat herself), nor whether she would have condoned its inclusion in the GALA collection. There is little public information about her life, and inquiries to her blood descendants have yielded scant information. The photographic album deposited in GALA is the only known record of her private life housed in a public archive. It became a primary source for queer history in 2000 when Hentie van der Merwe, a queer Johannesburg artist, "found an old photograph album in a junk-store that, to his eye, had a strong lesbian subtext."[5] Presuming that Liddicoat owned the album until her death in the 1980s, its provenance from then until 2000 remains unknown. A closer examination of the album's captions identified Liddicoat as its original owner. She was already well known to the GALA archive for her 1956 dissertation "Homosexuality: Results of a Survey as Related to Various Theories," and other publications.[6] In the words of sexuality historian Marc Epprecht, her work "helped to temper the wilder homophobic sentiments being expressed by South African politicians and police in the 1960s."[7] When GALA staff interviewed Liddicoat's former professional colleagues to confirm that it was her in the album, they also confirmed her queerness and recalled her as "being quite open about being lesbian."[8] GALA's work in acquiring the album preserved a valuable documentation of the negotiation of white lesbian identity in South Africa in the 1940s.

While Liddicoat appears to have been a gay-rights advocate, the album is also a source for the pre-history of apartheid ideology. Her livelihood was bound up in furthering the apartheid state. During her doctoral training in psychology at the University of Witwatersrand, one of Liddicoat's supervisors was the founder of the National Institute for Personnel Research (NIPR), an institution that worked to maximize economic output and managerial efficiency. The NIPR effectively provided, "the 'scientific' basis for the inferiorization of Blacks," as psychologist and anti-apartheid activist Sathasivian Cooper has written.[9] Liddicoat worked for the NIPR until the 1980s, and published articles in the late 1960s that involved contrasting IQ and motor skills in white English, white Afrikaner, and amaZulu children.[10] Thus, her legacy is a complicated one.

The black, leather-bound album was a mass-produced Kodak product. It contains approximately 260 black-and-white images, organized over 74 pages. Most photographs are about 3.5 by 5 inches and were arranged two-to-six per page. The pages are black, and she mounted the images with black corners. The album documents the years of her life in South African Women's Auxiliary Army Services (WAAS) from 1941 to 1945, when she was stationed mostly in Cairo. On every page, Liddicoat added handwritten captions in clear printing with white pencil to refer to the page in general, or to specific photographs. On the back of about half of the photographs are more extensive captions, some written by Liddicoat, and others by someone else (possibly by Mary Wilkie, who is in about fifteen of the photographs). It is not certain whether Wilkie and Liddicoat were lovers, but Wilkie's presence infuses the album. Liddicoat is in at least 26 photographs, and presumably was the photographer for the majority of the 260 images. In a few of the back-side captions, Liddicoat comments on how she had intended the image to look, and she points out two photographs (of "General" and "Mrs. Smuts") that she obtained from someone else.[11]

It is plausible that Liddicoat, and perhaps Wilkie, took and developed the photos, and then sent them home to South Africa throughout the war. For 1941, the underside captions are numerous, detailed, chatty, and occasionally written in the second person: "My first visit to the Pyramids was by moonlight, & I must say they look more impressive than shown in the gleaming sun. You can compare for yourself when Mary sends on the others."[12] Perhaps the "you" Liddicoat referred to was her father. He would die in Johannesburg in September of 1942, while she was deployed. After his death, Liddicoat's captions decrease in their chattiness, and Wilkie wrote more of them. After December of 1943, the captions stop altogether. It is plausible that Liddicoat came home from the war, collected the 1943 photos from her father's belongings, and put them in an album. It is also possible that she and/or Wilkie created pages as they developed the photographs, and rearranged the album at some point after the war.

Liddicoat's training as a psychologist in the 1950s suggests that the album might have helped to fix an image of her for both her own gratification and for the consumption of others. The album displays an awareness of "frontstage" and "backstage" modes of self-presentation, and of the "conscious" and "subconscious" expressions of identity, as well. The first page introduces the self-conscious protagonist at a protean moment in her development. Under the hand-written heading "1941," she arranged three photographs in a horizontal sequence. The left is of Liddicoat, smiling and confidently posed, wearing an army shirt over the caption "Off duty." The middle image shows rows of women in military uniforms marching past a building with the caption "Retreat Ceremony rehearsal at Oumashoop (Pta.)." The third is of a man and Liddicoat standing rigidly side-by-side, both in full military uniform. The caption reads "Dad" and "Self." Psychologically, "Self" is defined vis-à-vis the subject's father, which perhaps spoke volumes. Discourses at the time of the album's making argued that lesbianism stemmed from "gender trouble" posed by a girl's identification with her father instead of her mother, a discussion that Liddicoat explored and ultimately rejected in her dissertation, concluding that "indifference to parents was more prevalent (on the subjects' conscious level) than cross-parent fixation."[13]

But psychology is only one register of the motifs of social-scientific observation alive in the album. Each page after the first can be divided into one of two categories: "army life" and "the imperial explorer abroad." The "imperial explorer" pages make up well over half of the album, and they contain dozens of composed shots of buildings and scenes in Cairo, Aswan, Jerusalem, Bethlehem, Beirut, Damascus, Haifa, Khartoum, Alexandria, and parts of Algeria. Her views are reminiscent of the work of Roger Fenton and other Western commercial photographers offering touristic city views, such as the ones in Liddicoat's "Street Scenes of Old Jerusalem" and "Cairo Scenes."[14] In this section of the album, Liddicoat employs "artistic" approaches to her photographs, including extended exposures taken at night and backlit silhouettes of subjects including sailboats. Captions reference her experiments with lighting and angles, and attest to Liddicoat's active consideration of the images' artistic merits.

Only twice does Liddicoat's album show both Egyptians and white South Africans together, demonstrating the continued segregation of the races beyond South Africa. Their separation also marks the divisions between colonizer and colonized, and between privileged tourist class and peasant locals. The "army life" pages ostensibly follow a strict chronology, while the "explorer" pages exist out of time, or in a non-modern stasis as Orientalist motifs. In an anthropological vein, they label their North African subjects as occupational "types," or as people engaging in specific rituals. Thus, the WAASies and Liddicoat convey a colonialist dynamic in both the "army life" and "explorer" pages, while also providing a subtext that situates the pages historically within nineteenth-century Orientalist visual culture. This narrative moves from subtext to text on page 48 with a portrait of Wilkie in a pith helmet in a boat on the Nile captioned: "Dr. Livingstone, I presume?"[15] Another caption from that section of the album uses a racist epithet to describe Egyptians. Thus, Liddicoat appropriates the viewpoint and gaze of colonizing white males. Visually, the album continually features Liddicoat in roles usually reserved for white males (indeed, roles her father could have filled): South African soldier, colonizing explorer, army bureaucrat, flâneur, artist, and social scientist.

Liddicoat adds "Self" labels to describe four more photographs in the album: an image of her smiling and posing with two other women in training camp; a photograph of Liddicoat sitting in the grass at the Cairo Zoo and scowling while she and a man named Eric gaze at her friend Kay; Liddicoat relaxed, beaming, and posed beside Wilkie, who has an arm on her shoulder; and on page 41, the photo of smiling, smoking, uniformed Liddicoat (Fig. 7.1), where "Self" (written under the photo) is not defined in relation to another person.[16] While the handwritten text on the back of the photograph mentions that the image began as a "tiny snap" that did not enlarge to the developer's liking (presumably because it looked faded and grainy), this is not referenced in the main caption.[17] This "Self" portrait was taken three months after the death of Liddicoat's father.

Her father must have been a major figure in her life. Ancestry databases reveal that her mother died when she was four years old, leaving her with her father (John) and her brother, who was older by two years. As late as 1939, Liddicoat traveled to

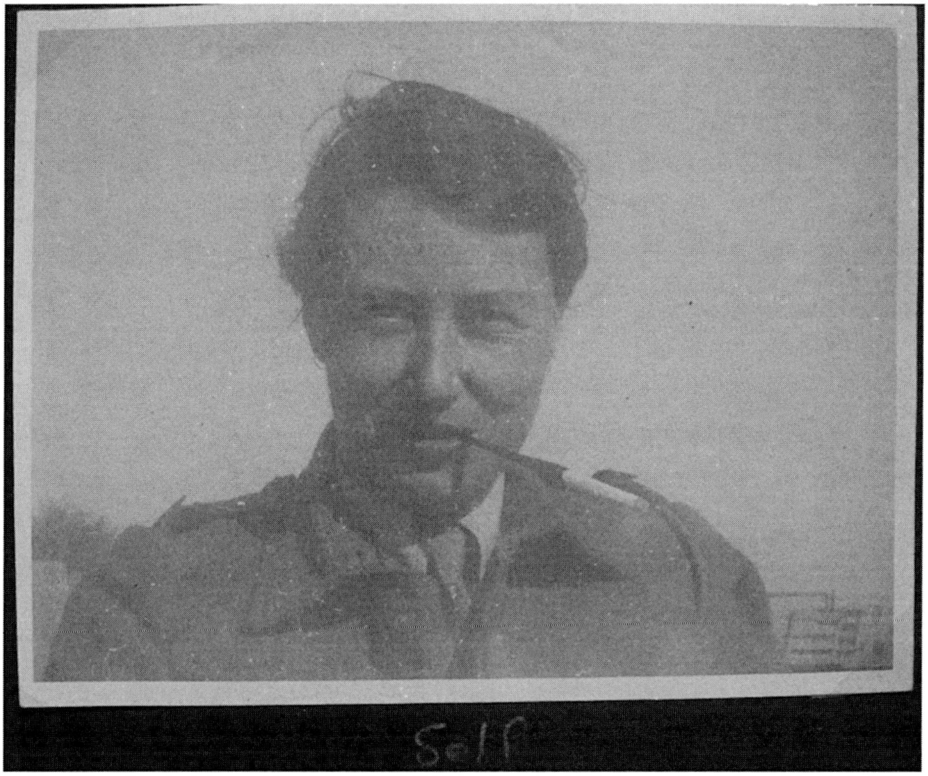

Figure 7.1 *Self*, 1942, black-and-white photograph, 4 1/2 × 6 in. GALA Queer Archive, Johannesburg, South Africa, Renée Liddicoat Collection (AM2800). Photograph by Danielle Kinsey.

Cornwall, England with her father, where the United Kingdom Registry recorded their presence for the War Office. It lists her occupation as "Elementary School Teacher – Retired," and her marital status as "single."[18] This information allows us insight into details that casual viewers of the album might not have known. While she was deployed in Cairo in 1942, her father died in Johannesburg. After learning about his death, Liddicoat and Wilkie went on leave to Damascus, where "Self" (Fig. 7.1) was taken. In this image, Liddicoat gazes intently at the camera. She looks tired, older, and a bit disheveled, but confident. It is tempting to view the photograph as a turning point in the narrative of her life. Perhaps the death of her father and possible estrangement from her brother freed her to go to graduate school, study homosexuality in sympathetic ways, and eventually lead a life "out of the closet." Liddicoat's dissertation argued that homosexuals felt indifference toward parental figures, and her album reveals the steady and stable presence of her father. Yet it also displays a kind of indifference about his loss conveyed by the lack of explicit information about his death, and a smiling, confident "Self" pictured not long after her father's passing.

Other conclusions in her dissertation seem to be anticipated by the album. Her research was a study of "50 male and 50 female homosexuals" and found that "No single environmental factor was … common to all cases."[19] Other conclusions included debunking any connections between homosexuality, neuroses, and psychopathy. Her study found homosexuals not to be any more neurotic than heterosexuals, and discovered that "the mean IQs of the homosexual groups were significantly higher than those of the control groups."[20] For the gays and lesbians in her sample group, "instability in the family was pronounced in only a few cases," and "the homosexual group was as stable as the control group in regard to employment." In addition, "there was little support for the general contention that all homosexuals are emotionally unreliable and sexually promiscuous" and "there was nothing in the appearance or build of 93% of these homosexuals to distinguish them from any normal group of people."[21] She noted that many of her dissertation's findings were "contrary to popular belief and warrant further investigation."[22] In the album, photograph after photograph of women training, working, and managing together during wartime attest to competence and stability. There is no discord, only camaraderie. Liddicoat's position among them signals an "in plain sight" presence of queerness in the album. Yet, the unknown gender-attraction status of the other women prefigures Liddicoat's findings that appearance does not indicate sexual orientation. Moreover, the album maker's cleverness and academic grooming are reflected through conscious mimicry of artistic and anthropological genres.[23]

What was the "lesbian subtext" in the album that drew van der Merwe to contact GALA? Perhaps the homosociality? Although, to be fair, males are present in about 30% of the photographs including people. Yet, many photographs of women present a familiarity that suggests intimacy. In his book on dissident sexuality in southern Africa, Marc Epprecht included four photos from Liddicoat's album, including "Last Lap" (Fig. 7.2), which shows reclining women relaxing in the sun. In "Last Lap," Liddicoat rests her body on Wilkie's legs, and Wilkie's left-hand scratches Liddicoat's left ankle. Another woman, labeled on the previous page as "Rookie," sits behind them, also with her leg and hand resting on Wilkie's body. "Last Lap" is in the "Homeward Bound" denouement of the album that covers Liddicoat's journey back to South Africa in October 1945, though the photograph has no date on it.[24] That image has a hand-written caption on the back that begins: "For all its horrors, World War II, for white gays and lesbians, was also a time of fun, discovery, and coming out."[25] "Last Lap" is perhaps the most candid view of LGBTIQ desire in the album.

Perhaps van der Merwe was also responding to the hairstyles in photographs of Liddicoat and Wilkie after June 1942, which feature each with especially short hair (even shorter than in "Self," Fig. 7.1), particularly in comparison to their fellow WAASies. The album shows that Liddicoat maintained the short haircut until 1945. A longer-haired Liddicoat starts off the album, is supplanted by the Liddicoat in "Self," Fig. 7.1, who in more officious guises stays for the remainder of the war. She then reverts to a longer haircut for post-war civilian times.

Taken as a whole, the album gives the casual viewer an easy narrative to follow: a woman joins the army, follows in her father's footsteps, sees exotic places, and she and her friends/colleagues make the most of it. Adventures were had, danger was not imminent, and Liddicoat made it home safe and sound. It is only by physically engaging with the album and reading the captions on the back of each photograph, which perhaps only the maker and other intimates would do, that a greater understanding is gained. In those captions on the backs of photographs we learn that Liddicoat's and Wilkie's lives were intertwined throughout the war, and Wilkie likely

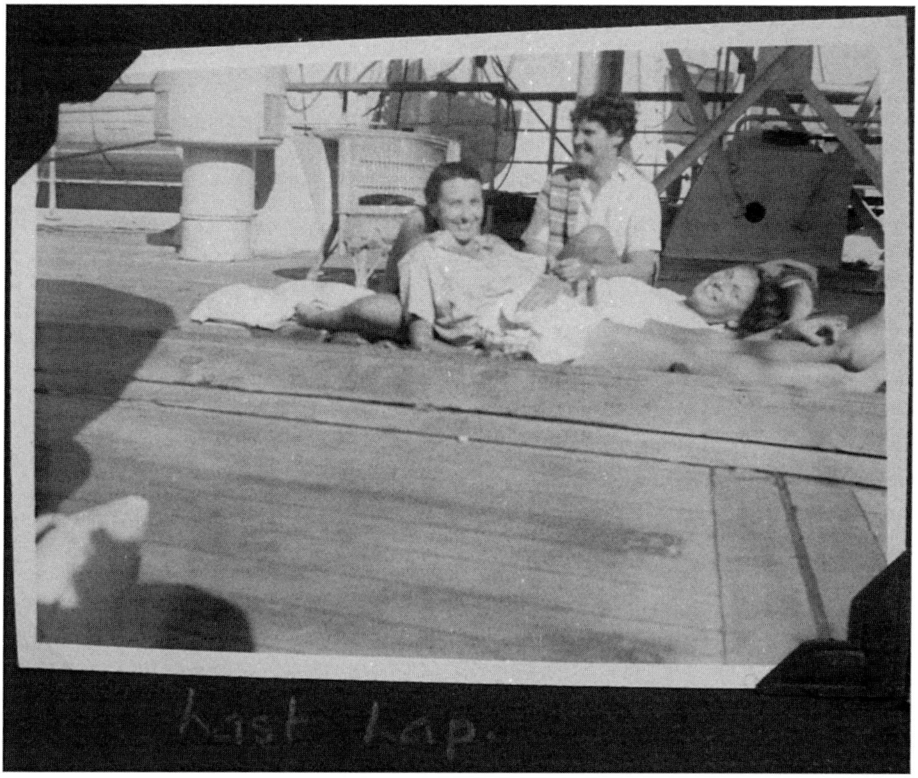

Figure 7.2 *Last Lap*, 1945, black-and-white photograph, 3 × 5 in. GALA Queer Archive, Johannesburg, South Africa, Renée Liddicoat Collection (AM2800). Photograph by Danielle Kinsey.

was the author of many of the verso captions, as well as an occasional photographer. Wilkie's presence is constant throughout the album, which speaks of *their* experience of World War II. We do not know the extent of their relationship, but the album contains lesbian subtext and/or homosociality. The album's textual and implied narratives express both Liddicoat's emerging queer identity in a homosocial atmosphere of important work but also her conformity with colonialist, Orientializing nationalism. Of course, we want to know more about Liddicoat: her views on her own gender identity, racism and class, her sexuality, apartheid, gay rights, her father, the roles of women in war, equality between the sexes, her relationship with Wilkie, and the other women with whom she served. We have her academic publications, which she intentionally published for public consumption, and this photograph album, which became an item of public record by chance, from which to draw information.

Album of "David, A Sailor, 1950s"[26]

The only thing we know about the maker of this second album, "David, A Sailor," comes from the album itself. Its ambiguous and hidden narratives stand on their own.

The album was received by the GALA archives as a donation from someone who found it at a collectibles shop in Cape Town around the year 2000. It is the same size as the Liddicoat album, suggesting that it also was made in the 1950s, using mass-market-available material such as black-and-white film, the album itself, mounting corners, and white pencil. Captions are written in cursive. However, "David's" album has about 35 pages, the photographs are substantially smaller (2.5 by 3.5 inches) than those from Liddicoat's album, most pages have a crowded layout of nine images per page, and at least 40% of the photographs are missing.

"David's" album is not as sophisticated in terms of composition and subject matter as Liddicoat's. It consists of medium- or full-length photographic portraits of men posing in front of a building or piece of technology. Whereas Liddicoat's album encompassed four years, suggesting that she probably had other albums covering earlier periods, "David's" begins with his early childhood and covers his entire life until his military service at sea, suggesting it may have been "David's" only photographic album. There is no notation of "Self" in "David's" album, nor is there any photojournalistic attention to recording dates or places. Instead, the reader is introduced to a family: "Me age 6" (missing image), "Granny" (missing photograph), "Ma and Aunt Gerta" (missing image), "My dog Eland," and "PA" on the first page. The next seven pages create a familiar coming-of-age story. Unnarrated photos of "David" in his adolescence show him posing with other boys and men. A hidden caption on the underside of a picture of a youth holding a peacock introduces the youth as "David." Seven photographs (only three of which remain) on page five are "From Pa's funeral," and on page six, a teenaged "David" poses in front of a car named "Old Betsy." The next page shows an adolescent male, perhaps "David," wearing swimming trunks "At the Y." An uncaptioned page eight shows an adult "David" in his sailor uniform, posing in front of a small house. Subjects in the photos are smiling and the car speaks to a certain level of affluence.

The remaining pages show smiling sailors, ships, the sea, and presumably, the locations in which the seamen were stationed. It is full of homosocial camaraderie but in a military context. Such images were not unusual in post-war visual culture. However, on page 11 (Fig. 7.3), the narrative takes a turn. It features five photographs: "David" (top left) with his arm around another sailor; a similar pose involving two different sailors (middle); another affectionate, same-gender pair appears (bottom left); an unexplained image of the sea (top right); and finally, a photograph of a shirtless soldier posed in the middle with two others leaning on him (bottom right). Under the image of the trio is the handwritten caption: "Sex Mad!" For a viewer determined to see the album's narrative as heteronormative, the caption could be explained as sailors longing for female company. But captions on the back of the photographs reveal an entirely queer narrative. On the back of "David's" "At the Y" photograph is a written caption: "The other pic is better. You can even see your cock in it (very tasty). I'm keeping that one for myself!" The photo of "David" posing in uniform on page eight hides the verso caption: "what a handsome chap you are!" The photograph in Figs. 7.3–7.4 (top left) of "David" with his arm around another sailor bears the following caption written on back: "Me: 'Behave yourself!'" On page 14, on the back of an image of a sailor leaning forward, is written: "Yes, I take it like a man." And page 15 shows a photograph of someone who looks like that same sailor, with his arm around the neck of a younger sailor. That image is accompanied by the caption: "Sandy's new 'wyfie.' She's already sucked off half of Durban,

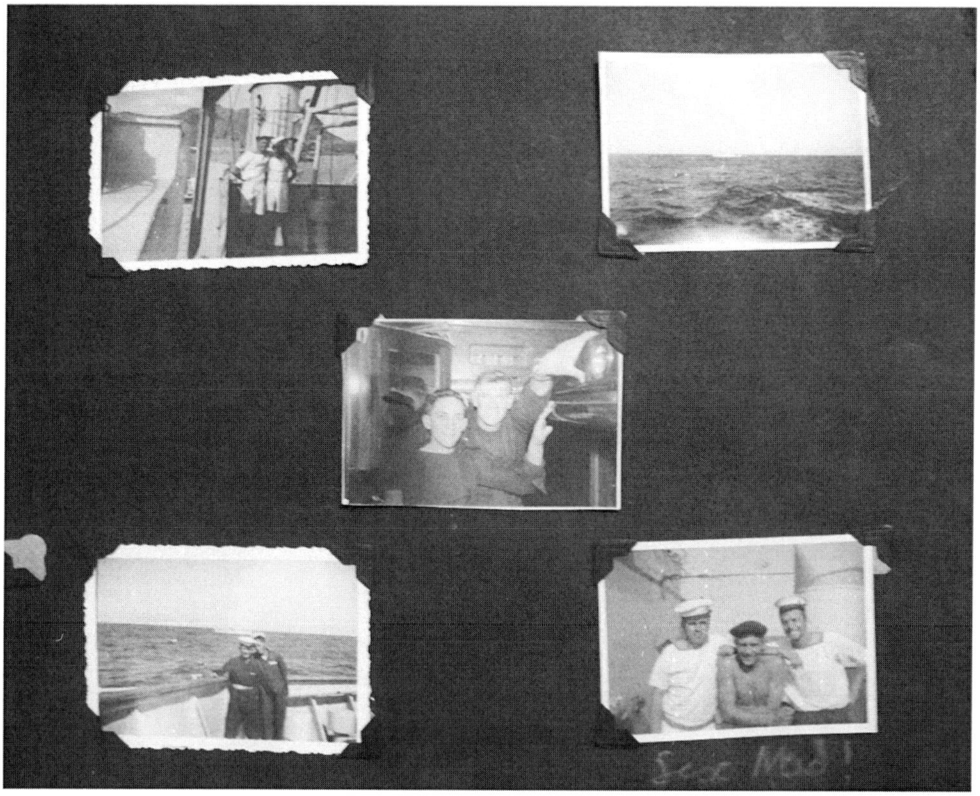

Figure 7.3 *Sex Mad!*, album page, 11 × 16 in. GALA Queer Archive, Johannesburg, South Africa, the personal photographic album of David, a Sailor (AM2823). Photograph by Danielle Kinsey.

but he don't care so much." Finally, page 19 shows a photograph captioned "David and Scarlet O'Hara," and of "David" beside another sailor. After page 19, all captions cease.

Archivist Anthony Manion, who catalogued the album, suggests that the handwriting on pages seven and eight might be different than that on pages 11 and 14. He thus introduces the idea that someone other than "David" wrote some of the more salacious captions.[27] It is also possible that the captions were written as jokes, perhaps in the maker's time or later to insinuate gay, illegal (in the military) relationships between sailors. This could have ridiculed specific individuals or played upon popular stereotypes. Given the illegality of being "out" in the military in the 1940s and 1950s, the navy presumably would condemn the male cohort the album both documented and potentially created.

In the absence of any evidence, we can speculate. Perhaps "David" gave the album to another man to examine, and they kept one of the photos of him at the "Y" for themselves, and wrote on the underside of the other, which remained in the album. And perhaps "David" wrote a caption on the back of a photo on page 11 to be seen by the other person, as they discussed their physical attractions, as well as each others' sex lives. If this were the case, the album served as a way to have a possibly

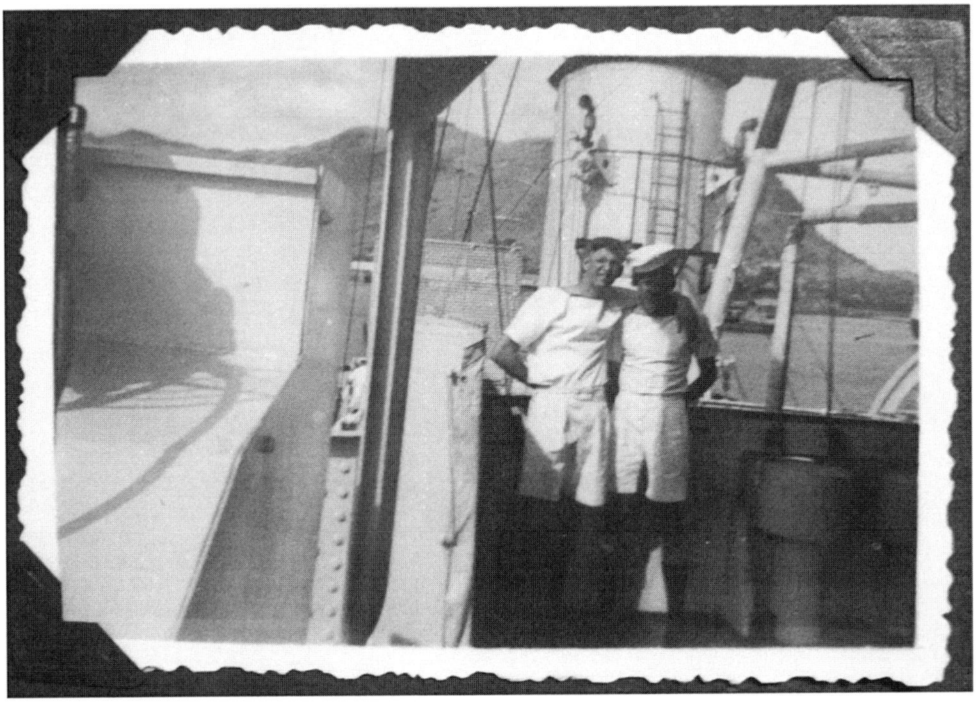

Figure 7.4 *Behave Yourself!*, n.d., black-and-white photograph, 2 × 3 in. GALA Queer Archive, Johannesburg, South Africa, the personal photographic album of David, a Sailor (AM2823). Photograph by Danielle Kinsey.

asynchronous, possibly clandestine, conversation between the two. The idea of someone taking a photo to satisfy their own desires underlines the tactile experience offered by photographic albums, not only for the maker but other interactors. The captions make explicit how the photographs evoked sexualized bodies and sex acts. The experience of leafing through the same pages also drew reader and maker together in physical and imagined ways, creating a sense of not just queer sexuality but queer community.[28] That is only one scenario. "David" could have also removed the images, carried them in his pocket, or given them to someone. Or the photographs could have simply fallen out.

The captions' hiddenness (on the backside of the images), their specificity, and their relative sparseness suggest that they give voice to queer experience and identity of some kind, even if these narratives do not correspond to the people in the photos. The captions were not just about male-male sex, but they also represented seemingly more committed relationships by talking about someone as a "wyfie." This word casts this relationship in heteronormative and binary terms by characterizing one partner as "male" and the other "female," or perhaps makes reference to roles assumed during sex. The irreverence of the captions, as well as their accuracy, would have been for the maker and viewers to determine. The album reveals the potential of the album to make a sub-community by building specific and relatable narratives, as well as by expressing binary genderism in queer and non-queer communities alike, in accord with its social and historical contexts.

Like Liddicoat's narratives, the surface and underside captions in "David's" album tell two different stories. The "in plain sight"/"surface" reading only reveals that the photographs are a working-class white man's personal collection of photos of his youth and time as a sailor. The hidden captions, however, reference queer lust, sex, and, perhaps most importantly, sub-community. Created in a context of the military's persecution of homosexual males, the album itself has a (mostly) hetero-passing "frontstage" and an explicitly queer "backstage," making it both an empowering and closeting experience. The sub-community-building aspect of the album is amplified exponentially by its inclusion in the GALA collection. Whether the captions were written in earnest or satire, they and the repetitive visuals of sailors happily in close contact are almost utopic, recalling Epprecht's characterization of mid-century military service as liberating for queer white soldiers. Each maker's enjoyment of a queer- and class-inclusive environment that was not welcoming to other races and non-binary genders, is palpable in both Liddicoat's and David's albums. Together they compel a historical consciousness about South Africa's queer white community.

The Oral History Project: Michel/le Bruno Photograph Album[29]

The format of a 1972 photographic album kept by white South African hairdresser Michel/le Bruno is also typical of commercial albums widely available at the time of its making. It is a mass-produced, vinyl-covered book of nine spiral-bound adhesive sheets protected by plastic covers. It contains about 74 items, the majority (93%) of which are photographs in either color or black-and-white, ranging in size from 2.5 by 2.5 inches to 5 by 7 inches. Bruno is in about 45% of the photographs. These images document eight parties Bruno attended, including "Xmas '72 at Mother's," a braai (barbeque) with friends, and large costume galas. Unlike Liddicoat's and "David's" albums, Bruno's has no hidden captions. Five full-page captions label the event but provide no further commentary. He wrote all captions in black marker and organized the photographs according to event. Yet, he did not present the events in chronological order, although presumably, they all happened in the same year. Bruno worked with GALA staff prior to his death in 2016 and chose items from his personal archive to become part of the collection. Many loose photos and some loose album pages by Bruno are inventoried by GALA, but this is the only complete album he chose to make public.

Made a generation after Liddicoat's and "David's," Bruno's album is so different that, in the context of an archive, it instantly compels a consciousness about the scale of change that occurred in South Africa between the 1940s and 1970s. Politically, this involved the continuous reinvention of the apartheid state alongside movements that fought against it. Socially and culturally, it was what might be characterized as the beginning of South Africa's sexual revolution. In that regard, the album purposely documents Bruno's life as an openly gay, gender-queer person who was integrated into the liberal white community of Johannesburg. Bruno was famous for his parties, and the album shows that they were just as much a part of his work and the way he carved out a space for himself in Johannesburg society as his hairdressing career.

In 1997, South African author and journalist Mark Gevisser interviewed Bruno about his life. GALA's archives hold the transcript. It offers insight into the role photographs played in Bruno's career as a public queer person. Among the events he recounted was his formative experience of being arrested and publicly shamed following the Forest Town Raid on January 22, 1966, in which police raided a private suburban garden party. Police claimed that they were cracking down on illegal drug use but also arrested men for "masquerading as women."[30] Bruno and eight others were arrested. This event galvanized the gay rights movement.

Bruno described that he arrived at the party and:

> I had my back to the rest of the room when out of the corner of my eye I saw flash bulbs going and I thought well someone's taking photographs. I didn't realize it was a plain-clothes policeman which had infiltrated the party. .... And the next thing someone tapped me on the shoulder. It was actually very amusing and [he] said excuse me lady, you're under arrest for masquerading. But he did say lady.[31]

Bruno and the other men were taken to police headquarters and photographed again. They were forced to strip down to their underwear. Bruno stood before the officers in a black, padded bra, a red-suspender belt holding up his stockings, and in men's underwear. He recalled: "If you were ever caught wearing women's underpants, the charge would be more. It was somehow better to be caught wearing men's underpants; we knew this."[32]

After admitting to his crime, Bruno paid the fine and was released. The next day his name was announced over the radio in connection with the raid. Bruno told Gevisser that this was "the worst moment of his life."[33] The police released their material to the newspapers soon thereafter, "outing" the arrestees. As Bruno recalled,

> On that first Sunday, *Die Beeld* [the image] came out with all our photographs but they put this thing over our eyes. And they did give me a very nice write-up I must say under my photograph. I was wearing an outfit any woman would give her eye teeth for.[34]

Bruno's album sits in contrast to photographs of him in police and newspaper archives. It shows how he took a tool of state oppression – party photography – and made it a touchstone of personal identity, political resistance, and queer acceptance and visibility. The first page introduces the subject matter of the album: parties. It contains two invitations Bruno and friend Peter Brückl printed for their costume party, "Bal Orientale: An Exotic Night in Persepolis," on June 4, 1972, in Craighall. Newspaper clippings on page two show Bruno and others at the gala, and record that it was "Johannesburg's 'Party of the Year,'" where "false eyelashes fluttered amid the glitter and a 'deevine' time was had by all."[35] A dozen color photos follow, showing Bruno among partygoers, and wearing a curly wig, elaborate jewelry, and a decadent robe. Page six displays another gala invitation, this one for a "Harem Whetting" in Hillbrow, on December 11. Guests were encouraged to "Come in Your Eastern Splendour."[36] Sixteen color photographs attest to the same lively atmosphere as the previous party, and Bruno is shown hobnobbing with the liberal social scene. The overt sexuality of orientalist galas created an alibi for Bruno's and others' brand of sexual fluidity in the event of a police crackdown (which were rarer after 1969). He was savvy about inhabiting roles and spaces that allowed him to be himself, in plain sight. As Bruno told Gevisser when asked if he ever felt discriminated against:

> I actually fought to do the job, start that work as a hairdresser. So I didn't feel as discriminated against as others who were working, who are people I knew in the bank who really had to watch their guard you know and not be overtly gay. I could let my hair down. ... I was lucky to do hairdressing and sort of be myself also at the same time I knew not to go over the top.[37]

Bruno carved out places where he would be accepted and managed his outward appearance at work.

Without the veneer of exoticism that the parties enabled, as the album attests, Bruno still managed to be himself in liberal company, such as at "Claudie's Birthday Nov 10th 1972." Photographs show him wearing a feminine shirt with his naturally long hair and women's jewelry. This is not Bruno dressed for a drag show but in his everyday style. At the "Opening of PLAKA Restaurant Nov 72," photographs show Bruno in a suit and tie, but with feminine styling and tailoring. More caption-less black-and-white photographs show him in flowing silks, perhaps at another costume party.

The thirteenth page initiates another sequence of party photographs. This series shows a more subdued version of Bruno: "Xmas '72 at Mother's." For the family party, he dresses conservatively in a white t-shirt with half-length short sleeves and jeans. Gevisser asked Bruno if his mother knew about his sexual orientation and he responded:

> My mother knew all about it obviously from my sisters. But we never, it was unspoken between my mother and I. It was only in later years before she died that she actually came out with that she knew all the time ... She was very cool about it.[38]

Other family pictures in the album show Bruno holding a baby and being a loving and accepted member of his family, while wearing subdued – but not closeted, per se – clothing.

The next sequence is "Brian's party," and a series of black-and-white snapshots of another costume party (Fig. 7.5). This series is typical of the party photographs in the album. A group poses for the camera; a man kisses Bruno's cheek, hamming it up for the camera; Bruno is caught slightly unaware and dressed in his gender-queer "party" way, circulating among the party guests; and everyone is having a good time. Was he still concerned about raids? The pictures create an impression that Bruno was at ease, enjoying himself in the crowd as the crowd enjoyed him.

The last gathering presented in the album is "Braai at Dudley's," an outdoor cookout and pool party with about six or seven other white men, most of them shirtless and in bathing suits. In one photograph, Bruno leans against a tree. The photograph was shot from ground level, and Bruno's pose mimics sexualized bathing-suit photographs of women in provocative magazines. He wears what appears to be women's bikini bottoms and no top. It is the epitome of gender-bending in the album.

The album as a whole attests to Bruno's extensive social networks and how he was embraced by Johannesburg's "it" crowd, as well as by his family and friends. The album's celebration of queer-inclusive community presumably affirmed Bruno's self-acceptance and encouraged self-acceptance for others with whom he may have shown the album. It could also say as much to police and other state authorities, who could have seized the album in the event of another crackdown. As a portable, yet substantial, carrier of evidence as well as personal narrative, a party album such as Bruno's could have been taken to a police station and used to testify about the

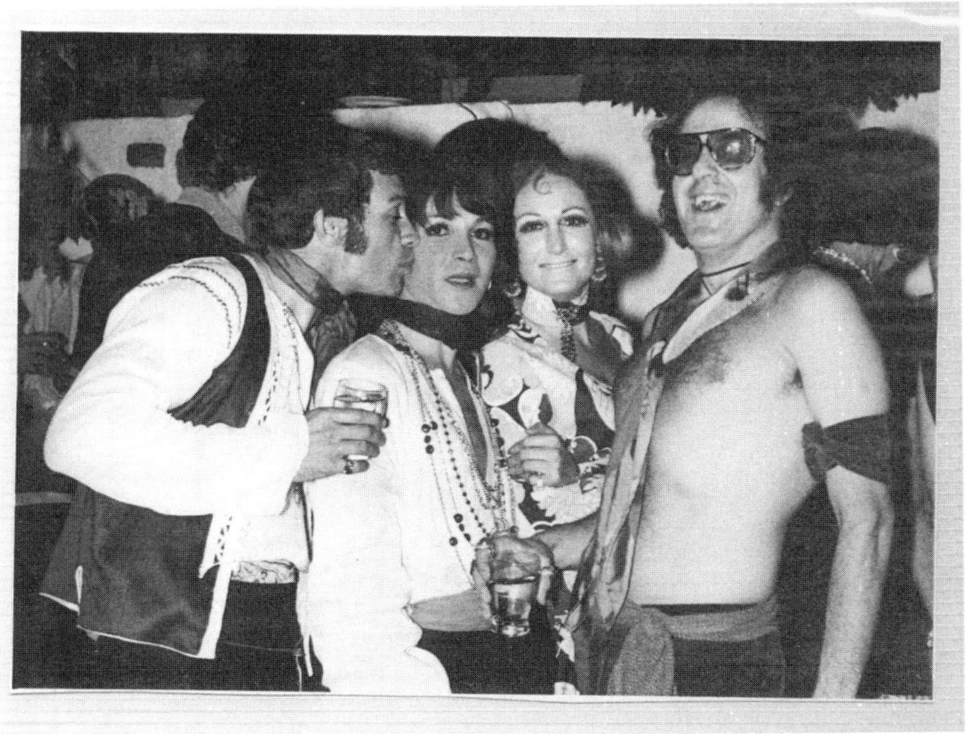

Figure 7.5 *Bruno at a Party,* 1972, black-and-white photograph, 4 × 6 in. GALA Queer Archive, Johannesburg, South Africa, The Oral History Project Collection (AM2709), GALA Queer Archive, Johannesburg, South Africa. Photograph by Danielle Kinsey.

support he found in the white middle-class community. It bore witness to how he lived his life in plain sight as a gender-queer socialite – with no hidden captions necessary. In that way, it perhaps functioned as an insurance policy, detailing social networks that could have been called into action if Bruno were ever arrested again. The public-facing quality of the album, important from its inception and content, is amplified exponentially by its presence in GALA's collection and accessibility to researchers. The album functions not only as part of Bruno's personal legacy but also as part of LGBTIQ activist history in South Africa. In this manner, it backs up the headline for Gevisser's obituary of Bruno in the *Mail & Guardian*: "Gay Rights Pioneer Who Blazed a Trail in Jozi Leaves SA Richer."[39]

Historicizing Queer Visibility

Together, Liddicoat's, "David's," and Bruno's albums show queer visibility and conformity in mid-twentieth-century South Africa. "David's" album underpins how evasive sources are for writing queer history. Liddicoat's liberatory legacy is tempered by her perception that her security as an "out" lesbian professional was predicated upon her furthering of the apartheid state. The LGBTIQ archive's mandate compels a much more textured analysis of it than would be the case in a different framework, such as one dedicated to women, war, or the history of apartheid. Bruno's album is the stuff of progressive national history in the context of GALA, with the backdrop of the rise of the gay-rights movement underwriting its intake into the collection. Taken together, these amateur photographic albums showcase an interplay between frontstage and backstage that perhaps best delivers a sense of negotiation between being "in" and "out" of the "closet" during apartheid South Africa.

Acknowledgments

This research was supported by Social Sciences and Humanities Research Council of Canada Insight Grant 435-2013-1324. I would like to thank Linda Chernis for her help, and James Warren and Erica Fraser for their comments.

Notes

1 As of June 14, 2021, GALA used "LGBTIQ" for the identities that they were representing. I use their designation here because it is specific to these albums' South African context. For a discussion of frontstage/backstage sociological dramaturgy, see: Erving Goffman, *The Presentation of Self in Everyday Life* (New York: Doubleday, 1959).

2 Patrizia Di Bello, "Mrs. Birkbeck's Album: The Hand-Written and the Printed in Early Nineteenth-Century Feminine Culture," *Interdisciplinary Studies in the Long Nineteenth Century*, Vol. 19, No. 1 (October 1, 2005): 23.

3 In everyday life, Bruno was flexible with his own gender pronouns, but in an interview with journalist Mark Gevisser, he said that he preferred male pronouns in print. I will continue that convention here. See: Mark Gevisser, "Gay Rights Pioneer Who Blazed a Trail in Jozi Leaves SA Richer," *Mail & Guardian* (May 19, 2016). Accessed April 5, 2021: https://mg.co.za/article/2016-05-19-gay-rights-pioneer-who-blazed-a-trail-in-jozi-leaves-sa-richer/.

4 Renée Liddicoat, "The Renée Liddicoat Album," n.d. AM 2800, GALA.

5 "Newsletter of the Gay and Lesbian Archives of South Africa (GALA)," Issue 3 (Johannesburg: GALA, 2002), 3. Accessed April 8, 2021: https://gala.co.za/wp-content/uploads/2019/03/Newsletter3.pdf.

6 Renée Liddicoat, "Homosexuality: Results of a Survey as Related to Various Theories," PhD Diss., University of Witwatersrand, Johannesburg, 1956.; Renée Liddicoat, "Homosexuality," *British Medical Journal,* Vol. 2, No. 5053 (November 9, 1957): 1110–1111.; Renée Liddicoat, "A Study of Non-Institutionalized Homosexuals," *Journal of the National Institution for Personnel Research,* 8 (1961): 217–249.; Renée Liddicoat, "Homosexuality," *South African Journal of Science,* Vol. 58 (1962): 145–149.

7 Marc Epprecht, *Hungochani: The History of a Dissident Sexuality in Southern Africa*, 2nd ed. (Montreal: McGill-Queen's University Press, 2013), xviii–xix.

8 Anthony Manion and Carol Preston, "Inventory – AM 2800 Renée Liddicoat Collection Ca. 1942–1962," 2000 and 2014, GALA.

9 Sathasivian Cooper, "A Synopsis of South African Psychology from Apartheid to Democracy," *American Psychologist* 69, No. 8 (2014): 839.; Wahbie Long, "Rethinking 'Relevance': South African Psychology in Context," *History of Psychology* 16, No. 1 (February 2013): 20.; Norman Duncan and Brett Bowman, "Liberating South African Psychology: The Legacy of Racism and the Pursuit of Representative Knowledge Production," in *Psychology of Liberation*, Christopher C. Sonn and Maritza Montero, eds. (New York: Springer, 2009), 101.

10 Renée Liddicoat, "The Effects of Maternal Antenatal Decompression Treatment on Infant Mental Development," *South African Medical Journal*, Vol. 42, No. 9 (1968): 203–211.; Renée Liddicoat, "Letter to the Editor," *Developmental Medicine & Child Neurology*, Vol. 11, No. 6 (1969): 821–822.

11 Liddicoat, "The Renée Liddicoat Album," 9, 10, 41.
12 Liddicoat, "The Renée Liddicoat Album," 9.
13 Liddicoat, "Homosexuality: Results of a Survey as Related to Various Theories," 49, 56, 62, 102–103, 219. Quotation is from: 228.
14 Liddicoat, "The Renée Liddicoat Album," 18, 35.
15 Liddicoat, "The Renée Liddicoat Album," 48. In 1869, explorer Henry Morton Stanley was dispatched by the *New York Herald* to find missionary David Livingstone, who was presumed missing in Africa. Stanley's reports of his travels and his "discovery" of Livingstone were news sensations. Henry Morton Stanley, *Stanley's Dispatches to the New York Herald, 1871–1872, 1874–1877*, Norman R. Bennett, ed. (Boston: Boston University Press, 1970). See Clare Pettitt, *Dr Livingstone, I Presume? Missionaries, Journalists, Explorers and Empire*, (Cambridge: Harvard University Press, 2007), 13–14.
16 Liddicoat, "The Renée Liddicoat Album," 1, 2, 20, 21, 41.
17 Manion and Preston, "Inventory," 9.; Liddicoat, "The Renée Liddicoat Album," 41.
18 The National Archives [United Kingdom], 1939 Register. Reference: RG 101/6687D. Kew, London, England.
19 Liddicoat, "Homosexuality: Results of a Survey as Related to Various Theories," 228.
20 Liddicoat, "Homosexuality," 228.
21 Liddicoat, "Homosexuality," 228–229.
22 Liddicoat, "Homosexuality," 229.
23 Her academic cleverness can to some extent be attributed to her middle-classness rather than to a measurably high IQ.
24 Liddicoat, "The Renée Liddicoat Album," 48, 49.
25 Epprecht, *Hungochani*, xviii.
26 David, "Personal Photograph Album of David, A Sailor; ca. the 1950s," n.d. AM 2823, GALA.
27 Manion, "Inventory – AM 2823 Personal Photograph Album of David, a Sailor," February 2001, GALA.
28 Patrizia Di Bello, *Women's Albums and Photography in Victorian England: Ladies, Mothers and Flirts* (Aldershot: Ashgate, 2007), 3. Di Bello discusses tactility and women's experiences in making and viewing albums to affirm identity. I am applying her ideas here to show a different kind of identity and community-building.
29 Michele Bruno, "Photo Album," 1972, AM 2709: The Oral History Project: A.1.7, GALA.
30 Gevisser, *Lost and Found in Johannesburg, A Memoir* (New York: Farrar, Straus and Giroux, 2014), 156.
31 Michele Bruno, Interview by Mark Gevisser (September 3, 1997). AM 2709: The Oral History Project - Mark Gevisser, ca. 1930s to 2000: A.1.7 Transcript, GALA.
32 Gevisser, *Lost and Found in Johannesburg, a Memoir*, 157.
33 Gevisser, *Lost and Found in Johannesburg, A Memoir*, 157.
34 Bruno, "Interview," 8.
35 Bruno, "Photo Album," 2.
36 Bruno, "Photo Album," 6.
37 Bruno, "Interview," 13–14.
38 Bruno, "Interview," 11.
39 Gevisser, "Gay Rights Pioneer Who Blazed a Trail in Jozi Leaves SA Richer."

Bibliography

Bruno, Michele. Interview by Mark Gevisser, September 3, 1997. AM 2709: The Oral History Project – Mark Gevisser, ca. 1930s to 2000: A.1.7 Transcript. GALA.

Bruno, Michele. "Photo Album," 1972. AM 2709: The Oral History Project: A.1.7. GALA.

Cooper, Sathasivian. "A Synopsis of South African Psychology from Apartheid to Democracy." *American Psychologist*, Vol. 69, No. 8 (2014): 837–847.

"David." "Personal Photograph Album of David, a Sailor; ca. the 1950s," n.d. AM 2823. GALA.

Di Bello, Patrizia. "Mrs Birkbeck's Album: The Hand-Written and the Printed in Early Nineteenth-Century Feminine Culture." *19: Interdisciplinary Studies in the Long Nineteenth Century*, No. 1 (October 1, 2005). doi: 10.16995/ntn.435

Di Bello, Patrizia. *Women's Albums and Photography in Victorian England: Ladies, Mothers and Flirts*. Aldershot: Ashgate, 2007.

Duncan, Norman, and Brett Bowman. "Liberating South African Psychology: The Legacy of Racism and the Pursuit of Representative Knowledge Production," in *Psychology of Liberation*, Christopher C. Sonn and Maritza Montero, eds. (New York: Springer, 2009), 93–113.

Epprecht, Marc. *Hungochani: The History of a Dissident Sexuality in Southern Africa*. 2nd ed. Montreal: McGill-Queen's University Press, 2013.

Gevisser, Mark. "Gay Rights Pioneer Who Blazed a Trail in Jozi Leaves SA Richer." *Mail & Guardian*, May 19, 2016. Accessed July 5, 2021: https://mg.co.za/article/2016-05-19-gay-rights-pioneer-who-blazed-a-trail-in-jozi-leaves-sa-richer/

Gevisser, Mark. *Lost and Found in Johannesburg, a Memoir*. New York: Farrar, Straus and Giroux, 2014.

Goffman, Erving. *The Presentation of Self in Everyday Life*. New York: Doubleday, 1959.

Liddicoat, R. "Homosexuality." *British Medical Journal*, Vol. 2, No. 5053 (November 9, 1957): 1110–1111.

Liddicoat, R. "Letter to the Editor." *Developmental Medicine & Child Neurology*, Vol. 11, No. 6 (1969): 821–822.

Liddicoat, R. "The Effects of Maternal Antenatal Decompression Treatment on Infant Mental Development." *South African Medical Journal*, Vol. 42, No. 9 (1968): 203–211.

Liddicoat, R. "A Study of Non-Institutionalized Homosexuals." *Journal of the National Institution for Personnel Research*, Vol. 8 (1961): 217–249.

Liddicoat, R. "Homosexuality." *South African Journal of Science*, Vol. 58 (1962): 145–149.

Liddicoat, R. "Homosexuality: Results of a Survey as Related to Various Theories." PhD, University of Witwatersrand, 1956.

Liddicoat, R. "The Renée Liddicoat Album," n.d. AM 2800. GALA.

Long, Wahbie. "Rethinking 'Relevance': South African Psychology in Context." *History of Psychology*, Vol. 16, No. 1 (February 2013): 19–35.

Manion, Anthony. "Inventory - AM 2823 Personal Photograph Album of David, a Sailor," February 2001. GALA.

Manion, Anthony and Carol Preston. "Inventory - AM 2800 Renee Liddicoat Collection ca. 1942 to 1962," 2000 and 2014. GALA.

"Newsletter of the Gay and Lesbian Archives of South Africa (GALA) Issue 3." Johannesburg: GALA, 2002. https://gala.co.za/wp-content/uploads/2019/03/Newsletter3.pdf

Pettitt, Clare. *Dr. Livingstone I Presume? Missionaries, Journalists, Explorers, and Empire*. Cambridge: Harvard University Press, 2007.

Part III

Retelling National and International Histories

8 "We Carry the Weight of a 150-Year Legacy": Sharing the Memories of a Civil War Photograph Album

Michèle Gates Moresi

The most photographed man of the nineteenth century, Frederick Douglass, espoused the strength of photography. For Douglass, the photographic portrait was an empowering, effective tool in the endeavor to shape one's identity and influence how one would be seen, understood, and remembered. In the midst of the U.S. Civil War, Douglass pointed to photography as essential in the efforts to challenge racism in society.[1] Photographs were shared as mementoes among lovers, beloved family, cherished friends, and admiring acquaintances. As part of the historical record, Americans can now view portraits like the ones in the Civil War-era microphotography album owned by Captain William A. Prickitt, and read them as messages from the past. Each portrait conveys what the sitter wanted the viewer to see: a confident human being.[2] Such portraits speak to us more than a century and a half later and prompt us to imagine the inter-relations of Black and white servicemen beyond the dichotomies of superior and subordinate, or liberator and liberated. Portraits of Union soldiers bring the epic events of the Civil War to human scale.

Captain Prickitt's photograph album of African American soldiers allows us to consider the meaning of not only the service of an officer and his troops in the Civil War but also the meaning of its legacy for Prickitt's heirs and even for a broader national memory. Captain Prickitt led the 25th Regiment, Company G, of the United States Colored Troops (USCT) in the Union Army. Until 2014, his descendants still held in their possession the album he had kept – a miniature album containing mostly micro-tintypes and a few albumen prints of African American soldiers. Family members recall that their great-grandfather attributed his survival during the war to his men who attended to him when he battled a deadly illness. Measuring only about 2 inches by 1 inch, and less than 1-inch thick, the album contains photographs of 17 African American soldiers who served under Captain Prickitt (Fig. 8.1). (There are 18 photographs, but one man is depicted twice.) All but one of the men is identified by name. Each portrait is nestled in a page with an oval-shaped opening showing the sitter from the shoulders up in his uniform with hand-tinting on brass buttons and epaulets. Each soldier looks directly at the camera, unsmiling, as was the convention at the time.

Remarkably, a white family's exploration into its own genealogical history led to the addition of this album to the collection at the Smithsonian National Museum of African American History and Culture. The national museum, with a mission to tell the American story through the lens of African American experiences, aims to humanize the stories of ordinary people whose lives are shaped by, and who take part in shaping, major events in American history. To do so, museum curators conduct the important, and often delicate, work of transitioning private histories into compelling case studies relevant to broader,

DOI: 10.4324/9781003157427-12

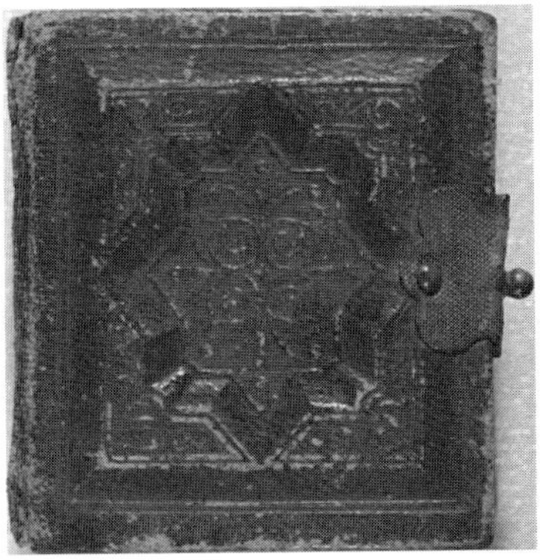

Figure 8.1 *Album Cover*, 1864–1865, 2 × 1 13/16 × 7/8 in., photographic album of William A. Prickitt, 25th Regiment of the United States Colored Troops soldiers. Collection of the Smithsonian National Museum of African American History and Culture, Gift of Aneita Gates, on behalf of her son, Kameron Gates, and all the descendants of Captain William A. Prickitt.

national narratives. Captain Prickitt's album encompasses the stories of a white officer who led Black soldiers in the Civil War to preserve the Union and end American slavery. Each portrait infuses a monumental historic event with humanity.

Service in the Union Army

The outbreak of the Civil War demanded that civilians step up and choose to serve, to take a side and defend the Union, or support secession of the Southern states. Most white Northerners supported efforts to preserve the Union and thousands of men, Black and white, stepped up to enlist. Initially, the Federal Government refused the service of African American volunteers. Although the war was fostered over fundamental disagreement about "free" versus "paid" labor, it was not initiated as a war to free enslaved people. President Abraham Lincoln and leaders of the Union Army were reluctant to enlist the aid of African American soldiers. Federal laws prevented Black people from serving in state militias, and repeated petitions by Black people to serve were refuted on the grounds that it was not legal. It was feared that organized Black militias would incite mob violence.[3] Public opinion was shaped by an enormous prejudice against African Americans and arming Black men was simply not palatable.[4]

Although not authorized to enlist to serve officially as soldiers, African Americans provided services to the Union Army in other capacities such as servants and laborers.[5] However, there was a general disbelief that Black soldiers could be effective on the battlefield. Indeed, racism played a significant role in the delay to enlist African American soldiers.[6] With the onset of the reality of the war – that it would not be quickly and neatly won – the tide shifted. The eventual decision to authorize the enlistment of African American soldiers in 1863 was for strategic military reasons.[7]

William Prickitt had volunteered to serve in the Union Army in August 1862, and enlisted at the age of 23 in the 14th New Jersey Volunteer Infantry, Company G, as a Corporal.[8] Identified as a teacher when he enlisted, Prickitt's education and profession was typical of that of white officers who commanded the USCT.[9] Given the sense of trepidation to enlist African American soldiers, the Army sought to develop a system to ensure that the officers leading Black troops were not only qualified to manage and adequately control the troops, but that the officers held a sincere commitment to train and lead these men. The Army had set up a special Board of Examination for Officers with a review process to screen for officers to lead the USCT. The Board tested each candidate with a "fair but rigorous examination as to physical, mental, and moral fitness to command."[10] Ironically there was a genuine effort by the Army to seek success for the USCT in the challenging atmosphere of racist attitudes and a deep-seated belief in African Americans' innate inferiority. Although the military chose to deny opportunities to African American men to serve as officers based on their merit, the screening process established to appoint white officers of the USCT often resulted in highly qualified and dedicated leaders.[11]

We know from the family story of Captain Prickitt, and from the evidence of the photograph album, that he felt a close connection to the men in his Company. This former teacher is described as an intelligent, accomplished, and compassionate man.[12] A report from the field indicates he sought to ensure his men had opportunities to learn to read. In describing the daily life of USCT soldiers stationed in Florida, Sergeant Milton Harris stated, "[The officers] take a deep interest in the boys of the 25th, and endeavor to make everything as pleasant and comfortable as possible." In particular, Harris calls out Captain Prickitt for returning to the camp with numerous books for his men: "He has been furnishing them with books so that a great many of them could learn to read and write." Sergeant Harris goes on to describe how other captains then sought books for their men, and he mentions plans to start a regular school.[13] The role and status of African American men after the war was a matter of concern and debate for many. Perhaps Captain Prickitt and the white officers felt compelled to provide the men with basic tools to begin a journey toward citizenship. These officers' efforts suggest that they recognized their soldiers as men with potential.

African American Union Soldiers

For African Americans, the decision to enlist was not a simple choice, given how resistant the government had been to use them as soldiers in the first place. The prospect of engaging in a long, protracted war with intense hardships was no less appealing for Black soldiers than it was for whites. Black enlisted men were paid at a lower rate than their white counterparts. An added deterrent was the fear of capture in battle. In May of 1863, the Confederate Congress had authorized that any captured officers of the USCT would be put to death, and captured soldiers would be executed or enslaved. The fact that African Americans would not be commissioned as officers to lead troops was particularly galling. Douglass stated that

> It is a little cruel to say to the black soldier that he shall not rise to be an officer of the United States whatever may be his merits; but I see that though coupled with this disadvantage colored men should hail the opportunity of getting on the United States uniform as a very great advantage.[14]

Nonetheless, the government solicited the help of several Black leaders to actively recruit African American soldiers, including Douglass, Henry Highland Garnet, and Martin Delany, who traveled the North, as far as Canada, to urge Black men to enlist.[15] Many heeded the call: the first African American regiment raised was the renowned 54th of Massachusetts. Lewis Douglass, a son of Frederick Douglass, was one of those early volunteers. He wrote to his "girl in waiting," Amelia Loguen, about his devotion to serve in the Union Army to end slavery, expressing his willingness to sacrifice his life. With the letter, he sent her his photograph showing him in his blue uniform.[16] Although they were finally allowed to enlist voluntarily, they were also drafted, like white men, and compelled to serve.[17] Ultimately nearly 200,000 African Americans served in the Union Army and Navy.

The 25th Regiment of the USCT was trained in Pennsylvania, then posted at Fort Pickens and Fort Redoubt in Florida. Although the 25th Regiment did not engage in battles, the role of holding fortifications in Florida was crucial to sustaining the upper hand for the Union. The safeguarding of coastal ports and inlets prevented Confederate blockades and required vigilant attention.[18] Federal troops secured the forts in Florida early in the war, and the USCT continued to guard them. Reports by soldiers published in newspapers described daily life as fairly quiet, although the occasional scouting expedition could result in a skirmish and even the capture of rebels and "contraband."[19] Enslaved persons who crossed Union Army lines were classified as property by the Army, and since enemy property was not returned, those who escaped slavery were considered contraband of war.

We can only guess why only 17 men appear in Prickitt's album from among 80 or so in his Company. Presumably, these are the men he felt some affinity and affection toward, some of whom may have cared for him during his illness. Two of the men pictured are documented to have been enslaved when they enlisted. George H. Watson and George H. Mitchell (Fig. 8.2) lived in Delaware, a slaveholding state that had not seceded and thus was not subject to the Emancipation Proclamation effective January 1, 1863. Remaining faithful to the concepts of ownership, the Federal Government compensated a slave owner up to $300 dollars for the enlistment of his enslaved person into military service with an accompanying deed of manumission and release.[20] Caleb Layton of Sussex County, Delaware, provided the necessary manumission and proof of title attesting his ownership of Mitchell. Layton enlisted Mitchell in the USCT, aged 19 years, on January 28, 1864, in Wilmington, Delaware, and received $300. With this arrangement, Mitchell would be free when he completed his military service and if he survived the war. Gazing determinedly into the camera, holding his musket upright, one may read Mitchell's expression as hopeful. He did survive the war. Census records document that Mitchell was illiterate and lived in southern Delaware in 1870 with his parents and seven brothers and sisters. Thus far, no record of his death has been discovered.[21]

Unlike the other soldiers portrayed in the album who all come from the mid-Atlantic states, Private John W. Walls hailed from Mississippi (Fig. 8.3). He enlisted in the USCT in Waterford, Pennsylvania, at the age of 19, and mustered out with his Company on December 6, 1865. It is unclear if Walls had previously been enslaved, but it is possible he had self-emancipated and had made his way to Pennsylvania. Walls wears a cap with insignia and holds his sword in his left hand. Walls' expression reads a combination of apprehension and resolve. Perhaps a fear of violence he may encounter in warfare, but an assurance of freedom fills him with courage. His

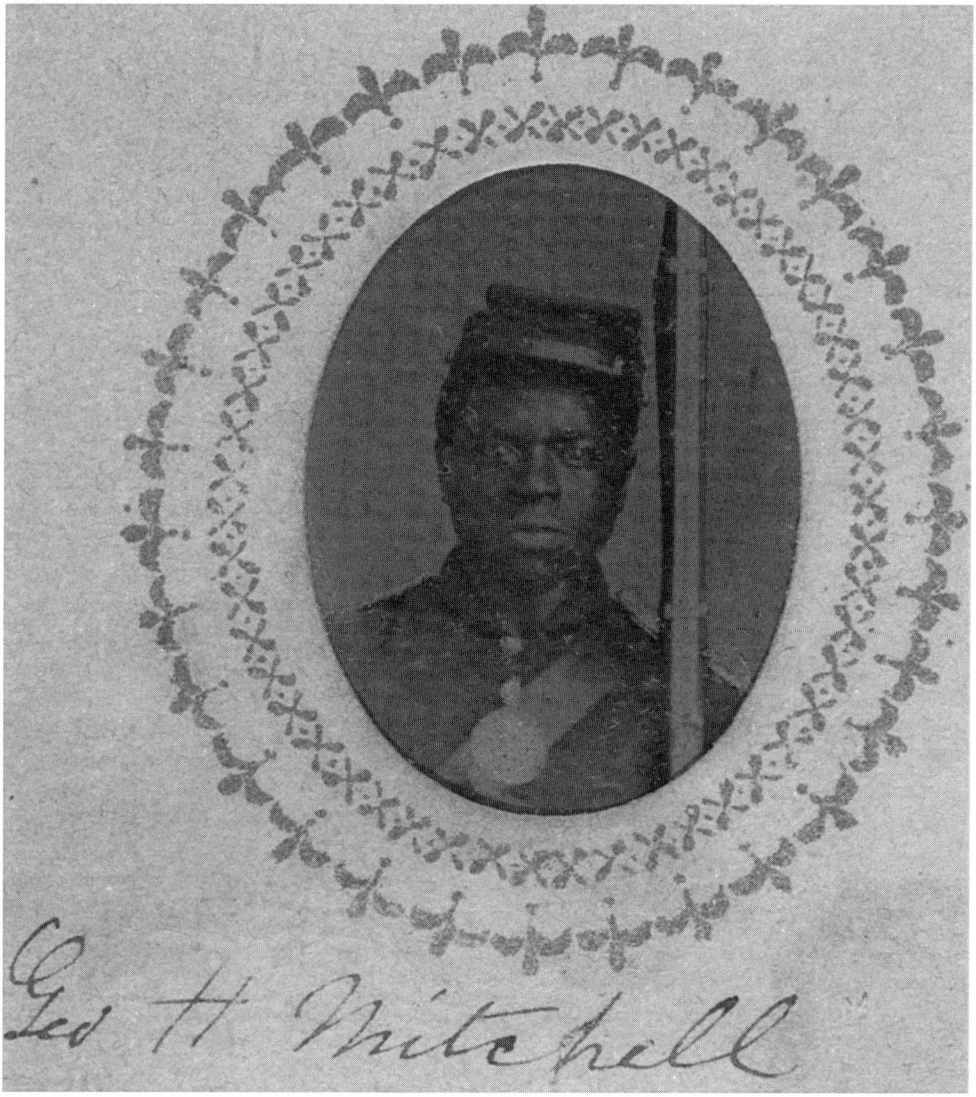

Figure 8.2 George H. Mitchell, 1864–1865, tintype, 1 3/16 × 7/8 in., photographic album of William A. Prickitt. Collection of the Smithsonian National Museum of African American History and Culture, Gift of Aneita Gates, on behalf of her son, Kameron Gates, and all the descendants of Captain William A. Prickitt.

occupation is listed as "farmer," which was common for many enlisted men as well as for those among Captain Prickitt's album. Military and census records indicate Walls returned to Mississippi, eventually moved to Tennessee, and had filed a Civil War pension application in January of 1891. Walls died on July 20, 1898, and his young widow received a pension.[22]

The soldiers pictured within the miniature album range in age from 15 to 50 years old. The eldest soldier is Private William H. Morris, who mustered in on February 1,

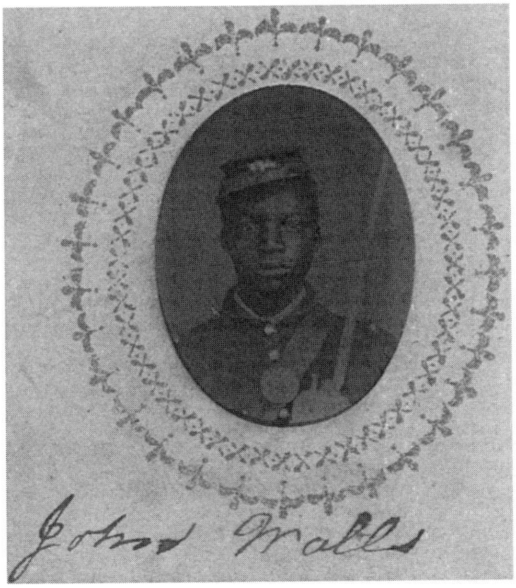

Figure 8.3 *John Walls*, 1864–1865, tintype, 1 3/16 × 7/8 in., photographic album of William A. Prickitt. Collection of the Smithsonian National Museum of African American History and Culture, Gift of Aneita Gates, on behalf of her son, Kameron Gates, and all the descendants of Captain William A. Prickitt.

1864, in Philadelphia (Fig. 8.4). Morris wears his cap slightly askew on his head, a careworn face etched with lines of a life of hard work and challenges. Yet his gaze conveys a sense of determination and even pride of a man who has survived and now wears a uniform with dignity. According to census records, Morris was a free man working as a farm laborer in Gloucester Township, New Jersey. The military records suggest Morris suffered an injury during his service in the USCT and filed for a pension in October of 1866. Census records identify his wife, Rebecca F. Chambers, and two of his three children, Isaac H. and Joseph B. Morris. Morris died on October 26, 1894.[23]

The occupations of the men at the time of their enlistment included farmers, farm laborers, laborers, a porter, and a waiter. One soldier's occupation is not identified in the record. Like many of the men who trained at Camp William Penn, the first Federal recruiting and training center for the USCT, many of the men came from Union states, and one man in the album had been born in the Deep South. Of the documentation located, more than half of them applied for a Civil War pension. While most of these stories are no longer remembered, and we can only piece together fragments of their lives, each troop member was an individual with a unique life history. Captain Prickitt's album is evidence of those lives and stories, and the start of recovering these men's histories.

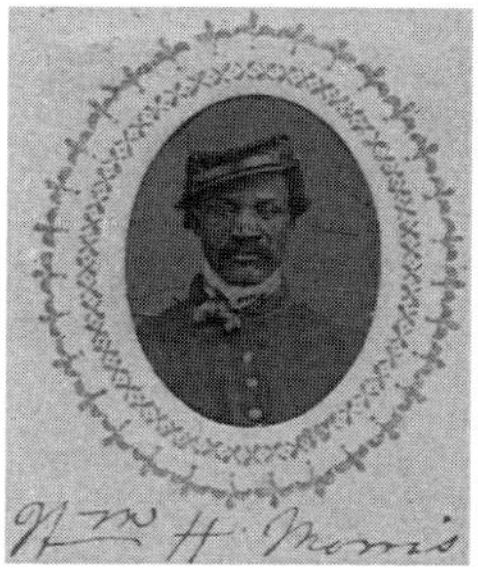

Figure 8.4 *William H. Morris*, 1864–1865, tintype, 1 3/16 × 7/8 in., photographic album of William A. Prickitt. Collection of the Smithsonian National Museum of African American History and Culture, Gift of Aneita Gates, on behalf of her son, Kameron Gates, and all the descendants of Captain William A. Prickitt.

From Family Legacy to National Collection

The story of exactly how Captain Prickitt's miniature photograph album of USCT soldiers was put together is not known and may never be discovered. But the narrative of the family's remembrance lives on and, with it, some semblance of the men who served under Captain Prickitt. Each of the soldiers made the choice to sit for a portrait, proudly wearing their uniform and then – perhaps individually, as a group, or requested by Prickitt himself – offering their portrait to their Captain as a memento. More than a century later, this family keepsake would transform into a national one when it was added to the permanent collection of the Smithsonian National Museum of African American History and Culture.

In 2013, three years before its grand opening, the burgeoning new institution was researching and gathering stories of individuals and communities to create exhibitions that would tell momentous stories of the American experience. Well-grounded in scholarship, museum exhibitions present artifacts used by ordinary people to tell such stories on an accessible, human scale. The museum first learned about this album by the offer of artwork created by Shayne Davidson, who had researched the album and was inspired to create illustrations based on the soldiers' photographic portraits. Davidson is an artist and genealogist and was engaged by the family to conduct research, provide a family history, and design a family tree. The family showed her the miniature album, which piqued Davidson's interest. We do not know for certain who created the album. Did Captain Prickitt collect the portraits during the war and bring them home to place in an album, or did a studio produce the album? Did he inscribe the names of the men he had commanded or did a family member assist in his recollections many years later? According to family lore, Captain Prickitt became deathly ill with influenza, and only through the care and attention of his own soldiers was he able to survive.

Davidson conducted diligent research to find the military and pension records in the National Archives for nearly all the men pictured. She was inspired as an artist to create large-format drawings of each soldier. She ultimately presented the color portraits in an art show in Grand Rapids, Michigan, in 2013, and published a brief monograph of her drawings and research.[24] Upon receiving an offer from Davidson to acquire the drawings, the museum declined but inquired about the original photographs, which led to a meeting between the institution, Davidson, and the descendants of Captain Prickitt at the museum's offices in Washington, D.C., in February of 2014. Aneita Gates and Cory Atwood, great-grandchildren of Captain Prickitt, were delighted to share the family story and were pleased the Smithsonian showed such a keen interest. The museum shared information about museum exhibition plans and argued for why the album should be in a museum. Most notably, it pointed to its goals for telling stories about white officers and Black soldiers that would be accessible to an international audience.

Davidson's efforts signaled the family's first steps toward publicly presenting these portraits that had been integral to their private history. The attention and interest revealed at the art competition in 2013 demonstrated the reach the images could have well beyond the family coffee table. In fact, Aneita Gates and Cory Atwood had urged the museum staff to reconsider Davidson's offer of prints of her drawings. However, the museum's collecting initiatives targeted original, authentic objects from the period and continued to press for a donation of the miniature album.

It was a friendly meeting and it ended with the understanding to continue the discussion. By telephone and email, we corresponded further, fielding questions about what would happen to the album, whether the family and subsequent generations would have access to the album, and ways we would present the album's story and make it accessible to the public. In her correspondence, Gates expressed the family's initial trepidation:

> We carry the weight of a 150-year legacy. This was never a trinket, but a valued remembrance of our great grandfather and these men … . We want the story to be shared. If the album ends up in your "attic," with the story untold, then even we, his descendants, will no longer be able to pass down this story (as we hand down the album) to each new generation's custodian. If it just goes into the Smithsonian's "attic," the story dies. And we will have let Capt. Prickitt and these men down.[25]

Clearly, Gates and other family members felt the weight of history and a responsibility to carry their story forward. They sought to remind future generations about their ancestor, and their very existence that was dependent upon his survival. She wrote, "[w]ere it not for one of these men, our branch of the family would have died out in the Civil War and none of us would be here today."[26] It is always a delicate balance with potential donors to reassure them that they can have a connection to their personal materials after donating while also being clear that they are indeed letting it go, and that ownership is transferring to the museum. By asking the family to donate a family treasure, we were asking them to let go of the material evidence connecting their heritage and existence directly to the survival of Captain Prickitt.

We continued to reassure the family that the album would not be "lost" among the heaps of materials in the museum collection. We cited especially online access to the collection database that (for all intents and purposes) would be "eternal" and have a life beyond the exhibition display planned for the album. We also expressed our goals to tell stories that are uniquely American, that are indeed human, and transcending of race.

In this story about a war fought over foundational issues of freedom – freedom to decide what and who is property, freedom to demand of your government rights and equal treatment as professed by the founding fathers – Captain Prickitt's experience presented a story of his personal contribution to the Union cause that was fundamentally dependent upon the Black soldiers he led. Captain Prickitt served because he cared – and he survived because his troops cared. They were all free because they all fought in a war to preserve not only the Union but also the principles of freedom and justice. As Douglass asserted at the time, "We are all liberated by the Proclamation, ... Everybody is liberated. The white man is liberated, the Black man is liberated, the brave men now fighting the battles ... are now liberated."[27]

Gates expressed eloquently the family's decision to relinquish ownership of the album to the National Museum of African American History and Culture:

> I think about my great grandfather, late in life, carefully adding these names below the men's images. Why? What sense of urgency did he feel? And then, the job done, carefully putting the album back into storage.
>
> The album, then, going down to his youngest daughter. And that daughter passing it on to her youngest niece, who passes it on to her daughter. All the while it is carefully stored away. Remembered but safely hidden from sight.
>
> So why, now, does it emerge from its hiding place? Just when your Museum is ready for it? We were oblivious of your new museum's birth. Unaware of our albums interest to anyone outside our family. Yet here it is. Our time as its Caretaker has come to its end. It is time to pass it on into your care.
>
> You are ready. You will take good care of it. It is time.[28]

The family decided their personal history was larger than their own family legacy. They had not made their decision lightly. The family had to grapple with the meaning of the object for their legacy, what it meant to physically hold it and hand it over to the next generation. The miniature album, alongside other family photographs and albums, shaped their understanding and remembrance of their own heritage. For the story that had been passed down through generations was that Captain Prickitt had served in the Union Army, indeed had volunteered to serve, and had survived sickness and an almost certain death only because of the care and attention of his men, African American soldiers of the USCT.

The Union Army was forced to recognize the humanity and potential of Black men out of military necessity, and the war to preserve the Union had transformed into a war of liberation. Ultimately, both were bound up with one another. This was intimately played out in the relationship between a white officer and Black troops; Captain Prickitt recognized the humanity and potential of his men by commanding them with respect and compassion. The men in turn recognized his decency and respected his leadership. Captain Prickitt only survived the ravages of war because the men cared for him, attended to him through his illness and nursed him back to health. The Union was only preserved because of the essential military role played by, and sacrifices made by, African American enlisted men. The descendants of Captain Prickitt only came to be because of the role of those very same Black troops. One hundred and fifty years later, by placing the miniature album in a public repository, the 18 images of soldiers who served in the Union Army would be known to all who care to learn.[29]

Photographic Albums and Memory Making

Recovering memory is an ongoing project pursued through many endeavors at the museum, and photography albums like these are among them. The artifacts and photographs in the collection tell a variety of stories in different ways. Photographs are especially powerful in that they bring both known and unknown characters to life – in the formal portraits we see their faces, demeanor, and the public persona the sitter aimed to present to the world. One of the 18 soldiers in the album is not identified (Fig. 8.5). He wears a cap with insignia and a stiff, white collar pokes out from under his brass-buttoned uniform. He stares intently into the camera, jaws set firmly, and he has a clean-shaven youthful face. While we cannot attribute a name to the soldier, his photograph is nevertheless significant. The names of hundreds of thousands of African Americans who endured slavery and the hardships of racism and discrimination, may not be evident, but many of their images are not lost. Portraits like this one project heroism, convey the sitter's humanity, and restore their dignity.[30]

Indeed, such portraits were an effective tool in projects to bring about social change. Equally important is the very personal and individual role that creating albums could play in these broader social projects. By creating evidence of personal worth, in themselves, their family, colleagues and friends, African Americans developed and built a vision of self-confidence that was necessary to live their lives with dignity. In albums created by non-African Americans, we see better the reality of the times – the races were not always so segregated and divorced from shared experiences. In raising awareness of albums like this and considering their meanings, we enrich our own understanding of the past. As part of our jobs as historians, we aim to collect, preserve, and show these interior lives and experiences of the past, as it enables us in our strategies to use visual culture today in constructive and effective ways.

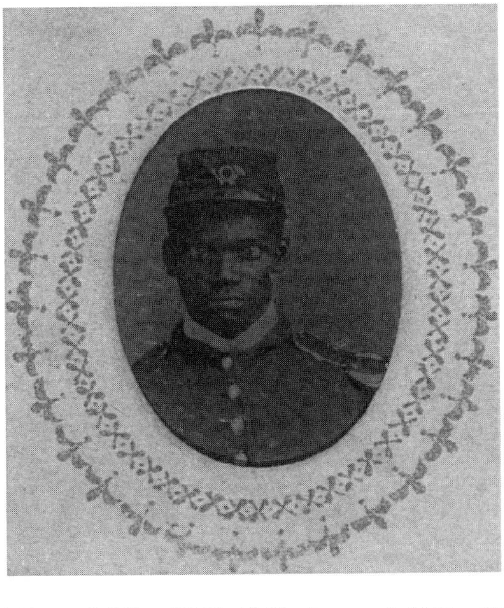

Figure 8.5 *Unidentified Union Soldier*, 1864–1865, tintype, 1 3/16 × 7/8 in., photographic album of William A. Prickitt. Collection of the Smithsonian National Museum of African American History and Culture, Gift of Aneita Gates, on behalf of her son, Kameron Gates, and all the descendants of Captain William A. Prickitt.

Notes

1 Frederick Douglass, "Pictures and Progress," in *Picturing Frederick Douglass: An Illustrated Biography of the Nineteenth Century's Most Photographed American*, eds. John Stauffer, Zoe Trodd, and Celeste-Marie Bernier (New York: W. W. Norton & Company, 2015), 161–173. The authors argue that the Civil War inspired Douglass to write and speak about photography and estimate Douglass wrote this speech sometime between November 1864 and March 1865.
2 Deborah Willis, *Reflections in Black: A History of Black Photographers 1840 to the Present* (New York: W. W. Norton & Company, 2000), xvii.
3 James M. McPherson, *The Negro's Civil War: How American Blacks Felt and Acted During the War for the Union* (1965) (New York: Vintage Books, 1993), 21–23.
4 Joseph T. Glatthaar, *Forged in Battle: The Civil War Alliance of Black Soldiers and White Officers* (Baton Rouge: Louisiana State University Press, 2000), 7. Glatthaar describes the chaotic episodes where generals sought to use Black troops as laborers as well as soldiers in the months before authorization from the War Department: Glatthaar, *Forged in Battle,* 6–10.
5 Glatthaar discusses the instances of Union generals employing the use of escaped or captured enslaved people to perform manual labor of military fortifications: Glatthaar, *Forged in Battle,* 6–9.
6 McPherson, *The Negro's Civil War,* 180–81; Glatthaar, *Forged in Battle,* 11–12.
7 Glatthaar, *Forged in Battle,* 6–8; James Oakes, *Freedom National: The Destruction of Slavery in the United States, 1861–1865* (New York: W. W. Norton & Company, 2014), 223–224; McPherson, *The Negro's Civil War,* 167.
8 Shayne Davidson, *Civil War Soldiers: Discovering the Men of the 25th United States Colored Troops* (Charleston: Create Space Independent Publishing Platform, 2013), 8. All of the research on Captain Prickitt and the soldiers depicted in the album was conducted by Shayne Davidson.
9 Glatthaar, *Forged in Battle,* 15–16.
10 Glatthaar, *Forged in Battle,* 48. Glatthaar cites: War Department General Order No. 144, Adjutant General's Office May 22, 1863. *OR* III 3, 216.
11 Glatthaar, *Forged in Battle,* 48, 59. For instance, Glatthaar cites testimony from Major General Silas Casey, "I have no hesitation in saying that the officers of the colored troops, *who passed the Board*, as a body were superior to them [volunteers in white units], physically, mentally, morally."
12 Davidson, *Civil War Soldiers,* 7.
13 Letter 61, Milton Harris, Orderly Sergeant, Company F, 25th USCT, Fort Redoubt, Florida, November 21, 1964, *Christian Recorder*, December 17, 1864, in *A Grand Army of Black Men: Letters from African-American Soldiers in the Union Army, 1861–1865*, ed. Edwin S. Redkey (1992; Cambridge: Cambridge University Press, 1993), 95–96. Note that while this letter presents a positive portrayal of white officers leading their Black troops, some reports by Black soldiers in the field indicate harsh treatment at the hands of white officers. Redkey finds letters from soldiers that show a "consistent picture of mistreatment by officers who objected to any efforts of the men to assert their pride," Redkey, ed., *A Grand Army of Black Men,* 156.
14 McPherson, *The Negro's Civil War,* 175–177, 178. McPherson quotes a letter from Douglass to Gerrit Smith, dated March 6, 1863, Smith Papers, Syracuse University Library.
15 McPherson, *The Negro's Civil War,* 175.
16 David W. Blight, *Frederick Douglass: Prophet for Freedom* (New York: Simon & Schuster, 2018), 396–397. In fact, two of Douglass' sons were among the first recruits from New York into the 54th Regiment of Massachusetts. McPherson, *The Negro's Civil War,* 176.
17 The Enrollment Act of March 3, 1863, also known as the Draft Act, was the first national conscription law to compel men to military service. Oakes, *Freedom National,* 225–232, discusses the impressment of enslaved Blacks into service with the Union Army.
18 Redkey, ed., *A Grand Army of Black Men,* 13.
19 Letter 60, A. J. Bedford, 25th USCT, Fort Pickens, Florida, November 7, 1864, *Christian Recorder*, March 4, 1865, in Redkey, ed., *A Grand Army of Black Men,* 94–95.
20 Davidson, *Civil War Soldiers,* 13; Jackie Budell, "The 150th Anniversary of the United States

Colored Troops," May 22, 2013, from "Pieces of History," U.S. National Archives, accessed May 16, 2021: https://prologue.blogs.archives.gov/2013/05/22/usct-service-records-digitization-project-completed-on-150th-anniverisary-of-united-states-colored-troops-may-22/. Enslaved persons did not have a choice to serve or not, unless they chose to run away and successfully crossed the Union line. The Federal Government offered an incentive to the slaveowner to receive compensation and to do so while the government offered it, as there was no guarantee the government would do so after the war ended.

21 Davidson, *Civil War Soldiers,* 24, 58, 73–75.

22 Davidson, *Civil War Soldiers,* 50, 71.

23 Davidson, *Civil War Soldiers,* 38, 65.

24 Davidson's drawings were shown at ArtPrize 2013 in Grand Rapids, Michigan, where her entry was recognized in the top 25 of more than 1,500 entries: Davidson, *Civil War Soldiers,* 5–6.

25 Correspondence, Aneita Gates, March 4, 2014, Object Record 2014.88, Smithsonian National Museum of African American History and Culture.

26 Correspondence, Aneita Gates, March 4, 2014.

27 Blight, *Frederick Douglass,* 388.

28 Correspondence, Aneita Gates, March 6, 2014.

29 It is noteworthy that Davidson's drawings of the men's portraits have been displayed several times since that first presentation in the Michigan art show in 2013. The larger-than-life color portraits (each measuring approximately 21 × 29 inches) continue to play a role in sharing the story of the USCT, ensuring they are accessible beyond the museum display, the museum catalog, or the published monograph. The Evergreen Museum and Library in Baltimore, Maryland, hosted a display of the drawings in December of 2016, Jill Rosen, "Evergreen Museum displays portraits of Civil War Soldiers History Overlooked," *Johns Hopkins Magazine*, December 14, 2016. Accessed May 16, 2021: https://hub.jhu.edu/2016/12/14/evergreen-exhibit-black-civil-war-soldiers/. The National Park Service displayed the drawings in Pensacola, Florida: Auriette Lindsey, "Fort Pickens Exhibit Recognizes African American Troops," ABC3 WEARE-TV, December 11, 2019. Accessed May 16, 2021: https://weartv.com/news/local/fort-pickens-exhibit-recognizes-african-american-troops. More recently, the Lewes History Museum in Delaware opened a show of the drawings in February of 2021 and was scheduled to remain on display for one year. "Black Soldiers of Civil War Exhibit to Open Feb. 12," *Cape Gazette*, February 10, 2021. Accessed May 16, 2021: https://www.capegazette.com/article/black-soldiers-civil-war-exhibit-open-feb-12/215297.

30 Deborah Willis, *The Black Civil War Soldier: A Visual History of Conflict and Citizenship* (New York: New York University Press, 2021), 116; Lonnie G. Bunch III, "Foreword," in *Pictures with Purpose: Early Photographs from the National Museum of African American History and Culture,* eds. Laura Coyle and Michèle Gates Moresi (Lewes, England: D. Giles Ltd., 2019), 7.

Bibliography

"Black Soldiers of Civil War Exhibit to Open Feb. 12," *Cape Gazette*, February 10, 2021. Accessed July 20, 2021: https://www.capegazette.com/article/black-soldiers-civil-war-exhibit-open-feb-12/215297.

Blight, David W. *Frederick Douglass: Prophet for Freedom*. New York: Simon & Schuster, 2018.

Budell, Jackie. "The 150th Anniversary of the United States Colored Troops," May 22, 2013, from "Pieces of History," U.S. National Archives. Accessed July 20, 2021: https://prologue.blogs.archives.gov/2013/05/22/usct-service-records-digitization-project-completed-on-150th-anniverisary-of-united-states-colored-troops-may-22/.

Bunch III, Lonnie G. "Foreword." In *Pictures with Purpose: Early Photographs from the National Museum of African American History and Culture*. Laura Coyle and Michèle Gates Moresi, eds. (Lewes: GILES, 2019), 7–9.

Davidson, Shayne. *Civil War Soldiers: Discovering the Men of the 25th United States Colored Troops*. Charleston: Create Space Independent Publishing Platform, 2013.

Glatthaar, Joseph T. *Forged in Battle: The Civil War Alliance of Black Soldiers and White Officers*. Baton Rouge: Louisiana State University Press, 2000.

Lindsey, Auriette. "Fort Pickens Exhibit Recognizes African American Troops," *ABC3 WEARE-TV*, December 11, 2019. Accessed July 20, 2021: https://weartv.com/news/local/fort-pickens-exhibit-recognizes-african-american-troops.

McPherson, James M. *The Negro's Civil War: How American Blacks Felt and Acted During the War for the Union. 1965*. New York: Vintage Books, 1993.

Oakes, James. *Freedom National: The Destruction of Slavery in the United States, 1861–1865*. New York: W. W. Norton & Company, 2014.

Redkey, Edwin S., ed. *A Grand Army of Black Men: Letters from African-American Soldiers in the Union Army, 1861-1865*. Cambridge: Cambridge University Press, 1993.

Rosen, Jill. "Evergreen Museum Displays Portraits of Civil War Soldiers History Overlooked." *Johns Hopkins Magazine*, December 14, 2016. Accessed July 20, 2021: https://hub.jhu.edu/2016/12/14/evergreen-exhibit-black-civil-war-soldiers/.

Stauffer, John, Zoe Trodd, and Celeste-Marie Bernier. *Picturing Frederick Douglass: An Illustrated Biography of the Nineteenth Century's Most Photographed American*. New York: W. W. Norton & Company, 2015.

Willis, Deborah. *The Black Civil War Soldier: A Visual History of Conflict and Citizenship*. New York: New York University Press, 2021.

Willis, Deborah. *Reflections in Black: A History of Black Photographers 1840 to the Present*. New York: W. W. Norton & Company, 2000.

9 The Politics of Floating: Space and Experience in G. Prat Photograph Album of China and Japan, 1874–1900

Xinyue Yuan

Trading ports such as Canton (Guangzhou) in southern China have long fascinated eighteenth- and nineteenth-century Western travelers as "floating cities" famous for their river scenery and sizable boat-dwelling populations. In travel accounts and visual representations, the Pearl River at Canton was always crowded with local boat-dwellers living on sampans floating as international trading ships and steamers passed them by. This view is affirmed in a photographic album made from 1874 to 1900 by French silk inspector G. Prat, who worked in late-nineteenth-century Canton and represented this "floating city" and others in China, in addition to several in Japan.[1] In the album, "floating" is conveyed literally by the presence of waterscapes, but also by evoking the physical sensations of either floating on a boat, or riding in a sedan chair carried by laborers. This chapter considers "floating" as a key metaphor in Prat's album for evoking sensory experiences, and for highlighting the fleeting nature of time, which ironically is expressed by movement.

Prat, like other European and U.S. businessmen in the Canton during the tense colonial era, was subjected to great restrictions to his mobility in this area. Recent studies on architecture and urban landscape in late-nineteenth-century Canton have established that firm spatial divisions separated the areas inhabited by Europeans from those of the city's dominant Chinese population.[2] Architectural historian Johnathan Andrew Farris elaborates that the construction of the "concession," or "international zone," of Shamian – an isolated manmade sand-bank island built to lodge foreign businessmen – was purposefully kept at a distance from the mainland by a canal traversed by two bridges. Prat lived on Shamian between 1877 and 1884, during a period of increasing spatial segregation between the Euro-American and Chinese districts.[3] Nevertheless, late-nineteenth-century Western expatriates such as Prat used photographic travel albums to privately negotiate their experiences with the political and geographic boundaries that preconditioned their "floating tours." This chapter demonstrates that Prat's photographic album-making engaged multi-layered spaces to deal with his real-life limitations and the precariousness of his access to other zones.[4]

A "Floating" Journey Between Pages

Prat's album contains 140 pages of 151 albumen photographs, most of which are full-page photographs of water-, land-, or cityscapes in China and Japan. In contrast to the brightly colored, dragon-decorated, exquisite lacquered album covers that bound many souvenir albums from Canton and Yokohoma from the same period, Prat's album conforms to

DOI: 10.4324/9781003157427-13

European conventions. It is half bound in dark-green leather with gold-stamped decorative banding.[5] G. Prat's handwritten name is inscribed on the front endpaper.

The album's contents reveal a tension between the matter-of-fact documentary photographic aesthetic found in his Cantonese views in the first half of the album, and an exoticism seen in the latter half of the album's Japanese views. Both styles were common in images featured in nineteenth-century Western travel photo albums. Existing scholarship on photographic albums made of China and Japan by nineteenth-century Western travelers, such as those made by Italian-British photographer Felice Beato in the 1860s and 1870s, points out that two general categories of images of remote places were popular with European and North American customers: scenic views and genre scenes (everyday-life scenes).[6] Prat's album reflects those tendencies. Many ready-made souvenir albums targeted at globetrotters constructed their photographic sequences so that viewers visually jumped from one famous site to another as they turned pages – and so did Prat's album, which includes some ready-made souvenir photography.

Prat's album is unusual among travel albums for its elaborate captions and annotations that circle each photographic print. All written in French, these texts combined the writing styles of ethnographic record-keeping and personal narration. Prat recorded local details like climate, population, and customs, and he added notes about his personal perceptions and living experiences within expatriate communities. Some captions directly addressed certain details in the photographs, and/or pointed out connections between a sequence of images in the album. This suggests that the target audience of the album may not have included only Prat himself, but his fellow expatriates, and his families and friends back in France.

Even though the photographs are dated in captions, the progression of pages in Prat's album does not follow a chronological order. The first page starts with the year 1878. But the pages then bounce between a variety of years from 1874 to 1896. The album's last page ends with the year 1877.[7] Instead of a chronological schema, Prat grouped his photographs by the city he visited, or where he lived. For example, he selected photographic views that centered on China's Pearl River Delta, including 98 views of Canton; six of Hong Kong; 11 of Macau; one of Nagasaki; two of Kobe; one of Lake Biwa; five of Yokohama; four of Tokyo; one of Osaka; and three of Mount Fuji. This organization implies that, for the album's target audience, visual sequencing of scenic views and their spatial mapping takes precedence over the historically accurate linear timeline. The dominance of scenic views in this personalized album also suggests that Prat's understanding of his cross-cultural experiences might be first and foremost a spatial one.

He only included three genre scenes of Japan, which indicates Prat's greater interest was in curating an itinerary of scenic views of places, rather than in collecting genre scenes. The remainder of the photographs featured Canton Amateur Theatrical Society's (CATS) productions, and showed a glimpse into recreational activities within the confines of the Shamian Island later during his stay. There are eight blank pages in the middle of the album, marked only with page numbers in pencil, and one blank page at the very end, suggesting that Prat perhaps constructed the album's narrative from the front and back toward the middle.

Views of "floating" scenes along the waterfronts of Canton in Prat's album possess strong documentary and unconstructed qualities. In contrast to spectacular panoramas and picturesque riverscapes carefully designed by late-nineteenth-century Western photographers such as John Thomson (1837–1921), Prat's images are not oriented around primary landmarks that draw album viewers' eyes through a striking composition. Instead, viewers' attention moves around among scattered watercrafts. Often shot from a high camera angle, these photographs bring viewers nearer to the surface of the water and allow for a closer observation of the life on the boat. For instance, the full-page photograph on page 70 reveals two narrow boats, or sampans, in the foreground that appear to be floating toward the camera. Part of the first sampan has moved off the frame, evoking the feeling of drifting in space and time. Below the image, Prat's French caption reads: "*Canton: Vue prise de la riviere des Perles*, 1883 pouvant donner une idee du mouvement continuel qui y existe et de l'importance de la population flotante"[8] ("*Canton: The View of Pearl River, 1883 may give an idea of the continuous movement that exists there and the importance of the floating population*").[9] Prat was drawn to the fleetingness, liveness, and the theme of floating implied by this image.

Three consecutive images of Prat's album, from pages 41 to 43 (Figs. 9.1–9.3), not only exemplify his fascination with local riverscapes but also show how the album mobilizes vision for reader-spectators by photographing spatially continuous waterways. These photographs were taken at the canal that separates the western suburbs of Canton

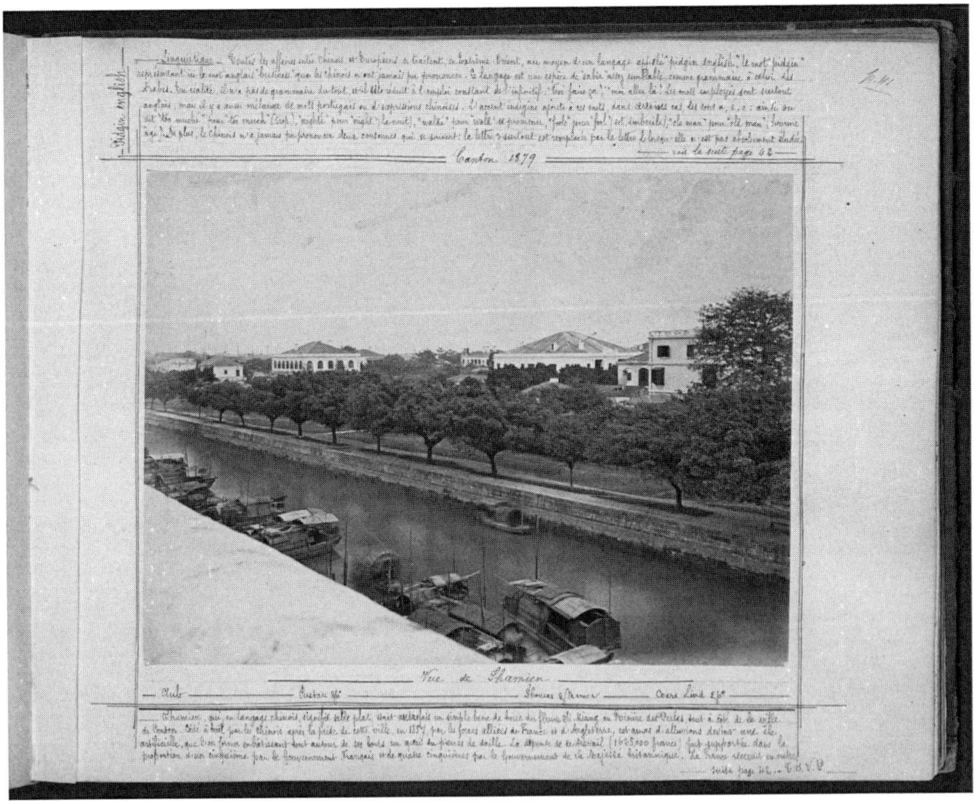

Figure 9.1 G. Prat, *Canton: Vue de Shamien*, 1879, album page with albumen print and notes, 12.8 × 15.3 in., photographic album of China and Japan. Getty Research Institute, Los Angeles, CA.

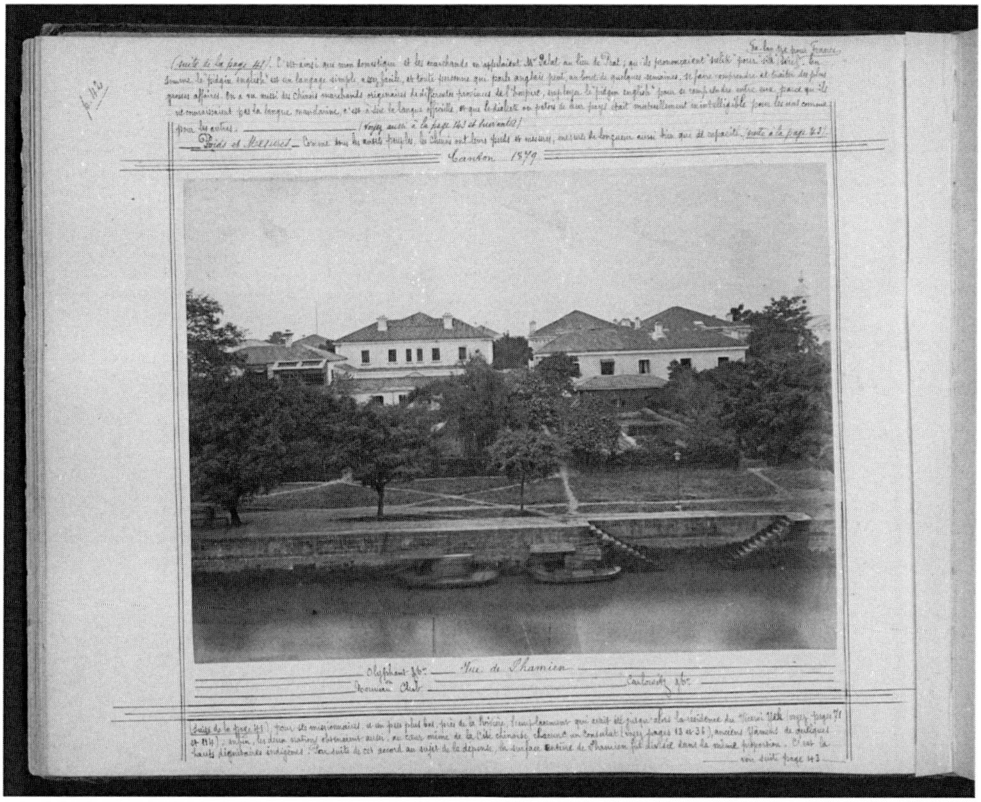

Figure 9.2 G. Prat, *Canton: Vue de Shamien*, 1879, album page with albumen print and notes, 12.8 × 15.3 in., photographic album of China and Japan. Getty Research Institute, Los Angeles, CA.

from the Shamian island, one of many geographic enclaves at trading ports given over to foreign powers under Imperial China.[10] The camera on page 41 (Fig. 9.1) was positioned at an oblique angle, looking toward the southeast. On the next page (Fig. 9.2), the camera faces right toward the riverbank, while the camera on page 43 (Fig. 9.3) takes an oblique view toward the southwest. Drifting sampans appear in each photograph, evoking the sense of movement of travelers through space and time. This implied movement underscores the photographic album's function as a pre-cinematic way of animating photographs and placing them in time. The series of still photographs almost suggests the movement of sequential frames in a movie camera (which would not be invented until the 1880s), panning along the river.

Prat applied a similar strategy to his transitional pages between views of China and Japan in the middle of the album. The section devoted to Canton first pauses at a photograph on a flower boat – a type of floating brothel and a subject often appeared in Cantonese export paintings – on the Pearl River, dated 1883.[11] Then the album drifts along to depart from the South China Sea and glides into the port of Nagasaki. From pages 91 to 93 dated 1896, Prat selected three hand-colored panoramic prints

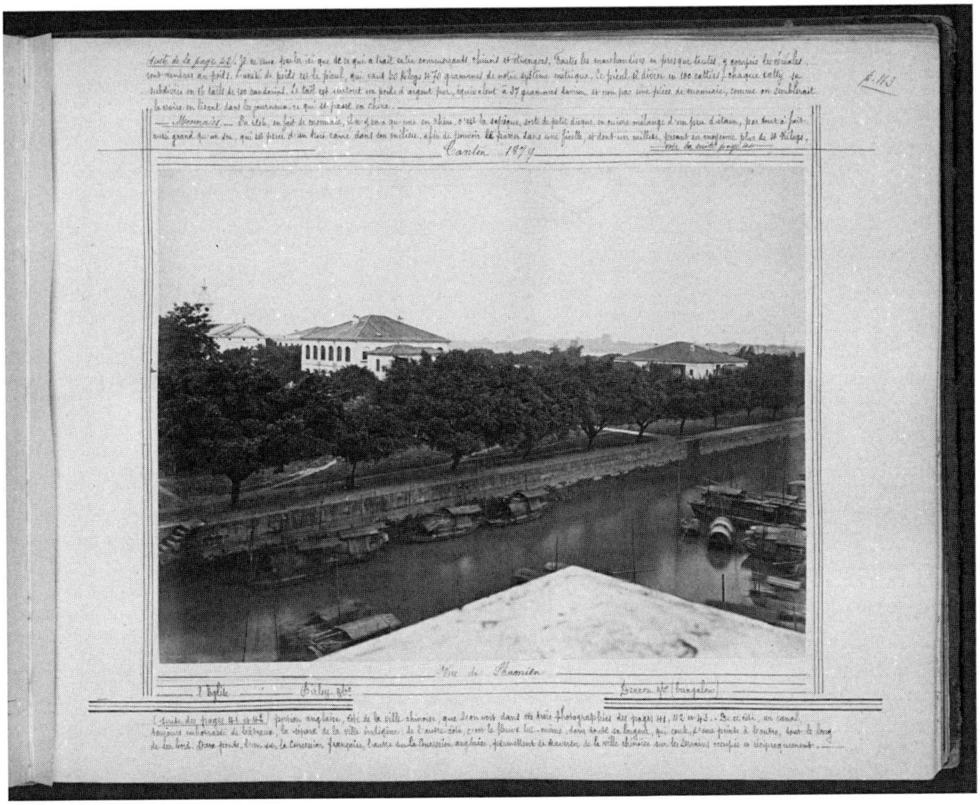

Figure 9.3 G. Prat, *Canton: Vue de Shamien*, 1879, album page with albumen print and notes, 12.8 × 15.3 in., photographic album of China and Japan. Getty Research Institute, Los Angeles, CA.

of seascapes. With each successive page, the horizon line drops slightly lower. Ships across the images proceed in the same direction, again suggesting a voyage of spatial continuity. On page 93, the blurred passing of a craft as it flees the frame is stilled for our later recurrent enjoyment.

In addition to reproducing the dynamic visual experience of tourism, Prat often selected multiple photographs of the same place that were produced by both unidentified amateur photographers and commercial photographic studios, but taken from different points of view. This gives album viewers a more comprehensive understanding of the spatial environment. Two full-page photographs presented on facing pages 16 and 17 show the Huaisheng Mosque in Canton from drastically different angles. Page 16 looks down at the mosque from a long distance, and situates it within a panoramic cityscape. Whereas, on page 17, Prat chose to present a close-up of the mosque shot from a low camera angle, to simulate the experience of moving viewers nearer to observe the mosque's decorative details. The images of Canton from pages 12 to 40 in Prat's album featured typical staged shots of famous places, sharing some characteristics with contemporaneous souvenir photographic albums.

Yet Prat further mixed and re-sequenced views of landscapes and ships to mimic travel on specific touristic routes. For instance, a photograph on a steamship on page ten follows the opening pages showing the European concession areas of Canton (where Prat lived). The steamship named *Jinshan*, according to Prat's annotations below the image, traveled between Hong Kong and Canton.[12] Immediately following it on the next page is a bird's-eye view of Hong Kong, implying that it is the steamship's travel destination. For most reader-spectators of Prat's album, who have never been to Canton, turning pages across tourist sites is a dynamic visual and tactile experience that recreates the experience of "floating" from one city to another, through the sensation of looking at shifting vantage points, views, and the lenses of various photographers.

Expatriates as Middlemen in Tourist Photography Business

In the late-nineteenth century, photography businesses influenced visual conventions in the tourism industry, as well as Euro-American tourists' expectations for their travel experiences. Prat was a consumer of the heterogeneous visual economy and tourist industry in semi-colonial regions, and repeated some of its tropes. For example, pages 12, 13, and 14 each feature a monumental pagoda, the most iconic type of traditional monumental architecture in Chinese Canton, and which was celebrated in touristic visual culture. The Pa-choc (Pazhou) Pagoda near Wampoa (Whampoa Island) appeared as the first view of Prat's Cantonese tour. But imposing pagodas in southern China also popularly appeared as a book illustration for Johannes Nieuhof's travel accounts in 1665, they inspired William Chambers' ambitious imitation in the Grand Pagoda at Kew in London in 1762, and they were the subject of William Alexander's watercolor renderings of his journey with the Macartney Embassy in the 1790s.[13] The pagoda was also possibly the first landmark that travelers looked forward to seeing when they entered the sea near Canton, and it reveals the influences of touristic visual culture on Prat.

Yet Prat utilized annotations to enrich the commercial photographs by adding his personal narratives to them. For instance, the first view of his Cantonese tour, the Pa-choc (Pazhou) Pagoda, was most likely a reproduction from the Hong Kong-based Pun Lun Studio of commercial photography.[14] Yet, he added the caption: "One meets her [the pagoda] on the left when one goes from Hong Kong to Canton," and "at the foot of the pagoda are some scattered stones on the flank of the hill."[15] His captions show his own sensitivity to the experience of movement and spatial shifts correlated with the visual references in the image.

As a long-time dweller in Canton, Prat visited Japan merely as an itinerant traveler. Although he possessed a less Westernized vision of China and Japan than many foreign transitory tourists, the Japanese views he included in the album also are typical of those in nineteenth-century tourist photographs. From pages 105 to 107, Prat inserts three photos sold by the Yokohama-based Kusakabe Kimbei photographic studio, which look at Mount Fuji from Yoshiwara, Hakone's Lake, and Otometoge, respectively. Also produced by Kimbei, the images on pages 108, 109, and 110 feature Japanese girls in costumes, sometimes eating. Kimbei enjoyed great success during the 1880s and 1890s as a major exponent of *Yokohama shashin* (literally, "Yokohama photographs") which were famous for their vibrant hand-painted colors. They replaced the popularity of woodblock prints, known as *ukiyo*-e, literally meaning "pictures of the floating world."

These photographs followed many *ukiyo*-e conventions such as the representation of romantic and staged scenes of beauty, pleasure, indulgence, and transience. Prat likely was drawn to the hand-tinted photographs due to their accentuated liveliness and transience, and – more importantly – the added sense of authenticity they offered for describing the experience of Japan. Furthermore, Prat's annotations emphasize ethnographic details such as climate, housing, and attire worn in Japan, which lead viewers to conduct an ethnographic reading of the images and associate the staged genre-scene representations with authentic lifestyles.

Chinese photographer Lai Fong (c.1839–1890) produced the images featured by Prat on pages 28, 29, 34, 72, 73, and 77. In recent studies on Lai, curator Kate Addleman-Frankel examines Lai's album of 95 photographs of Beijing from the collection of the Cornell University Library and argues that instead of taking one perfect picture at one place, Lai preferred taking multiple views at one site, creating a sense of really "being there."[16] Curator/collector Stacey Lambrow identified a photograph dated to 1869 as Lai's darkroom tent.[17] In the picture, the sampan carrying Lai's photographic equipment rests on the surface of a river in the Fujian province, revealing a floating cameraman at work. The innovative working methods such as shooting a photograph on a boat along the river by Chinese photographers like Lai might have contributed to the aesthetics of the "floating" scene and the emphasis of movement in commercial photographs of the period.

However, Kimbei and Lai did not necessarily reflect a distinct "Japanese" or "Chinese" way of looking at the landscape, genres, or people. Kimbei started out as a photographer as an apprentice to Italian-British photographer Felice Beato.[18] Lai hired European assistants to develop his photography business.[19] These cross-cultural contacts suggest that the West and East did not necessarily develop distinct and divergent photographic traditions, but that both co-influenced each other. Moreover, local photographers' well-received tourist photographs were shaped by the tastes of their cosmopolitan and sometimes global clientele. In particular, previous scholarship has rarely touched upon how European-U.S. expatriates in East Asia such as Prat could act as the middlemen between global travelers and local photographic studios. Expatriates' modes of experiencing local spaces could potentially shape the practices of commercial photographers, who were receptive to their customers' changing tastes and perceptions.

A manuscript list with descriptions from the GRI collection reveals that Prat hoped to act as a broker, by acquiring photographs from local Chinese photographers and selling them to globetrotters as souvenirs. He pointed out that a Chinese photographer would not want to miss out on making this huge profit by selling to a more global audience.[20] Dated after 1884, the manuscript describes 18 photographs of Canton that Prat wished to acquire. Photographs on the list include views of French and English concessions on Shamian, views of the Bocca Tigris, views of varied watercrafts on the Pearl River, and views within the Chinese city of Canton.[21] In several descriptions, Prat specifies more than just the desired subject matter of these photographs but also mentions his preferences for camera angles, and the times of day when those photographs ideally should be taken. In other words, the list seems to be a shooting script for a photographer, rather than an order for existing photographs. However, Prat's descriptions can be viewed as instructions for helping local photographers how to adapt their products for Western customers.

For instance, number 17 on Prat's list is a photograph of the Dragon Boat Festival, which can only be taken in May or June.[22] Prat suggests that the best two places to take this view will be from the Dutch Folly, or while aboard flower boats, since rows of boats passing are visible from both places.[23] Prat highlights that "La photographie pourrait prendre en enfilade la Riviere de Canton." ("The photograph could capture a series of the Cantonese river.")[24] Prat's predilection for fleetingness and movement perhaps may have urged local photographers to experiment with an alternative style that was less static and timeless – as many Chinese landscapes appeared in commercial photographs. Existing commercial photography in China apparently was not fully meeting the demands of expatriates like Prat, who either tried to commission photographs to match his own perceptions or who utilized textual annotations to further refine and redefine the meanings of commercial photographs. We might further guess whether Prat's album could operate both as a commemorative album of his own expatriate life, and a product sample for global travelers who spent limited time in port cities. The "immersive" experience conveyed by serial photographs taken from multi-angle points of view express Prat's unique expatriate spatial memories, and also compensating global travelers for their lack of enduring exploration.

Crossing Borders with Album Making

The sequence of different locations represented in the album, charted in Chart 9.1, show Prat's movements between areas within and outside the city's European concession, and freely across various political entities and boundaries.[25] Prat centered his "floating" journey around the borders of the European concession.[26] Originally from France, Prat

Pages 1 to 9	Cityscape views of Canton (inside the concession)
Page 10	Views of steamship "Jinshan" traveling between Hong Kong and Canton
Page 11	Cityscape view of Hong Kong
Pages 12 to 40	City-and landscape views of Canton (outside the concession)
Pages 41 to 43	Cityscape views of Canton (borders of concession)
Pages 44 to 76	City-and landscape views of Canton (inside the concession and seascapes around the concession)
Pages 77 to 81	City-and landscape views of Canton (outside the concession)
Pages 82 to 90	No photographic prints; page numbers handwritten by pencil
Pages 91 to 110	City-and landscape views of Nagasaki, Kobe, Yokohama, Tokyo, Osaka
Pages 111 to 119	Portraits of European-U.S.expatriates
Pages 120 to 121	Views of steamships
Pages 122	Portraits of European-U.S.expatriates
Pages 123 to 129	Cityscape views of Hong Kong
Pages 130 to 131	Portraits of European-U.S.expatriates
Pages 132 to 142	Cityscape views of Macao
Pages 143 to 148	Portraits of European-U.S.expatriates

Chart 9.1 Xinyue Yuan, A Page-By-Page Look at G. Prat's Album Subjects (Chart), 2021.

worked as a silk inspector for Russell & Co. – the largest United States trading company dealing in tea, silk, and opium in late-nineteenth-century China – for a year and a half, and then worked for the English firm Thomas, Rowe & Smith for five-and-a-half years. The album's non-commercial, amateur-made photographs of Prat's communities testify to his active presence in the European-U.S. social circles at Shamian. He appears in a number of group portraits across 16 of the album's pages. On page 44, Prat and his fellow "junior men" who were employed by European trading companies as silk inspectors, tea tasters, and accountants, posed on the second-story balcony and on a seat near the front gate of the house Thomas, Rowe & Smith rented for their employees. Prat's captions identify his male friends' names and positions, including accountant J. D. Monro, and tea tasters E. W. Michell and A. B. Tomkins.[27] Some other group portraits show Prat and his communities' enclaved lifestyles and leisure activities, including theater performances, masquerade balls, and lawn tennis.

The foreign quarters of Canton had lost their dominance in conducting foreign trade by the time Pratt lived there.[28] According to Farris, between 1860 and 1905, when Shamian was constructed, the second phase of Western habitation in Canton began.[29] After the Second Opium War (1856–1860), Shamian was developed into a residential district for European and American trading houses.[30] An artificially built canal divided the Shamian island and the western suburbs of Canton. Separated from the Chinese city in Canton, Shamian only was accessible by two gated bridges on the north and east sides of the island. In her book *Wanderings in China* (1886), Scottish travel writer and painter Constance F. Gordon-Cumming described Shamian in 1879 as "a very smart, purely foreign settlement, as entirely isolated from the native city as though they were miles apart, instead of only being divided by a canal, which constitutes this peaceful green spot an island."[31] The geographic enclosure and seclusion of Prat's physical milieu was at odds with the spontaneous and far-reaching floating tour represented in his album.

The late-nineteenth century not only witnessed the increasing isolation of the Western settlement in Canton, but a decrease in the population of European-U.S. expatriates there due to the increased number of cities on coastal China that were opened for foreign trade. By 1873, only 300 Western residents remained in Canton, whereas the Chinese population was estimated to be 1.5 million.[32] After the Treaty of Nanjing, female residents only were allowed in concession areas with family friendly urban plans, including public gardens, parks, and tennis courts. These comforts, in turn, encouraged and reinforced these families' isolated lifestyles.[33] After the Second Opium War, foreigners such as Prat were allowed to enter the city wall of Chinese Canton. Yet, the hostility of the sizable Chinese population toward them made this journey intimidating. European and U.S. expatriates thus heavily relied on local tour guides to navigate historic Cantonese sites.

A group photograph on page 144 features a masked ball held by Mr. and Mrs. G. M. Smith at the garden of the London-headquartered Matheson & Co. house in January of 1879 (Fig. 9.4). According to Prat's annotations, balls provided outdoor entertainment during the warm winter in Canton.[34] The Matheson & Co. masquerade started at 10 p.m. and lasted throughout the night. Guarded by the walls of the Shamian island's private gardens, hosts and their guests set up a boundary within the boundary. These events were exclusive to Europeans, U.S. citizens, and other white people, making the border not only spatial but also racial. However, paradoxically, white attendees staged fantasized intercultural encounters within their safe zones, as can be seen from the image, a bearded man wearing a cross holds a crutch

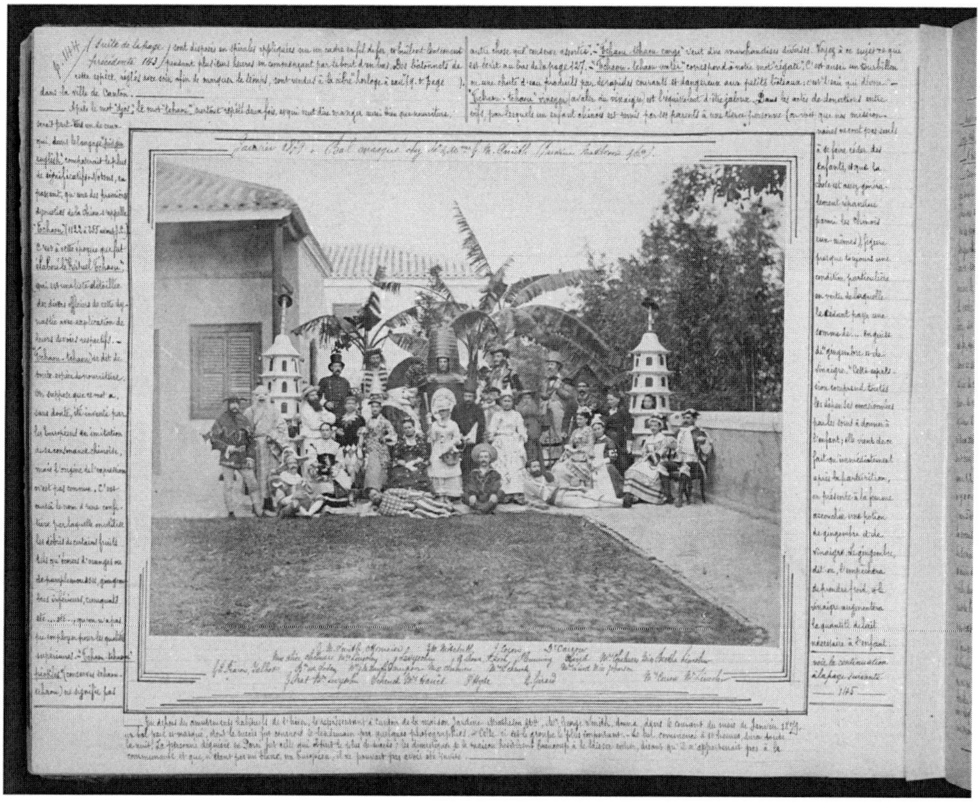

Figure 9.4 G. Prat, *Bal Masqué Chez Mr. & Mm. G. M. Smith (Jardine, Matheson & Co.)*, 1879, album page with albumen print and notes, 12.8 × 15.3 in., photographic album of China and Japan (Prat is seated on far left.) Getty Research Institute, Los Angeles, CA.

with a gourd associated with Daoism. Other subjects don a hodgepodge of Parsi, Indian, Chinese, and European attires. Prat sat in the front row, wearing a pirate captain's hat. The group's carefree gestures, gazes, and organization in the portrait were similarly cacophonous. The guests scaled to human height the Huaisheng Mosque in the middle and a pair of pagodas, culturally appropriating these monuments as playful costumes. Perhaps this was the only way European and American travelers felt that they could safely "embody" the experience of Chinese Canton. under the careful watch of local powers.

Even the comfortable cocoon of Shamian was constantly under the threat of natural disaster or the potential violence from local populace outside of the boundary. Prat's album opens with a series of photographs of a building complex in Shamian that was hit by the notorious 1878 typhoon. Six full pages of photographs of urban ruins follow, offering multiple views of the same typhoon's damage. It is not clear who took these images. Historian of photography Claire Roberts has discussed how the identities of original photographers of typhoon photos were ambiguous because the same set of negatives might change hands between commercial photographers, and/or be passed down the generations.[35] Nevertheless, photographic records of sensational disasters like this one found a huge market among Western travelers. Pratt may have purchased this set of typhoon photos from a photography studio. Despite that, his captions such as "view of the house of W. Pustau & Co.," "the warehouse of Messrs. Siemssen & Co.," and "view of the house garden of Matheson & Co.," authenticate his spatial experience of the event by identifying the names of the companies that owned the destroyed buildings.[36] This identification personalizes the typhoon, and was likely meaningful to Prat and potential album viewers among the European-U.S. communities on Shamian, since their daily lives were interconnected.

More importantly, the typhoon sequence was succeeded by three images of order, leisure, and tranquility in photographs of a well-maintained church, courtyards, and porches within the Shamian island. Thus, the album-viewing was designed to reveal new buildings reborn from the architectural ruins. The last photograph in the sequence on page nine was amateur-made and featured the "veranda of the Russell & Co. company."[37] The two men relaxing in the open-air gallery are also identified by Prat's captions as F. Koch and T. B. Cunningham, Russell & Co. employees. His annotations below the image tell us that both Koch and Cunningham were old friends of Prat's whom he knew well during his nine years in Canton.[38] Prat's intentional combination of commercial and amateur photographs and the authoritative tone of his annotations blur the boundaries between the more universally-accessible touristic spaces of commercial photographic representations and Prat's real experiences and images for album viewers.

In addition to weathering natural catastrophies, anti-foreigner sentiments among the Chinese population sparked conflicts. The imperialist expansion of nineteenth-century China was a spatial negotiation. Thus, buildings of foreign companies within the concession island became the most reasonable target for the anti-foreigner movement. On September 10, 1883, against the backdrop of Sino-French War (1883–1885), anti-foreigners attacked and set on fire buildings on the eastern end of the Shamian island. Photographs between pages 55 and 68 in Prat's album concentrate on the destruction of Shamian during the 1883 riot. Prat presented a series of photographs that document the open wounds and remaining skeletons of architecture at varied locales on the island in the aftermath of the event. Many of the photographs depict spaces important to Prat's everyday life that the riot radically altered. These sites would no longer be identifiable were it not for the accompanying captions.[39]

Pages 64 (Fig. 9.5) and 65 feature post-riot side and front views of the same building presented on pages 44 and 45. The photograph on page 44 shows the facade of the Thomas, Rowe, & Smith building, dotted with small figures of the companies' employees, including Prat. The photograph on page 45 offers a closer look at the arched inner gate where Prat, his colleagues, and their Asian servants gathered. Written on page 44, Prat's text highlights the contrasting black-and-white colors of the wall paint. In his annotations on page 45, he concludes that this house was completely destroyed in the riot on September 10, 1883, which he further instructs the album viewers to look at on pages 64 and 65.[40] Page 65 uses a similar ground-level angle to photograph the building's front door shown on page 44. The striking visual contrast between human presence and absence in the same space reveals the fragile conditions of their rootless sojourn. However, Prat's captions on pages 64 and 65, contrary to expectations, narrate the riot in an unemotional tone.[41] The power of the explanatory text over the image assures viewers of a recovery.

One month later after the riot, the noted U.S. art collector and world traveler Isabella Stewart Gardner (1840–1924) ventured to Canton. She stayed at the house of Russell &

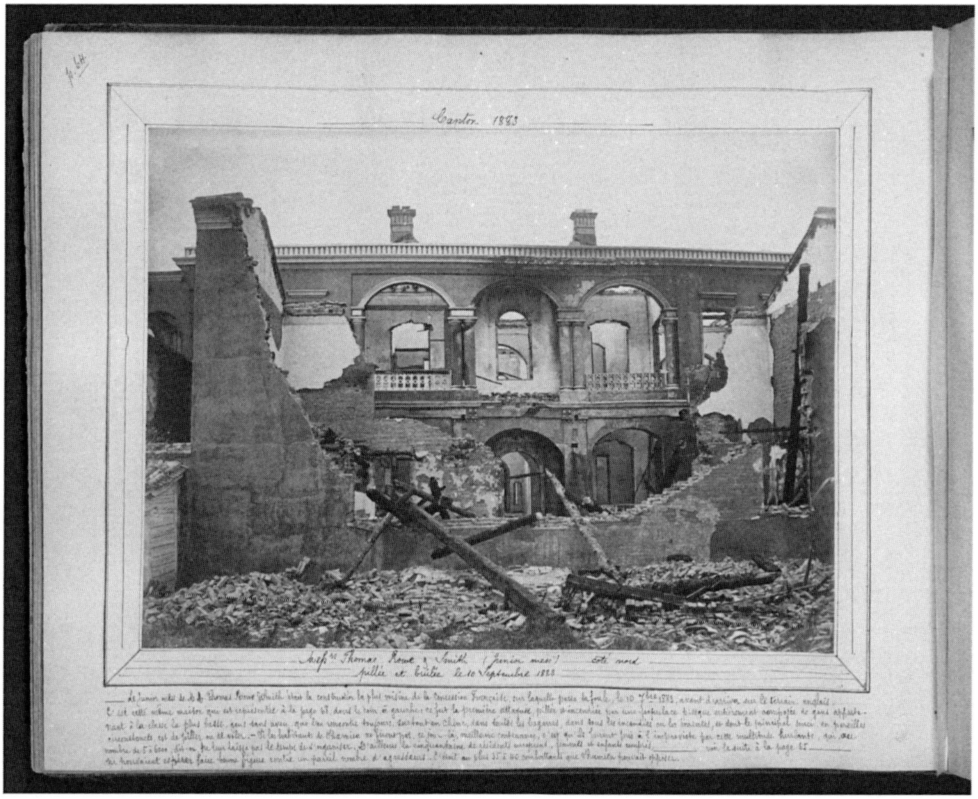

Figure 9.5 G. Prat, *Canton: Messrs. Thomas, Row & Smith (Junior Men) Coté Nord, Pliée et Brûlée le 10 Septembre 1883*, 1883, album page with albumen print and notes, 12.8 × 15.3 in., photographic album of China and Japan. Getty Research Institute, Los Angeles, CA.

Co., and dined with Mr. Prat. Gardner wrote in her journal about the hidden anxieties over spatial boundaries and the political threats directed at European-U.S. communities. On October 30, 1883, she articulated her feelings of excitement and uneasiness about sightseeing abroad. Arriving in "a town of boats" – the city of Canton – Gardner eschewed wandering its local and historic core, to instead make haste to Shameen (Shamian).[42] There, a boat owned by Russell and Co. picked her up to ferry her to the house. Gardner recorded having tea with Cunningham, who appeared in photograph on page 9, and she recalled that Prat joined their dinner. At their gathering, Gardner learned that the house next door had been burned down by local Chinese during a riot the previous month and had "only the shell standing."[43] Being particularly aware of the spatial divisions between the Shamian island and the Chinese city of Canton on the other side of the canal, she wrote:

> We went to bed under the protection of the gunboats that are now lying in a line in front of us. And it is still undecided about our going into the town. The verandah of our rooms opens on the canal and the Chinese town on the other bank is as merry as lights, music, and fire crackers [sic] can make it.[44]

In the next day's journal entry, Gardner recorded that although the Chinese authorities did not want foreigners to go into the Chinese Canton, the U.S. Consul Charles Seymour (1821–1903) said he would go with her and "test the people."[45] Guided by the servant "Mac," they managed to travel in sedan chairs and visit the Chin-chan Guild Hall (Chen Clan Ancestral Hall) located within the Chinese city, and they dined with Prat again after returning to Shamian. On November 1, 1883, they started in sedan chairs carried by sixteen "coolies," and visited various sites outside the Euro-American settlement area including White Cloud Mountains, the City of the Dead, the Monastery, the Mohammedan Tomb, the five-storied Pagoda, the Flowery Pagoda, the English Consul's grounds, and then the Guild Green Tea Merchants.[46] Gardner described how her fear about potential dangers was overcome by the mesmerizing "floating" tour in sedan chairs: "through it all was the spice of fear. I never was so frightened as for the first half-hour, but got accustomed and ended by total forgetfulness of all danger."[47]

How might travel restrictions in late-nineteenth-century Canton have stimulated demand for images of an unrestricted floating tour? Previous scholarship has established that Western travelers followed advertisements published in guidebooks to inspect photographic studios' collections before they visited the actual tourist attractions and potentially purchased photographs.[48] In extreme cases, Sebastian Dobson argues, purchasing one of these souvenir albums "could even act as a substitute for the experience of traveling itself."[49] As an examination of exemplary images from the Prat album suggests, photography quenched a strong desire for the experiential real, for seeing the fleeting nature of life and the environment, for moving in and through spaces, and for embodied contact. By curating an amalgam of commercial photographs, amateur photographs, and adding text, Prat engaged spaces in photographic representations, textual spatial mapping, the space of a travel album, and real living spaces in Canton and other Asian cities. For potential viewers of Prat's album such as global travelers and European-U.S. expatriate communities on Shamian, "the floating tour" in his album flies over boundaries of European concessions and tours around within the city wall of Chinese Canton with ease. This tour's therapeutic power reveals European and American foreigners' deep anxieties over spatial isolation and political threat in contact zones. The case study of Prat's album offers a glimpse into how individual lives and objects were shaped by mobility and encounters in the global nineteenth century.

Acknowledgments

I would like to thank Roberta Wue, Molly Katharine Thrailkill, Asako Katsura, Edward Dimendberg, Mary Trent, and Kris Belden-Adams for their insightful feedback on earlier versions of this chapter.

Notes

1 In Japan, the term "Floating World," or "ukiyo," has additional meanings. During the Edo Period (1615–1868), the "Floating World"/"ukiyo" also referred to a pleasure-oriented urban lifestyle and culture focused on play and entertainment. It was naughty, hedonistic, and transgressive.

2 Johnathan Andrew Farris, *Enclave to Urbanity: Canton, Foreigners, and Architecture from the Late Eighteenth to the Early Twentieth Centuries* (Hong Kong: Hong Kong University

Press, 2016); Patrick Conner, *The Hongs of Canton: Western Merchants in South China 1700-1900, As Seen in Chinese Export Paintings* (London: English Art Books, 2009); Peter C. Perdue, "Rise & Fall of the Canton Trade System - II: Macau & Whampoa Anchorage," *Massachusetts Institute of Technology - Visualizing Cultures*. Accessed June 1, 2021: https://visualizingcultures.mit.edu/rise_fall_canton_02/cw_essay01.html; Peter C. Perdue, "Rise & Fall of the Canton Trade System - III: Canton & Hong Kong," *Massachusetts Institute of Technology - Visualizing Cultures*. Accessed June 1, 2021: https://visualizingcultures.mit.edu/rise_fall_canton_03/cw_essay01.html.

3 Farris, *Enclave to Urbanity*, 67–144.

4 On the notion of contact zones, see Mary Louise Pratt, "Arts of the Contact Zone," *Profession* (1991): 33–40. http://www.jstor.org/stable/25595469.

5 Allen Hockley, "Felice Beato's Japan: Places: An Album by the Pioneer Foreign Photographer in Yokohama," *Massachusetts Institute of Technology - Visualizing Cultures*. Accessed June 1, 2021: https://visualizingcultures.mit.edu/beato_places/index.html; Allen Hockley, "Globetrotter's Japan: Places: Foreigners on the Tourist Circuit in Meiji Japan," *Massachusetts Institute of Technology - Visualizing Cultures*. Accessed June 1, 2021: https://visualizingcultures.mit.edu/gt_japan_places/ga2_essay01.html; Photo Album "Pictures of Canton," 1899, the Getty Research Institute, Los Angeles, Accession no. 2007.R.17, 2772-713.

6 Hockley, "Felice Beato's Japan."

7 After the first page, the subsequent pages move (in order) to the years: 1874, 1879, 1878, 1879, 1881, 1883, 1881, 1877, 1883, 1896, 1882, 1883, 1882, 1883, 1879, 1881, 1879, 1878, and 1877.

8 G. Prat Photograph Album of China and Japan, 1874–1900, The Getty Research Institute, Los Angeles, Accession no. 98.R.14, Box 1, p. 70.

9 G. Prat Photograph Album of China and Japan, 1874–1900, The Getty Research Institute, Los Angeles, Accession No. 98.R.14, Box 1, p. 70.

10 Photographer unidentified.

11 G. Prat Photograph Album of China and Japan, 1874–1900, The Getty Research Institute, Los Angeles, Accession no. 98.R.14, Box 1, p. 81.

12 G. Prat Photograph Album of China and Japan, 1874–1900, Box 1, p. 10.

13 Johannes Nieuhof, *La Tour de Porcelaine*, 1669, British Museum, London, Registration No. 1867,1012.599; William Chambers, (*Pagoda at Kew*) *A View of the Wilderness with the Alhambra, the Pagoda and the Mosque*, 1763, British Museum, London, Registration No. 1863,0509,281; William Alexander, *South Gate of the City of Ting-Hai*, 1798, British Museum, London, Registration No. 1899,0713.72.

14 The same imagery appeared in different formats such as carte-de-visite produced by Pun Lun studio. See inscriptions:"Par Chou Pagoda, Chinese Pagoda near Canton, China. Hong Kong China, 1868," and "Pun-Lun, Photographer & Ivory Painter. No. 56, Queen's Road, Upstairs. Opposite the Oriental Bank. Hong Kong," Clark Worswick Collection of Photographs of China and Southeast Asia, The Getty Research Institute, Los Angeles, Accession No. 2003.R.22, Box 1.

15 G. Prat Photograph Album of China and Japan, 1874–1900, Box 1, p. 12.

16 Kate Addleman-Frankel, "Who Is Lai Fong? New Perspectives on 19th-Century Photography in China," Unpublished Paper, Presented at the Annual Stoikov Lecture on Asian Art, Cornell University, Ithaca, N.Y., October 15, 2020. Accessed June 15, 2021: https://museum.cornell.edu/exhibitions/lai-fong-photographer-china.

17 Stacey Lambrow, "Who Is Lai Fong? New Perspectives on 19th-Century Photography in China," Unpublished Paper, Presented at the Annual Stoikov Lecture on Asian Art, Cornell University, Ithaca, N.Y., October 15, 2020. Accessed June 15, 2021, https://museum.cornell.edu/exhibitions/lai-fong-photographer-china.

18 Hockley, "Felice Beato's Japan."

19 Roberta Wue, *Picturing Hong Kong: Photography 1855–1910* (New York: Asia Society, 1997), 17.

20 G. Prat Photograph Album of China and Japan, 1874–1900, Box 1, Sheet 1.

21 Bocca Tigris is a narrow strait about 40 miles from the mouth of the Pearl River.

22 The Dragon Boat Festival occurs on the fifth day of the fifth month of the lunar calendar.

23 The Dutch Folly is an oval fort built by Dutchmen on a sand bar in the Tigris in the Pearl River.

24 G. Prat Photograph Album of China and Japan, 1874–1900, Box 1, Sheet 1.
25 After their loss in two Opium Wars with British and French armies, imperial China was forced by "unequal treaties" to lease out more territory in treaty port cities such as Guangzhou as part of the concession occupied by foreign powers.
26 G. Prat Photograph Album of China and Japan, 1874–1900, Box 1, p. 9.
27 G. Prat Photograph Album of China and Japan, 1874–1900, Box 1, p. 44.
28 The dominance of trade in the port at Canton lasted from the late 1700s until the First Opium War (1839–1842). Peter C. Perdue, "Rise & Fall of the Canton Trade System - I: China in the World (1700–1860s)," *Massachusetts Institute of Technology - Visualizing Cultures*. Accessed June 1, 2021: https://visualizingcultures.mit.edu/rise_fall_canton_01/cw_essay01.html.
29 Farris, *Enclave to Urbanity*, 3.
30 This new site measured 2,850 feet from west to east and 950 feet from north to south. See Conner, *The Hongs of Canton*, 243.
31 Gordon-Cumming is cited in: Farris, *Enclave to Urbanity*, 67.
32 Terry Bennett, Anthony Payne, and Lindsey Stewart, *History of Photography in China: Chinese Photographers, 1844–1879* (London: Quaritch, 2013), 113.
33 Farris, *Enclave to Urbanity*, 84–85.
34 G. Prat Photograph Album of China and Japan, 1874–1900, Box 1, p. 144.
35 Claire Roberts, *Photography and China* (London: Reaktion Books Limited, 2013), 42.
36 G. Prat Photograph Album of China and Japan, 1874–1900, Box 1, pp. 1–3.
37 G. Prat Photograph Album of China and Japan, 1874–1900, Box 1, p. 9.
38 G. Prat Photograph Album of China and Japan, 1874–1900, Box 1, p. 9.
39 G. Prat Photograph Album of China and Japan, 1874–1900, Box 1, p. 55, 64–65.
40 G. Prat Photograph Album of China and Japan, 1874–1900, Box 1, p. 44, 45.
41 G. Prat Photograph Album of China and Japan, 1874–1900, Box 1, p. 55, 64–65.
42 Gardner is quoted in: Alan Chong, Noriko Murai, and Christine Guth, *Journeys East: Isabella Stewart Gardner and Asia* (Boston: Isabella Stewart Gardner Museum, 2009), 222.
43 Gardner is quoted in: Chong, Murai, and Guth, *Journeys East*, 222–225.
44 Gardner is quoted in: Chong, Murai, and Guth, *Journeys East*, 222–225.
45 Gardner is quoted in: Chong, Murai, and Guth, *Journeys East*, 226.
46 "Coolies" is an offensive name for Asian laborers. Gardner is quoted in: Chong, Murai, and Guth, *Journeys East*, 226.
47 Gardner is quoted in: Chong, Murai, and Guth, *Journeys East*, 226.
48 Allen Hockley, "Packaged Tours: Photo Albums and Their Implications for the Study of Early Japanese Photography," in *Reflecting Truth: Japanese Photography in the Nineteenth Century*, eds. Nicole Coolidge Rousmaniere and Mikiko Hirayama (Amsterdam: Hotei, 2004), 66–85; Sebastian Dobson, "Yokohama Shashin," in *Art & Artifice: Japanese Photographs of the Meiji Era*, eds. Sebastian Dobson, Anne Nishimura Morse, and Frederic A. Sharf (Boston: MFA Publications, 2004), 15–16.
49 Dobson, "Yokohama Shashin," 16.

Bibliography

Behdad, Ali, and Luke Gartlan. *Photography's Orientalism: New Essays on Colonial Representation*. Los Angeles: Getty Research Institute, 2013.

Bennett, Terry, Anthony Payne, and Lindsey Stewart. *History of Photography in China: Western Photographers, 1861–1879*. London: Quaritch, 2010.

Bennett, Terry, Anthony Payne, and Lindsey Stewart. *History of Photography in China: Chinese Photographers, 1844–1879*. London: Quaritch, 2010.

Chong, Alan, Noriko Murai, and Christine Guth. *Journeys East: Isabella Stewart Gardner and Asia*. Boston: Isabella Stewart Gardner Museum, 2009.

Cody, Jeffrey W., and Frances Terpak. *Brush & Shutter: Early Photography in China*. Los Angeles: Getty Research Institute, 2011.

Conner, Patrick. *The Hongs of Canton: Western Merchants in South China 1700–1900, As Seen in Chinese Export Paintings*. London: English Art Books, 2009.

Dahlgren, Anna. "Dated Photographs: The Personal Photo Album as Visual and Textual Medium," *Photography & Culture*, Vol. 3 (July 2020): 2.

Dahlgren, Anna, Petersson, Dag, and Vestberg, Nina Lager. *Representational Machines: Photography and the Production of Space*. Aarhus: Aarhus University Press, 2013.

Dobson, Sebastian, Anne Nishimura Morse, and Frederic A. Sharf. *Art & Artifice: Japanese Photographs of the Meiji Era*. Boston: MFA Publications, 2004.

Farris, Johnathan Andrew. *Enclave to Urbanity: Canton, Foreigners, and Architecture from the Late Eighteenth to the Early Twentieth Centuries*. Hong Kong: Hong Kong University Press, 2016.

Gartlan, Luke and Roberta Wue. *Portraiture and Early Studio Photography in China and Japan*. Oxon: Routledge, 2017.

Hockley, Allen. "Expectation and Authenticity in Meiji Tourist Photography." In *Challenging Past and Present: The Metamorphosis of Nineteenth-Century Japanese Art*, Ellen P. Conant, ed. (Honolulu: University of Hawaii Press, 2006), 114–131.

Hockley, Allen. "Felice Beato's Japan: Places: An Album by the Pioneer Foreign Photographer in Yokohama." *MIT Visualizing Cultures*. Accessed June 1, 2021: https://visualizingcultures.mit.edu/beato_places/index.html

Hockley, Allen. "Globetrotter's Japan: Places: Foreigners on the Tourist Circuit in Meiji Japan." *MIT Visualizing Cultures*. Accessed June 1, 2021: https://visualizingcultures.mit.edu/gt_japan_places/ga2_essay01.html

Hockley, Allen. "John Thomson's China—1: Illustrations of China and Its People, Photo Albums (1873–1874)." *MIT Visualizing Cultures*. Accessed June 1, 2021: https://visualizingcultures.mit.edu/john_thomson_china_01/ct_essay01.html

Perdue, Peter C. "Rise & Fall of the Canton Trade System - I: China in the World (1700–1860s)." *MIT Visualizing Cultures*. Accessed June 1, 2021: https://visualizing-cultures.mit.edu/rise_fall_canton_01/cw_essay01.html.

Perdue, Peter C. "Rise & Fall of the Canton Trade System - II: Macau & Whampoa Anchorage." *MIT Visualizing Cultures*. Accessed June 1, 2021: https://visualizingcultures.mit.edu/rise_fall_canton_02/cw_essay01.html.

Perdue, Peter C. "Rise & Fall of the Canton Trade System – III: Canton & Hong Kong." *MIT Visualizing Cultures*. Accessed June 1, 2021: https://visualizingcultures.mit.edu/rise_fall_canton_03/cw_essay01.html.

Roberts, Claire. *Photography and China*. London: Reaktion Books, Limited, 2013.

Rousmaniere, Nicole Coolidge and Mikiko Hirayama, eds. *Reflecting Truth: Japanese Photography in the 19th Century*. Amsterdam: Hotei, 2004.

Schwartz, Joan M. and James R. Ryan. *Picturing Place: Photography and the Geographical Imagination*. London; New York: I.B. Tauris, 2003.

Wilson, Alona C. "Felice Beato's Japan: People: An Album by the Pioneer Foreign Photographer in Yokohama." *MIT Visualizing Cultures*. Accessed June 1, 2021: https://visualizingcultures.mit.edu/beato_people/fb2_essay01.html

Wu, Hung. *A Story of Ruins: Presence and Absence in Chinese Art and Visual Culture*. London: Reaktion Books, Limited, 2011.

Wue, Roberta. *Picturing Hong Kong: Photography 1855–1910*. New York: Asia Society, 1997.

10 Collecting the Indian Congress: Reframing Indigenous Photography Albums from the Trans-Mississippi and International Exposition

Karen Barber

Upon opening the small photo album labeled "American Indians Photographs" in a combination of handwritten and embossed script, the first image we encounter depicts a young woman with long black, wavy hair holding her infant child in a willow cradleboard (Fig. 10.1; and hand-tinted version on this book's cover). She is framed against a nondescript, slightly blurred painted backdrop, of the sort often seen in the studios of nineteenth-century photographers. Seated with her baby in her lap, the woman's shirt is plain, but she wears a long, striped, woolen blanket that contrasts with the checkerboard pattern of the baby's blanket. The cradleboard, made of twigs and twine, cuts a diagonal line across the composition. The portrait is striking because the young woman gazes out at us earnestly. But even more arresting, the infant, shrouded in blankets and secured to the cradleboard, looks out at us as well. It is as if they know we are looking at them and seeking to understand what their lives were like at this particular moment, and what brought them on this day to the studio of Omaha photographer Frank A. Rinehart. The "Photographs" album, of the sort used to collect family snapshots, does not identify the woman or provide her name. It tells us nothing of her or her child, other than their tribal affiliation, which is included in a hand-written caption reading *Wichita Woman and Child in Cradle*, located just below the sepia-toned photograph.

At approximately 6 ½ by 8 inches, the photograph of *Wichita Woman and Child in Cradle* and its caption fill the album page. It is positioned vertically below a handwritten "List of Tribes," thus necessitating a turn of the album from a horizontal to a vertical viewing position. This positioning requires the viewer to take them in at once, suggesting a relationship between the two and that perhaps she is an iconic representation of *all* Indigenous peoples included in the album. In an album that favors representations of men, particularly of Chiefs and warriors, it is remarkable that a photograph of a woman and child appears on the first page. The photograph exudes a certain exoticism with its focus on the woman and her cradleboard, a form of mobile cradle that swaddles the infant and is worn on the mother's body, allowing the mother to continue her work and suggesting, in keeping with stereotypes, that she is "closer to the land." Viewed from a white European-American perspective, this sort of baby-wearing would have been understood as "exotic," as outside the norm, which at this moment would have included a baby carriage in which infants were held, quite literally, at arm's length.

As the first image in "American Indians Photographs" (hereafter AIP), *Wichita Woman and Child in Cradle* was thus exemplary of the album's theme, connoting

DOI: 10.4324/9781003157427-14

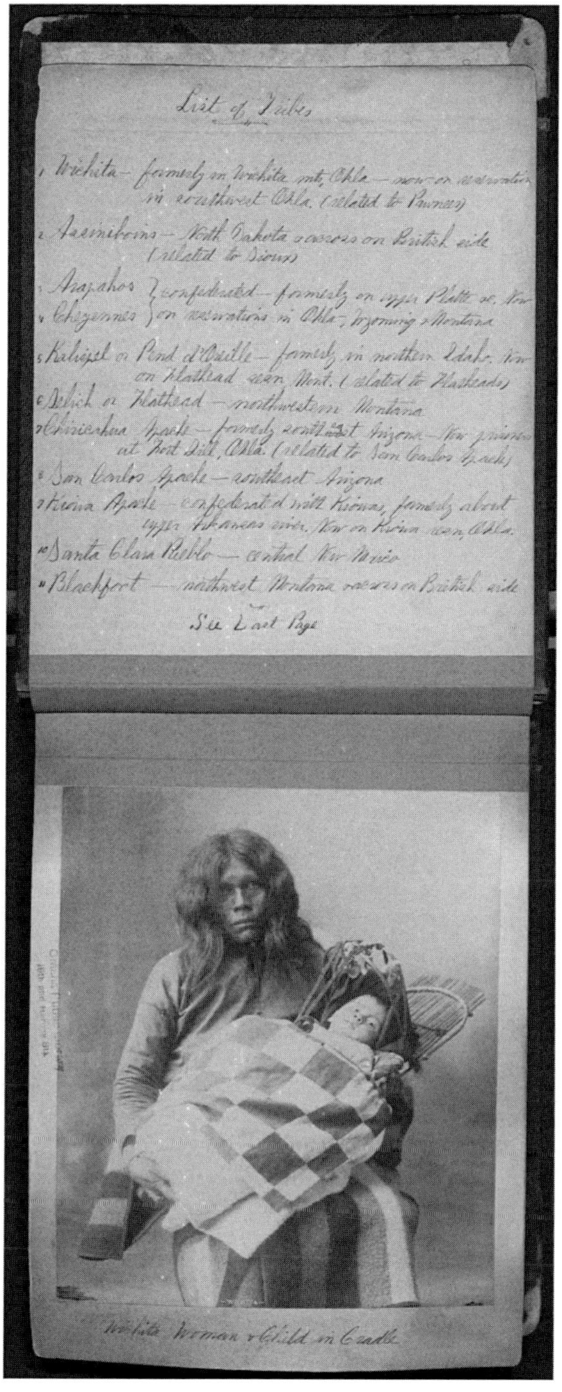

Figure 10.1 Double-page album spread with handwritten "List of Tribes" and *Wichita Woman and Child in Cradle*, photograph by Frank A. Rinehart and Adolph Muhr, 1898, 22.8 × 8.26 in., American Indians Photographs album. Courtesy of Omaha Public Library. Public Domain.

"*Indianness*" to the compiler of the album. As Gerald Vizenor (Minnesota Chippewa Tribe, White Earth Reservation) has stated,

> [t]he decorative feathers, beads, leathers, woven costumes, silver, turquoise, bone, and other tribal representations have turned humans into the mere objects that bear material culture in photographs. Moreover, peace pipes, medals, trade axes, bows and arrows, rifles, and other weapons, are the obscure simulations of *Indianness*.[1]

Lacking identification, but stressing those aspects of material culture that simulate "*Indianness*," such images (like the *Wichita Woman*) are "mere ethnographic simulations, silences without names or narratives ... the coincidence of discoveries and the causes of dominance."[2]

In the Western imagination, the photograph also makes reference to the long-standing trope of the Madonna and child, but instead of focusing on motherhood as a potential common ground shared by many women, there is an emphasis on "Othering" the Wichita Woman and her child. An example of the delegate photographs taken by Rinehart and his assistant Adolph Muhr during the 1898 Indian Congress, *Wichita Woman and Child in Cradle*, was taken at the request of the Bureau of American Ethnology (BAE) for ethnographic purposes. But it does not necessarily read that way. Instead, it appears representative of "American Indians" as a "vanishing race," and thus, it reflects a desire to document Indigenous Americans before they disappeared. Ironically though, the inclusion of an infant child that gazes back at us, indicates otherwise. It suggests persistence and continuation, rather than a "vanishing." The photograph is thus indicative of the complex, intertwined, and sometimes conflicting narratives that inscribe both the photographs and the album.

Although the authorship of the album's photographs has never been in question – they are the work of Rinehart and his assistant Muhr – the ownership and authorship of the AIP album is less certain. The captions, "List of Tribes," and the organization of the photographs suggest that the album was compiled by someone with knowledge of the information compiled by Rinehart, Muhr, and the BAE. Perhaps its maker and keeper was Rinehart himself. The divergent intentions and interests of Rinehart and the BAE, which vacillate from commercial to ethnographic portraiture, are central tensions of the project. These conflicting intentions underlie my reading of the AIP album and its photographs. As such, this chapter addresses the AIP album, and a small sampling of its constituent photographs, contextualized as part of a larger project that seeks to deepen our understanding of the conflicted and problematic history of photographic representation of Indigenous peoples. This reading necessarily explicates the album and its photographs within the context of the fin-de-siècle moment in which they were created, accounts for the attitudes of those involved, and contextualizes the public reception of the photographs by both Indigenous and non-Indigenous audiences. It is important to create a historical framework for these photographs as a means of interrogating what they can tell us about late-nineteenth-century perceptions of Indigenous culture (i.e., the mythology of the "vanishing race"), Federal Indian policy, and the photographic legacy of the BAE. As well, a better understanding of these images can clarify the connections between the other large-scale photographic projects on Native North America initiated under the auspices of the BAE and Edward S. Curtis's massive *North American Indian* project in the early decades of the twentieth century.[3]

The photographs of the Indian Congress, which are the basis of the AIP album, mark a turning point from the BAE's emphasis on recording ethnographic "types" toward capturing romanticized images of the timeless "Indian," as seen later in the work of Curtis and Joseph Kossuth Dixon. As such, photographs by Rinehart and Muhr draw on both tendencies to create a body of work that foregrounded those aspects of Indigenous culture that were marketable as albums or individual photographs to curious audiences. Although the initial intent of the Indian Congress portraits was to educate and give visible tangible form to "types," the style and appearance of the romanticized, soft-focus photographs were also emblematic of "*Indianness*," and thus the commercial interests of the photographer. This was due largely to Adolph Muhr's aesthetic flair, which would be further transformed when Muhr left Rinehart's employ to work in the studio of Curtis, who would shortly thereafter begin his monumental project *The North American Indian*. Because the AIP album's photographs have appeared in a variety of contexts since their appearance in 1898, the end of this chapter will consider some of the ways that they have been circulated, and importantly, how they have been reconsidered and reimagined recently by Indigenous artists and scholars.

Photography albums of this sort, it should be remembered, were often made *of* Indigenous Americans in the nineteenth century, but far fewer were made *by* Indigenous Americans. This is not to say that Indigenous sitters did not also collect their likenesses and save them for posterity, because that would be inaccurate, but with improvements to photographic technology (and especially with the emergence of the carte-de-visite) the individual needs of the sitter took a backseat to the commercial interests of the photographer.[4] The collection and compilation of Indigenous portraits, many of which made their way into photography albums, fed the nineteenth-century fascination with "Indians" and "*Indianness*," thus taking their place, as historian Martha Sandweiss notes, "within a single overarching narrative story – the inevitable decline of the nation's native cultures, the determinist tale of a 'vanishing race.'"[5] Thus, the power relations at play within the operations of this and other albums compiled by white Americans of Indigenous sitters are important to acknowledge. This is not a family album, but a racialized compilation of photographs that illustrated more nefarious narratives. But the circle is completed, or at least continues, when Indigenous peoples take back these albums for their own purposes. As Carole Nez (San Carlos Apache/Navajo), remarks

> [t]he moment a photo album opens, memories flood back. Smells, sights, sounds, energy surge forth instantaneously from the photographs. The setting and even the comfort level of the photographic subjects return to haunt the photographer.[6]

Although Rinehart's photographs are historical documents that reference a specific event and moment in time, they are not static documents with closed meanings and interpretations. On the contrary, 809 original glass-plate negatives by Rinehart and Muhr were purchased in 1975 by the Alumni Association of Haskell Indian Nations University, an Indigenous university born out of the troubling legacy of the United States Indian Industrial Training School (also known as Haskell Institute) – which was part of the U.S. government's damaging assimilationist policies that sought to stamp out Indigenous culture and "civilize" Indigenous peoples.[7] The presence of the Rinehart negatives, which seem to traffic so appallingly in racial stereotypes, have been a source of research for current Indigenous students and a way of countering the very notion on which Rinehart's images were predicated: that Indigenous American people and culture were vanishing. These photographs are also an important means of bringing young students at Haskell Indian Nations University into conversation with their ancestors, creating a new sort of family album. At the end of this chapter, I will consider some of the ways that photographs by Rinehart and Muhr have been reimagined by contemporary Native artists like Wendy Red Star (Apsáalooke). Red Star's recent exhibition at the Joslyn Art Museum in Omaha, Nebraska, carried forward the idea of the photographic album to create a large-scale, multi-layered work that returns agency to the sitters of Rinehart's and Muhr's photographs, providing a contemporary commentary on the idea that Indigenous peoples at the Omaha Fair were displayed as exhibits to be consumed and purchased (through photographs and other memorabilia). In sum, this chapter will address the specificity of the AIP album and its complex narratives, but also the shift that has occurred over time, from past to present, in reading its attendant photographs.

The AIP Album in Context

To return once again to the album, a turn of the page and a rotation of the album reveals further "simulations of *Indianness*," this time in a vertically oriented double portrait, captioned *Wichita Young Men, Fred Carruth and John Tatum*, in which two men are posed, one standing and holding a rifle, and the other seated with hands clasped in his lap, against a similarly plain painted backdrop (Fig. 10.2, left). They stare at the camera, but do not smile. Although the young men wear Western shirts and vests, signs of their partial assimilation, they are wrapped at the waist in woolen blankets, Tatum wears moccasins, and both men's long, braided hair, is embellished with feathers and other ornamentations. The two men, as noted in the caption, are identified by name, while the "Wichita Woman" is not.

Another rotation of the album reveals, on the facing page, a group portrait that includes Carruth again, along with five other adults (three women and two men) and four children. The caption tells us that this is a *Group of Wichitas, Chief Tawáconi* [Tawákoni] *and Wife at Center* (Fig. 10.2, right). The men, all of whom wear Western dress suggesting a degree of assimilation, are posed behind the women, who are seated, with patterned blankets wrapped around their bodies. The older children stand with the men and the younger children sit in front of their mothers. Perhaps not surprisingly, the only figure identified is Chief Tawákoni, which on the one hand suggests the public's fascination with "Indian Chiefs" but, on the other, indicates the gender difference between images of men, many of whom are identified, and those of women, who, often are not. As is the case in many of the photographs in the album, gender hierarchies appear in the posing of groups and in the organization of the subjects in photographs. Men stand, strong and assertive, while the women are seated and wrapped in blankets, seemingly weak and submissive. The pairing of this group portrait with a portrait of two men of the Wichita "type" is repeated elsewhere in the album among the various tribes. With a few exceptions, many of the women and children appear toward the end of the album.

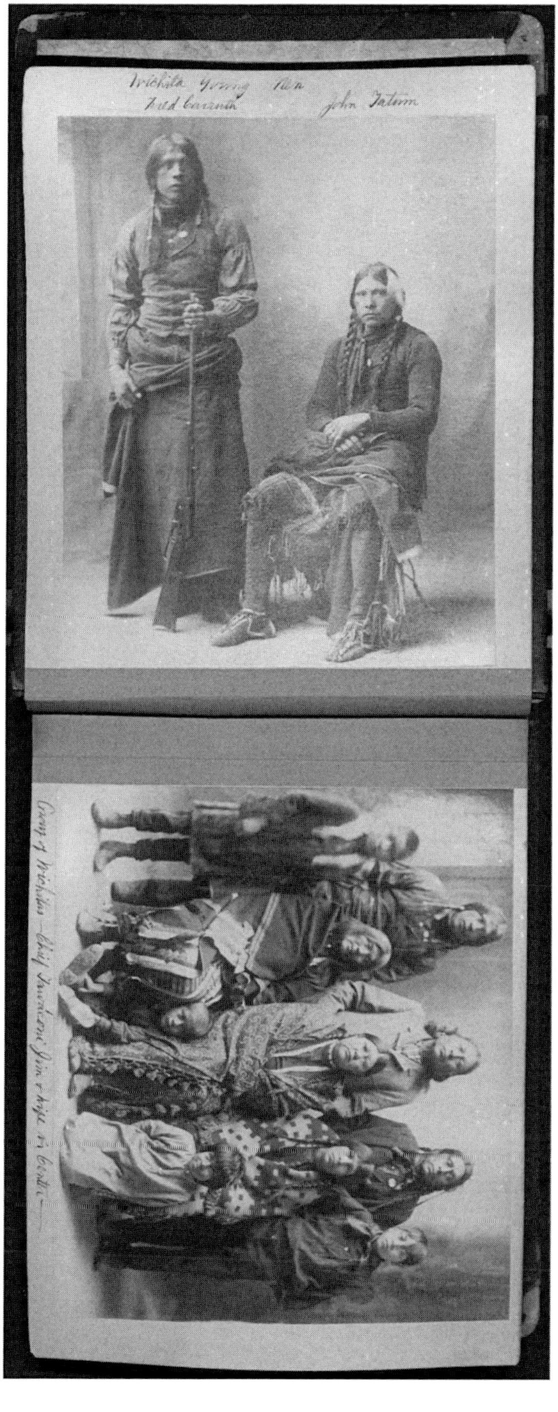

Figure 10.2 Double-page album spread with *Wichita Young Men, Fred Carruth and John Tatum* and *Group of Wichitas, Chief Tawaconi Jim and Wife in Center*, photographs by Frank A. Rinehart and Adolph Muhr, 1898, 22.8 × 8.26 in., American Indians Photographs album. Courtesy of Omaha Public Library. Public Domain.

This group of photographs of the Wichita tribe and others from the album were taken during the 1898 Indian Congress held at the Trans-Mississippi and International Exposition.[8] As official photographers of Omaha World's Fair, Rinehart and Muhr had been contracted by Frank Mooney of the BAE to photograph the delegates in attendance at the Indian Congress during the final weeks of the Fair, to create a set of negatives for historical posterity for the BAE's archives.[9] While the initial mission of the photographs was ethnographic, Rinehart and Muhr were studio photographers. Although they shared an interest in Native American cultures, their primary concern was the creation of a set of photographs that could be marketed and sold later as part of the so-called "Indian craze."[10] Rinehart and Muhr (but mostly Muhr) made portraits of many of the 500-plus delegates from 36 tribes in attendance at the Omaha Fair, providing an important document of Indigenous cultures west of the Mississippi at the turn of the century. Their soft-focus, romanticized photographs such as the portraits of the Wichitas present an approach to representing their subjects that operates somewhere between formal commercial studio portraits and anthropological documents. As such, they tell us about contemporary perceptions of Indigenous cultures, and the mythology of the "vanishing race" prevalent in the late-nineteenth and early-twentieth centuries.[11]

After all, the Indian Congress took place at a moment when Indigenous Americans were subject to U.S government assimilationist policies that included education in "Indian" boarding schools and life on reservations. Despite persevering in the face of such devastating circumstances, the "vanishing race" trope was everywhere, and was evident at the Fair and in these photographs. As scholar Philip Deloria (Standing Rock Sioux Tribe) has stated, "[a]fter Indian removals, Americans often denied the physical and social presence of real Indians, reimagining vanishing Indian savages as now-noble parts of a unified American past."[12] The timing of the Indian Congress, just eight years after the massacre at Wounded Knee and five years after historian Frederick Jackson Turner declared the frontier closed, marks a shift in perception toward a view of Indigenous Americans as nostalgic symbols of a fabled past that was quickly disappearing – a view perpetuated by both photography and ethnology.[13] The photographs in the "American Indian Photographs" album reflect the tension between the "noble savage" of the popular imagination and the racialized "portrait types" of ethnographic and anthropological photography.[14] As Elizabeth Edwards has stated,

> In broad nineteenth century anthropological usage, the 'type' represented the general form or character which distinguishes a given group and was accepted as standard; it was also the person or thing which exhibits these qualities, or at least some of them.[15]

The conflicted nature of these photographs – part anthropological documents, part romanticized portraits – is perhaps not surprising when viewed in the context of the Omaha Fair, which also trafficked in mixed messages about the fate of Indigenous Americans.

Indeed, it is important to situate these photographs within the larger thematics of the Omaha World's Fair, which located its ideological underpinnings in imperialism (in this case, Manifest Destiny) and in colonialist settler narratives that celebrated industrialization and ingenuity as evidence of (white) racial superiority.[16] The presence of the Indian Congress, which continued the tradition of featuring living anthropological exhibits of people of color established at previous World's Fairs, was evidence of broader international racist ideologies.

At the Omaha Fair, Indigenous American tribes lived and performed in the so-called "Indian encampment" displays that were accompanied by other exhibitions elsewhere at the Fair that highlighted the successes of, for example, "Indian schools." The Indigenous tribes in attendance for the Indian Congress were thus part of the World's Fairs' embrace of ethnology – the study of different peoples and the relationships between them – made possible by the involvement of Frank Mooney and the BAE. This organization's involvement was part of a larger strategy to educate an American public beyond the reach of the Omaha Fair's attendees about the customs, religions, traditional dress, music, manners, and other distinctive characteristics of Indigenous groups. The seemingly positive desire to "educate" the public was countered by the more sinister "display" of Indigenous American tribal groups for entertainment purposes, thus encapsulating the fear and desire of "the Other." Importantly, the photographs also implicitly sought, like the Fair itself, to highlight the perceived "success" of the U.S. government's policies of forced assimilation by demonstrating that Indigenous peoples could be "civilized" through education, much as the wild west had been tamed by the technological advances brought by Western settlers. The nostalgia for a "dying race," perceived by some as a result of westward expansion and innovation, provided a stark contrast to the positivist underpinnings of the Fair as a whole. The AIP album is thus reflective of the conflicting discourses at work in the planning and implementation of the Fair.

The AIP album positions sitters both as romanticized and timeless, but also as exemplary of Indigenous "types." The album, with its hand-written "List of Tribes," is related to the practice of making photography albums of "racial types," such as *Portrait Types of the Midway Plaisance*, created during the World's Columbian Exposition, which featured overtly racist photographs of living inhabitants seen at the fairs.[17] These albums, compiled by Peabody Museum director Frederic Ward Putnam, allowed visitors to bring them home as "souvenirs" to be kept and viewed in posterity. Though it lacks the embossed cover of an officially assembled photography album, the AIP album is similarly concerned with the impulse to collect "souvenirs" of the Fair. Built into this desire to "collect," was the nostalgic longing for what will soon fade away and the feeling that one was part of a far-reaching historical event. As Susan Sontag once noted, "When we are afraid, we shoot. But when we are nostalgic, we take pictures."[18] The nostalgia Sontag is referencing finds its parallel in the collecting of ethnographic photographs, which allowed viewers to "possess" the sitters literally and symbolically. Sontag continues:

> Still, there is something predatory in the act of taking a picture. To photograph people is to violate them, by seeing them as they never see themselves, by having knowledge of them they can never have; it turns people into objects that can be symbolically possessed.[19]

Possession took the form of photographs collected in souvenir albums like the one that is the focus of this chapter, but it also relates to the collection of images of racial/tribal "types" by the BAE and its photographers.[20] The delegate portraits from the Indian Congress are closely related in format to the photographic style established by the BAE for formal delegate portraits taken in Washington, D.C., from the mid-nineteenth century, which included a frontal bust view, a profile view, and a full-length portrait of each delegate, as well as group portraits of each tribal group.[21] In fact, Mooney, acting as representative for the BAE, was responsible for overseeing the delegate portraits at the

Omaha Fair in order to ensure the necessary views and information (name, tribal affiliation, and biographical data) were obtained.[22] The photographs thus exist at the intersection of several discourses around anthropology and racial "types," the "vanishing race," and American imperialism at the World's Fairs.

The AIP Album

The photographs in the AIP album, and the work of Rinehart and Muhr more generally, signal a shift away from the photography of ethnographic "types" (while still borrowing from their conventions) to represent the romanticized and timeless, but no less racist, images of the "vanishing Indian" that would influence the work of Curtis and others in the 1910s and 1920s. Indeed, the album does not include the systematic frontal and profile views, often shown side-by-side, typical of anthropological albums (though other "American Indian" albums in the Omaha Public Library's collection do). Instead, the poses of the sitters, which differ from individual to individual, are those that offer what the photographers believed to be the individual's or group's "best view," or their most "descriptive view," the view that marks them, first and foremost, as different from (or less than) the presumably white, Western viewer and Fair-goer. Whether in the focus on the cradleboard and boldly patterned blankets of the *Wichita Mother and Child in Cradle,* or the long braids, blankets, feathers, and rifle seen in the photograph of *Wichita Young Men, Fred Carruth and John Tatum*, the emphasis is on those aspects of Indigenous identity that were being systematically stamped out by U.S. government assimilationist policies and so-called "Indian Schools" – tribal dress, long hair (among men), and other adornments associated with tribal identity – the "simulations of *Indianness*" described by Vizenor (Figs. 10.1 and 10.2).

Little is known about the origins of the AIP album, but records at the Omaha Public Library indicate that the album entered their collection not long after the Omaha Fair closed in 1898/1899.[23] Labeled in cursive script on the cover with the words "American Indians" over embossed gold lettering that reads "Photographs," an otherwise nondescript small black photography album contains 69 portraits of individuals and groups, representing 15 of the 36 Native tribes present at the Omaha Fair's Indian Congress (Fig. 10.3). Each of the 69 photographs is captioned above or below with the sitter or group's identifying information, in some cases with the names of those included and their tribal affiliation. A list of tribes on the title page (which continues on one of the endpapers) determines, approximately, the album's organization. The list, which includes brief descriptions of each tribe and their ancestral lands, also indicates that the album was compiled in 1899, a year after the conclusion of the Indian Congress. Now in the collection of the Omaha Public Library, just a few miles from the location where the photographs were originally taken, the album is one of four albums containing delegate portraits from the 1898 Indian Congress. Although there is some repetition of images among the four albums, the three other albums are larger in scale and the album covers are embossed in gold lettering with the words "American Indians 1898." The larger scale of these albums allowed for the inclusion of larger photographs and more of them, in some cases bringing together frontal and profile views of sitters (in keeping with the BAE's methods described earlier) on the same page with handwritten captions below. While the AIP album is the smallest of the four (at 11 ¾ × 8 ¼ in.), it is in the best condition.

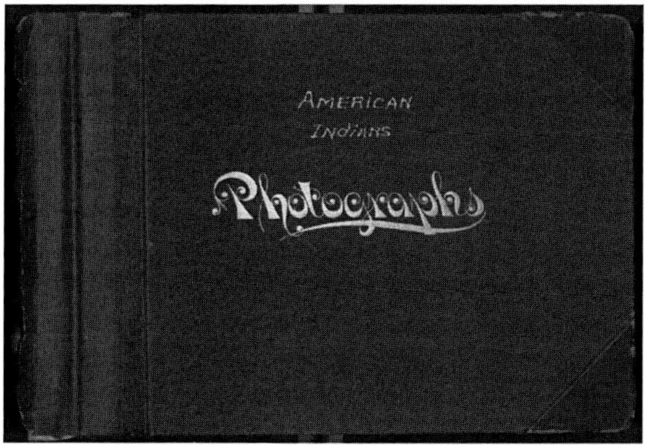

Figure 10.3 Cover, 1898, 11.4 × 8.26 × 1.96 in., American Indians Photographs album. Courtesy of Omaha Public Library. Public Domain.

With their unknown provenance, the three larger "American Indians 1898" albums may have been compiled to commemorate the Indian Congress, the most popular attraction at the Omaha World's Fair. With their embossed covers and more formal titles, they appear more official. It is possible that they were compiled for the Fair organizers and supporters as visual mementos and reminders of the success of the Fair. Given that Rinehart was the official Fair photographer and had every intention of selling and publishing the portraits taken of the Indian Congress delegates, it seems likely that he would have created a series of photography albums at the behest of his employers. In fact, the initial agreement between Rinehart, Mooney, and the fair organizers stipulated that the BAE would receive the negatives and the organizers would receive two sets of prints.[24] Although the agreement was not honored, Rinehart's continued presence in Omaha and his continued marketing of the photographs seem to indicate that he sold and distributed the images in a variety of ways. This practice would have been in keeping with previous World's Fairs and their publication of commemorative photography albums, such as the aforementioned overtly racist images of World's Columbian Exposition's *Portrait Types of the Midway Plaisance*.[25] If gatherings of "exotic" peoples were intended to bring people to the World's Fairs, then photography albums allowed people to collect mementos of them to take home.

The handwritten label on the cover of the smaller AIP album might indicate that it was compiled by a different individual, in a less official capacity. It is also the only one of the four albums that includes a list of tribes, which is also curious. As noted earlier, although *Wichita Woman and Child in Cradle* is the first photograph in the AIP album, it is not the first page. The first and last pages feature something of a table of contents that does not list the names of the sitters but a "List of Tribes" with generalized information about each tribe's location prior to removal and where they currently reside. A total of fifteen tribes are listed, many of whom were then living on reservations, a stark reminder to the reader that the album's portraits represented the last vestiges of a "dying race." The list also references, obliquely, the idea prevalent at the time that Indigenous peoples existed outside of time and place. The album thus positions the sitters in the liminal space between then (pre-contact with white settlers) and now (after Wounded Knee and the close of the frontier), but it also points to the fact that White Americans likely had little idea about the original inhabitants of the land they now resided.

The "List of Tribes" reads as follows:

1 *Wichita – formerly in Wichita mts, Okla – now on reservation in southwest Okla. (related to Pawnees)*
2 *Assiniboins – North Dakota & across on British side (related to Sioux)*
3 *Arapahos [and] 4. Cheyennes – confederated – formerly on upper Platte & Now on reservations in Okla, Wyoming, & Montana*
4 *Kalispel or Pend d'Oreille – formerly in northern Idaho. Now on Flathead resn. Mont. (related to Flatheads)*
5 *Selish or Flathead – northwestern Montana*
6 *Chiricahua Apache – formerly southeast Arizona – Now prisoners at Fort Sill, Okla. (related to San Carlos Apache)*
7 *San Carlos Apache – southeast Arizona*
8 *Kiowa Apache – confederated with Kiowas, formerly about upper Arkansas River. Now on Kiowa resn., Okla*
9 *Santa Clara Pueblo – central New Mexico*
10 *Blackfoot – northwest Montana & across on British side. See Last Page List of Tribes (continued from first page)*
11 *Sauk – (confederated with Foxes) – Formerly in eastern Iowa & adjoining parts of Illinois & Wisconsin. Now chiefly on reservation in central Oklahoma.*
12 *Pottawatomi – formerly about upper Lake Michigan. Now chiefly on resns. in Okla. & Kansas*
13 *Omaha – Formerly and still in northeastern Nebraska*
14 *Winnebago – Formerly in Wisconsin. Now partly there; partly on Omaha resn, Neb. 1899.*[26]

This list provides the approximate organization of the album, but it also reflects the diversity of tribes represented and the tendency to view the individuals represented as "types" – *Wichita Woman and Child, Wichita Young Men, Group of Wichitas.* Other titles/captions make this point (for example, *Assiniboine Warriors, Chief Wets It in Center, Group of Assiniboines, Dan Martin in Center, Assiniboine Children, Kalispel or Pend d'Oreille, Kalispel Women, Winnebago Group of 9, Winnebago Men, Winnebago Women).* As this list demonstrates, the photographs in the album also tend to follow a pattern of sorts: a photograph of one individual or two is followed by a group portrait from the same tribe, which reinforces the idea that these are "portrait types" meant to represent specific tribes. In most cases, the images of men appear before the images of women and children, which appear toward the end of the album. So, while the *Wichita Woman and Child in Cradle* opens the album, it is followed by *Wichita Young Men* and *Group of Wichitas.* Another photograph of the Wichita, *Wichita Woman, Wife of Tawáconi* [Tawákoni] *Jim*, which shows a seated woman in profile, appears later in the album in a section that included images of women and children, many of whom are not identified by name (Fig. 10.4).

The information included in the above "List of Tribes" suggests that the compiler of the album had some level of specialized knowledge of the tribes present during the Indian Congress and their respective histories. In fact, the information provided is

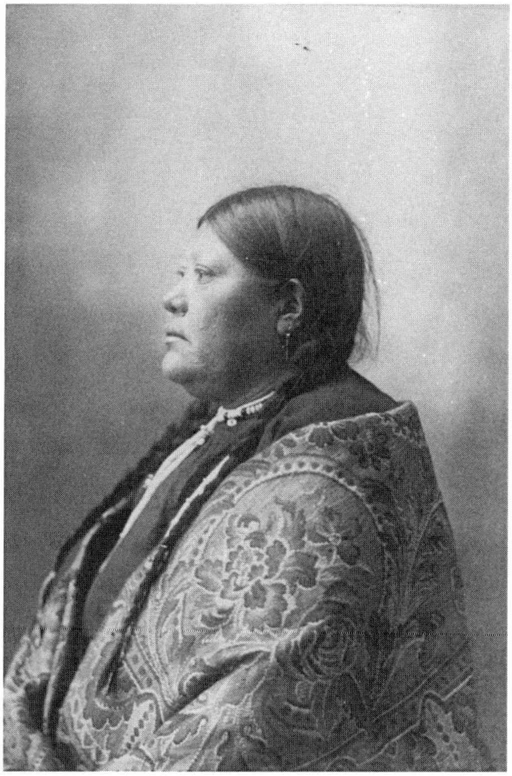

Figure 10.4 Frank A. Rinehart and Adolph Muhr, *Wichita Woman, Wife of Tawaconi Jim*, American Indians Photographs album, 1898, 4.3 × 6.29 in. Courtesy of Omaha Public Library. Public Domain.

remarkably similar to both Muhr's published recollections and James Mooney's report on the Indian Congress published in *American Anthropologist* in January of 1899.[27] Although his report only references in detail "some of the tribes" he deemed "most interesting," his discussions of the tribes included their linguistic group, their current numbers, their historical homelands, where they currently reside, the sort of dwellings they inhabit, whether they were agricultural people, the crops they cultivated, and their physical characteristics.[28] As an ethnologist, Mooney was particularly interested in the Wichita tribe. He assisted the Wichita in their visit to the Fair and encouraged them to bring along the materials necessary to build a grass lodge on the grounds of the Fair (which they did).

Given that the photographs were shot under Mooney's supervision, while Mooney himself collected the necessary anthropological data (some of which is included in the "List of Tribes," and in the captions), it is possible, even likely, that the AIP album came directly from Rinehart's Omaha studio. The focus in the early part of the album on the Wichita can thus be related to Mooney's interest in the Wichita tribe during the Fair, but also to the fact that Rinehart himself viewed the photograph of the *Wichita Woman and Child in Cradle* as one of his most popular, and most marketable, images. It is thus not surprising that the album would open with an image that was so popular among Rinehart's photographs that it was used as part of a marketing campaign for the Indian Congress, due to its "simulation of *Indianness.*" Taken for anthropological purposes but marketed by the Rinehart studio to feed the ongoing fascination with the "noble savage," which, as Philip Deloria has argued, "juxtaposes and conflates an urge to idealize and desire Indians and a need to despise and dispossess them," the photograph of the Wichita woman and others in the AIP album illustrates this tension.[29]

Mooney had accompanied the Wichita delegates from Oklahoma, and from his perspective, they were among the most interesting participants in the Indian Congress. During the Fair, they constructed a grass lodge in the "Indian encampment," a project in which Mooney was involved. During the planning of the Congress, Mooney traveled to Oklahoma, where he "paid the [Wichita] group to repair the oldest Wichita house remaining in Indian Territory, take it down, transport it, and reconstruct it on exposition grounds."[30] This was an expression of Mooney's aspirations that the Congress would be educational and have some ethnological benefit. The work of reconstructing the grass lodge, done mostly by women, took place over the course of a week, which provided opportunities for Mooney to observe, document, and take notes. Anthropologist Nancy Parezo has noted that during the Fair, the Wichita "discussed corn agriculture and demonstrated corn grinding with stone metates and wooden mortars, pottery making, and cooking in pottery vessels."[31] At the close of the Fair, Mooney purchased the lodge, along with corn-grinding tools, and the furniture, for the U.S. National Museum in Washington, D.C.[32]

In his report on the Omaha Fair, Mooney spoke in some detail about the Wichita tribe and their history, noting that they are "like all the tribes of the Caddoan stock ... an agricultural people ... [who] raised large quantities of corn, which they ground into meal upon stone metates or in wooden mortars, or boiled in pottery of their own making."[33] As if to remind the reader that the Wichita were "good," he reiterated that "they have never been at war with the whites."[34] Mooney went on to describe the composition of the Wichita delegation and their physical attributes:

> The party had been carefully selected, and included several noted runners distinguished in the ceremonial foot-races of the tribe, two Kichai woman, still retaining their peculiar language, and one of them with the old-style tattooing upon her face and body, and a mother with an infant in a cradle of willow rods. Physically the Wichita are dark and generally of medium size, with flowing hair inclined to waviness. They are accompanied by their chief, known to the whites as Tawákoni Jim, a man of commanding presence and fluent eloquence, and in former years a scout in the service of the government.[35]

With this extensive, generalized, description in mind, it is illustrative to look again at the photographs of the Wichita delegation in the AIP album. The details provided in Mooney's report reference the individuals and groups that appear in the album, including the *Wichita Woman and Child in Cradle* and *Group of Wichitas, Chief Tawáconi* [Tawákoni] *Jim and Wife at Center*. The Wichita woman and her child described by Mooney were thus chosen because they represented the Wichita "type": "dark and generally of medium size, with flowing hair inclined to waviness." But they also were chosen because the use of a cradleboard made of willow rods represented

"*Indianness*" and the "exotic" for the non-Native viewer. The cradleboard, which was used by a range of Indigenous cultures, served a practical purpose for many Indigenous women, allowing them to swaddle and secure their infants to a cradle that was easily transportable, and often carried on their backs (Fig. 10.1).

Mooney also speaks of Wichita Chief Tawákoni Jim, who is featured in a group portrait alongside his family, noting his "commanding presence and fluent eloquence" (Fig. 10.2). By referencing Chief Tawákoni Jim's work for the government as a scout, Mooney reiterates that he is both a Chief (which would have appealed to white Fairgoers and their fascination with "Indian Chiefs") and a "good Indian" who worked with, rather than against, the government. Like the young men to his left and right, he stands proudly, looking stoically toward the camera with his hands resting on the chair behind his wife (who is unnamed). He appears to wear a Western shirt and vest, but his long, wavy hair and gold ear ornaments are Wichita tribal dress. He is thus a representative of Native perseverance, on the one hand, and evidence of the presumed strides of government assimilationist policies, on the other. The information we are given about the sitters tells us very little about them or their lives, but nevertheless constructs a narrative about "*Indianness.*" The group is posed formally against a painted studio backdrop. The men stand behind the three seated women, and the young children pose at the sides and in front of the women. As noted earlier, the arrangement of individuals and groups is similar, stylistically, to the BAE's longstanding tradition of delegation photography. While some delegation portraits followed the procedures established by anthropology for the posing of sitters, others sought the most "picturesque" view (through pose, clothing, and props) that thoroughly captured, as seen in this album, the sitter or tribe's characteristic traits and adornments.

This tendency to depict sitters with props that simulated "*Indianness*," and hence the trope of the "vanishing race," can be seen most directly in the photograph of *Wichita Young Men – Fred Carruth and John Tatum*. Fred Carruth stands at left with a rifle in hand, while John Tatum is seated with hands clasped in his lap. Both men wear Western dress, but their long hair (adorned with feathers and other adornments), blankets, and moccasins, are emblematic of their Wichita culture. The presence of the rifle in this instance is intriguing. While it recalls the damaging stereotypes of Indigenous Americans as "savages" addressed at the beginning of this chapter, it also relates to the requests by the Fair organizers for Native groups to bring "implements and emblems of war."[36] The rifle was the weapon of choice for both the Western settler and the U.S. military, and therefore speaks on some level to assimilation. But it is also possible that the rifle is merely a prop intended to further demonstrate the simulation of "*Indianness.*"

Although the photographs and texts in the AIP album make clear reference to the ethnological aspects of the fair, as put forward by Frank Mooney and the BAE, Rinehart and Muhr's photographs were also indicative of the increasing fascination with the romanticized "Indian" as part of a "vanishing race." The image of the *Wichita Woman and Child in Cradle* was, undoubtedly, one of Rinehart's best-known and most frequently reproduced photographs. It provides an interesting case study for the various ways that this image was presented and circulated in the years following the Indian Congress by Rinehart and others. As previously discussed, the album caption titles the photograph *Wichita Woman and Child in Cradle* and includes no other identifying information, aside from the description of the Wichita. In other examples, including in his 1899 publication *Rinehart's Indians*, the woman is identified as "Ahahe. – Wichita." The book further notes that "This picture of mother and child is well known as the Indian Madonna."[37] The opening pages of *Rinehart's Indians* include a table of prices for "Rinehart's Productions of Indian Subjects," which range from platinum prints of individual images, to color reproductions of eighteen of his best subjects and reproductions of his catalogue (*Rinehart's Indians*). The suggestion that he *produced* his "Indian subjects" is interesting here. This is in keeping with his combination of anthropological tropes with romanticized images of the "vanishing race" for marketing purposes, but the reference to the "Indian Madonna" also alludes to Western pictorial tradition and hence to Rinehart's creation of his own, perhaps more marketable, version of *"Indianness."* The cover image for this book is one of Rinehart's color (re)productions, which was adapted from the original negative and later used as advertisement for Rinehart's work, but also the Indian Congress. The Wichita woman and her child thus came to represent Rinehart's own particular conception and commodification of the "Indian" and *"Indianness."*

Rinehart's marketing of the Indigenous photographs can be understood as part of a long history of exploitation at the hands of nineteenth-century photographers in the Western U.S., seeking to capitalize on ongoing battles between Indigenous tribes and the military over treaties, territories, and Native sovereignty.[38] His publication of the portraits taken at the Indian Congress was also part of the larger trend in the early-twentieth century that American art historian Elizabeth Hutchinson has referred to as the "Indian craze," in which Americans collected all manner of Indigenous cultural objects, including photographs, to include in their so-called "Indian corners."[39] The "Wichita Woman" was so popular among Rinehart's images that it was turned into a collectible poster, with added color and a border featuring stereotypical "Indian" objects – a peace pipe, feather headdress, arrows, and a drum – to market the Indian Congress during the run of the Fair.[40] With the frontier "closed" and Indigenous peoples now safely out of the way and on reservations, the American public sought souvenirs, often photographs, of the cultures and lifeways they had done their best to destroy. Ironically, by 1898, when these photographs were taken, it was a challenge for the Congress organizers to find individuals who still fit the part of the disappearing "Indian" that Americans wanted them to play. It fell to Rinehart and Muhr to highlight in their photographs and albums those aspects of Indigenous culture that would appeal, not just to Fairgoers and those seeking mementos of the Indian Congress, but also to those who sought to possess and collect the last vestiges of a "vanishing race." The AIP album, and certainly others like it, promised the sort of comprehensive overview, thanks to the inclusion of an archive of portraits classified by "type"/tribe, that might allow the viewer to know, and also – importantly – to possess, the "Indian." While one could certainly collect the individual photographs, and arguably many did, the small scale of the AIP album provided a portable museum of sorts that could be viewed and possessed over time and space.

Photographing the Indian Congress

In the final weeks of the Omaha Fair, Mooney had grown dissatisfied with the commercialized atmosphere (focused on souvenir collectibles and living Indigenous people on display as exhibits), eventually lamenting to W. J. McGee, John Wesley Powell's assistant at the BAE, "in this place an ethnologist's time is wasted & his labor lost."[41] There were, for Mooney, a few redeeming aspects of the Fair and the

Indian Congress, including his field work with the tribes in attendance. But the main reason he stayed on was to ensure that the BAE got its set of delegate portraits from Rinehart, who had up to this point been engaged with photographing other aspects of the Fair in his role as official photographer. The delegate portraits were taken in the final weeks of the Fair, after Mooney reached out to the BAE in Washington, D.C., and proposed that the Bureau allocate funds for the project that would be matched by the Fair organizers. A deal was struck between Rinehart and the BAE, with Mooney overseeing the photography of the delegates in attendance. The format of the photographs followed the longstanding BAE procedures for photographing Indian delegations in Washington. In exchange for funding the photographs, Rinehart would relinquish all of the negatives to the BAE for their archives.[42] In the end, the BAE was unhappy that Rinehart kept 100 negatives of the most marketable "Indian" portraits taken during the Congress, including a portrait of Geronimo, which they later had to request to use for a BAE annual report.[43]

Usually, such ethnographic photography projects were undertaken either by an anthropologist or under their direct supervision.[44] The BAE, which was under the control of the Smithsonian, also had an established tradition of studio portrait photography dating back to the Indigenous American delegation photographs made in the mid-nineteenth century by studio photographers such as Alexander Gardner. Although the systematic photography of Indigenous American delegations predates the founding of the BAE, the establishment of a government studio (or laboratory) in 1870 helped to codify a set of practices that would continue through the turn of the century. According to Paula Richardson Fleming and Judith Luskey:

> In the laboratory, visiting Indians were photographed against artificial backdrops or other known objects to permit physical measurements of sufficient accuracy for practical purposes, and special attention was given to recording the subjects in exact portrait, profile, and full-face, 'with the view of permitting the extension of measurement to the facial angle, form of cranium, and other anthropometric elements.'[45]

This approach became the standard for subsequent photography of Indigenous American tribes by the BAE and its affiliated photographers. Rinehart and Muhr, at least in terms of the "portrait types" requested by the BAE, were subject to this set of standards. Rinehart spoke of his role in this regard, noting that during the Indian Congress, he was

> ever busy recording scenes and securing *types* of these interesting people, who with their savage finery are rapidly fading away. In a remarkably short time education and civilization will stamp out the feather, beads and paint – the sign language, the dancing – and the Indian of the past will live but in memory and pictures.[46]

Although working in an official capacity for the Fair and the BAE, Rinehart and Muhr shared an interest in photographing Indigenous American cultures and capitalizing on the results. Rinehart, who was born in Illinois, moved to Denver, Colorado, in 1878, where he came into contact with photographer William Henry Jackson. With Jackson's assistance, Rinehart honed his photography skills and developed an interest in Indigenous American culture. Jackson, it should be noted, had also worked with Powell and the BAE, and went on to compile the voluminous album entitled *Photographs of Indians Selected from the Collection in the Possession of the U.S. Geological Survey of the Territories, Representing 70 Tribes*, in 1877.[47] Interestingly, the photography albums at the Omaha Public Library are in keeping with albums created by and for the BAE, and their inclusion of photographs and portraits organized by tribal affiliation.[48] Because some, but not all, of Rinehart's negatives were handed over to the BAE at the end of the Fair, they became part of the Bureau's pictorial record of Indigenous North American tribes. This and other albums of the sort provided models for Rinehart's "Indian" photographs and for the AIP album. Rinehart later moved to Omaha, Nebraska, in 1886, where he opened a studio specializing in commercial portraits. Rinehart was already a successful studio operator in Omaha when he was appointed official photographer of the Exposition in 1898. His photographs of the Fair range from images of buildings and grounds, exhibitions mounted by the states in attendance, the various events and happenings, and, of course, the so-called "Indian encampment."[49] Given Rinehart's vast responsibilities with regard to photographing the Fair, photographing individual delegates fell primarily to his assistant, Adolph Muhr. Unfortunately, because Muhr was Rinehart's assistant rather than his partner, Muhr's role in the production of the Indian Congress portraits was largely ignored. Muhr, who had significant one-on-one interactions with Indigenous delegates, and likely made most of the individual and group portraits, found himself shut out of the monetary gain from the photographs he took. Muhr later contested the copyright of the photographs, and in 1903, he left Rinehart's studio to work for Curtis.[50]

Muhr, then, played an important role in making the portraits of the delegates, and it is therefore his work that appears in the AIP album, even if Rinehart had a hand in compiling it. Muhr wrote about the experience of photographing the delegates in the catalogue *Rinehart's Platinum Prints of American Indians*:

> Being employed by Mr. Rinehart, the official photographer, to the writer was assigned the task of photographing the Indians, into which he carried the zest of a novel experience. They [the Indians] were timid at first, hung back like children, but a little coaxing and a better acquaintance soon made smooth sailing ... the acquaintance ripened into many warm friendships, and it is from conversations through the interpreters, that the information contained in this catalogue is compiled. The Ethnological Introduction for each tribe is written from notes made at that time and verified from the limited sources at hand. I trust any inaccuracies will be pardoned.[51]

Mooney is not mentioned in Muhr's description, but the reference to ethnology and the notes taken during the photography sittings suggests that he was working closely with Mooney. In his recollection of events, Mooney mentions:

> The work was done according to a systematic plan, the Indians being photographed in costume in tribal groups and singularly, in bust, profile, and full length, resulting in one of the finest collections of Indian portraits in existence ... at the same time, the Indian name of each individual was obtained with its

interpretation, and some points of information concerning the tribe, with brief vocabularies of each language.[52]

Rinehart later adapted the notes taken by Muhr and Mooney during the portrait sittings for use in his captions in the 1899 catalogue *Rinehart's Indians*. Given that this information appeared in a variety of contexts in Rinehart's published and unpublished photographic catalogues, it is perhaps not surprising that these brief captions, often ethnocentric in nature, are similar to those in the AIP album and its "List of Tribes." The photographs taken by Muhr and Rinehart, and the later compilation of the AIP album, reflect, as noted previously, the complex narratives surrounding American imperialism, Manifest Destiny, and Federal Indian policy, on view at the Omaha World's Fair and its Indian Congress.

The Indian Congress at the Trans-Mississippi and International Exposition

> The Exposition has become the instrument of civilization. Being a concomitant to empire, westward it takes its way – The Crystal Palace, the Centennial, the World's Fair, the Trans-Mississippi Exposition.[53]

The aforementioned statement, given by John N. Baldwin at the opening ceremony of the Trans-Mississippi and International Exposition of 1898, clarifies the broader imperialist concerns of the Omaha World's Fair, which foregrounded the achievements and character, in rather lofty terms, of white settlers in the western U.S., "who overcame the 'wilderness' and converted the 'desert' into a garden of benefits."[54] A range of scholars in history and anthropology have addressed the imperialist underpinnings of the Omaha Fair, which played out against the backdrop of the Spanish-American War.[55] Following on the heels of the 1889 Paris Universal Exposition and the 1893 Chicago World's Columbian Exposition, the Trans-Mississippi and International Exposition was held from June 1 to October 31, 1898 in Omaha. Mounted during a time of great political and economic uncertainty, the Omaha Fair went on to become the most popular U.S. World's Fair up to that point. Intended to showcase the development of the West, and the success of the American imperialist project, the Omaha Exposition was introduced by the organizers in the official guidebook:

> We believe that an Exposition of all the products, industries and civilization of the States west of the Mississippi River, made at some central gateway where the world can behold the wonderful capabilities of these great wealth-producing States, would be of great value, not only to the Trans-Mississippi States, but to all the home-seekers in the world.[56]

It was also hoped, according to historian Robert Rydell, that the Fair "would restore popular faith in the basic soundness and rightness of the American economic system."[57] The Fair would include exhibits that featured examples of industry, agriculture, and mining from states west of the Mississippi River.

Perhaps not surprisingly, given the desire to bolster the economy and showcase American prosperity in the West, the two individuals responsible for the planning of the Fair were Omaha businessmen: Gurdon Wattles, a local banker (who became the

Exposition's president), and Edward Rosewater, founder and editor of the local newspaper, the *Omaha Daily Bee*. Rosewater was particularly important in garnering federal support for the Fair, but he was also responsible for developing the idea of the Indian Congress, which he believed would be a major commercial and educational attraction at the Fair, rivaling the famed Midway at the Chicago World's Columbian Exposition.[58] The inclusion of an Indian Congress promoted, on the one hand, the narrative of "progress" in the American West, and the triumph of American imperialism and Manifest Destiny. But it also repeated tropes of previous fairs and expositions, which similarly foregrounded ethnology as part of their promotion of imperialist and, in the case of the American fairs, heroicized colonialist settler narratives of American history and culture. For Rosewater, the presence of Native Americans would be the highlight of the Fair, or its signature achievement that set the Omaha Fair apart from previous World's Fairs. In order to avoid allusions to amusement and Wild West shows (which had limited educational benefit), Rosewater opted to call the gathering an "Indian Congress."

The Omaha Fair thus became a performative site where Native American tribes were showcased in ethnological "living exhibits," as they lived and acted for the crowds. Displays of "Indians" at World's Fairs, which started with the Chicago World's Columbian Exposition in 1893, and continued at the 1901 Pan-American Exposition in Buffalo, New York, and the 1904 Louisiana Purchase Exposition in St. Louis, sought to capitalize on Indigenous Americans' popularity while highlighting ethnology and expansionist thematics.[59] In planning for the Indian Congress, Nebraska U.S. Senator William V. Allen made allusions to colonial exhibits at European fairs, particularly those of France and Belgium – in which groups of colonized peoples were displayed as living exhibits.[60]

The Indian Congress brought to Omaha 545 Indigenous delegates from 36 tribes. In Rosewater's remarks about the planning of the Congress, he invoked the then-popular belief that this gathering of Indigenous North American peoples might be the last time that such a meeting would occur before the tribes disappeared altogether. In an article for the *Omaha Daily Bee*, he noted that a plan was afoot for "an extensive exhibit illustrative of the life, customs and decline of the aboriginal inhabitants of the western hemisphere."[61] He went on to suggest that this opportunity "would undoubtedly be the last gathering of these tribes before the bronzed sons of the forests and plains, which resisted the encroaching of the white man, are gathered to the happy hunting grounds."[62] By positioning the Indian Congress as comprised of those who had "resisted the encroaching of the white man," it could be said that his approach ran counter to the federal government's assimilationist policies, which sought to "civilize" the "savage Indian." Although Rosewater's explicitly racist statements were intended to engender public support for the Congress, he also hoped that by positioning it as educational and as a significant historical event, he could petition the federal government for the funds necessary for such an undertaking. Since tribes were deemed wards of the U.S. government, it was also necessary to gain government approval to permit individuals to leave their reservations to travel to Omaha for the Fair. Rosewater also cited his collaboration with the BAE to bolster his case. Viewing the Indian Congress as a unique opportunity to bring together and document Indigenous tribes, Powell, BAE's Director, agreed to bring the resources of the Bureau to the organization of the Congress. And indeed, when the BAE signed on to participate in the Fair, Powell similarly relied on the "vanishing Indian" argument – which was embedded in the sort of "salvage ethnography" that was at the heart of the BAE's mandate – when seeking federal funding for the Congress, noting that it would provide an opportunity to study languages, rituals, and artifacts that would soon disappear.[63]

The educational goals of the Indian Congress were reiterated by Sen. Allen, who, in his petition to the U.S. Congress, viewed the gathering as "an effective means of educating the people on the advancement made by the Indians under the system adopted by the Government."[64] In other words, the Indian Congress would educate Americans on the effectiveness of the government's assimilationist policies. As further evidence of these presumed successes, Harvard anthropologist Alice Fletcher organized a separate exhibition at the Fair, an "Indian School" display, that celebrated "Native industry through collections of children's handiwork and presented the Indians' successful assimilation through education."[65] The Fair thus put forward conflicting messages about the place of Native American peoples in the American story: as nearing extinction or assimilating.

The Indian Congress was organized "to make an extensive exhibit illustrative of the mode of life, native industries, and ethnic traits of as many aboriginal American tribes as possible."[66] The plan, according to the federal Indian Office (later called the Bureau of Indian Affairs), was to

> bring together selected families or groups from all the principal tribes, and camp them in tepees, wigwams, hogans, etc., on the exposition grounds, and there permit them to conduct their domestic affairs as they do at home, and make and sell their wares for their own profit.[67]

Although the goal (for Rosewater anyway) was to represent as many tribes west of the Mississippi as possible, Mooney, in his report on the Indian Congress, later lamented that the vast majority represented "but a single type, the ordinary tipi tribes of the plains," and thus excluded tribes in California, Oregon, and New Mexico, among others.[68] For Rosewater, the planning for a comprehensive gathering of Indigenous American tribes eventually gave way to his belief that those "who had seldom come in touch with whites would prove a more attractive feature" at the Fair.[69] The goal, it seems, was to include those individuals and groups who exuded what Vizenor has called "simulations of *Indianness*," even if the task of finding representative "types" proved difficult. The Indian Office directive went on to state that the encampment at the Fair

> should be as thoroughly aboriginal in every respect as practicable, and that the primitive traits and characteristics of the several tribes should be distinctly set forth. This point should be constantly kept in view in the selection of the Indians and in the collection of materials.[70]

When the funds for the Indian Congress were appropriated by the U.S. Congress a month after the Omaha Fair opened to the public, Captain William A. Mercer, acting agent of the Omaha and Winnebago Agency, pushed Indigenous agents to invite delegations to participate in the Congress.[71] Despite the allocated funds, the participants of the Congress would not be paid for their involvement, or for their travel. On top of that, they were expected to wear their traditional dress, and bring materials for constructing their houses, objects to sell at the Fair, and "implements and emblems of war."[72] The Omaha Fair trafficked in the sort of spectacle that brought white fairgoers to see "sham battles," ceremonies, and dances that harkened back to times past (including the Ghost Dance that had precipitated the massacre at Wounded Knee). Although Indigenous groups would be able to keep any funds made from the sale of objects, many declined to participate because they believed it to be a risky financial endeavor. Some invited delegates considered participating because it would allow them to leave the reservation at a time when their mobility was seriously curtailed. Indeed, some scholars have suggested that despite the motives for organizing the Indian Congress, it was, in fact, evidence of cultural persistence.[73]

With the BAE's involvement secured through Powell, James Mooney was approached to take the lead in organizing the Indian Congress. Mooney, who had participated in the ethnographic exhibitions at previous World's Fairs, supported its potential educational and ethnographic benefits: "Briefly they want to show our nativ [sic] tribes & their arts & life on a more complete scale then has ever been attempted hitherto."[74] Mooney was assisted by Mercer, who was largely responsible for overseeing the delegates when they arrived in Omaha and set up their encampments on the Midway. It was Mercer who helped organize the popular Wild West style "sham battles" that ensued, much to the chagrin of Mooney. In the days that followed the Indian Congress's opening parade on 4 August, visitors could walk freely through the "Indian encampments," where they could watch delegates – who were identified by name and tribal affiliation on signage placed in front of tepees and tents – living, working (often, creating objects for sale at the Fair), or engaging in ceremonies, dances, and horse races.[75] The Wichita tribe, at the urging of Mooney, brought a grass house to the encampment and built it on site, a process photographed by Mooney and observed by fairgoers.[76] The delegates were thus performing their "Indigeneity" on a daily basis, for the amusement of fairgoers. It was not long before the approach shifted from one focused on education, and on the strides made by U.S. Indian policy (i.e. assimilation), to one of entertainment and spectacle, taking cues from Wild West shows.[77]

The idea for "sham battles" that pitted Indigenous Americans against whites, and sometimes against one another, originated with a fraternal order of white men known as the Improved Order of Red Men. This Order of non-Native, white men who liked to "play Indian," hoped to camp on the grounds of the Fair and envisioned two battles between whites ("cowboys") and "friendly Indians" – all of whom would be played by members of the Order. They, in turn, would be pitted against the "hostile Indians" (those not yet fully assimilated), played by delegates of the Indian Congress.[78] The idea was received enthusiastically by Mercer, who even agreed to participate in the battle. Although the Order had to back out at the last minute, Mercer moved forward with plans, gathering upward of 700 white and Indigenous performers. The monumental battle, which took place in the "Indian" encampment with guns and fake cartridges, involved simulated scalpings, fictional acts of torture, chases, dancing, and gun battles, ending with Mercer leading the "Indians" to the reservation. The symbolism was clear: it is all fun and games during the Fair, but when it is over, delegates will be returned to their respective reservations. These sham battles were repeated many times over the next several months for thousands of eager visitors. Mooney, however, was particularly affronted by such attempts to position the Indian Congress as a form of entertainment in the eyes of the public, which he believed would undermine the educational possibilities of such a gathering. From this point forward, Mooney noted that the Indian Congress "has degenerated into a Wild West show with the sole purpose of increasing gate receipts."[79] The Indian Congress, and by extension the AIP album, visualized these conflicting narratives, representing at one and the same time the spectacle of Indigenous Americans enacting their disappearance, the presumed progress made by assimilationist policies, and the ethnological interests of the BAE and Fair organizers. Viewed from our contemporary moment, the AIP album and its attendant photographs have more to tell us about new approaches to the commemorative or family album. Recent projects by contemporary Indigenous American students, scholars, and artists suggest new ways of reading these photographs that acknowledge their troubled past and seek to re-interpret them in more empowering ways as symbolic not of disappearance, but of survivance.

Contemporary Reframings

> When we, as Indians, venture through our past by viewing early photographs, we probably look at the faces, apparel, and settings to seek recognition or link to kinship that is long gone. We minutely study every detail of earrings, hairstyles, necklaces, beadwork designs, and featherwork. As I search through these early photographs, I wonder just what the subjects would say to me, and I to them, if we were able to converse if only for a minute.[80]

The aforementioned quote by Kiowa/Delaware author Linda Poolaw makes clear that while historic photographs of Indigenous American peoples, such as those by Rinehart and Muhr at the Omaha Fair, are problematic in their allusions to "*Indianness*," they are also important documents of Native perseverance. Although long inscribed by popular and anthropological narratives, as discussed above, the photographs of the Indian Congress have, in recent years, been reconsidered and reimagined by Indigenous authors, curators, scholars, and students, seeking recognition and dialogue with past generations. Immensely popular and frequently reproduced, Rinehart and Muhr's photographs are now included in the collections of many important libraries, museums, and archives such as the Omaha Public Library, the Getty Museum, the Smithsonian's National Anthropological Archives, and Haskell Indian Nations Museum, among many others. The diversity of this list provides some indication of the types of institutions that keep and collect photographs of Indigenous North Americans.

As noted briefly at the start of this chapter, in 1975, the Alumni Association of Haskell Indian Nations University, once the Haskell Indian boarding school, purchased a collection of 809 original glass plate negatives made by Rinehart and Muhr in order to further "a conversation between the people photographed over one hundred years ago and American Indian people today."[81] The photographs have thus become the centerpiece of Haskell's "American Indian" research materials, with which students can engage with and explore their past. As photographer Shan Goshorn (Eastern Band Cherokee) has articulated,

> [u]nlike many non-Natives who view lineage as a line with no connection from one end to another, we see ourselves as belonging to a spiral, with ancestors and descendants ever winding, almost touching – illustrating the impact and relationship our generations have upon each other.[82]

Viewing lineage as a spiral, Goshorn stresses continuity, rather than change or rupture, when descendants engage with photographs of their ancestors, which is particularly relevant for Haskell students seeking connections with cultural traditions. Haskell was at the center of the U.S. government's assimilationist policies, and because Rinehart and Muhr's photographs are important documents relating to Native survivance in the face of forced assimilation, it is apt that they should have found their way to Haskell. Although the Indian Congress photographs are highly problematic for perpetuating the mythology of the "vanishing race" and racist "types," they have been a source of inspiration and learning for Indigenous scholars, artists, and students, at Haskell and beyond. The exhibition and book, *Beyond the Reach of Time and Change: Native American Reflections on the Frank A. Rinehart Photograph Collection,* illustrates the Indian Congress photographs alongside a series of reflections written by Indigenous Americans in 2004. These images are thus able to speak across time to new generations of Indigenous individuals seeking understanding of their cultures, their past, and their ways of life. Much as Haskell has become a place of reconnection and re-engagement, the Indian Congress photographs have been similarly reimagined as a way of understanding the past. Although still inscribed by the racist narratives that determined their reception at the turn of the century, they are being continuously reinscribed and reconsidered by future generations seeking to create their own family albums and narratives.

In 2021, contemporary Apsáalooke artist Wendy Red Star created a project for the Joslyn Art Museum featuring photographs from the 1898 Indian Congress.[83] The immersive, site-specific installation, swathed in patriotic red, white, and blue bunting, included hundreds of cut-outs of photographic portraits by Rinehart and Muhr taken during the Indian Congress. The cut-outs of Indigenous delegates were organized in rows of "exhibits" and displayed in an exposition case of the sort used to showcase objects at the Fair. Much as the delegates had been "on display" as part of "living exhibits," Red Star's installation, which removes them from time and space, further suggests that Native American delegates, were, in essence, objects (likenesses) for sale. Her figure cut-outs have removed the backdrop and other extraneous details, so the delegates appear to stand or sit on the display case, now engaging in conversation with one another. The cut-outs are grouped by nation on the tiered display table to demonstrate the sheer magnitude of the gathering. For Red Star, the process of cutting out the Indigenous figures was akin to creating a family album on a grand scale.

The process of creating this grand family album was personal for Red Star, since many of Rinehart and Muhr's subjects were from the Apsáalooke Nation (though none appear in the AIP album that is the subject of this chapter). Although many of the photographs used by Red Star were taken at the Omaha Fair, some were taken by Rinehart during a later visit to Apsáalooke lands in Montana, where Red Star herself grew up decades later. A large-scale, contemporary color photo mural peeking out from behind red velvet curtains, perhaps a reference to Charles Willson Peale's *The Artist in his Museum*, depicts a sacred site on Apsáalooke lands. Red Star's gathering of Indigenous delegates is transformed into a celebratory affair on Indigenous lands that acknowledges tribal sovereignty and survivance, thus shifting the focus away from the colonialist settler narrative that initially inscribed them. By reimagining the problematic history of these photographs and rejecting racist stereotypes, Red Star's project reinscribes them with the agency initially denied to the sitters.

Red Star's imaginative reimagining of the family album through the work of Rinehart and Muhr brings us full circle, back to the Indian Congress delegate portraits presented in the AIP album, allowing us to consider how the album has been viewed over time. Although the original work of the AIP album, which, as discussed above, acted as a discreet collection or mini-archive that encapsulated the totalizing, Westernized knowledge of a race believed to be vanishing, its meanings and interpretations are not fixed. The AIP album presented Indigenous North Americans as objects to be looked at and collected, as photographic specimens of popular and ethnographic interest. It reflected the complex and conflicting narratives around the popular and ethnological/anthropological that were embedded in both the Indian Congress and the photographs taken of the delegates. These operations have shifted with Red Star's cut-outs, removing the photographs, literally and metaphorically, from their original nefarious context. Instead, she presents them in such a way that they engage with and converse with one another as spirits returned to ancestral/tribal land as part of a multi-generational community. The silence that inscribed the sitters in the AIP album has been given a new voice by Red Star, as she lifts them from the pages of the album and invites the viewer to engage with them as a reunited community of elders on sacred Apsáalooke lands. The sitters' eyes no longer engage ours. They now engage each other's.

Indeed, as Vizenor has argued,

> the fugitive poses in simulations are the eternal critics of photography; all the more vehement because the simulations of *Indianness* have overturned the real presence of the tribes. Watch the shadows of the eyes to hear the narrative of continuous presence.[84]

For Vizenor, in photographs like those in the AIP album, it is in the eyes that presence (as a form of survivance) is revealed, not in the costume which is merely a simulation that traps the sitter in "fugitive poses." "The eyes of the wounded fugitives in photographs are the sources of stories, the traces of tribal survivance ... [they] are the narrative presence of the tribes."[85] Red Star's installation re-configures the notion of the photo album as a collection of portrait "types" to be sold and circulated for popular and scientific purposes. She returns Rinehart and Muhr's sitters to their continuous presence, ensuring that the Indigenous delegates that gathered together in the summer of 1898 would be forever linked, not to "simulations of *Indianness*," but to Indigenous lands and Indigenous presence.

Notes

1 Gerald Vizenor, "Fugitive Poses," in *Excavating Voices: Listening to Photographs of Native Americans* (Philadelphia: University of Pennsylvania Museum, 1998), 10.
2 Vizenor, "Fugitive Poses," 11.
3 Edward S. Curtis, *The North American Indian Being a Series of Volumes Picturing and Describing the Indians of the United States and Alaska*, ed. Frederick Webb Hodge (Cambridge, MA: The University Press, 1907–1930).
4 This shift occurs, according to Martha Sandweiss, when "the portrait that once memorialized a personal, private moment is easily reimagined as a public commodity, the record of a specific historical event reembraced as an ahistorical visual metaphor." See Martha Sandweiss, *Print the Legend: Photography and the American West* (New Haven: Yale University Press, 2002), 215.
5 Sandweiss, *Print the Legend*, 217.

6 Carole Nez, "Unless You Were There," in *Beyond the Reach of Time and Change: Native American Reflections on the Frank A. Rinehart Photograph Collection* (Tucson: The University of Arizona Press, 2004), 124.

7 Although Haskell Indian Nations University was born from a troubling legacy, today it serves for many young students as a cultural touchstone, allowing Indigenous students to reconnect with their indigeneity after generations of forced assimilation and, for some, a loss of their ancestors' cultural traditions.

8 In the pages that follow, in keeping with the original title given to the gathering of Indigenous tribes at the Trans-Mississippi and Universal Exposition, I will use the now-outmoded term "Indian" when referring to the "Indian Congress." Elsewhere, I will use the term Indigenous Americans, rather than Native Americans, which is falling out of favor, to describe Indigenous tribes in the United States.

9 Although the Bureau of American Ethnology also collected photographs, the collection of negatives allowed the Bureau to print photographs for later use in reports and other U.S. government publications. On Frank Rinehart, see Royal Sutton, *On the Edge of Distinction* (Bloomington, IN: AuthorHouse, 2013); Frank A. Rinehart, *The Face of Courage: The Indian Photographs of Frank A. Rinehart* (Fort Collins, CO: Old Army Press, 1972); Simon J. Ortiz, *Beyond the Reach of Time and Change: Native American Reflections on the Frank A. Rinehart Photograph Collection* (Tucson: University of Arizona Press by arrangement with Haskell Indian Nations University, 2004); Robert Bigart and Clarence Woodcock, "The Rinehart Photographs: A Portfolio," *Montana: The Magazine of Western History*, Vol. 29, No. 4 (Autumn, 1979): 23–37; Roger Watson, "Photographs by Rinehart and Muhr of the 1898 Omaha Indian Congress," *America in Britain*, Vol. XL (2002): 21–29.

10 The term "Indian craze" has been used by Elizabeth Hutchinson to describe the interest in and collection of Native American objects and images at the turn of the century. Elizabeth Hutchinson, *The Indian Craze: Primitivism, Modernism, and Transculturation in American Art, 1890-1915* (Durham: Duke University Press, 2009).

11 The narrative trope of the "vanishing race" was so prevalent in the late-nineteenth and early-twentieth centuries that it was used as the title of Joseph Dixon's 1913 book of photographs: Joseph K. Dixon, *The Vanishing Race: The Last Great Indian Council* (Garden City, NY: Doubleday, 1913). However, as will be discussed later in this essay, the narrative of the "vanishing race" was perpetuated in both popular culture and anthropology, particularly by the Bureau of American Ethnology and its emphasis on what is known as "salvage ethnography." In "salvage ethnography," there is an emphasis on recording the practices and folklore of cultures threatened with extinction. Nancy Parezo has suggested that the presence of the Indian Congress at the Omaha Fair would allow visitors to engage in their own "salvage ethnography." See Nancy Parezo, "Exposition Anthropology," in *The Trans-Mississippi and International Expositions of 1898–1899: Art, Anthropology, and Popular Culture at the Fin de Siècle* (Omaha: University of Nebraska Press, 2018), 301.

12 Philip Deloria, *Playing Indian* (New Haven: Yale University Press, 1998), 90.

13 Frederick Jackson Turner gave his famous address, in which he declared the frontier closed, at a meeting of the American Historical Association in Chicago on July 12, 1893, at the World's Columbian Exposition. Turner's essay can be read here: https://www.historians.org/about-aha-and-membership/aha-history-and-archives/historical-archives/the-significance-of-the-frontier-in-american-history-(1893)

14 Although the term "ethnology" relates to the study of the characteristics of various peoples and the relationships between them, as Curtis Hinsley notes, ethnology was "the general term for anthropological work at the time." Whereas, the term "ethnography" relates to the detailed study of a particular group. See Curtis Hinsley, *The Smithsonian and the American Indian: Making a Moral Anthropology in Victorian America* (Washington, DC: Smithsonian Institution Press, 1981), 29.

15 Elizabeth Edwards, "Photographic 'Types': The Pursuit of Method," *Visual Anthropology*, Vol. 3, No. 2–3 (1990): 240.

16 For more on this aspect of the Omaha fair, see Robert Rydell, *All the World's a Fair: Visions of Empire at American International Expositions, 1876–1916* (Chicago: University of Chicago Press, 1984); Wendy Jean Katz, ed., *The Trans-Mississippi and International Expositions of 1898–1899: Art, Anthropology, and Popular Culture at the Fin de Siècle* (Omaha: University of Nebraska Press, 2018); Bonnie M. Miller, "The Incoherencies of Empire: The "Imperial" Image of the Indian at the Omaha World's Fairs of 1898–99," *American Studies*, Vol. 39, No. 3/4 (Fall/Winter 2008): 39–62.
17 Melissa Banta and Curtis M. Hinsley, *From Site to Sight: Anthropology, Photography, and the Power of Imagery* (Cambridge, MA: Peabody Museum Press, 1986), 61.
18 Susan Sontag, *On Photography* (New York: Anchor Books, Doubleday, 1990), 15.
19 Sontag, *On Photography*, 14.
20 The approach taken by the BAE in their photographs of Native American tribes conforms (in terms of posing the sitter in frontal, profile, and full-body views) to the larger genre of "types" or "portrait types," which, as Elizabeth Edwards has noted, existed in a variety of formats and styles, extending "from anthropometric studies by scientists that rendered the human body as a measurable and comparable object ... to a wide range of 'curiosities', exotica and racial and cultural stereotypes ... . As it was expressed through photography, 'type' brought together, variously and in different degrees, the aesthetics of the western concept of portraiture and that of the scientific specimen. Arranged in the picture space for visibility and legibility, such types found their meanings in relation to assumed racial hierarchies. The idea of the 'type' was premised not on human individuality, but on the production of exemplars of racial categories ..." See Elizabeth Edwards, "Evolving Images: Photography, Race and Popular Darwinism," in *Endless Forms: Charles Darwin, Natural Science, and the Visual Arts*, eds. Diana Donald and Jane Munro (New Haven: Yale University Press, 2009), 168–169. See also Elizabeth Edwards, "Photographic 'Types': The Pursuit of Method."
21 The tradition of Native American delegation visits, as a form of diplomacy, goes back to the colonial period. Beginning in the mid-nineteenth century, a systematic effort was made to photograph delegations during their visits to Washington, D.C. The earliest delegation photographs date to 1851, but they continued throughout the nineteenth and early-twentieth centuries. The format and procedures for taking these photographs were codified with preference given to specific views (frontal, profile, and full-length) that would provide the best and most anthropological data. See Parezo, "Exposition Anthropology," 358. For more on Delegation photography, see Paula Richardson Fleming and Judith Luskey, *The North American Indians in Early Photographs* (London: Calmann and King Ltd., 2000).
22 Nancy Parezo, "Exposition Anthropology," 358.
23 Karen Barber, Email Correspondence with Archivist Martha Grenzeback, Omaha Public Library, August 21, 2021.
24 Parezo, "Exposition Anthropology," 359.
25 Banta and Hinsley, *From Site to Sight*, 61.
26 American Indians Photographs album, 1898, Omaha Public Library.
27 Mooney, "The Indian Congress at Omaha."
28 James Mooney, "The Indian Congress at Omaha," *American Anthropologist*, Vol. 1, No. 8 (1899): 133.
29 Philip Deloria, *Playing Indian*, 4.
30 Parezo, "Exposition Anthropology," 347. See note 40 above for information about viewing images of the construction of the Wichita grass lodge at the Omaha Fair.
31 Parezo, "Exposition Anthropology," 341.
32 Parezo, "Exposition Anthropology," 341.
33 Mooney, "The Indian Congress at Omaha," 131.
34 Mooney, "The Indian Congress at Omaha," 131.
35 Mooney, "The Indian Congress at Omaha," 133.
36 Parezo, "Exposition Anthropology," 334.
37 *Rinehart's Indians*, unpaginated.
38 For more on this, see Sandweiss, *Print the Legend*.
39 Hutchinson, *The Indian Craze*.

40 The Indian Congress poster, which is captioned "Ahahe, Wichita" in the negative, can be viewed on the Trans-Mississippi and International Exposition website: https://trans-mississippi.unl.edu/memorabilia/view/TMI05048.html
41 Mooney is quoted in: Parezo, "Exposition Anthropology," 353.
42 The government and the BAE had been producing and collecting photographs and negatives since at least the 1850s, which included photographs taken during delegation visits, the U.S. Geological Surveys, and fieldwork undertaken by BAE ethnologists. The collection of photographs of Native American tribes went hand in hand with the larger goals of the Bureau of American Ethnology and now forms part of the vast National Anthropological Archives at the Smithsonian's Natural History Museum. See https://www.si.edu/siasc/naa.
43 Bigart and Woodcock, "The Rinehart Photographs: A Portfolio," 24–25.
44 See, for example, Ira Jacknis, "In Search of the Imagemaker: James Mooney as Ethnographic Photographer," *Visual Anthropology*, Vol. 3, No. 2–3 (1990): 179–212.
45 Fleming and Luskey, *The North American Indians in Early Photographs*, 178.
46 Italics are my emphasis. Fleming and Luskey, *The North American Indians in Early Photographs*, 178.
47 William Henry Jackson, *Photographs of Indians Selected from the Collection in the Possession of the U.S. Geological Survey of the Territories Prof. F.V. Hayden in Charge. Representing 70 Different Tribes*, 1876. Jackson's album of photographs by Charles Milton Bell, Thomas Easterly, Alexander Gardner, Benjamin Gurney, William Jackson, James McClees, and Antonio Zeno Shindler, was accompanied by a "Descriptive Catalogue" that included brief histories of the represented tribal nations and biographies for each sitter. William Henry Jackson, *Descriptive Catalogue of Photographs of North American Indians* (Washington, DC: U.S. Department of the Interior Miscellaneous Publications, No. 9, 1877).
48 These albums included the work of multiple photographers employed or commissioned at one point or another to take (or supply) photographs of Native tribes for the BAE, and are now part of the National Anthropological Archives at the Smithsonian Institution. See, for example, https://sova.si.edu/record/NAA.PhotoLot.60; and https://archive.org/details/PhotographsOfIndiansSelectedFromTheCollectionInThePossessionOfThe/page/n3/mode/2up
49 Rinehart's photographs from the Trans-Mississippi and International Exposition (approximately 3,000 of them) can be viewed on the Omaha Public Library's website, which houses their digital collection. See: https://digital.omahalibrary.org/digital/collection/p16747coll1. To view additional photographs from the Indian Congress, see the Omaha Public Library's Indian Congress collection: https://cdm16747.contentdm.oclc.org/digital/collection/p16747coll2.
50 Bigart and Woodcock, "The Rinehart Photographs: A Portfolio," 23–37.
51 Adolph F. Muhr is quoted in: Frank Albert Rinehart, *Rinehart's Platinum Prints of American Indians* (Omaha: F. A. Rinehart, Photographer, 1899), 3.
52 Mooney, "The Indian Congress at Omaha," 147.
53 John N. Baldwin is quoted in his opening address to the Trans-Mississippi and International Exposition in: James B. Hayes, *History of the Trans-Mississippi and International Exposition of 1898* (St. Louis: Woodward & Tiernan Printing Co., 1910), 347.
54 Hayes, *History of the Trans-Mississippi and International Exposition of 1898*, 347.
55 See, for example, Bonnie M. Miller, "The Incoherencies of Empire"; Robert Rydell, *All the World's a Fair: Visions of Empire at American International Expositions, 1876–1916*; Wendy Jean Katz, ed., *The Trans-Mississippi and International Expositions of 1898–1899*; and Robert A. Trennert, Jr, "Selling Indian Education at World's Fairs and Expositions, 1893-1904," *American Indian Quarterly*, Vol. 11, No. 3 (Summer, 1987): 203–220.
56 *Official Guidebook to Omaha, Trans-Mississippi and International Exposition* (Omaha: Megeath Stationery Company, 1898), 9.
57 Robert Rydell, "Introduction: America's Jewel in the Crown," in *The Trans-Mississippi and International Expositions of 1898–1899*, 5.
58 Lester G. Moses, "Indians on the Midway: Wild West Shows and the Indian Bureau at the World's Fairs, 1893-1904," *South Dakota History*, Vol. 21, No. 3 (Fall 1991): 205–229.
59 See, for example, Moses, "Indians on the Midway," and Robert Rydell, *All the World's a Fair.*

60 William V. Allen to the Secretary of the Interior [Correspondence], December 5, 1897, Senate Report No. 397, *Senate Reports*, Vol. 1, No. 3620, 2–3.
61 Edward Rosewater, "The History of the Indian: Planning for an Interesting Exhibit at the Transmississippi Exposition," *Omaha Daily Bee* (August 16, 1897): 8.
62 Rosewater, "The History of the Indian," 8.
63 Miller, "The Incoherencies of Empire," 45.
64 William V. Allen is quoted in: Robert Bigart and Clarence Woodcock, "The Trans-Mississippi Exposition & the Flathead Delegation," *Montana: The Magazine of Western History*, Vol. 29, No. 4 (Autumn, 1979): 16.
65 Miller, "The Incoherencies of Empire," 49. A noted ethnographer, Alice C. Fletcher was an assimilationist who had helped conceptualize and draft the 1887 Dawes Act. In the exhibition, she hoped to demonstrate "the things the Indian mind was capable of," by bolstering the Indigenous art industry on certain reservations, and by showing that through education Indigenous children were capable of assimilation and citizenship. Alice Fletcher is quoted in: Nancy Parezo, "Exposition Anthropology," 318.
66 Mooney, "The Indian Congress at Omaha," 128.
67 Mooney, "The Indian Congress at Omaha," 128.
68 Mooney, "The Indian Congress at Omaha," 130.
69 Rosewater in Rydell, *All the World's a* Fair, 113.
70 Mooney, "The Indian Congress at Omaha," 128.
71 Rydell, *All the World's a Fair*, 113–114.
72 Parezo, "Exposition Anthropology," 334.
73 Josh Clough, "'Vanishing' Indians? Cultural Persistence on Display at the Omaha World's Fair of 1898," *Great Plains Quarterly*, 25 (Spring 2005): 67–86.
74 James Mooney is quoted in: Bigart and Woodcock, "The Trans-Mississippi Exposition & the Flathead Delegation," 16.
75 Rydell, *All the World's a Fair*, 114.
76 Photographs of the construction of Wichita Grass House can be viewed on the Trans-Mississippi and International Exposition website, which is administered by the University of Nebraska, Lincoln (https://trans-mississippi.unl.edu/photographs/view/TMI01004.html). The website (https://trans-mississippi.unl.edu/) includes a broad range of photographs, documents, press clippings, and publications related to the Omaha World's Fair, many of which are drawn from the archives of the Omaha Public Library.
77 The most popular of the "Wild West" shows was Buffalo Bill's Wild West Show, which opened, ironically, in 1883 in Omaha, Nebraska. Buffalo Bill's shows featured "cowboys" and "Indians" in raucous spectacles that re-enacted historical events like the Battle of Little Big Horn. Buffalo Bill was known for recruiting well-known Chiefs, including Sitting Bull, to participate in his shows. Interestingly, Buffalo Bill's Wild West Show had performed during the Chicago World's Fair, but beyond its gates, which much to the chagrin of the Fair organizers, had attracted visitors away from the Fair. The "sham battles" that ensued at the Omaha Fair were, in part, an attempt to keep Fairgoers at the Fair. See Rydell, "Introduction," in *The Trans-Mississippi and International Expositions of 1898-1899: Art, Anthropology, and Popular Culture at the Fin de Siècle*, 8.
78 For more on the tendency of white Americans to "play Indian," see Philip Deloria, *Playing Indian*.
79 Mooney was particularly frustrated with Mercer, who was paying delegates to participate in "sham battles." Mooney was concerned that Indigenous peoples were no longer compelled to engage in other aspects of the Indian Congress (producing objects and traditional wares) that would teach ethnography to the Fair-going public. James Mooney is quoted in: Rydell, *All the World's a Fair*, 117.
80 Linda Poolaw is quoted in: *Beyond the Reach of Time and Change*, x.
81 Bobbi Rahder, "Introduction," in *Beyond the Reach of Time and Change: Native American Reflections on the Frank A. Rinehart Photograph Collection*, ix.
82 Shan Goshorn (Eastern Band of Cherokee) is quoted in: Ortiz, *Beyond the Reach of Time and Change*, ix.
83 "Gallery Guide: Wendy Red Star, January 30–April 23, 2021," Joslyn Art Museum. Accessed

December 20, 2021: https://www.joslyn.org/Post/sections/52/Files/Wendy-Red-Star_gallery-guide-final.pdf. Additional information about Wendy Red Star's installation at the Joslyn Art Museum, including a link to an interview with Red Star, can be found on the museum's website: https://www.joslyn.org/collections-and-exhibitions/temporary-exhibitions/upcoming/details.aspx?ID=1606

84 Vizenor, "Fugitive Poses," 11.

85 Vizenor, "Fugitive Poses," 9.

Bibliography

Alison, Jane, ed. *Native Nations: Journeys in American Photography*. London: Barbican Art Gallery, 2000.

Banta, Melissa and Curtis M. Hinsley. *From Site to Sight: Anthropology, Photography, and the Power of Imagery*. Cambridge, MA: Peabody Museum Press, 1986.

Bigart, Robert and Clarence Woodcock. "The Rinehart Photographs: A Portfolio." *Montana: The Magazine of Western History*, Vol. 29, No. 4 (Autumn 1979): 23–37.

Bigart, Robert and Clarence Woodcock. "The Trans-Mississippi Exposition & the Flathead Delegation." *Montana: The Magazine of Western History*, Vol. 29, No. 4 (Autumn 1979): 14–23.

Clough, Josh. "'Vanishing' Indians? Cultural Persistence on Display at the Omaha World's Fair of 1898." *Great Plains Quarterly*, Vol. 25 (Spring 2005): 67–86.

Deloria, Philip. *Playing Indian*. New Haven: Yale University Press, 1998.

Dixon, Joseph K. *The Vanishing Race: The Last Great Indian Council*. Garden City, NY: Doubleday, 1913.

Edwards, Elizabeth. "Evolving Images: Photography, Race and Popular Darwinism." In *Endless Forms: Charles Darwin, Natural Science, and the Visual Arts*. Diana Donald and Jane Munro, eds. (New Haven: Yale University Press, 2009), 168–169.

Edwards, Elizabeth. "Photographic 'Types': The Pursuit of Method." *Visual Anthropology*, Vol. 3, No. 2–3 (1990): 235–258.

Fleming, Paula Richardson. *Native American Photography at the Smithsonian: The Shindler Catalogue*. Washington, DC: Smithsonian Books, 2003.

Fleming, Paula Richardson and Judith Luskey. *The North American Indians in Early Photographs*. London: Calmann and King Ltd., 2000.

Hayes, James B. *History of the Trans-Mississippi and International Exposition of 1898*. St. Louis: Woodward & Tiernan Printing Co., 1910.

Hutchinson, Elizabeth. *The Indian Craze: Primitivism, Modernism, and Transculturation in American Art, 1890-1915*. Durham: Duke University Press, 2009.

Hutchinson, Elizabeth. "From Pantheon to Indian Gallery: Art and Sovereignty on the Early Nineteenth-Century Cultural Frontier." *Journal of American Studies*, Vol. 47, No. 2 (May 2013): 313–337.

Jacknis, Ira. "In Search of the Imagemaker: James Mooney as Ethnographic Photographer." *Visual Anthropology*, Vol. 3, No. 2–3 (1990): 179–212.

Jackson, William Henry. *Descriptive Catalogue of Photographs of North American Indians*. Washington, DC: U.S. Department of the Interior Miscellaneous Publications, No. 9, 1877.

Johnson, Tim, ed. *Spirit Capture: Photographs from the National Museum of the American Indian*. Washington, DC: Smithsonian Institution Press in association with the National Museum of the American Indian, 1998.

Katakis, Michael. *Excavating Voices: Listening to Photographs of Native Americans*. Philadelphia: University of Pennsylvania Museum, 1998.

Katz, Wendy Jean, ed. *The Trans-Mississippi and International Expositions of 1898–1899: Art, Anthropology, and Popular Culture at the Fin de Siècle*. Omaha: University of Nebraska Press, 2018.

Lidchi, Henrietta and Hulleah J. Tsinhnahjinnie, eds. *Visual Currencies: Reflections on Native Photography*. Edinburgh: National Museums Scotland, 2009.

Lippard, Lucy, ed. *Partial Recall*. New York: New Press, 1992.

Miller, Bonnie M. "The Incoherencies of Empire: The "Imperial" Image of the Indian at the Omaha World's Fairs of 1898–99." *American Studies*, Vol. 39, No. 3/4 (Fall/Winter 2008): 39–62.

Mooney, James. "The Indian Congress at Omaha." *American Anthropologist*, Vol. 1, No. 8 (1899): 126–149.

Moses, Lester G. "Indians on the Midway: Wild West Shows and the Indian Bureau at World's Fairs, 1893–1904." *South Dakota History*, Vol. 21, No. 3 (Fall 1991): 205–229.

Official Guidebook to Omaha, Trans-Mississippi and International Exposition. Omaha: Megeath Stationery Company, 1898.

Ortiz, Simon J. *Beyond the Reach of Time and Change: Native American Reflections on the Frank A. Rinehart Photograph Collection*. Tucson: University of Arizona Press by arrangement with Haskell Indian Nations University, 2004.

Rinehart, Frank A. *The Face of Courage: The Indian Photographs of Frank A. Rinehart*. Fort Collins, CO: Old Army Press, 1972.

Rydell, Robert. *All the World's a Fair: Visions of Empire at American International Expositions, 1876–1916*. Chicago: University of Chicago Press, 1984.

Sandweiss, Martha. *Print the Legend: Photography and the American West*. New Haven: Yale University Press, 2002.

Shannon, Heather and Sky Campbell. "Prominent Americans: Photographs of Treaty Delegates at the Smithsonian." *American Indian*, Vol. 15, No. 2 (Summer/Fall 2014): 47–52. https://content.yudu.com/web/1q1ji/0A1r2jl/nmai-summerfall-2014/html/index.html?page=48.

Sontag, Susan. *On Photography*. New York: Anchor Books, Doubleday, 1990.

Sutton, Royal. *On the Edge of Extinction*. Bloomington, IN: AuthorHouse, 2013.

Viola, Herman J. *Diplomats in Buckskins: A History of Indian Delegations in Washington City*. Bluffton, SC: Rivilo Books, 1995.

Watson, Roger. "Photographs by Rinehart and Muhr of the 1898 Omaha Indian Congress." *America in Britain*, Vol. XL (2002): 21–29.

Whalen, Abby. "A Temporary Taming of the Wild West: The Events of the Trans-Mississippi and International Exposition of 1898." *Great Plains Quarterly*, Vol. 36, No. 3 (Summer 2016): 187–205.

11 Secrets from the Family Album: Official and Silenced Knowledge on Migration

Ya'ara Gil-Glazer

Author's Note: Names of workshop participants have been changed to protect students' anonymity.

> The discourse on the ... photos showed me how similar our stories were. When you see a family photo and listen to the personal story behind it, it makes you lose the sense of time, the sense of ethnic identity. Despite the fact that we are talking about our roots, it sort of shatters the boundaries between us, we are in a single space.
>
> – Hannan and Nadia, participants in the author's photo elicitation workshop

In the field of critical pedagogy, the term "official knowledge" refers to the explicit knowledge that constitutes a national curriculum; hence, the knowledge conveyed by teachers at school. As noted by Paulo Freire and Ira Shor, "the structure of official knowledge is also the structure of social authority."[1] And, as suggested by Peter McLaren, it is contradictory to "the pursuit of freedom and social justice."[2] According to this position, a national curriculum, which is usually constructed top-down by the hegemonic culture, reproduces social power relations and oppressive hierarchies.[3] In the Israeli context, the various Jewish and Palestinian migrations are central to what the official curriculum highlights and silences.

Nevertheless, migration can also be reconstituted pedagogically as a common denominator. Since its establishment in 1948, the hegemonic educational discourse and official knowledge in Israel has been Judeo and Eurocentric. This comes at the expense of the narratives of Palestinians as well as of Mizrahi Jews.[4] The history of both these groups is hardly represented in the national curriculum.[5] This exclusion reflects two major conflicts in Israeli society. The first, "one of the fundamental ills of the Jewish state,"[6] is related to the socioeconomic and cultural discrimination of the Mizrahi Jews by the Ashkenazi establishment.[7] That discrimination predated the establishment of the state of Israel and became exacerbated following the massive Mizrahi immigration in the late 1940s and early 1950s; even today, Mizrahi Jews are underrepresented in the economic, cultural, and academic spheres.[8]

The conflict with the Palestinians is rooted in the Jewish takeover of Palestine in 1948, involving the uprooting of most of its Palestinian population. This is an even deeper conflict than the Mizrahi-Ashkenazi one since the latter "lacks an ideological base, fundamental disputes, institutional separation, delegitimization of the other, and mass mobilization."[9] The conflict with the Palestinians who are Israeli citizens also has multiple contemporary implications: they are heavily discriminated against,

DOI: 10.4324/9781003157427-15

with the Jewish majority controlling the lion's share of resources and shaping the country's national character.[10]

Family albums in Israel testify to these enduring conflicts. While state archives structure the dominant national narrative, family albums are cultural artifacts that archive public histories and are particularly relevant as sources of cultural knowledge marginalized by official history.[11] Connecting personal interpretation to collective history, the meanings of personal images such as family photos are related to the positioning of the self with reference to past memories and are shaped by social meanings and public conventions involved in their production process.[12]

This chapter examines family narratives made up of memories elicited by family photos related to migration, as handed down to members of the second and third generations of the two conflicts described earlier. It is based on an analysis of materials developed in four workshops facilitated by the author with Israeli students representing Israel's multicultural population. As part of the Education through Art program at an academic college in northern Israel, all students had previously participated in a course on the critical analysis of photographs. For the workshop, participants brought in and discussed photographs taken from their family photograph albums.[13] This chapter focuses on a central theme that emerged in the workshop: official and silenced knowledge on migration and uprooting. The theme is discussed in terms of the alternative knowledge elicited from the albums, which challenges the divisiveness constructed by the conflicts mentioned above and has the potential to develop critical and empowered awareness and identity, and to promote social change.[14]

Photo Elicitation and Family Albums as Records of Marginalized History

Coined by John Collier, "photo elicitation" refers to photographs' potential to elicit thoughts, memories, and sentiments in viewers thanks to their polysemic quality.[15] The photograph provides rich information that stimulates thought and discussion while allowing a broad range of interpretations.[16] Photo elicitation, therefore, moves us "away from the task of documenting the social world to using images as tools via a dialogical process to gain an insight into the lifeworlds of those who participate in our studies."[17] Photo elicitation is increasingly used in education and is a research method in the social sciences.[18] It can encourage critical discussions, as well as the production of new knowledge, and provides a new and accessible way of communication. Such group discussions connect the self with society, culture, and history.[19] They also provide, according to Pablo Vila, a:

> possibility to delve in some depth into the complex collective process of identification ... because the different narrative plots that structure peoples' diverse identities come to the forefront in the process of making sense of the photos.[20]

As suggested by Gillian Rose, reanimating the photograph enables one to realize the multifaceted qualities and meanings inherent in it.[21] The discussions of family photographs created in the workshop rely on their quality to elicit thoughts, emotions, memories, and interpretations. The aspects of emotion and memory inherent to the discourse triggered by family albums are significant also as historical knowledge.[22] This has been recognized by Martha Langford, who refers to the family album as "an instrument of collective show and tell" that generates text that is actually a conversation.[23] In a similar vein, Glenn Willumson views family albums as cultural products that transcend the private and personal, and that are unique mainly in that the photos included in them have been carefully selected, highlighting the family history and the historical narrative encapsulated within it. Their activation by talking about the photos and flipping through them mark the albums as personal memoirs as well as cultural artifacts.[24] Marita Sturken also points to photographs' significant function in relating personal memory, cultural memory, and history, derived from their ability to straddle these different realms.[25] Family photos do more than connect private and public histories, however: they have the potential of archiving alternative public histories by providing visibility to those who have been marginalized from them. Intended to be reviewed in the future, Patricia Holland argues that albums offer "many possible pasts."[26]

Whereas reviewing the family album is usually associated with nostalgia, on a deeper level it also involves pain, silencing, and the absence of certain people or certain issues.[27] When it comes to migration narratives, the album as archive loses its direct connection with the past. Both Marianne Hirsch and Zofia Rosińska describe the trauma involved in this disconnection as a transgenerational experience: "Loss of family, of home, of a feeling of belonging and safety in the world 'bleed' from one generation to the next."[28] Rosińska describes the loss of sense of belonging as a melancholy sense of "no return," whether for political or economic reasons.[29] Hirsch discusses photography as a medium for transgenerational transfer of traumatic memories. She maintains that the next generation is able to take part in the creation of what she calls "postmemory," and she highlights its potential as a platform for activist engagement in cultural and political contexts. The cross-temporal potential of working with photographs is also suggested by Sturken, who argues that memory is created by, and therefore does not reside in, the photograph: "The camera image is a technology of memory, a mechanism through which one can construct the past and situate it in the present."[30]

From a critical-educational perspective, the historical narratives and memories captured in the family album can thus challenge the official knowledge provided by the curriculum. In its place, alternative narratives merge the personal and political, and uncover concealed and silenced local histories. The principles proposed by Ariella Azoulay in *The Civil Contract of Photography and Civil Imagination* also inform this discussion, particularly with regard to subject-spectator relations. According to Azoulay, "photography, while personal, is a mobile and global recording kit for contesting injuries to citizenship."[31] As I indicate later, the "revival" of historical family photos can be used in this way as a historical recognition tool.[32]

Official and Silenced Knowledge

Israel is a nation of migrants. Only two years after it became a state, in 1950, it passed the Law of Return that entitles every Jew who immigrates to Israel, almost without exception, to immediate citizenship, including the right to vote. Between 1948 and 1951, 700,000 Holocaust survivors from Europe, as well as Jews from Islamic countries, immigrated and doubled the young state's population, which was composed of first- and second-generation migrants. At the same time, Israel's resounding military victory in the 1948 Arab-Israeli war involved the fleeing and forced uprooting of 750,000 Palestinian Arabs. In addition to these refugees, tens of thousands were internally displaced.[33] Whereas Israel celebrates this victory on Independence Day, the Palestinians refer to their defeat as the Nakba, or Catastrophe.

According to Assaf Meshulam, the Israeli curricula are characterized by ethnic and social biases that reproduce the existing social power relations.[34] In particular, the official history curriculum studied in both Jewish and Arab schools emphasizes the various Jewish migration waves from Europe at the expense of Mizrahi migrations. The issue of refugeehood following the 1948 war is even more marginalized and discussed in the context of the Zionist narrative, if at all. These two exclusions are related in that they are part of an overarching framework of a Eurocentric curriculum, not only in history but also in literature and art.[35]

As part of that Eurocentric curriculum and its nation-building project more generally, Israel has used the memory of the Holocaust "to negate the Palestinian identity," as argued by Ilan Gur-Ze'ev. Moreover, local Holocaust studies are instrumentalized to deny the very legitimacy of "engaging and dialogically responding to the otherness of the Other."[36] Potential dialogical recognition, suggests Gur-Ze'ev, will address the history, suffering and aspirations of the local Others and promote a dialogue where the Palestinians will be called upon to recognize the historical injustice perpetrated against the Jews as well and recognize the uniqueness of the Holocaust on the universal moral level. With obvious differences, this also applies to the historiography of Mizrahi Jews, often also referred to as Arab Jews.[37] A report recently submitted to the Minister of Education states that Israeli students could finish high school "without learning even a single Mizrahi literary work." As for the history curriculum, "The general narrative ... is written from a European point of view that downplays the history of ... Mizrahi Jews."[38]

Beyond the near complete absence of Mizrahi Jews from the official curriculum, local historiography has documented multiple examples of a patronizing if not outright ethnophobic attitude toward them by the Ashkenazi hegemony. Key political figures in the history of Zionism and Israel, such as rightwing opposition leader Ze'ev Jabotinsky, Prime Ministers David Ben-Gurion and Golda Meir and Foreign Minister Abba Eban all referred to them as ignorant, primitive, and disease-ridden. In 1970, Meir, for example, said they "didn't know how to do anything" and in 1969, Eban said they had to be transformed, with the "Western spirit instilled into them."[39] Although such explicit statements are becoming rarer, ethnocentric attitudes have not disappeared. As recently as in 1997, for example, leading Israeli politician Ehud Barak found it necessary to apologize to the Mizrahim for the historical treatment against them, an apology that has failed to mend the rift.[40]

Secrets from the Family Album

"The question that needs to be asked is not which knowledge to teach, but rather whose," says Meshulam, paraphrasing Michael Apple's well-known concept of "official knowledge" described earlier.[41] Inspired by that statement, I designed four workshop meetings based on reanimating family photos to create alternative historical and cultural knowledge that belongs to the subaltern. The meetings were part of a voluntary extra-curricular activity on integrating the arts in education. Aged between 21 and 23, the participants represented the broad ethnic spectrum of Israeli society; all were members of the second or third generation of migration and/or uprooting. They included six women students of education through art and myself: two Arabs (a Christian and a Muslim) and four Jews, one of Ashkenazi origin and the rest, including myself, of mixed Ashkenazi-Mizrahi origin.[42] Animating the photos through open discussion in the context of migration harnessed the single photograph's power to awaken memories through a "communal practice." This practice combined "showing and telling, as well as looking, listening and touching," as discussed by Langford, with the ability to "see more clearly into the interstices of power, and understand the counterpoint family photographs can present to the deadening weight of the eye of the state," and to "uncover counter-archives," in Laura Wexler's words.[43]

Each session focused on one or two participants, each of whom selected a photo from their family albums as a basis for a group discussion involving photo elicitation. The discourse elicited by the photographs in the workshop included frequent and profound reference to the concealment of familial migration stories, echoed on the national scale by the concealment and silencing of Mizrahi and Palestinian histories in the history curriculum. These silenced aspects are given voice in the examples presented later, which connect the various marginalized narratives to create new and significant knowledge: a critical, alternative history.[44]

Accordingly, as we shall see, the discourse aroused by the photos illustrates Azoulay's suggestion that the contents of photographs are only seemingly frozen. The workshop participants followed Azoulay's imperative by moving "from the addressee position to the addresser's position," and taking public responsibility for the sense of those photographs.[45] This imperative is particularly relevant for a discussion of the dialogical potential of family photos that have political-historical meaning: expanding the communities of which the subjects are part or from which they are excluded, enabling the formation of new alliances.

"Lots of Shame and Much to Hide": Mizrahi Migration and Identity Crises

Three Jewish participants chose to discuss photos of their Mizrahi grandparents and parents, all taken before the migration to Israel, and all reflecting joy, family unity, and a sense of belonging. In that, the photos contradicted descriptions of the identity crisis experienced by the migrants after arriving in Israel, one of whose central themes has been shame.

Miriam (like the other participants, her name is an alias) described her mother's sense of inferiority with relation to the Ashkenazi hegemony and her attempts to adjust to it.

> My mother's Moroccan origin is not evident in her appearance ... and she concealed it for many years ... Only when I became an adult did I find out about the crisis they had undergone when they immigrated to Israel ... They were treated like they were stupid. My Grandpa was an intellectual ... My mother always had this Ashkenazi air to her, which involved tremendous disrespect for her mother and they were really disconnected. When [the grandmother] would come to visit the kibbutz [where my mother lived] unannounced, [my mother] would immediately send her back on the bus. She was ashamed.

The photograph Miriam picked, of her mother at age nine together with her family, was taken about a year before their immigration to Israel, on the beach in Casablanca.

Sigal's description of the image she selected of her grandfather raises similar issues:

> Ever since they came here, they did everything to integrate in Israeli society ... at a heavy cost of a sense of inferiority and shame. I would like to change the past and let them integrate in society while retaining their identity and culture without feeling inferior to the dominant culture. [My father] embraces the oppression warmly, as part of his coping. My father became Ashkenized ... That's something very powerful in our house: ... I want you to be like everyone else, I don't want you to suffer ... He has a lot of feelings of inferiority he never discusses – lots of shame and much to hide.

Sigal presented a photo in which his grandfather stands in the center of the frame and looks very dignified with all the family around him as a counterpoint to that sense of shame, by "representing the pre-immigration period – characterized by belonging."

The students' knowledge about their families' migrations comes mostly from their grandparents and parents, and also includes their own insights, having experienced the implications of the family crisis in the form of post-memory. Although they are increasingly becoming part of the public discourse in recent years, they remain absent from the history textbooks, whose hidden curriculum creates a hierarchy of identities, with the less valued ones being "ignored or even derided."[46]

"Grandpa Never Spoke It": Holocaust and Migration from Eastern Europe

Nadia and Galia talked about the silence of the grandfather, a Holocaust survivor, in a photo. Their photo elicitations reflect the nature of family album photographs as revealing ghosts from a long-gone world that enliven their subjects and enable us in the present "not only to see and to touch that past but also to try to reanimate it by undoing the finality of the photographic 'take.'"[47]

They selected, respectively, a photo representing the time before fleeing the country of origin and one that documents the moment of arriving in Israel. They focused on their grandfathers' post-immigration stories. Out of their photo descriptions emerged a narrative of family histories that restarted in Israel, and turned their backs on the diasporic past. Nadia, who chose a photo of her grandfather as an infant in his mother's arms, described a struggle for life and "rebirth." Galia, whose photo documented her father's family landing in Israel after managing to get out of the Soviet Union in 1971, described a kind of running from the past to a supposedly promising future. She asked her grandparents seen in the photo, "What did you expect? What did you run away from?" She went on to talk about her grandfather's integration difficulties: "He found it difficult to adjust to the Israeli language ... in the main, he didn't understand the culture ... Grandpa never spoke it ... but it was obvious. He was traumatized by World War II and had a difficulty integrating in this thing called Israel."

The Holocaust is a central part of history textbooks in Israel. Nonetheless, the personal histories of Holocaust survivors living in Israel have been mute for many years. They were silenced by survivors themselves, due to the extent of their traumas, as well as by the Zionist establishment, which sought to develop a heroic, militarized myth of redemption in a new land. Survivors' voices were redundant if not discrepant to "fresh start" mythologies.[48] Consequently, these narratives became posttraumatic secrets.[49] Only in the 1960s, after the Eichmann Trial, was their trauma legitimized by the Israeli public. Even then, however, and to this day, many have not told their harrowing personal stories to their family members, certainly not in full.

"You Can't Teach about the Nakba": Palestinian Uprooting and Migration

Whereas concealment and silence characterize the family histories of the Jewish participants, both inwardly and outwardly, the family histories of the Palestinian-Arab participants are spoken about in the privacy of the home, but silenced publicly. The Nakba is almost completely absent from the history curriculum. The discourse elicited by the photos suggested a yawning gap between the knowledge acquired in Israeli schools and the family stories of uprooting and migration, of which the Jewish participants were completely ignorant. The intimate, open atmosphere of the workshop led the Arab students to talk relatively freely about their family experience in the 1948 war. Nevertheless, they stressed that this subject had been taboo in their conversations with Jews prior to their academic studies, and largely remained that way in other contexts. In fact, they hardly met any Jews prior to attending college.

Dareen chose a portrait of her grandfather when he was about six. "They were tender of age but all grown from within, because of what they had experienced ... during the war." She shared her grandfather's stories about the sense of belonging to the land, to nature and to the village where he was born and from which his family was expelled, stories that had no room in the historical narrative taught in Israeli schools. The moral of her grandfather's story was nevertheless optimistic. All the country's inhabitants must live together in peace: "There's room for everyone."

In Hannan's photo, the year is 1994, at the height of the sanguine years of the Israeli-Palestinian Oslo Accords. Her grandfather shakes hands with Yasser Arafat and his transgenerational message is clear: "my grandfather ... was expelled from his village. That I'm a third-generation internally displaced person ... I connect those things because I'm opposed to wars over land." This knowledge came from him and other family members, not her school:

> You can't even say the word "Palestine" or anything like it. I remember that in eleventh or twelfth grade, I asked the civic studies teacher a question and he didn't answer me. I told my father and as a teacher and educator, he ... told me that the civics teacher was prohibited from answering such a question [by] the Ministry of Education's regulations. He can't say "Palestine," you can't teach about the Nakba.

The intensity of this fear, this norm of silencing, is echoed in Nadia's reaction to Hannan's story: "You say Nakba and that makes me afraid. It frightens me to talk about it ... Why should I not know what happened to your families?" The dialogue resulting from photo elicitation that developed between Hannan and Nadia connects Jewish and Palestinian history. It contained post-memories that reflect the transformative potential of creative storytelling of collective memories as a tool for promoting shared understanding of the past and formulating a vision for peace in the present and future, including identity questions about "who we are, where we belong, where we are going."[50] It represents the potential, described by Gur-Zeev,[51] for an alternative to the hegemonic discourse dictated by the formal education system, a discourse of recognition of the suffering of both sides, their common denominators that could lay the foundation for a future of equality.

Hannan: It's important for the next generation to know what happened ... The history we were taught in school was the "Jewish" history ... Every story has two sides and it's important that we know both.

Nadia: We all come from homes that have experienced significant pain involving migration ... There is no real discourse in Israel about this, not many opportunities like me and Hanan had, sitting in the same room talking – she about her Palestinian roots, me about my European roots.

Conclusion

According to Hirsch, family photos reduce distances and bring people closer. Photos of a world taken away by force do not only provide information or confirmation but also intimate emotional attachment.[52] This healing dialogue is in fact an extrapolation of Azoulay's "external eye," which "deterritorializes" the photographs, turning them into "a social, cultural and political instrument of immense power."[53] Although this eye had already been present in the encounter between the photographer and subject, it now gains additional meaning in the encounter with new spectators' eyes. The photo elicitation they practice activates family album photographs and reveals their power to awaken a discussion that merges memories, emotions, and interpretations. When it touches on cultural and political aspects, it can be a platform for promoting social change.[54]

In the examples discussed here, the photo dialogue breaks official silences behind the family stories and brought the participants closer, all members of the second or third generation of collective and individual traumas of external and internal uprooting. It gave room to a new knowledge that challenged the official knowledge taught to them at school. All of the Jewish students said that their historical knowledge about migration was extensive in the context of Jewish history, particularly the Holocaust, limited in the context of the migration of Mizrahi Jews and almost non-existent in the context of local Palestinian history – the stories of fellow students living right next to them in the same country. The Arab students, on the other hand, knew their local history from the stories of their families, and learned the traumatic European Jewish history at school. At the same time, the gaps in content and form between the personal-family knowledge delivered across the generations and the formal academic knowledge regarding all types of migration discussed in the workshop were similar in all cases.

Photographs and the intergenerational memories embedded in them played a key role in eliciting open and intimate dialogue about personal as well as conflictual issues. They even led the participants to return to their family homes and ask new questions, discover new secrets. Thus, the participants used the photos to create critical, alternative post-memories, "mediated," in Hirsch's words, "not by recall but by imaginative investment, projection and creation."[55] Their post-memories have the potential to construct a narrative that offers a better future for this, and the following, generations.

Notes

A version of this essay first appeared in: "Secrets from the Family Album: Official and Silenced Knowledge on Migration" (Y. Gil-Glazer, *Int. Journal for History, Culture & Modernity* 8/1, Brill 2020). Reproduced with permission of Brill Academic Publishers.

1 Ira Shor and Paulo Freire, *A Pedagogy for Liberation: Dialogues on Transforming Education* (Westport, CT: Praeger, 1987), 10.
2 Peter McLaren, "Revolutionary Pedagogy in Post-Revolutionary Times: Rethinking the Political Economy of Critical Education," in *The Critical Pedagogy Reader*, eds. Antonia Darder and Marta Baltodano (New York: Routledge, 2003), 173.
3 Michael Apple, *Official Knowledge: Democratic Education in a Conservative Age* (New York: Routledge, 2014); Maurianne Adams and Anne Bell Lee, eds., *Teaching for Diversity and Social Justice* (New York: Routledge, 2016); Shor and Freire, *A Pedagogy for Liberation,* 10, 44.
4 Mizrahi Jews immigrated to Israel from Islamic countries, while Ashkenazi Jews immigrated from Europe and the Americas to Israel. Julia Resnik, "Alternative Identities in Multicultural Schools in Israel: Emancipatory Identity, Mixed Identity and Transnational Identity," *British Journal of Sociology of Education*, Vol. 27, No. 5 (2006): 585–601, https://doi.org/10.1080/01425690600958782; Yaron Tsur, "Israeli Historiography and the Ethnic Problem," in *Making Israel*, ed. Benny Morris (Ann Arbor: University of Michigan Press, 2007), 231–232.
5 Ayman K. Agbaria, Mustafa Muhanad, and Yousef T. Jabareen, ""In Your Face" Democracy: Education for Belonging and its Challenges in Israel," *British Educational Research Journal*, Vol. 41, No. 1 (2015): 143–175, https://doi.org/10.1002/berj.3133; Avner Ben-Amos, "An Impossible Pluralism? European Jews and Oriental Jews in the Israeli History Curriculum," *History of European Ideas*, Vol. 18, No. 1 (1994): 41–51, https://doi.org/10.1016/0191-6599(94)90145-7; Ilan Gur-Ze'ev, "The Production of Self and the Destruction of the Other's Memory and Identity in Israeli/Palestinian Education on the Holocaust/Nakbah," *Studies in Philosophy and Education*, Vol. 20 (2001): 255–266, https://doi.org/10.1023/A:1010367128782; Yehuda Shenhav, "The History Textbooks of the People of Israel," *Mitzad Sheni*, Vol. 18 (1999): 22–25 (text in Hebrew).
6 Yaron Tsur, "Israeli Historiography and the Ethnic Problem," *Pe'amim,* Vol. 94 (2003): 7–56 (text in Hebrew), https://www.jstor.org/stable/234293637.
7 Sami Shalom-Chetrit, *The Mizrahi Struggle in Israel: 1948–2003* (Tel Aviv: Am-Oved, 2006) (text in Hebrew); Sami Shalom-Chetrit, *Intra-Jewish Conflict in Israel: White Jews, Black Jews* (New York: Routledge, 2010); Reuven Snir, "Who Needs Arab-Jewish Identity? Fragmented Consciousness, "Inessential Solidarity," and the "Coming Community" (Part 1)," *Journal of Modern Jewish Studies*, Vol. 11, No. 2 (2012): 169–188, https://doi.org/10.1080/14725886.2012.684864.
8 Tsur, "Israeli Historiography and the Ethnic Problem"; Sammy Smooha, "The Mass Immigrations to Israel: A Comparison of the Failure of the Mizrahi Immigrants of the 1950s with the Success of the Russian Immigrants of the 1990s," *Journal of Israeli History*, Vol. 27, No. 1 (2008): 1–27, https://doi.org/10.1080/13531040801902708.
9 Smooha, *"The Mass Immigrations to Israel,"* 10.
10 Ifat Maoz, "Does Contact Work in Protracted Asymmetrical Conflict? Appraising 20 Years of Reconciliation-Aimed Encounters between Israeli Jews and Palestinians," *Journal of Peace Research*, Vol. 48, No. 1 (2011): 115–125, https://doi.org/10.1177/0022343310389506. Note that the term "Palestinians in Israel" (also called "Palestinian citizens of Israel" or "Israeli Arabs") is used here to refer to the Palestinians living within Israel's sovereign territory, as opposed to the Palestinians living in the Occupied Territories.
11 Karen Cross and Julia Peck, "Editorial: Special Issue on Photography, Archive and Memory," *Photographies*, Vol. 3, No. 2 (2010): 127–138, https://doi.org/10.1080/17540763.2010.499631; Yvonne Singer, "The Veiled Room," in *Memory and*

Migration: Multidisciplinary Approaches to Memory Studies, eds. Julia Creet and Andreas Kirtzmann (Toronto: University of Toronto Press, 2011), 263–279.

12 Barbara Harrison, "Photographic Visions and Narrative Inquiry," in *Considering Counter-Narratives: Narrating, Resisting, Making Sense*, eds. Michael Bamberg and Molly Andrews (Philadelphia: John Benjamins Publishing, 2004), 113–136.

13 Due to their personal nature, the specific images cannot be reproduced in this chapter.

14 In a previous work, I describe additional themes and discuss the methods of working with the photographs (photo monologue and dialogue) as vehicles for critical educational discussion: Ya'ara Gil-Glazer, "Photo-Monologues and Photo-Dialogues from the Family Album," *Journal of Peace Education*, Vol. 16, No. 2 (2019): 175–194, https://doi.org/10.1080/17400201.2019.1587744. This chapter focuses on the theme of secrecy that has emerged as central to the conflictual experience elicited from the photographs using the photo monologue and dialogue methods, and as equally and powerfully relevant to the two conflicts experienced by the diverse student population.

15 John Collier and Malcolm Collier, *Visual Anthropology: Photography as a Research Method* (Albuquerque, NM: University of New Mexico Press, 1986); Douglas Harper, "Talking about Pictures: A Case for Photo Elicitation," Visual *Studies*, Vol. 17, No. 1 (2002): 15–26, https://doi.org/10.1080/14725860220137345.

16 Graeme Baxter et al., "The Use of PE to Explore the Role of the Main Street in Kirkwall in Sustaining Cultural Identity, Community and a Sense of Place," *Aberdeen Business School Working Paper Series*, Vol. 8, No. 1 (2015), http://hdl.handle.net/10059/1185.

17 Jon Prosser and Andrew Loxley, *Introducing Visual Methods* (Unpublished Paper) (Southampton, England: National Centre for Research Methods, 2008), http://eprints.ncrm.ac.uk/420/.

18 Nancy Brown, Robert Wiggins, and David Secord, "This Must Be a Suburban Classroom! Using Photographs to Investigate Teacher Candidates Developing Professional Identities," *Brock Education*, Vol. 18, No. 2 (2009): 49–65, doi:10.26522/brocked.v18i2.91; Harper, "Talking about Pictures"; Analia Inés Meo, "Picturing Students' Habitus: The Advantages and Limitations of Photo-Elicitation Interviewing in a Qualitative Study in the City of Buenos Aires," *International Journal of Qualitative Methods*, Vol. 9, No. 2 (2010): 149–171, https://doi.org/10.1177/160940691000900203; Veronica M. Richard and Maria K. E. Lahman, "Photo-Elicitation: Reflexivity on Method, Analysis, and Graphic Portraits," *International Journal of Research & Method in Education*, Vol. 38, No. 1 (2015): 3–22, https://doi.org/10.1080/1743727X.2013.843073; Pablo Vila, "The Importance of Photo-Interviewing as a Research Method in the Study of Identity Construction Processes: An Illustration from the U.S.-Mexico Border," *Visual Anthropology* 26 (2013): 51–68, https://doi.org/10.1080/08949468.2013.735187.

19 Harper, "Talking about Pictures"; Douglas Harper, *Visual Sociology* (New York: Routledge, 2012).

20 Vila, "The Importance of Photo-Interviewing," 53.

21 Gillian Rose, *Doing Family Photography: The Domestic, the Public and the Politics of Sentiment* (Farnham: Ashgate Publishing, Ltd., 2010).

22 Leora Auslander, "Reading German Jewry through Vernacular Photography: From the Kaiserreich to the Third Reich," *Central European History*, Vol. 48, No. 3 (2015): 300–334, https://doi:10.1017/S0008938915000771.

23 Martha Langford, *Suspended Conversations: The Afterlife of Memory in Photographic Albums* (Montreal: McGill-Queen's Press, 2001).

24 Glenn Willumson, "Making Meaning: Displaced Materiality in the Library and Art Museum," in *Photographs Objects Histories: On the Materiality of Images*, eds. Elizabeth Edwards and Janice Hart (London: Routledge, 2004), 66–68.

25 Marita Sturken, "The Image as Memorial: Personal Photographs in Cultural Memory," in *The Familial Gaze*, ed. Marianne Hisrch (Hanover, NH: University Press of New England, 1999), 178.

26 Patricia Holland, "Introduction: History, Memory, and the Family Album," in *Family Snaps: The Meaning of Domestic Photography*, eds. Jo Spence and Patricia Holland (London: Virago, 1991), 1.

27 Marianne Hirsch, *Family Frames: Photography, Narrative, and Postmemory* (Cambridge, MA: Harvard University Press, 1997); Singer, "The Veiled Room."
28 Marianne Hirsch, *The Generation of Postmemory: Writing and Visual Culture after the Holocaust* (New York: Columbia University Press, 2012), 112.
29 Zofia Rosińska, "Emigratory Experience: The Melancholy of No Return," in *Memory and Migration: Multidisciplinary Approaches to Memory Studies*, eds. Julia Creet and Andreas Kirtzmann (Toronto: University of Toronto Press, 2011), 34–35.
30 Marita Sturken, *Tangled Memories: The Vietnam War, the Aids Epidemic, and the Politics of Remembering* (Berkeley: University of California Press, 1997), 19–20.
31 Ariella Azoulay, *The Civil Contract of Photography* (New York: The MIT Press, 2008), 124.
32 Ariella Azoulay, *Civil Imagination: A Political Ontology of Photography* (New York: Verso, 2015), 47.
33 Hillel Cohen, "The Internal Refugees in Israel: The Struggle over Identity," *The New East* 43 (2002): 83–102 (text in Hebrew); Eli Reches and Arik Rudknitsky, eds. *The Arab Population in Israel: Basic Data, Arab Society in Israel: Information File* (Neve Ilan: Abraham initiatives, 2009), 1–54 (text in Hebrew).
34 Assaf Meshulam, "Critical Practices in Education and Their Implementation in Bilingual Schools in Israel," in *Critical Theory in Action: Critical Practices in the Social Sphere in Israel*, eds. Michal Krumer-Nevo, Idit Weiss-Gal, and Roni Strier (Tel Aviv: Resling, 2020), 33–67 (text in Hebrew).
35 The history curriculum for high school students in both the Jewish and Arab education systems requires a minimum of ninety hours, of which 50 are dedicated to the "History of the Jewish People" (10 hours), "The Holocaust" (30) and "The Establishment and History of the State of Israel" (10). Only 12 hours are dedicated to "Arabs and Islam" (5) and "The Arab World in the Nineteenth and Twentieth Centuries" (7). "Palestinian Arabs and Palestinian Nationalism" are included as a "sub-topic" within the latter. Yossi Yonah, Galia Zalmenson-Levy, and Chagit Gur-Ziv, "Also-and-Also Curricula at Kedma," in *Inequality in Education*, ed. Dafna Golan-Agnon (Tel Aviv: Bable, 2004), 188–208 (text in Hebrew).
36 Gur-Ze'ev, "The Production of Self," 256.
37 Anis M. Al-Qasem, "Arab Jews in Israel: The Struggle for Identity and Socioeconomic Justice," *Contemporary Arab Affairs*, Vol. 8, No. 3 (2015): 323–338, https://doi.org/10.1080/17550912.2015.1054613; Yehuda Shenhav and Hanan Hever, "'Arab Jews' after Structuralism: Zionist Discourse and the (De)formation of an Ethnic Identity," *Social Identities: Journal for the Study of Race, Nation and Culture*, Vol. 18, No. 1 (2012): 36, https://doi.org/10.1080/13504630.2011.629517.
38 Erez Biton et al., *Biton Committee Report on the Empowerment of the Sephardic and Mizrahi Heritage in the Education System* (Jerusalem: Biton Committee, 2016), 5, 32 (text in Hebrew).
39 Meir is quoted in: Shenhav and Hever, "'Arab Jews' after Structuralism", 106; Eban is quoted in Sammy Smooha, "The Loci of the Ethnic Problem in Israel Today," in *Half the Nation: Readings in the Culture and Status of Oriental Jews in Israel*, ed. Shlomo Deshen (Ramat-Gan: Department of Jewish History and Contemporary Jewry at Bar-Ilan University, 1986), 299.
40 Zion Zohar, *Sephardic and Mizrahi Jewry: From the Golden Age of Spain to Modern Time* (New York: New York University Press, 2005), 300–301.
41 Meshulam, "Critical Practices in Education."
42 The participants come from different communities in northern, central, and southern Israel. All have previously studied in the author's course on a critical gaze on photographic expressions in society and culture. They were selected for this study in view of their significant participation in the course in both the intellectual and the educational leadership respects, and volunteered to the experience described, designed to subsequently formulate a social-educational tool for a local corrective historical discourse that combines the personal and political.
43 Martha Langford, "Mrs Wagner's Aspirations: The Album as Monument," in *Photography Reframed: New Visions in Contemporary Photographic Culture*, eds. Ben Burbridge and Annebella Pollen (London: I.B. Tauris, 2018), 62–63; Laura Wexler, "The State of the

Album," *Photography and Culture*, Vol. 10, No. 2 (2017): 102–103, https://doi.org/10.1080/17514517.2017.1331561.

44 The participants provided sensitive personal details about themselves and their families in the workshop. The intimate conversation among them is an important source of knowledge that straddles the personal and political and challenges the official sociocultural knowledge in Israel. While their anonymity is protected by aliases, however, the photos cannot protect their privacy. Therefore, the photographs are not presented in the chapter.

45 Azoulay, *The Civil Contract,* 159–160; Azoulay, *Civil Imagination*, 54.

46 Meshulam, "Critical Practices in Education."

47 Hirsch, *Family Frames*, 115.

48 Yair Auron, *The Pain of Knowledge: Holocaust and Genocide Issues in Education* (New Brunswick, NJ: Transaction Publishers, 2005).

49 Tommy S. Steier, "Why Were They Silent Again? On the Mental Condition of Holocaust Survivors and their Treatment by Society and Therapists," *HaRefuah*, Vol. 148, No. 4 (2009): 219–223 (text in Hebrew).

50 Gill Scherto and Ulrike Niens, "Education as Humanisation: A Theoretical Review on the Role of Dialogic Pedagogy in Peacebuilding Education," *Compare: A Journal of Comparative and International Education*, Vol. 44, No. 1 (2014): 21. https://doi.org/10.1080/03057925.2013.859879.

51 Gur-Ze'ev, "The Production of Self."

52 Hirsch, *Family Frames,* 116.

53 Azoulay, *The Civil Contract of Photography,* 121.

54 Hirsch, *The Generation of Postmemory*, 6.

55 Hirsch. *The Generation of Postmemory*, 5.

Bibliography

Adams, Maurianne and Anne Bell Lee, eds. *Teaching for Diversity and Social Justice*. New York: Routledge, 2016.

Agbaria, Ayman K., Mustafa Muhanad, and Yousef T. Jabareen. "'In Your Face' Democracy: Education for Belonging and Its Challenges in Israel." *British Educational Research Journal*, Vol. 41, No. 1 (2015): 143–175. doi:10.1002/berj.3133

Al-Qasem, Anis M. "Arab Jews in Israel: The Struggle for Identity and Socioeconomic Justice." *Contemporary Arab Affairs*, Vol. 8, No. 3 (2015): 323–338. doi:10.1080/17550912.2015.1054613.

Apple, Michael. *Official Knowledge: Democratic Education in a Conservative Age*. New York: Routledge, 2014.

Auron, Yair. *The Pain of Knowledge: Holocaust and Genocide Issues in Education*. New Brunswick, NJ: Transaction Publishers, 2005.

Auslander, Leora. "Reading German Jewry through Vernacular Photography: From the Kaiserreich to the Third Reich." *Central European History*, Vol. 48, No. 3 (2015): 300–334. doi:10.1017/S0008938915000771.

Azoulay, Ariella. *The Civil Contract of Photography*. New York: The MIT Press, 2008.

Azoulay, Ariella. *Civil Imagination: A Political Ontology of Photography*. New York: Verso, 2015.

Baxter, Graeme, et al. "The Use of PE to Explore the Role of the Main Street in Kirkwall in Sustaining Cultural Identity, Community and a Sense of Place." *Aberdeen Business School Working Paper Series*, Vol. 8, No. 1 (2015): 1–32. http://hdl.handle.net/10059/1185.

Ben-Amos, Avner. "An Impossible Pluralism? European Jews and Oriental Jews in the Israeli History Curriculum." *History of European Ideas*, Vol. 18, No. 1 (1994): 41–51. doi:10.1016/0191-6599(94)90145-7.

Biton, Erez, et al. *Biton Committee Report on the Empowerment of the Sephardic and Mizrahi Heritage in the Education System*. Jerusalem: Biton Committee, 2016 (Hebrew).

Brown, Nancy, Robert Wiggins, and David Secord. "This Must Be a Suburban Classroom!

Using Photographs to Investigate Teacher Candidates Developing Professional Identities." *Brock Education*, Vol. 18, No. 2 (2009): 49–65. doi:10.26522/brocked.v18i2.91.

Cohen, Hillel. "The Internal Refugees in Israel: The Struggle over Identity." *The New East*, Vol. 43 (2002): 83–102 (Hebrew).

Collier, John and Malcolm Collier. *Visual Anthropology: Photography as a Research Method*. Albuquerque, NM: University of New Mexico Press, 1986.

Cross, Karen and Julia Peck. "Editorial: Special Issue on Photography, Archive and Memory." *Photographies*, Vol. 3, No. 2 (2010): 127–138. doi:10.1080/17540763.2010.499631.

Gil-Glazer, Ya'ara. "Photo-Monologues and Photo-Dialogues from the Family Album." *Journal of Peace Education*, Vol. 16, No. 2 (2019): 175–194. doi:10.1080/17400201.2019.1587744.

Gur-Ze'ev, Ilan. "The Production of Self and the Destruction of the Other's Memory and Identity in Israeli/Palestinian Education on the Holocaust/Nakbah." *Studies in Philosophy and Education*, Vol. 20 (2001): 255–266. doi:10.1023/A:1010367128782.

Harper, Douglas. "Talking about Pictures: A Case for Photo Elicitation." *Visual Studies*, Vol. 17, No. 1 (2002): 15–26. doi:10.1080/14725860220137345.

Harper, Douglas. *Visual Sociology*. New York: Routledge, 2012.

Harrison, Barbara. "Photographic Visions and Narrative Inquiry." In *Considering Counter-Narratives: Narrating, Resisting, Making Sense*, Michael Bamberg and Molly Andrews, eds. (Philadelphia: John Benjamins Publishing, 2004), 113–136.

Hirsch, Marianne. *Family Frames: Photography, Narrative, and Postmemory*. Cambridge, MA: Harvard University Press, 1997.

Hirsch, Marianne. *The Generation of Postmemory: Writing and Visual Culture after the Holocaust*. New York: Columbia University Press, 2012.

Holland, Patricia. "Introduction: History, Memory, and the Family Album." In *Family Snaps: The Meaning of Domestic Photography*, Jo Spence and Patricia Holland, eds. (London: Virago, 1991), 1–14.

Langford, Martha. *Suspended Conversations: The Afterlife of Memory in Photographic Albums*. Montreal: McGill-Queen's Press, 2001.

Langford, Martha. "Mrs Wagner's Aspirations: The Album as Monument." In *Photography Reframed: New Visions in Contemporary Photographic Culture*, Ben Burbridge and Annebella Pollen, eds. (London: I.B. Tauris, 2018), 62–73.

Maoz, Ifat. "Does Contact Work in Protracted Asymmetrical Conflict? Appraising 20 Years of Reconciliation-Aimed Encounters between Israeli Jews and Palestinians." *Journal of Peace Research*, Vol. 48, No. 1 (2011): 115–125. doi:10.1177/0022343310389506.

McLaren, Peter. "Revolutionary Pedagogy in Post-Revolutionary Times: Rethinking the Political Economy of Critical Education." In *The Critical Pedagogy Reader*, Antonia Darder, and Marta Baltodano, eds. (New York: Routledge, 2003), 151–184.

Meo, Analia Inés. "Picturing Students' Habitus: The Advantages and Limitations of Photo-Elicitation Interviewing in a Qualitative Study in the City of Buenos Aires." *International Journal of Qualitative Methods*, Vol. 9, No. 2 (2010): 149–171. doi:10.1177/160940691000900203.

Meshulam, Assaf. "Critical Practices in Education and their Implementation in Bilingual Schools in Israel." In *Critical Theory in Action: Critical Practices in the Social Sphere in Israel*, Michal Krumer-Nevo, Idit Weiss-Gal, and Roni Strier, eds. (Tel Aviv: Resling, 2020), 33–67 (Hebrew).

Prosser, Jon and Andrew Loxley. "Introducing Visual Methods." Unpublished Paper. National Centre for Research Methods: 2008. http://eprints.ncrm.ac.uk/420/.

Reches, Eli and Arik Rudknitsky, eds. "The Arab Population in Israel: Basic Data." *Arab Society in Israel: Information File*. Neve Ilan: Abraham initiatives, 2009 (Hebrew).

Resnik, Julia. "Alternative Identities in Multicultural Schools in Israel: Emancipatory Identity,

Mixed Identity and Transnational Identity." *British Journal of Sociology of Education*, Vol. 27, No. 5 (2006): 585–601. doi:10.1080/01425690600958782.

Richard, Veronica M. and Maria K. E. Lahman. "Photo-Elicitation: Reflexivity on Method, Analysis, and Graphic Portraits." *International Journal of Research & Method in Education*, Vol. 38, No. 1 (2015): 3–22. doi:10.1080/1743727X.2013.843073.

Rose, Gillian. *Doing Family Photography: The Domestic, the Public and the Politics of Sentiment*. Farnham: Ashgate Publishing, Ltd., 2010.

Rosińska, Zofia. "Emigratory Experience: The Melancholy of No Return." In *Memory and Migration: Multidisciplinary Approaches to Memory Studies*, Julia Creet and Andreas Kirtzmann, eds. (Toronto: University of Toronto Press, 2011), 29–42.

Scherto, Gill and Ulrike Niens. "Education as Humanisation: A Theoretical Review on the Role of Dialogic Pedagogy in Peacebuilding Education." *Compare: A Journal of Comparative and International Education*, Vol. 44, No. 1 (2014): 10–31. doi:10.1080/03057925.2013.859879.

Shalom-Chetrit, Sami. *The Mizrahi Struggle in Israel: 1948–2003*. Tel Aviv: Am-Oved, 2006 (Hebrew).

Shalom-Chetrit, Sami. *Intra-Jewish Conflict in Israel: White Jews, Black Jews*. New York: Routledge, 2010.

Shenhav, Yehuda. "The History Textbooks of the People of Israel." *Mitzad Sheni*, Vol. 18 (1999): 22–25 (Hebrew).

Shenhav, Yehuda and Hanan Hever. "'Arab Jews' after Structuralism: Zionist Discourse and the (De)formation of an Ethnic Identity." *Social Identities: Journal for the Study of Race, Nation and Culture*, Vol. 18, No. 1 (2012): 101–118. doi:10.1080/13504630.2011.629517.

Shor, Ira and Paulo Freire. *A Pedagogy for Liberation: Dialogues on Transforming Education*. Westport, CT: Praeger, 1987.

Singer, Yvonne. "The Veiled Room." In *Memory and Migration: Multidisciplinary Approaches to Memory Studies*, Julia Creet and Andreas Kirtzmann, eds. (Toronto: University of Toronto Press, 2011), 263–279.

Smooha, Sammy. "The Loci of the Ethnic Problem in Israel Today." In *Half the Nation: Readings in the Culture and Status of Oriental Jews in Israel*, Shlomo Deshen, ed. (Ramat-Gan: Department of Jewish History and Contemporary Jewry at Bar-Ilan University, 1986), 293–309.

Smooha, Sammy. "The Mass Immigrations to Israel: A Comparison of the Failure of the Mizrahi Immigrants of the 1950s with the Success of the Russian Immigrants of the 1990s." *Journal of Israeli History*, Vol. 27, No. 1 (2008): 1–27. doi:10.1080/13531040801902708.

Snir, Reuven. "Who Needs Arab-Jewish Identity? Fragmented Consciousness, "Inessential Solidarity", and the "Coming Community" (Part 1)." *Journal of Modern Jewish Studies*, Vol. 11, No. 2 (2012): 169–188. doi:10.1080/14725886.2012.684864.

Steier, Tommy S. "Why Were They Silent Again? On the Mental Condition of Holocaust Survivors and Their Treatment by Society and Therapists." *Harefuah*, Vol. 148, No. 4 (2009): 219–223 (Hebrew).

Sturken, Marita. *Tangled Memories: The Vietnam War, the Aids Epidemic, and the Politics of Remembering*. Berkeley: University of California Press, 1997.

Sturken, Marita. "The Image as Memorial: Personal Photographs in Cultural Memory." In *The Familial Gaze*, Marianne Hisrch, ed. (Hanover, NH: University Press of New England, 1999), 178–195.

Tsur, Yaron. "Israeli Historiography and the Ethnic Problem." *Pe'amim*, Vol. 94 (2003): 7–56 (Hebrew). https://www.jstor.org/stable/23429363.

Tsur, Yaron. "Israeli Historiography and the Ethnic Problem." In *Making Israel*, Benny Morris, ed. (Ann Arbor: University of Michigan Press, 2007), 231–277.

Vila, Pablo. "The Importance of Photo-Interviewing as a Research Method in the Study of

Identity Construction Processes: An Illustration from the U.S.-Mexico Border." *Visual Anthropology*, Vol. 26 (2013): 51–68. doi:10.1080/08949468.2013.735187.

Wexler, Laura. "The State of the Album." *Photography and Culture*, Vol. 10, No. 2 (2017): 99–103. doi:10.1080/17514517.2017.1331561.

Willumson, Glenn. "Making Meaning: Displaced Materiality in the Library and Art Museum." In *Photographs Objects Histories: On the Materiality of Images*, Elizabeth Edwards and Janice Hart, eds. (London: Routledge, 2004), 65–83.

Yonah, Yossi, Galia Zalmenson-Levy, and Chagit Gur-Ziv. "Also-and-Also Curricula at Kedma." In *Inequality in Education*, Dafna Golan-Agnon, ed. (Tel Aviv: Bable, 2004), 188–208 (Hebrew).

Zohar, Zion. *Sephardic and Mizrahi Jewry: From the Golden Age of Spain to Modern Time.* New York: New York University Press, 2005.

Part IV

Conclusions

12 Conclusions: Albums and Diverse Communities

Kris Belden-Adams

Each of the photographic albums and scrapbooks featured in this volume offered outlets for their various makers to express their unique life plights for an audience of family, friends, their subculture, or for themselves. Some of those makers' stories – contextualized and retold in this volume by an equally diverse range of scholars from different disciplines, using a variety of methodologies – made the album into a subversive vehicle that transformed their makers' liminal and marginalized "unbeings" into an undeniable "beings," using a visual language of the privileged hegemony.[1] This strategy is transformative and consequential, even if it has received little sustained examination in existing histories.

The authors in this volume have shed new light on how a diverse range of personal scrapbooks and albums spanning many time periods and gender identities/orientations address various dis/abilities, and a variety of global social/cultural contexts, reshape, record, and assert the makers' "selfhoods." In *The Queer Art of Failure*, Judith/Jack Halberstam suggested that for individuals whose identities are positioned outside of a white, male, cisgender, privileged, Western social and economic hegemony, recombining visual-culture artifacts enables not only the personal expression of marginalization but also provides an outlet for conveying the maker's frustration over their failure to meet society's ideals of "exceptionalism."[2] This process is potentially a rebellious act that embraces their "unbeing" in society and allows for the reassembling and reimagining of a hegemonic system (a mass-friendly photography) that accommodates their voices, according to Halberstam.[3] These expressions of self, Halberstam argue, are not "unduly optimistic, but nor are they mired in nihilistic critical dead ends."[4]

That holds true for many album-makers who adopted this form of expression for various rebellion-focused reasons, and employed variegated tactics to express their marginalization and to make room for their voices and stories, despite oppressive social and political climates. As they did so, many of the case studies in this volume also expanded on the hegemonic conventions of the photographic album/scrapbook. For example, the chapters in the first section of this volume, "Complicating Family Narratives," examined scrapbooks and albums that preserved, redefined, and enlarged the roles and norms of family narratives.

The stories of Chapter 2 by Visual Studies scholar Suryanandini Narain examined several photographic albums' revelations of generational shifts in the conceptions of "family." Her examination of travel albums and journal excerpts kept by a grandmother, mother, and daughter, based in Delhi, India, and Washington, D.C., took a closer look at how albums were used to express the shifting Indian conceptions of the

DOI: 10.4324/9781003157427-17

family unit's essential members, as well as its changing importance in an increasingly global, networked, diasporic society.

Interestingly, Narain discovered that while widowed and unmarried women risked unconformity with Indian marriage-oriented social and cultural norms, their single statuses also enabled them to assert a new sense of independence that inspired world travel by multiple generations. The albums provided a space where that marginality was confessed, selfhood was expressed, and "family" was redefined within and beyond the Indian diasporic community. They also allowed each traveler to anchor herself in domestic and familial cultural normativity, even though the emphasis of domesticity declined in albums by more recent generations in favor of a travel-focused narrative that no longer emphasized the diasporic community, but instead celebrated the bond of sisterhood. Thus, in the space of one generation, the album's focus changed to reflect the shifting conceptions of "familiality" among members of Generation X. These priorities departed from those of their mother, a member of the Baby Boomer generation.

Albums also were a bifurcated space for implying disappointment over one's single status, yet also for celebrating the freedom that being unfettered from raising children allowed. Documenting travel, however, conformed to existing travel-album-making norms. Photographs show subjects clustered before touristic scenery, organized in a linear manner to reflect "stops" made while traveling. In this sense, the albums conformed to travel-album norms as they also expressed normative expectations of family-album narratives (to show familial cohesion by revealing happy family members posing together and bonding while enjoying a common activity, travel). In the end, the albums across generations reaffirmed of the importance of both family bonding and marriage, the means of expanding bloodline-based families.

Narain's study of generational shifts and continuities in analog, or pre-digital, photographic albums has not been a significant focus of recent discourses on the history of albums and scrapbooks. But her chapter suggests the further promise of continuing to examine the influences of globalism and the maintenance of previous social/cultural expectations after diaspora. In addition, Narain's cross-generational study involving family members who were raised with analog albums suggests another avenue for further studies. It raises questions about the influence of digital technology on generations that were born into the sharing of *digital* photographic albums (instead of analog, paper-bound ones) for "Millennials" and "Generation-Z" album-keepers on social media. An extended study that assesses the ways in which digital albums have departed and conformed with the habits and conventions of analog norms holds much promise for future study in a book focused instead on digital albums. Moreover, as generations who have had hands-on experience making analog photographic albums give way to born-digital generations, it is intriguing to ask: *Does the analog photographic album – with its specific conventions – evolve into something different, or does it disappear? If it evolves into something new, how might digital albums compare and extend upon the dialogues proposed by albums such as the analog ones featured in this volume?* Such questions comprise a next step beyond this volume to address digital albums, inspired by essays such as Narain's.

Some of the album-makers whose works were featured in this volume were located demographically within the hegemonic majority, but experienced reversals of cultural power dynamics when their circumstances shifted. For example, a scholar of social policy James W. Trent, in Chapter 3, took a closer look at a scrapbook kept by white middle-class parents Emily and Bernhard Kress about their son Bernard ("Bernie"), who had Down syndrome. The books chronicle his time in residence at a state mental institution in New Jersey. While institutionalizing children with Down syndrome such as Bernie may have been the norm for middle-class parents of their generation, the Kresses' albums reflect deep ambivalence over that decision. The Kresses compiled albums commemorating Bernie's life and environment at the institution, their support and involvement with the institution, clippings about scandals, and other ephemera that raised questions about the humane treatment of patients.

Trent's reading of the Kress family's scrapbook offered a counter-narrative to the optimism conventionally offered in hegemonic family albums filled with optimistic milestone moments and celebratory narratives. Instead, Trent suggested that a more honest expression of the task of parenting might reveal our copious moments of deep regret, contradictory feelings, and insecurities. The Kresses – able-bodied and able-minded, hegemony-representing parents – expressed their alternating experiences of connection and frustrated disconnection with their son Bernie, as well as their misgivings about the decisions they made about his care. Compared to existing hegemonic norms in albums and scrapbooks for optimistically and sentimentally chronicling the growth of children, the Kresses offer a deeply honest and vulnerable counterpoint to the views of perfect families with neurotypical, seemingly well-behaved children who grow up and gain full independence. The Kresses' album subverted the typical representations of the family – whether or not it originally was intended to do so – using a forum of representation that gave this normative expectation its repeated reiteration and social/cultural potency as a personal mythology.

In Chapter 4, art historian Mary Trent offers an alternative conception of family that challenges the presumption that it necessarily be based on bloodline, or even, living beings. Careful study of the orphaned Chicago self-taught artist/author/hospital janitor Henry Darger's lushly illustrated, autobiographical albums bring a vivacious, imaginary cast of family members to life. Darger, who grew up in an orphanage and in a psychiatric hospital, creates his own "family" in the absence of actual kin. For example, Darger integrates images of natural oddities taken from a *Life* magazine series addressing ways various species (desert cacti, Galapagos lizards) adapt to survive harsh environments. Trent suggests that these "characters" are analogies for how marginalized individuals such as Darger navigate a society that has outcasted them. In these animals and plants, Darger found a chosen family that was like him and understood his struggles.

Darger's albums also feature a team of transgender "children" fugitive heroes that triumph in a challenging world. Thus, he recasts his albums into a different kind of "family album" – one that subverts the notion of the "perfect" family or idyllic life, and leaves room for LGBTQI+ and neurodivergent voices such as Darger's. As Darger's heroes – themselves outcasts and marginalized figures in a beautiful but inhospitable environment – are incessantly challenged by a harsh world, they triumph fantastically. The constructed, collaged realities in Darger's albums thus invert the power structures to allow figures like him to not only survive, but thrive.

Despite being multiple-marginalized (LGBTQI+, financially insecure, and neurodivergent), Darger creates an imaginary world that not only accommodates him, but celebrates him. As such, he takes the photographic album from being a space for celebrating hegemonic homogeny into a space that appreciates the diversities of another kind of species: his. By extension, the album is appropriated for all people who are also twice marginalized by mainstream society. And to accomplish this, he adopts two visual languages by which hegemonic society communicated its messages about family values, the photo album and by clipping images from the mass press.

Indeed, each of the case studies in the section "Complicating Family Narratives" subverted the mainstream album-making tradition of showcasing idealized representations of bloodline-related families who share upbeat moments and milestones like birthdays and vacations. Instead, these albums make room for the commemoration of women traveling freely to visit family members in diasporic Indian cultures, for reflecting a shifting relationship to the Indian community, and for reconceptualizing familial bonds in an increasingly global society. They create a space for the expression of imperfect parenting experiences, regret, and frustration over disconnection. They redefine a "family" as a community that reaches across cultural boundaries, gender binaries, neurodiversities, and even material realities. The albums featured in this section implicitly argue for an expanded view of the possibilities of the album and its normative expectations.

The second section of this book, "Stepping Out of the Closet, Privately," featured case studies that considered how albums and scrapbooks have been used as a private, candid forum for the free expression of "closeted," societally marginalized, LGBTQI+ identities in the face of a cisgender hegemony. The case studies in this chapter not only addressed these album-makers' subversion of the cisgender-family-oriented conventions, but they also examined the complications that these albums and scrapbooks posed after they left private ownership and their subcultural coding spoke to a public audience that may miss the visual cues and that also assumes (by default) the makers' normative cisgender orientations.

The upper-class, Victorian-era practice of women-crafted albums in the United States and Europe has been well-explored in our histories as expressions of fulfilling gender-dictated destinies. Masculine counterpart practices are rare, but also offer alternative narratives about the pageant of cisgender courting among the upper classes. In Chapter 5, I took a closer look at the 1880s college albums by William Belcher Whitney, whose hairpin photomontage seemingly celebrates the robust dating life of a promising young marriage prospect.

Only at a closer look does this narrative falter. Literal and metaphoric "dropped hairpins" – gestures that let other gay men know that Whitney was ready to "let his hair down" – appear in the album. His engagement in homosocial/sexual relationships are expressed by then-familiar subcultural visual codes, and in photographs that reveal less subtle evidence: sultry gazes and copious bodily contact. This essay recovered Whitney's album narratives – both in overt symbolism (to imply that he was chasing and courting multiple women – as would have been expected of a man of his social class), and through the lens of gay-subcultural codes. As such, Whitney's albums expressed his struggle to conform to cisgender norms, as a man of status whose professional profile and family name required him to "pass," or "conform," as "straight."

While appearing to perform "conformity," Whitney actively complicates "conformity" itself, and allows us to consider the convention-laden album's role in kindling that expressive discourse. For example, while women's albums from the same era sentimentally record upper-class courting rituals and underscore the importance of marriage, keeping the family social profile, and having children, the Whitney album coopts the "courting pageant" album's expectations to insert gay-cultural lingo and visual codes in plain sight. Whitney, who had no heirs, may or may not have considered how these albums might be interpreted in historical posterity. While Whitney's albums originally were made for the viewing and enjoyment of their maker and his close confidants, their passage into the Amherst College Archives allows for the rediscovery of these hidden messages, and for the historicizing of marginalized LGBTQI+ voices in upper-class, late-nineteenth-century society.

In addition, this study of the Whitney albums raised methodological issues inherent in hindsight readings of cisgender hegemony onto the albums, discussed the risks of allowing LGBTQI+ album-/scrapbook-makers' queerness to remain unexamined, and advocated for the visibility of these individuals' stories to avoid keeping subjects "closeted" in historical perpetuity. Albums embedded with LGBTQI+ sub-cultural visual codes such as Whitney's, I have suggested, adopt mainstream scrapbook vernacular language to hide in plain sight. As we write new contributions to history, we are obligated not to keep their voices hidden, but to celebrate them instead.

Sometimes, the album- and scrapbook-makers themselves denied their invisibility and insisted instead on celebrating his LGBTQI+ status in direct defiance of social and cultural norms – but for a private viewing audience of chosen peers. In Chapter 6, American Culture Studies scholar and archivist James Kaser analyzed several multimedia albums, scrapbooks, and journals kept by Ogden Salmon from throughout his life. Salmon, a gay Chicago/New York City man, copiously documented his social life and affirmed his emerging identity as a gay man by appropriating images from mainstream culture and mixing them with artwork, prose, and images from his own social world. Salmon's albums colorfully projected his inner fantasies on romance-prone celebrity divas who famously engaged in socially inappropriate behavior (public nudity, stealing fiancés, and murder), appropriated news clippings, validated a gay gaze, celebrated military life, and documented his own supportive gay community in New York. His albums chronicle the life of a man navigating gayness in a homophobic culture.

As Halberstam argued, to embrace and celebrate a maker's liminal "unbeing" in society, as Salmon does in his albums, allows for the reassembling and reimagining of a hegemonic system that accommodates and celebrates his voice and his world.[5] Thus, Salmon finds freedom and agency to write his own honest narrative "out of the closet" – in the private world of his albums and scrapbooks – even though he lived a "closeted" existence in the public eye. His albums were previously kept for personal viewing and for enjoyment of his friends, lovers, and confidants. But their passage into Kaser's personal collection allowed Salmon's stories of gay subculture to enjoy broader reach, and to contribute his creative voice to the tapestry of our LGBTQI+ historical narratives. Like Whitney, Salmon also posthumously enjoys release from his "closet" after his albums were shared after his death.

Historian Danielle Kinsey's look at three personal photograph albums from the Gay and Lesbian Memory in Action archive in Johannesburg showed a conflicting view of both subversive queer visibility and conformity in apartheid and pre-apartheid South Africa. In Chapter 7, Kinsey looked at LGBTQI+ albums by three very different subjects. In the first, a white woman of privilege who served in World War II expressed outright affection for her female partner, yet later was complicit in the scientific aims of the apartheid state in South Africa. The second album was constructed by "David, a Sailor," an anonymous serviceman who explored gayness in and out of the closet during his time in World War II military service. The third example featured the memories of a socialite hairdresser who attended glamorous

LGBTQI+ parties and periodically was arrested and shamed for his attendance – along with others from high society. In all three cases, the album provided a means for admitting one's own truth, one's loves and "lusts," documenting one's own subculture, and expressing oneself – honestly.

However, as Kinsey points out, just because an album-maker is a member of the LGBTQI+ community does not make them an agent for a humanist, civil-rights-minded agenda in all areas of life. One was complicit in the development of apartheid, and all three benefitted from white privilege under apartheid. Their whiteness no doubt mitigated the oppression they endured for their LGBTQI+ status, while members of the Black LGBTQI+ community suffered greater injustices. As such, the albums in Kinsey's study reveal the complicated politics of marginalization in South Africa. Nevertheless, these albums are brazenly honest self-expressions that could have been used to oppress their makers, had they fallen into the wrong hands.

Regardless of the time period, album-/scrapbook-making offered all of the practitioners in the section "Stepping Out of the Closet, Privately" a safe space to express their identities within an object that was shared only with a trusted audience with whom they were "out." As such, keeping a private album still maintained its makers' quiet inhabitation of the "closet." Perhaps only in the eyes of history and in the hands of historians, after these albums have left their original makers, are their marginalized narratives able to be more fully explored and discussed with impunity and without fear with an expanded public audience. The implications of normalizing and historicizing the LGBTQI+ experience and encouraging its free expression are potentially transformative for our histories. We hope this volume will encourage further examinations of this sort, perhaps also expanding into digital realm.

In addition, many of the albums in this section employed photomontage and collage techniques. The acts of slicing, recombining, overlaying, and recomposing of objects from the external world and reassembling them enabled LGBTQI+ album-makers to create new, liminal spaces with a hybrid (and more accommodating) reality. These new worlds are ones with fewer boundaries that abide by rules of the album-keeper's making. As artifacts now separated from their makers, the albums assert for the eyes of history that their makers *did* exist – even if they might not have left behind progeny to pass along the stories of their lives and challenges.

This book's section, "Retelling National and International Histories," presented case studies of albums and scrapbooks that represented narratives that visualized their makers' and subjects' emotional navigations of the boundaries of "self" and "other" across contested and liminal boundaries of cultural/political "insider" and "outsider." These albums and scrapbooks renegotiated the geographic positioning of their makers' precarious public economic, political, and/or cultural identities, and relationships.

For example, in Chapter 8, Michèle Gates Moresi, a scholar of American Civilization and Supervisory Museum Curator of Collections at Smithsonian National Museum of African American History and Culture, told the story of how a rare microphotography album of portraits of members of Company G of the 25th Regiment of the United States Colored Troops kept by U.S. Civil War Captain William A. Prickitt came to be part of the collection at the Smithsonian's National Museum of African American History and Culture. The album, Gates Moresi suggests, tells a story of interracial interdependence and respect that rarely finds expression in our histories. According to family lore, Prickitt kept the miniature portrait album to remember the men who saved his life during a bout of illness during the war.

As Gates Moresi recounts the story of the family's donation of the album to the NMAAHC, the loss of the album as a springboard for family storytelling figured into Prickitt's descendants' concerns as the object passed from being a privately kept object to an artifact of public and national history. They worried that the album's absence would prompt a loss of their own personal sense of connection to Prickitt himself, and to broader historical narratives. This concern underscores the importance that albums hold as sites for connecting our own life narratives to broader stories, so that we might find deeper personal meaning in our connection to them.

However, as a museum-kept object, the microphotography album now is accessible to a broader number of researchers who may uncover new stories about it, such as learning more about the 17 African-American soldiers whose portraits are affixed to the album pages, and who fought with Prickitt for the Union in the Civil War. Thus, the album's passage into the NMAAHC's archives invites further research into the stories of the pictured soldiers themselves, and into the inter-racial history of co-operation, caring, and mutual respect during the war. In time, these soldiers' stories may be recovered, so their voices may assume their rightful places in history. The album itself is a tangible testament to the merit of finding and acting on compassion and common humanity, across racial divides. Its ongoing historicization naturally will lead to an enriched history that accentuates these values. That is a history I look forward to reading.

In Chapter 9, Visual Studies scholar Xinyue Yuan's study of French silk inspector G. Prat's photographic album examined how a late-nineteenth-century Western businessman abroad used the photographic travel album to negotiate the political boundaries of foreign concessions within semi-colonial cities such as those in East Asia. For travelers like Prat, the assemblage of the album took on therapeutic power to deal with real-life precariousness and geographical restrictions in strange lands. Following the Sino-French conflicts between 1883 and 1885, the album, however, undercuts optimistic tourist narratives and provides hints of the European visitor's reality: outsiders were not allowed free access to parts of East Asia. Nevertheless, as Prat rebuilds a deceptively "normal" looking "floating world" tour of China and Japan from a blend of studio and vernacular photographs, hints of rupture appear. The album, then, becomes a way of letting these fissures take hold in the ever-so-slight departures from the normative expectations of tourist albums, which confirm and commemorate the presence of the album-keeper at important sites. Instead, Prat's album offers telltale views of his difficulties adapting to a world far from his home, one that operated by different rules.

Prat only was allowed access to certain areas of China, rendering useless any power and privilege he may have elsewhere enjoyed as a European man in a period of colonization. His albums suggest that power does not only flow one way, from the colonizer to the colonized. Often, the colonized passively resist and actively assert their authority – marginalizing individuals such as Prat, and keeping them from touristically and economically colonizing China, as well. For Prat, photography (whether it was purchased, made by the album-keeper, or clipped from the mass press) provided a way to explore their ill sense of belonging, their efforts to adapt, and their incessant feeling of "foreign-ness" in worlds in which they did not belong. Prat's album was a safe place for escaping these concerns, that allowed him to retreat into a fantasy world of idyllic "floating" tours, and to revel in the beauty of touristic scenes that he was able to access through commercial photographers who could – and did – travel where he was not welcome to go. Thus, Prat could enjoy the album's narrative of full touristic agenda, even though the commercial images provided his closest thing to experiencing those sites firsthand. As such, the album itself becomes a witness to scenery the maker did not see.

Likewise, in Chapter 10, art historian Karen Barber examined images and an album made to commemorate the 1898 Indian Congress held at the Trans-Mississippi and International Exposition in Omaha, Nebraska, by Frank A. Rinehart and his assistant, Adolph Muhr, for the Bureau of American Ethnology. The albums were intended to document this "living exhibition" of the more than 500 Indian Congress delegates from 35 Native-American Nations at the Omaha fair in soft-focus, romanticized photographs that operated in a liminal space between commemorative, sentimentalizing formal studio portraits and "othering" anthropological documents of this "vanishing race" of indigenous people. More than two million visitors viewed Exposition displays, toured indigenous encampments, and attended "Wild West"-inspired shows that were part-anthropological, part-entertainment, and celebrated Indigenous assimilation as well as the United States's expansion into indigenous lands.

Rinehart's albums, Barber argues, helped encourage a larger cultural fascination with indigenous North Americans that was fueled by other World's Fair album-making practices and photographic projects by William Henry Jackson, Alexander Gardner, John K. Hillers, and Edward S. Curtis. Photographs by Rinehart helped form hegemonic and enduring views of "types" of Indigenous North Americans. However, one resulting Omaha Fair album, titled "American Indians Photographs," also speaks to gender relations, assimilation into U.S. culture, and it calls into question the curatorial practice of hosting "living exhibitions" of Indigenous peoples, for entertainment purposes.

As Barber notes, Rinehart's delegation photographs (mostly made by assistant Muhr) have been interrogated, reconfigured, re-narrated, and exhibited by indigenous scholars at Haskell Indian Nations University (owner of an original set of negatives). For younger Indigenous generations, these connections to Indigenous traditions may have been lost over the decades to *too much* assimilation. Barber also notes artist Wendy Red Star (Crow/Apsáalooke), whose 2021 installation *The Indian Congress* recreated an Exposition booth in an honorific manner that humanizes, re-narrativizes, and celebrates indigenous individuals' stories, rather than reframing the delegates as entertaining "Others," offers a new lens through which to view these photographs. Unveiling and confronting harmful stereotypes, as Red Star's installation did, is a step toward acknowledging the audacity of the Exposition, the fin-de-siècle's "Indian craze," and its documentation with the intent of fueling the material possession keeping of such images of an "Other."

But discursive tensions and purposes – vacillating from honorific, historic, and sentimental views to ethnological "types" – were in the albums all along, Barber suggests, in her reading of a "souvenir" photographic album based on Rinehart's images of selected groups Indigenous peoples. As such, the album's legacy is conflicted. It is an act of historical commemoration and nostalgia, and offered rare photographic views of indigenous figures – some of whom endure in U.S. folklore, such as Apache Chief Geronimo.

Scholar of Visual Culture and Art Education, Ya'ara Gil-Glazer, suggests that photographic albums can help heal divisions between "self" and "other." In Chapter 11, Gil-Glazer recounts the experiences of a "photo elucidation" project involving students whose album-keeping family members were on differing sides of decades of Palestinian conflicts spanning generations. Gil-Glazer encouraged students to recover family histories and memories by selecting a series of family photographs and sharing the recollections they evoked across generations. Frequently, the students' narratives addressed common experiences of migration, uprooting, religious difference, and strife – no matter which side of the conflict engaged students' various family members. They realized that not only their own families' experiences were worthy of respect, but their classmates were, as well. This project, Gil-Glazer suggests, helped students move beyond the histories taught in school and the hand-me-down memories of strive and division to see commonalities with classmates whose families had the "Other" groups' experiences.

Gil-Glazer's project illustrates the potential of revisiting photographic albums to find common ground, compassion, and humanity among groups of young people who may have been taught to fear or hate each other without further question. Her work points to one way by which the social work of historicizing and re-contextualizing of albums and vernacular photographs can transform reality and perhaps even heal divisions, especially as instabilities in Palestine persist.

As the last four chapters suggest, the study of photographic albums tied to macro-historical events (race relations during the U.S. Civil War, colonialism in east Asia, the "vanishing" of indigenous populations as the U.S. West was settled, and Palestinian conflicts) has much to teach us about ourselves, about others, about "othering," and about discovering, through individual stories, humankind's commonalities. All these projects dare us to imagine more inclusive, enriched histories that forge into a future in which the "othering" of marginalized people is no longer a normative tendency. Gil-Glazer even leaves us with a kernel of hope: that re-interpreting photographic albums might potentially lead to our discovery of a common humanity. After all, as Margaret Vendryes reminds us in the "Afterward" essay that follows this one: "[a]cknowledging difference – one's own and that of others – is what makes an engaged life worth recording." To those ends, we hope that you have found the various essays in this volume to be persuasive of the photographic album's/scrapbook's potency as a place of rebellion, fantasy, celebration, introspection, and confession – where mainstream conventions give way to something richer and more vibrant.

Notes

1 Judith/Jack Halberstam, *The Queer Art of Failure* (Durham, NC: Duke University Press, 2011), 4–8, 23.
2 Halberstam, *The Queer Art of Failure*, 2–3, 10–11.
3 Halberstam, *The Queer Art of Failure*, 4–8, 23.
4 Halberstam, *The Queer Art of Failure*, 24.
5 Halberstam, *The Queer Art of Failure*, 4–8, 23.

13 Afterword

Margaret Rose Vendryes

The rising tide of the feminist movement since the 1960s has demanded change that some – no, *many* – were unprepared to face or support. That powerful rallying cry of "the personal is political" has maintained its currency and can stand as an overarching thesis for the essays found in this volume. Family photograph albums and scrapbooks are considered, to anyone other than those close to their creation, ephemera. Those that end up preserved in archives and museums are exceptions. For art historians, locating one of these artifacts in one's area of research can be like winning the lottery. So much can be learned about the album maker and their eras by interrogating their contents.

Scrapbooks beg to be studied in their own right rather than to play a merely supporting role to scholarship focused on other topics. For example, Alexander Gumby's (1885–1961) collection of more than 300 scrapbooks, some made by him and some made by others, that document Black lives from 1901 to 1960 is one splendid example. Gumby was a charismatic aesthete who settled in Harlem after turning away from an education in law. His collection at Columbia University is particularly useful for research on the Harlem Renaissance. For example, documentation on the sculptor Richmond Barthé was hiding within the collection (Fig. 13.1). The work of turning the pages to find such gems represents unforgettable experiences with past material culture. Writer Ben Neihart understood what Gumby's collection represented when describing it as "a physical representation of the longing to participate and comment on the American cultural state."[1]

Social and racial segregation was particularly detrimental to Black intellectuals like Gumby, who faced anti-Black discrimination when attempting to publicly share his thoughts and theories about Black life. The staggering magnitude of his collection testifies to the importance of capturing and preserving what was going on around him. During Gumby's lifetime, only Black people understood how much Black lives matter. Change is a long time in coming, but it has arrived in the wake of lost Black lives. Change is also inevitable as histories are resuscitated and rewritten using heretofore marginalized material. What curator and author Susan Tucker states about collecting is irrefutable. She asserts that revision is central to all collecting regardless of its public or private position.[2]

The albums and scrapbooks of marginalized subjects disrupt established histories and complicate the dominant narrative. Brown-skinned peoples, differently abled artists, migrants, exiles, queers – those pushed to the periphery before today's resuscitated civil rights movement for diversity, equity, and inclusion – are taking the

DOI: 10.4324/9781003157427-18

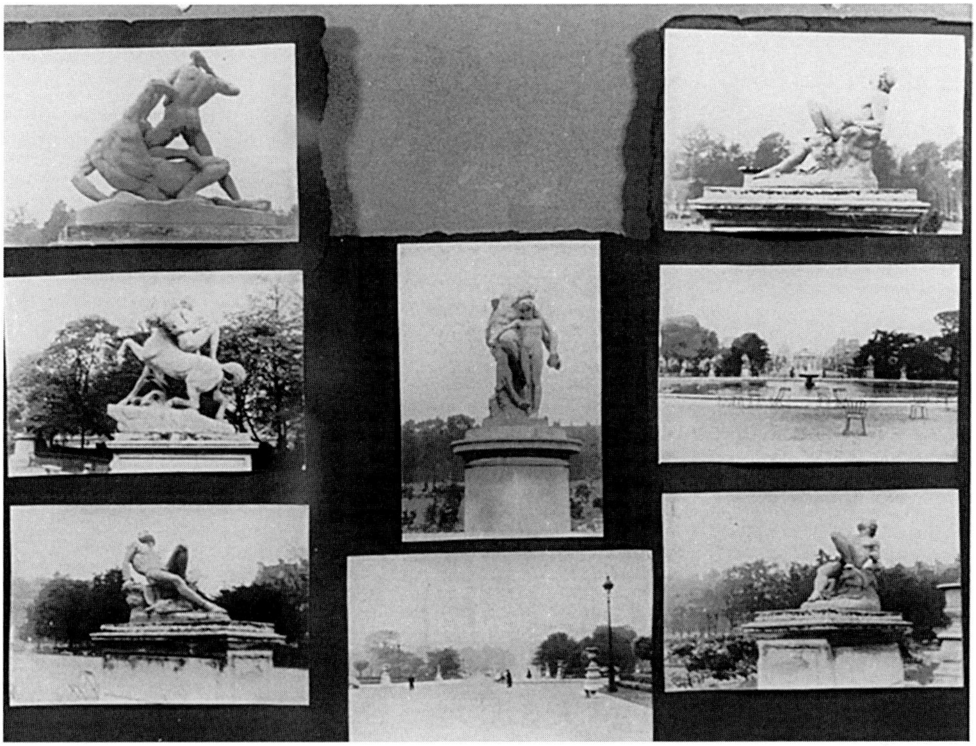

Figure 13.1 James Richmond Barthé, page from Barthé's Photograph Album (Paris, France), 1934, 12 × 14 inches. Richmond Barthé Papers, Amistad Research Center, New Orleans, Louisiana.

center. And it is about time that things got shaken up, particularly in academia, where the future leaders of communities, countries, and corporations are soaking up information found in texts like this one. Interdisciplinary research – social/political, science, art history, psychology, literature, etc. – must include artifacts like those discussed here. The charge has been taken up in earnest. A cursory search for published sources on the self-driven artist Henry Darger yields over 1,200 hits covering an impressive diversity of disciplines. His work can be treated like one expansive scrapbook, in which Darger expressed a world that existed only for him.[3] Like Darger, we are all self-taught, vernacular, folk, and "outsider" artists when we compile and curate albums of life as we wish to memorialize it. We have authority over what gets in and what does not.

For example, Ogden Salmon's third-person auto-narratives, written with annotated photographs as if he were a popular-culture journalist, reveal a nonconformist individual's desire to leave a trace of his truths between those book covers. His scrapbooks were autofiction writ large beyond a diary or journal: illustrated, coded, but revelatory, once read by a like-minded viewer.[4] The empathetic viewer is James A. Kaser who "saw" Salmon even though no photographs of or by the scrapbooks' creator are extant before he was 29 years old, and after many books had already been filled. As cultural historian Ellen Gruber Garvey asserts, "you could see something about people's responses to what they read by how they pasted it down."[5] This sensibility guided Kaser's reading of Salmon's stories. In fact, making scrapbooks during the early years of the civil rights struggle was a form of activism for women and African Americans. For Salmon, it was "coming out," curated on scrapbook pages.

Few of us would consider our family albums as historical, archive-worthy treasures. A professional photograph made by a professional photographer becomes "history" seconds after it is taken, but the snapshots that fill our material memorials of personal events are exempted from such reverence, even when someone inadvertently takes a "really good" photograph. This has become even more relevant in our digital age when thousands of photographs are uploaded to a "cloud" server, held in an application, posted to a web page, or uploaded to social media, rather than printed and arranged in a physical album. A particular photograph can be easily located without having to physically search through pages of photographs. The journey is abbreviated much like no longer needing that folding map to find your way to a new place. The Global Positioning System (GPS) is so common now that the art of getting lost is, well, lost.

The tactile quality of leafing through a family album, like reading a hard-copy book, is very much a part of the experience. Album makers often include the out-of-focus photographs of this or that person or place or event because that photograph might be the only evidence that exists, and because the memories of those present in that moment are, in the end, unreliable. This collection of essays transforms and complicates the understanding of what those personal artifacts represent. The album/scrapbook becomes a telling space, and for some, a home. It is a place of belonging, owned and acted upon with agency and authority.

When discarded photographs of Black men found their way to a bin in a gay bookstore where visual artist Glenn Ligon found them, a project of populating an ideal family album for himself, and perhaps other Black queer men, was born. He identified potent material in these cast-off pictures, declaring that, "We can still use the images, inhabit and change them, read against their intended meanings, critique ourselves with them, place our stories alongside them, use them to talk about our histories and desires."[6] Found objects can become family. For Ligon, the original intention or purpose of the photographs becomes tangential as his ownership has given the artist control over their meaning. Is this the plight of visual ephemera? How confident can we be regarding access to information, purpose, or meaning held in such unexplained and orphaned visual materials?

About a decade ago, there was a resurgence of interest in scrapbooking. The arts-and-crafts stores created new aisles for merchandise to accommodate this retro activity: blank, bound, large-format books, glues, labels, and tiny photograph corners like the ones used in earlier eras, only now they are acid-free. Often, scrapbooks were made as gifts, and were consciously composed to offer a guided experience of its contents. I was not taken with the neo-scrapbook fad, but when my mother died, I designed a digital memorial "scrapbook" presentation (Fig. 13.2). I recall the difficulty of choosing photographs of watershed events in her life (as I understood them), to be projected in a loop at the wake. A CD of the scrapbook was given to those in attendance because I understood that many, if not most of them, wanted something

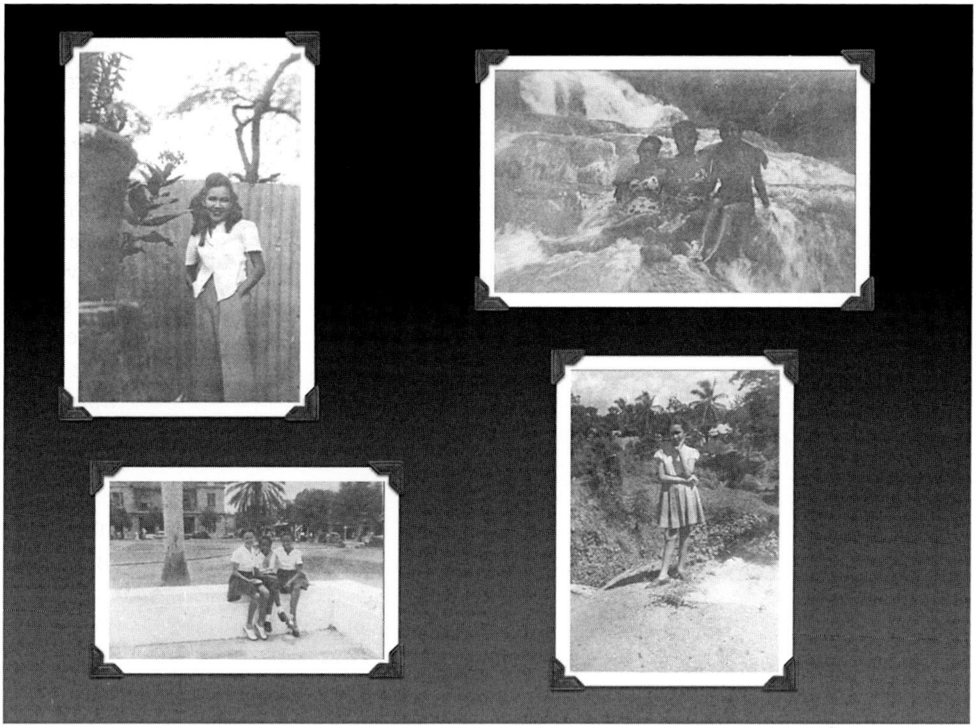

Figure 13.2 Margaret Rose Vendryes, page from Lena Amabel Vendryes (1933–2012), 2012, digital memorial scrapbook.

to hold on to, something they could place in their personal archive. Even so, guests overarchingly wished that I had printed it. The lure and legacy of leafing through a family album is hard to beat with a digital product. It did not matter that such a family album was non-existent outside of my digital compilation. This is but one example of how the "thing," the tactile object itself, is deeply significant.

A number of the authors here write of "touch." Specifically, they discuss handling a photograph as an object to be scrutinized and discussed from an album's extended narrative – what Ya'ara Gil-Glazer refers to as a conversation becoming a text through "photo elicitation." That text then becomes a contestation of "official knowledge" sanctioned for dissemination in schools. Discussing photographs can acknowledge difficult life changes brought on by uprooting and migration, displacement and the loss of belonging. Family albums document essential communal experiences. The value of this project confronts, for example, the exclusion of the Arab migration from classrooms and textbooks. Discussions that transpire over an album or scrapbook, and not always by its maker, make sense of its content and give it context. But, more often than not, the telling remains in the moment. So much oral history has been lost to us. That kind of loss makes projects like Gil-Glazer's valuable beyond its academic relevance. The content of this volume will find its way into the curriculum and the minds of learners who will likely have more access to make change than the "common" folks who make such artifacts and leave them behind to memorialize "regular" lives. There are so many unexplained events (secrets taken to the grave) held in photographs, scraps of paper, and scribbled notes that will remain out of sight because research is conducted on lives identified as significant to established, mainstream representations of community or society. The cogs that everyday people represent are too many and too small to note until someone on the inside, a scholar perhaps, makes relevant the example of an uncelebrated person's life story to enrich that mainstream picture.

Visual artists employ to great effect traditional design formats of scrapbooks or family albums to evoke the homey familiarity of a personal artifact when opening a published book. We scrutinize the pages differently than the customary exhibition catalog, in which type-set words frame illustrations. For example, Ligon's project makes use of faded, hastily composed snapshots to reveal unspoken sentiments and relationships made invisible through censorship. Another example is Kara Walker's tissue separators that, when lifted, unveil auto-fictional events, such as sexual abuse, that some viewers may wish she had left secret. Family albums can be fraught with pain: gatherings shared before divorce, deceased lovers' smiles, myriad entanglements brought back to life by a 5 × 3-inch piece of paper.

How might this volume's spilled ink change the landscape of intolerance for difference? This study enables the reader to come face to face with diversity spirited away inside of personal albums. Acknowledging difference – one's own and that of others – is what makes an engaged life worth recording. Artists like Darger realized this when feeling compelled to release his ideas – fantasies – into real time and space. Is it "art," as those who encountered his "albums" decided it was? Does it matter? Is reading them through a psychological lens appropriate? How much of what we take away from these albums, accessed without the benefit of the maker's explanations, is valid?

As a historian, and a biographer by default, I lay claim to years of research laced with self-reflection. The photograph albums of Barthé, the premiere 20th-century African American figurative sculptor, are important to the telling of his travels and relationships. Held in the archives of the Amistad Research Center in New Orleans, Barthé's albums lack annotations, leaving the viewer responsible for making connections with what is there. Those albums, more than any other evidence of documenting his life, revealed Barthé's queer identity. Scholars are warned of walking on precarious ground by trusting what is found in photographs or works of art for that matter. But, there is something to be said for gut reactions, even though there is danger in posthumously delving into lives long ended before we open a private album made public.

I wonder, and at times worry, what will be made of my not-particularly-orderly photography albums. Should I preserve them for access to me after I die? Will reading a page such as this one, filled with photographs taken during the awakening years of my lesbian identity, be understood as moments in my rite of passage? (Fig. 13.3). Or will imaginations run wild and counter to what I had documented on these, and many other, pages for my own enjoyment? The people in most of those photographs are strangers, but they are important historical markers. This I write as a historian and collector who purchased in a thrift store an old family album created by a person unknown to me just because I can freely imagine an existence not my own.

These authors engaged *Diverse Voices in Photographic Albums: "These Are Our Stories"* with care and made their perspectives accessible. As we read their

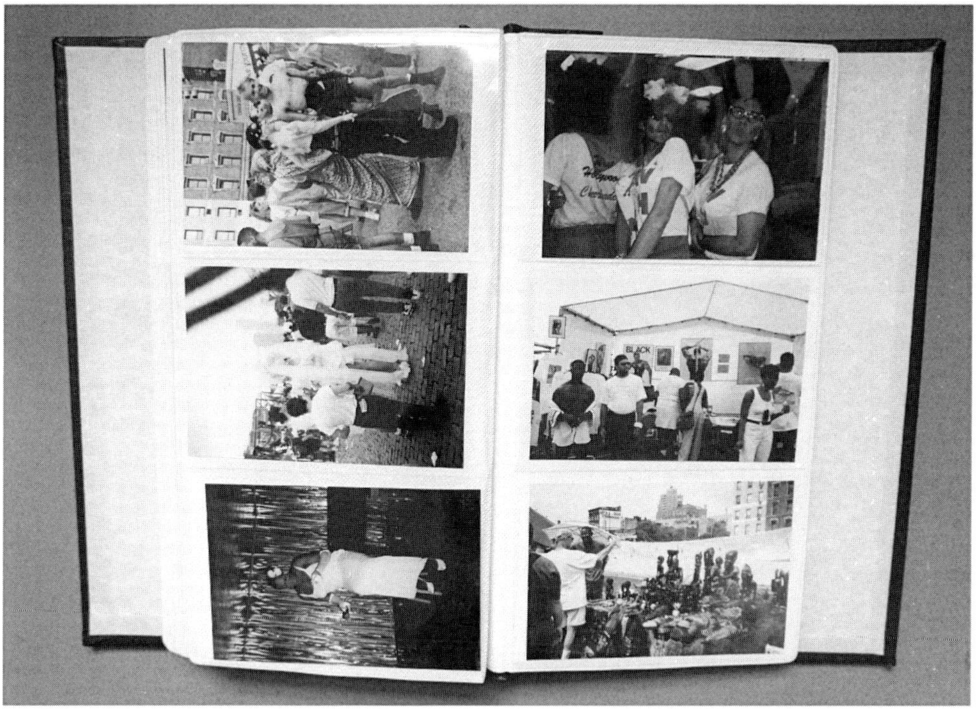

Figure 13.3 Margaret Rose Vendryes, *New York City Pride*, page from author's photograph album, June 1995, 13 × 18 inches.

interpretations of personal visual material, be it true to their lives or fictional, it all becomes factual, because the truth is that someone made those objects as evidence of a conscious life lived. How we use it – what we make of it – is on us.

Notes

1 Ben Neihart is quoted in Anna Imperial, "The Archived Memory in Alexander Gumby's Collection of Negroiana: A Commentary on the Curious Meanderings of the American Temperament," *Diesis: Footnotes on Literary Identities*, Vol. 2, Issue 2 (Spring 2012): 3. For a closer look at the Alexander Gumby Collection, visit "The Unwritten History": Alexander Gumby's African America, Columbia University Online Exhibition. Accessed May 5, 2021: https://exhibitions.library.columbia.edu/exhibits/show/gumby.

2 Susan Tucker, "Telling Particular Stories: Two African American Memory Books," in *The Scrapbook in American Life*, eds. Susan Tucker, Katherine Ott, and Patricia P. Buckler (Philadelphia: Temple University Press, 2006), 220–234.

3 Mary Trent, "Henry Darger and the Unruly Paper Dollhouse Scrapbook," in *Phallacies: Historical Intersections of Disability and Masculinity*, eds. Kathleen M. Brian and James W. Trent, Jr. (Oxford, UK: Oxford University Press, 2017), 44–64.

4 For an insightful study on scrapbooks as historical records, see Ellen Gruber Garvey, *Writing with Scissors: American Scrapbooks from the Civil War to the Harlem Renaissance* (Oxford: Oxford University Press, 2012).

5 Claire Parfait, "Interview with Ellen Gruber Garvey," *Transatlantica*, Vol. 2 (April 2014): 1.

6 Glenn Ligon, "A Feast of Scraps," in *The Masculine Masquerade: Masculinity and Representation*, eds. Andrew Perchuk and Helaine Posner (Cambridge, MA & London: The MIT Press, 1995), 89.

Bibliography

Columbia University Library. ""The Unwritten History": Alexander Gumby's African America." Accessed May 5, 2021: https://exhibitions.library.columbia.edu/exhibits/show/gumby.

Garvey, Ellen Gruber. *Writing with Scissors: American Scrapbooks from the Civil War to the Harlem Renaissance*. Oxford: Oxford University Press, 2012.

Imperial, Anna. "The Archived Memory in Alexander Gumby's Collection of Negroiana: A Commentary on the Curious Meanderings of the American Temperament." *Diesis: Footnotes on Literary Identities*, Vol. 2, No. 2 (Spring 2012): 2–14.

Parfait, Claire. "Interview with Ellen Gruber Garvey." *Transatlantica*, Vol. 2 (April 2014): 1.

Perchuk, Andrew and Helaine Posner, eds. *The Masculine Masquerade: Masculinity and Representation*. Cambridge, MA & London: The MIT Press, 1995.

Trent, Mary. "Henry Darger and the Unruly Paper Dollhouse Scrapbook." In *Phallacies: Historical Intersections of Disability and Masculinity*, Kathleen M. Brian and James W. Trent, Jr., eds. (Oxford, UK: Oxford University Press, 2017), 44–64.

Tucker, Susan. "Telling Particular Stories: Two African American Memory Books." In *The Scrapbook in American Life*, Susan Tucker, Katherine Ott, and Patricia P. Buckler, eds. (Philadelphia: Temple University Press, 2006), 220–234.

Index

Note: Page numbers followed by "f" indicate figure.

actors 102–103, 103f, 104, 107–109
Addleman-Frankel, Kate 154
Adolph Greenburg /Adrian 108
Adrian /Adolph Greenburg 108
Agassiz, Louis 10
albums: elitism 7, 9–10; etymology 8; and fine art 6, 8; hegemonic standards 4, 6–7, 9–12; loss of 18; narrativity 3, 11–12, 195–197; revision of 8; tactility 6, 9, 18, 222–223; temporality of 5, 196; viewing experience 8
Alexander, William 153
Allen, William V. 181–183
American Anthropologist 175
American Association on Mental Deficiency 46–47
Amherst College 15, 77, 78f, 79, 80f, 84–85, 88–89, 215; baseball team 87f, 88f
anthropological portraits 169, 176, 176–179, 185, 218
anti-foreigner sentiments 158
Apache 167, 218; Kiowa 174; San Carlos 174
Apple, Michael 197
Apsáalooke /Wendy Red Star 17, 168, 186–187, 218
Arab Israeli War 196
Arafat, Yasser 200
Arapahos 174
archive 7–8
Art Institute of Chicago, The 62
Ashkenazi Jews 194–199
Assiniboins 174; children 174; warriors 174
Asylum for Insane Criminals/Illinois State Penitentiary at Menard 102, 104
Atlantic City 31, 35
Atwood, Cory 142–143
"aura" 31
autograph book 7
Azoulay, Ariella 196, 198, 201

Baerenholdt, Jørgen Ole 28
Baldwin, John N. 181
Ballet Russe 105
Barak, Ehud 197
Barthé, Richmond 220, 223f, 224
Barthes, Roland 12
Batchen, Geoffrey 12
Beato, Felice 149, 154
Beijing, China 154
Ben-Gurion, David 197
Bérubé, Alan 108
Bethesda, Maryland 29, 32f
Blackness: Black studies 8; Black women and marginality from history 4; vernacular photography about 13, 220, 222
Blackfoot 174
Blackfriars 106
Black militias 136
Blake, Grace C. 82
Block Island 82
Bocca Tigris 154
bodybuilders 109, 111
Boston, Massachusetts 81–82, 84
Bourdieu, Pierre 11, 66
Brown, Ellen Cort 80
Brown, Elspeth 5, 13
Brückl, Peter 126
Bruno, Michel/le 115–120, 125–129, 128f
Bureau of American Ethnology 166–167, 170–172, 177–179, 183–184
Bureau of Indian Affairs/Indian Office 17, 182, 218

cabinet of curiosities 8
cacti 59, 68, 213
Caddoan peoples 176
Cairo, Egypt 117–119

Callaghan, John 102, 108
Cambridge University 81
Camp William Penn 141
Campt, Tina 9, 13, 63, 65, 69
Canton Amateur Theatrical Society 149
Canton (Guangzhou), China 16, 148–160, 217–218
Capetown, South Africa 122
Carruth, Fred 168, 169f, 172, 177
Carson Pirie Scott & Co. 104
carte-de-visite 7
Carter, Mary A. 82
Casablanca, Morocco 198
Catastrophe/Nakba 196, 200
Catholicism 70
celebrity culture 104
Chalfen, Richard 11
Chambers, Rebecca F. 141
Chambers, William 153
Charleston, South Carolina 5
Chase, Aquila 85
Chase, Charles Amherst 77, 85–89, 86f, 87f, 88f
Chatton, Sydney 108
Chauncey, George 85, 105
Cherokee 184; Eastern Band 185
Cheyennes (Indigenous North Americans) 174
Chicago Civic Opera 100, 104–105
Chicago Daily Tribune 107
Chicago, Illinois 14, 56, 62–63, 66, 97–98, 102, 104–107, 213, 215; "Boul Mich" 104; "Towertown" 104; "Fairytown" 104
Chief Tawákoni 168
Chin-chan Guild Hall (Chen Clan Ancestral Hall) 160
Chippewa (indigenous North Americans) 166
Chiricahua Apache 174
chromolithography 7
Churchill, David S. 107
Civil War, U.S. 15, 135–145, 216–217, 219; Black Union soldiers 135–145, 216–217; soldier portraits 139f, 140f, 141f, 144f
Coca-Cola 11
Collier, John 195
colonization 10, 14, 16, 118, 120, 217–219
coloring book 60
Columbia University 220
commercial photography studios 8, 158, 160, 170
Cooper, Sathasivian 117
Confederate blockades 139
coronavirus xv
Cornwall, England 119
costume parties 126, 154, 157f
Craft, Ellen 5
Crystal Palace 181
Cunningham, T. B. 158
Curtis, Edward S. 167, 172, 218; *North American Indian* project 167, 172
Cusco, Peru 13

Damascus, Syria 119
Danielli, Charles 100, 100f, 101–102
Daoism/Taoism 157
Day, James 107
Darger, Henry 14–15, 56–74, 213, 220, 224; *The Story of the Vivian Girls, in What Is Known as the Realms of the Unreal, of the Glandeco- Angelinnian War Storm, Caused by the Child Slave Rebellion*, or *In the Realms of the Unreal* 56, 57f, 58f, 59, 69; Table with source materials 61f; Vivian, Annabelle Aronberg 63, 64f, 66
Darwin, Charles 69–71
Davidson, Shayne 142
Davison, Gale Franklin 107
de Certeau, Michel 11, 65, 69
Deitcher, David 89
D'Emilio, John 108
Delany, Martin 139
Delhi, India 14, 29, 38, 211
Deloria, Phillip 170, 176
Dewan, Deepali 13
Diaspora: from South Asia 27–39, 211–212, 214
di Bello, Patrizia 9, 115
Dick and Jane readers 59
Dick Tracey 63
Diggs, Marylynne 90
Disney films 106
divas 15, 98, 99f, 100, 100f, 101–102, 111, 215
Dixon, Joseph Kossuth 167
Dobson, Sebastian 160
domesticity 4, 7–9, 11–13, 31–33
Douglass, Frederick 135, 137–138, 143
Douglass, Lewis 138
Down Syndrome 14, 43, 54, 213
drag 83, 97–99, 107, 111, 126; oblique 101, 109
Dragon Boat Festival 154
"dropped hairpins" 77–78, 78f, 79–96, 214
du Bois, Raoul Pene 108
Durban, South Africa 122
Dutch Folly 155

Eastman Kodak Co. 7, 11, 40, 66, 117
Eban, Abba 197
Edwards, Elizabeth 31, 170
Eichmann Trial 199
"elegants" 105
Elledge, Jim 63

enslavement 5, 10, 59, 62, 64–65, 136, 138, 144
Esquire 107
Epprecht, Marc 116, 120, 125
ethnography 166–167, 170, 172, 174–175, 180–182, 218
eugenics 15, 45, 47, 62–63, 92; forced sterilization 15, 45
Eurocentricity 197
Evanston, Illinois 104
evolution 68
exoticism 164
expatriates 153–156, 160, 217

Facebook 17
family album 11–12, 14, 17, 27–39, 43–54, 56, 61, 64, 66, 70–71, 122, 127, 168, 194–201, 211–214, 220, 221f, 221–222, 224–225
family photographs 11–12, 14, 17, 122, 127, 211–214, 220, 221f, 221–222, 224–225
Farris, Johnathan Andrew 147, 156
feminist movement 220
Fenton, Roger 118
figure drawing 104
Fiske, Dwight 104
flâneur 28, 40
Flathead 174
Fleming, Paula Richardson 179
Fletcher, Alice 183
"floating world" 16, 148–160, 217
Flowery Pagoda 160
Forest Town Raid 126
Fort Jay, New York 108
Fort Pickens 138
Fort Redoubt 138
Fong, Lai 154
Foxes (Indigenous North Americans) 174
Franks, Robert "Bobby" 107
Freire, Paulo 194
friendship book 7
"front stage"/"back stage" behavior 115–129

Gardner, Alexander 179, 218
Gardner, Isabella Stewart 158–160
Garfield, John 108
Garnet, Henry Highland 138
Garvey, Ellen Gruber 221–222
Gates, Aneita 142
Gay and Lesbian Memory in Action LGBTIQ Archive 15, 115–116, 122, 125, 129, 215
gaze, the: familial 11; gay male 77–91, 97–111, 122–124, 214–216; lesbian 116–120, 128, 216
"gender bending" 100, 105–106, 117–118, 127, 214–216
gender expectations 3, 9, 84–85, 90–91, 98, 106–107, 111, 117–118, 120, 124, 127, 168, 214–216
Geronimo 178, 218
Getsy, David 90
Getty Museum 185
Gevisser, Mark 125–128
Ghost Dance 184
Gloucester Township, New Jersey 141
"Golden Age of Photojournalism" 7
"good Indian" 177
Google Photos 17
Gordon-Cumming, Constance F. 156
Goshorn, Shan 185–186
Grand Pagoda at Kew, London 153
Grecian Guild Pictorial 98
Grossi, Anthony J. 49
Guild Green Tea Merchants 160
Gumby, Alexander 220
Gur-Ze'ev, Ilan 197, 200–201

Hakone Lake /Lake Ashi 152
Halberstam, Judith/Jack 211, 215
Harlem Renaissance 220
Harris, Milton 137
Haskell Indian Nations University / Haskell Institute 167–168, 185–186, 218
Hartman, Sadiya 4; "wayward knowledge" 4
Harvard University 10, 79, 84–85, 183
hill stations 36
Hillers, John K. 218
Hills, Emily 83–84
Hirsch, Marianne 12, 196, 201
Hellzadamarung 102
heteronormativity 66, 78, 89, 111, 115–129, 214–216
Holland, Patricia 11–13, 196
Holmes, Oliver Wendell Sr. 90–91
Holocaust 196–197, 199, 201
homophobia 14–15, 89, 107, 211, 214–216
homosexuality 14–15, 49, 63, 77–91, 97–111, 115–129, 214–216
"homosocial" 14–15, 88–89, 104, 117–120, 122, 214–216
hooks, bell 13
Hong Kong, China 153–155
Huaisheng Mosque, Canton, China 152, 157
Hulburt, Katherine 81
Hunter, Jane H. 81
Hutchinson, Elizabeth 178
Hyde Park Art Center 65

Illinois Asylum for Feeble-Minded Children 62
"imperial explorer"/"imperial tourist" 117–118, 120, 148–160, 217
Improved Order of Red Men 184

Indiana Dunes 104, 107
Indian Congress 164–187, 218
"*Indian craze*" 170, 178, 218
"*Indianness*" 166–187, 218
Indian Office/Bureau of Indian Affairs 183
"Indian School" 183
"Indigeneity" as performance 184, 218
Indigenous Americans 17, 101, 105, 106f, 164–187, 218; and perseverance 17, 185, 218
institutionalization (mental) 14, 43–54, 102
intellectual disability 14, 43–54, 56–74, 212–214
Israel 194–201
Israeli-Palestinian Oslo Accords 200

Jabotinsky, Ze'ev 197
Jackson, William Henry 179–180, 218
Jenkins, Henry 11
Jerusalem 118
Johannesburg, South Africa 15–16, 115–129, 215–216; during apartheid 115–129; lesbianism 116–117; LGBTIQ oppression 115–129; politics 115–116, 125; sexual revolution 125–127, 128f
Johnson, Allen 81
Joslyn Art Museum 167, 186

Kalispel 174; women 174
Kashmir 37, 37f
Kennedy, John F. 50
Kichai 176
Kidder, Mabel 79
Kimbei, Kusakabe 153–154
Kincaid, Jamaica 12
Kiowa 174; Apache 174
Kobe, Japan 149, 155
Koch, F. 158
Kodak 7, 11, 40, 66, 117
Koestenbaum, Wayne 98, 102–103
Kress, Berhard Jr 14, 43–54, 213
Kreutzberg, Harald 105

Lake Ashi /Hakone Lake 153
Lambrow, Stacey 154
La Paz Opera 98
Lady Godiva 102
Lake Biwa, Japan 149
Lake Shore Athletic club 104
Langford, Martha 8–9, 195, 198
Lanier, Tamara 10
Law of Return 196
Layton, Caleb 139
Leaf, Munro 105
Lefebvre, Henri 10–11
Leonard, G. 83–84
Leopold, Nathan and Loeb, Richard - trial 97, 107
Lerner, Nathan 56, 65
Liddicoat, Renée 115–119, 119f, 120, 121f, 122, 128–129; "Homosexuality: Results of a Survey as Related to Various Theories" 116, 119–120
Life magazine 59, 61f, 66–70, 102, 213
Ligon, Glenn 222, 224
Little Annie Rooney 60, 66
Littlefield, Catherine 105
LGBTQIA+/LGBTIQ 10, 15–16, 49, 63, 77–91, 97–111, 115–129, 213–214, 222, 224, 225f, 225
Loguen, Amelia 138
Luskey, Judith 179

Macartney Embassy/Macartney Mission 153
Macau, China 149, 155
Madonna and Child trope 166, 178
Manifest Destiny 170, 181–182
Manion, Anthony 123
marital status 27–28, 31, 33–36, 39, 56, 119, 122–124, 212
Marcus, Sharon 104
Martin, Dan 174
masculinities: and album-making 3; "pansy" type 107, 109; "homosexual" type 109
Matheson & Co. 156, 157f, 158
May, Elaine Tyler 90
McGee, W. J. 178
McLaren, Peter 194
Meir, Golda 197
memory 28, 38–39, 195
Men's Grille, The 104
mental illness 14, 43–54, 56–74, 101
Mercer, William A. 183–184
Meshulam, Assaf 197
microphotographs 15, 138f, 139f, 140f, 143f
microphotography album 15, 135–144, 216
migration 194–201
Miller, Daniel 11
Mitchell, E. W. 156
Mitchell, George H. 138, 139f
Mizrahi Jews/Misrahim /Arab Jews 194–201
Mohammedan Tomb 160
Monette, Paul 109
Monro, J. D. 156
Moon, Michael 63
Mooney, Frank - cover 170–172, 175–179, 183–185
Morgan Park Academy 97
Morley, Robert 107
Morris, Isaac H. 141
Morris, Joseph B. 141
Morris, William H. 139–140, 141f

Mount Fuji 149, 153
Mount Holyoke 79, 80f, 81–82
Muhr, Adolph 17, 166–187, 165f, 169f, 175f, 218

Nagasaki, Japan 149, 151, 155
Nakba/Catastrophe 196, 200
National Anthropological Archives, Smithsonian, U.S. 185
National Archives, U.S. 141
National Association for Retarded Children (NARC) 47, 48f
National Institute for Personnel Research 116
National Museum of African American History and Culture, Smithsonian 16, 135, 141, 216
Navajo 167
Neihart, Ben 220
Nelson, Lura W. 83
New England Conservatory of Music 82–83
New Jersey Parents Group for Retarded Children/Jersey ARC 47–48, 52, 52f
New Jersey Training School at Totowa 46
New Salem Academy 84
New Women 81
New York City 97, 104–105, 107–108, 215
Nez, Carole 167
Niagara, Canada 31, 35, 35f
Nieuhof, Johannes 153
Noble, Hannah 82
"noble savage" 176–177, 182, 218

Obernai, Serre 100–101, 100f
"official knowledge" 194, 197, 200–201
Omaha and Winnebago Agency 183
Omaha Daily Bee 182
Omaha (Indigenous North Americans) 174
Omaha Public Library 165f, 170f, 173f, 175f, 185
Omaha World's Fair/Trans-Mississippi and International Exposition (1898) 17, 168, 170, 218
opera 15, 98; singers 15, 98, 99f, 100f
Opium War, Second 156
oral narration/oral tradition 9, 28, 32–33
Orientalism 118, 126, 171, 173–174, 176–177, 218, 219
orphans 14, 56, 57f, 59–60, 62–64, 66, 213
Orr, Maddie 82–84
Osaka, Japan 149, 155
O'Shea, Michael 108
Otometoge, Japan 153
Overlees, Frank 106

Pa-choc (Pazhou) Pagoda 153
Palestine 17, 194–201, 218; Jewish and Arab relations 17, 194–201
Pan Am Airlines 67f
panorama 151–152
parenthood 43–54, 70, 117–119, 213
Parsis 157
"passing" 85, 214
Pasternak, Gil 12
Peabody Museum 171
Peale, Charles Wilson 186
Pearl River 148–151, 154
Peirce, Leona 81
Pend d'Oreille 174
Philadelphia Ballet, The 105
photo elicitation 194–201, 222
Phu, Thy 5, 13
Pinney, Christopher 10, 13, 16
Ponca 106; dance 106
Poolaw, Linda 183
Poole, Deborah 13
Pope Pius XII 70
"postmemory" 196
Pottawatomi 174
Powell, John Wesley 178, 180, 182, 184
Power, Tyrone 103
Prickitt, Captain William A. 15, 135–144, 216–217; illness 141; relationship to Black soldiers 141, 216–217; soldier portraits 139f, 140f, 141f, 144f
Progressive Era 14, 62
Protestants 91
Pueblo (Indigenous North Americans) 174; Santa Clara 174
Puritans 90
Puss 'n' Boots 66
Pustau & Co., W. 158
Putnam, Frederick Ward 171

racial stereotypes 1, 168, 170–173, 176, 216
Raft, George 103
Rinehart, Frank A. cover 17, 164–187, 165f, 169f, 175f, 218; *Rinehart's Indians* 177–178, 181
riots 158
Red Star, Wendy (Apsáalooke) 17, 168, 186–187, 218
Robinson, Paul 100–101
roll film 7
Rose, Gillian 27, 31, 195
Rosewater, Edward 182–183
Rosińska, Zofia 196
Rundquist, Leisa 68
Russell & Co. 154, 158, 160
Russell, Rosalind 108
Rydell, Robert 181

Sabu 103
sailors 115–116, 121–123, 123f, 124, 124f, 125, 128–129, 215

Salmon, Ogden 15, 97–98, 99f, 100f, 100–103, 103f, 104–106, 106f, 107–110, 110f, 111, 215, 220–222
Samper, Amelia 100–101
Sandweiss, Martha 167
Sauk 174
Schloeder, William 63
Sekula, Allan 11–12
Selish 174
servants 158
Sexual Psychopath Law, Illinois 104
Seymour, Charles 160
"sham battles" 184–185, 218
Shamian 16, 148–149, 150f, 151f, 152f, 154, 158–159
Shapiro Studio 106f
Shawn, Ted 106f
Sheehan, Tanya 13
Shor, Ira 194
Shriver, Eunice Kennedy 50
Siegel, Elizabeth 9
Siemssen & Co. 158
Silverman, Kaja 90
Sino-French War 158, 217
Sioux (Indigenous North Americans) 170, 174
Smith College 77, 81–82
Smith, G. M. 156, 157f
Smith-Rosenberg, Carroll 79, 88
Snyder, Stephanie 9
Sontag, Susan 171
South African Women's Auxiliary Army Services 115, 117
souvenirs 171, 173, 178, 218
Soviet Union 199
Spanish-American War 181
State Colony Association for New Lisbon Boys 47–49, 54
State Colony for Boys (New Lisbon, N.J.) 43–54, 44f, 50f, 51f; "Jail" 51f; New Lisbon Cottage 44f; train 50f
stereotypes of race 3, 168, 170–173, 176, 216
Steward, Samuel M. 105
Stokes, Leslie and Sewall 107
Sturken, Marita 196
subcodes, cultural 77–79, 211, 214–216
survival 68–69
Swallow, Beatrice 101–102, 104

Taoism/Daoism 157
Tatum, John 168, 169f, 172, 177
Tawákoni, Chief Jim 168, 169f, 174, 176–177, 175f
Taylor, Delia 10
Taylor, Renty 10
Taylor, Robert 103, 107
Ted Shawn and His Male Dancers 105
Temple, Shirley 63, 66
theater performances 154
Thomas, M. Carey 80
Thomas, Rowe & Smith 156, 158, 159f; Junior Men 159f
Thompson, James 85
Thomson, John 150
Tokyo, Japan 149, 155
Tomkins, A. B. 156
Tosca 101
tourist "gaze" 27, 29–30, 32, 39–40, 66, 117–118, 148–160, 211, 214, 217–218
tourist photography (commercial) 118, 148–149, 153, 158, 160, 217–218
transgenerational trauma 196, 199–201
Trans-Mississippi and International Exposition / Omaha World's Fair (1898) 168, 170
Treaty of Nanjing 156
Tucker, Henry G. 82
Tucker, Susan 220
Turner, Frederick Jackson 170
typhoon 157–158
typological studies 174, 183, 186–187, 218

ukiyo-e 153–154
Uncle Tom's Cabin 61–62
United States of America: assimilationist policies (toward Indigenous populations) 167–168, 170–171, 177–178, 181–182, 185–186, 218; expansionist policies 181
United States Colored Troops, U.S. Army 15, 135, 217–217; salary 137, 140
United States Indian Industrial Training School 167, 168
University of Chicago 84; *Pulse* 103f
University of Witwatersrand 116

van der Merwe, Hentie 116, 120
"vanishing race" 166–168, 170–173, 177–178, 182–183, 218
Verdi, Marion 100–102
Vicinus, Susan Martha 88, 90
Vila, Pablo 195
Vizenor, Gerald 166, 172, 186

Walker, Kara 224
Walls, John 139, 139f
Walton, Alice 83
Wampoa (Whampoa) Island 153
Washington, D.C. 27–29, 33, 30f, 34f, 142, 171, 179, 211
Washington Monument 30f, 34, 34f
Waterford, Pennsylvania 138
Wattles, Gurdon 181
weightlifters 109, 111

Welch, Jeannette C. 83–84
Wellesley College 77, 83–84
West, Mae 103
Wexler, Laura 4–5, 198
White Cloud Mountains 160
White, Ludlow 108
Whitney, William Belcher 15, 77–78, 78f, 79–86, 86f, 87–96, 214
Wichita (indigenous North Americans) - cover 164, 165f, 166, 168, 169f, 170–175, 175f, 176–177, 184; Ahahe cover image 165f, 178; women cover image 165f, 174, 175f, 176
Wilde, Oscar 107
Wild West Shows 181, 184–185, 218
Wilkie, Mary 117–118, 120, 121f
Willis, Deborah 13
Willumson, Glenn 195
Wilmington, Delaware 138
Winchell, Walter 107
Winnebago (Indigenous North Americans) 174; men 174; women 174
Works Progress Administration 104
World War I 100
World War II 98, 108–109, 110f, 115, 117–121, 121f, 122–125, 199, 215; Scrapbooks/albums of 98, 110f, 117–121, 121f, 123f, 124f
World's Fair: Louisiana Purchase Exposition, St. Louis, Mo. (1904) 182; New York City (1939) 102, 108; Pan-American Exposition, Buffalo, N.Y. (1901) 182; positivist rhetoric of prosperity in the West 181–182, 218; Universal Exposition, Paris (1889) 181; World Columbian Exposition, Chicago (1893) 173, 181–182; World's Fair / Trans-Mississippi and International Exposition, Omaha (1898) 17, 168, 170–189, 218
Wounded Knee 170, 174, 184

Yale University 81
Yokohoma, Japan 148–149, 153–155
Yoskiwara District, Tokyo, Japan 153

Printed in Canada
PGIL2024USA